NEURAL NETWORKS AND ARTIFICIAL INTELLIGENCE FOR BIOMEDICAL ENGINEERING

IEEE PRESS SERIES IN BIOMEDICAL ENGINEERING

The focus of our series is to introduce current and emerging technologies to biomedical and electrical engineering practitioners, researchers, and students. This series seeks to foster interdisciplinary biomedical engineering education to satisfy the needs of the industrial and academic areas. This requires an innovative approach that overcomes the difficulties associated with the traditional textbook and edited collections.

NEURAL NETWORKS AND ARTIFICIAL INTELLIGENCE FOR BIOMEDICAL ENGINEERING

Donna L. Hudson

UCSF Medical Education Program
University of California, San Francisco

Maurice E. Cohen

UCSF Medical Education Program
University of California, San Francisco
California State University, Fresno

IEEE Engineering in Medicine and Biology Society, *Sponsor*

IEEE
PRESS

IEEE Press Series in Biomedical Engineering
Metin Akay, *Series Editor*

The Institute of Electrical and Electronics Engineers, Inc., New York

This book and other books may be purchased at a discount from the publisher when ordered in bulk quantities. Contact:

IEEE Press Marketing
Attn: Special Sales
Piscataway, NJ 08855-1331
Fax: (732) 981-9334

For more information about IEEE Press products, visit the
IEEE Press Home Page: http://www.ieee.org/press

Printed in the United States of America

10   9   8   7   6   5   4   3   2   1

ISBN 0-7803-3404-3
IEEE Order Number PC5675

Library of Congress Cataloging-in-Publication Data

Hudson, D. L. (Donna L.)
    Neural networks and artificial intelligence for biomedical
  engineering / Donna L. Hudson, Maurice E. Cohen.
        p.   cm. — (IEEE Press series in biomedical engineering)
    Includes bibliographical references and index.
    ISBN 0-7803-3404-3
    1. Artificial intelligence—Medical Applications.   2. Neural
  networks (Computer science)   3. Expert systems (Computer science)
  4. Biomedical engineering—Computer simulation.   I. Cohen, M. E.
  (Maurice E.)   II. Title.   III. Series.
  R859.7.A78H84   1999
  610' .285'63—dc21   99-30757
                                                              CIP

To our parents
David and Elvera Hegquist Harder
and
Elias and Katie Hey Cohen
for instilling in us at an early age the importance of knowledge

Contents

Preface

The purpose of this book is to cover a broad range of topics relevant to computer-assisted techniques for biomedical decision making. The book consists of three parts: neural networks, artificial intelligence, and alternative approaches. Part I provides a basis for understanding the theoretical and practical approaches to the development of neural network models and their implementation in modeling biological systems. At each stage, theoretical techniques are presented, followed by algorithmic development and application to specific problems in biomedicine. The objective is to allow the reader to see how each technique works in practice. A broad range of neural network techniques and learning algorithms are discussed. At the end of Part I, comparative analyses of different approaches are given. Part II addresses topics in artificial intelligence and their applicability to problems in biomedicine. Topics include knowledge-based acquisition and representation, knowledge-based systems, and searching strategies. Part III deals with other methodologies, including genetic algorithms, probabilistic systems, fuzzy systems, and hybrid systems in which two or more techniques are combined. The concluding chapters include a case study, analysis of the symbolic versus the numerical approach, and future perspectives. The exercises range from straightforward problems that measure comprehension of basic concepts to more challenging problems that permit the development of practical models using the theoretical techniques. In addition to the exercises in the book, problems related to each chapter in the text that can be solved using the MATLAB software package are available by FTP. If you have web access, use ftp://ftp.ieee.org/uploads/press/Hudson. If you are using an ftp command,

    ftp ftp.ieee.org
    login: anonymous
    password: (your email address)
    cd uploads/press/Hudson.

Although a number of published texts describe decision-making strategies, this book focuses on the use of these methods in conjunction with medical and biological data and the unique problems they pose. The book is intended for upper division or graduate students in medical informatics, biomedical engineering, and allied fields, as well as for researchers who require an up-to-date and broad-based overview of the field. Extensive references are included to relevant literature, allowing the student or researcher to investigate specific topics in depth.

This book can be used in a number of ways for different course structures. Part I can be used on its own for a one-quarter graduate or one-semester undergraduate course on neural networks. Part II can be used similarly for an artificial intelligence course. The entire book is appropriate for a full-year (three-quarter or two-semester) graduate course on decision-support strategies at an upper division or graduate level. For a general one-quarter or one-semester overview course, topics can be selected from each section. A sample course could include Part I: Overview, Chapters 1–3; Part II: Chapters 9–10; and Part III: Chapters 14–17. In addition, within each chapter, depending on the level of sophistication, the mathematical treatment and algorithm development can initially be omitted.

The book is intended to give a broad overview of the complex area of decision-support systems and their uses in medicine and biology. It contains sufficient theoretical material to provide a deep understanding of the techniques involved. For researchers in the field, the book is an important tool for initiating in-depth studies on specific topics, hopefully producing new and interesting theoretical and practical developments.

Donna L. Hudson
Maurice E. Cohen

Acknowledgments

We extend our thanks to a number of individuals: first, our spouses, Dr. Samuel Hudson and Odette Cohen, for their patience and assistance in proofreading the manuscript. We also appreciate the assistance of Ronna Mallios, Michael Tilden, and Thomas Dickerson in the preparation of some of the figures in the book. Finally, we thank the referees who reviewed the manuscript and made numerous constructive suggestions.

Donna L. Hudson
Maurice E. Cohen

Overview

0.1 EARLY BIOMEDICAL SYSTEMS

0.1.1 History

Since the early 1960s, the computing community has made predictions regarding the imminent emergence of powerful systems for dealing with medical and biological data, only to be proven wrong. At the same time, many highly successful systems have been created in other areas. There are a number of explanations for this lack of success in the biomedical area. Early computer programs were successful for well-defined systems, the extreme case being physical models that are accurately described in mathematical terms, including many problems in engineering and physics. The further away the application is from the physical sciences, the less defined the model becomes. In general, biomedical systems have some components that are well defined, along with numerous others that are only partially understood. Straightforward mathematical or algorithmic modeling in biomedical systems is only possible for some subsystems. As a result, new techniques need to be developed to deal with biomedical applications.

One early approach utilized pattern recognition techniques. Today pattern recognition is more closely associated with image processing, but in the early years, in the 1960s and 1970s, pattern recognition referred to algorithms that allowed the computer to search for data patterns. These patterns could be images or groups of parameters associated with specific diseases. The latter application now is more commonly called *pattern classification,* with the term pattern recognition reserved for searching for patterns in images. Several successful systems were developed using pattern classification methods. Early pioneers in this area included de Dombal et al. (1972), Patrick, Stelmock, and Shen (1974), Raeside and Chu (1978), Kulikowski (1979), and Cohen, Hudson, and Deedwania (1985).

In the 1970s, spurred by an article by Gorry (1973), interest increased in the potential use of artificial intelligence (AI) techniques in medical systems. AI techniques had been under development since the advent of computers (Jackson, 1974). The AI

1

approach became popular because of the drawbacks associated with pattern classification. These disadvantages included the seemingly black-box nature of the algorithms that provided physicians with only a result, along with the inability of the systems to provide explanations for their conclusions. It was felt that the AI approach would allow the inclusion of expert input as well as address the above shortcomings. For a decade, AI systems in medicine abounded (Miller, 1988), again with limited practical results. Although several excellent systems emerged, few were used in practice, including the most famous of these systems, MYCIN (Shortliffe, 1976). In the mid-1980s, neural network models began to reemerge as an alternative to the AI systems. These models had much in common with the early pattern classification systems in that their knowledge was derived from data rather than from experts. Chapter 1 gives an overview of the historical development of neural networks, and Chapter 9 presents an overview of artificial intelligence.

0.1.2 Medical Records

In addition to the problems involved in developing appropriate paradigms for biomedical systems, another major difficulty centers on the form of the medical record. Medical data are inherently complicated because so many diverse components are important: quantitative test results, analog output such as electrocardiograms and electroencephalograms, pictorial output such as radiographs, computed tomography (CT), magnetic resonance imaging (MRI), nuclear medicine scans, and ultrasound, as well as handwritten notes. Types of medical data are treated in detail in Section O.2 of this chapter. In addition to the complexity of data types, medical records are traditionally handwritten in free form and contain many comments. Specific test results, history, and clinical findings are typically found within the written comments. For the last forty years, numerous attempts have been made to organize these diverse data types into a format that can be easily automated.

Greenes et al. (1969) at Massachusetts General Hospital did early work in the development of the computerized medical record. They developed the computer-based medical record system (COSTAR) system, organized as a hierarchical database. PROMIS (problem-oriented medical information system), developed at the University of Vermont (Schultz, 1976), focused on the problem of organization of medical data, as well as feedback on medical action. Medical information is organized in frames. The ARAMIS system (Fries, 1972), developed at Stanford University in the 1970s, built on some of the ideas in PROMIS but in addition introduced the important concept of the time-oriented data record (TOD) to display the progress of a patient and to permit the development of causal relationships. The goal of the HELP program developed by Warner, Rutherford, and Houtchens (1972) was to assist in medical decision making. The system provided access to raw data, as well as all currently relevant decisions previously made on the patient. Miller began development of the MEDUS/A system (Ben Bassat et al., 1980) at Harvard in 1977 using frames, as did PROMIS. (These systems are discussed in more detail in Chapter 9.)

Researchers continue to struggle with the problem of computerizing medical records. It is a topic of interest at most conferences dealing with computers in medicine. For example, at the 1996 American Medical Informatics Association Fall Symposium, one of the major topics was the computer-based patient record. New graphical techniques allow the inclusion of visual data directly in the patient record. With the advent of the Internet, new pressure has arisen for standardization of the medical record so that it can be utilized at remote sites. Other advances permit the inclusion of magnetic strips on cards so that individuals can carry their medical records with them. New technologies have given rise to new issues, including privacy concerns, particularly as they relate to the transmission of medical records on the Internet. Recent work is concentrating on information sharing, security, standards, and appropriate uses. In many locations, however, the paper record remains the primary source of information, especially for patient history and physical exam parameters.

O.1.3 Drawbacks of Traditional Approaches

Strict algorithmic approaches to decision support in medicine have not been successful because in most instances complete models that describe biological system functioning are not known. The lack of deterministic models was recognized early, leading to the development of pattern recognition approaches to address classification problems, such as differential diagnosis. These models allowed the computer to search for patterns in the data. Approaches based solely on accumulated data present a number of drawbacks. The most obvious problem is that not only is the model dependent on the accuracy of the data, but also it is limited by the applicability of the data to other populations. For example, if the data were collected on a male population between the ages of 18 and 25, a common occurrence in military hospitals, any models generated probably could not be generalized to the population as a whole. This problem plagues many medical studies. A study done on heart disease in Finland, which has a largely homogeneous population, may not apply in the United States, with its extremely diverse population. The knowledge-based approach avoids this problem by using expert input as its knowledge base. The knowledge-based approach has inherent problems. Using only one or a small number of experts as consultants to develop the knowledge base may reveal differences of opinion and may produce knowledge bases that are not in agreement with other experts. An additional problem with expert-derived knowledge bases is the development of methods for incorporating rapidly developing new knowledge.

O.1.4 Numerical versus Symbolic Approaches

Experts continue to debate whether the symbolic approach (knowledge-based systems using expert input) or the numerical approach (pattern recognition and neural networks using data-derived knowledge) is the proper route for accommodating biomedical data. Recently, a number of hybrid systems have been developed that take advantage of both data-derived information and expert-supplied knowledge (Kandel and Langholz, 1992; Cohen and Hudson, 1992). These hybrid systems rely on two or more techniques that are brought to bear on solving a single problem. (Hybrid systems are discussed in Chapters 17 and 18.)

O.2 MEDICAL AND BIOLOGICAL DATA

Medical and biological data are inherently complex. In most medical records, a number of types of data are encountered, including items that describe patient history, physical exams, laboratory tests, pathology reports, imaging reports, and electrocardiogram reports. The types of data that are present must be examined carefully because they influence the kind of analysis that can be done.

O.2.1 Binary Data

Binary data have two possible responses, usually yes/no, but also male/female, present/absent, and so on. Binary data usually assume the values 0 and 1. A variation on binary data is bipolar data in which the variable can assume the values of -1 and 1.

O.2.2 Categorical Data

Categorical data have more than two responses. An example would be progression of severity of symptoms: decrease, no change, increase. A special type of categorical is ordered categorical in which responses can be ranked from worst to best or vice versa. An example of a categorical variable is type of cardiac drug taken. Categories may assume values such as calcium channel blocker, beta-blocker, and anti-arrhythmic agent. The categories are then numerically coded. The progression of symptoms as defined above represents an ordered categorical variable.

O.2.3 Integer Data

Examples of integer data include variables such as blood pressure where an inherent ordering is present, but only integer rather than real values can be assumed. In general, integer data items can be treated the same as continuous data.

O.2.4 Continuous Data

Mathematically speaking, continuous data are the best behaved of all data types and can be easily manipulated in any type of model. However, a few words of caution are due here. In most data, and especially biomedical data, the precision and accuracy of the number must be considered.

O.2.5 Fuzzy Data

A test result depends on the precision of the instrument. The level of precision is usually given in the manual. A hemoglobin level of 14.3 may have a ± 0.1 factor due to the precision of the instrument. The number 14.3 is generally used as a crisp number. An alternative is to define a fuzzy number that attempts to include the imprecision information in the model. First we will consider continuous fuzzy data. An example of continuous data is a test result or an instrument reading such as body temperature or potassium level. A potassium level of 4.2 may have been obtained. However, all instrument readings and test results are subject to some degree of uncertainty, it may therefore be more accurate to represent the potassium level to be in the interval (4.1, 4.3). In other words, it can be considered to be a fuzzy number. In the crisp case, this interpretation would degenerate into (4.2, 4.2) or just the number itself. An example of a fuzzy number representing a test result is shown in Figure O.1 (Hudson and Cohen, 1994). Fuzzy numbers are represented by membership functions that are generally considered to be either triangular or trapezoidal. A triangular membership function has only one value with full membership (a value of 1.0). A trapezoidal membership function has a range of values with full membership. (Techniques for inclusion of these data in the neural network models are discussed in Chapter 16.)

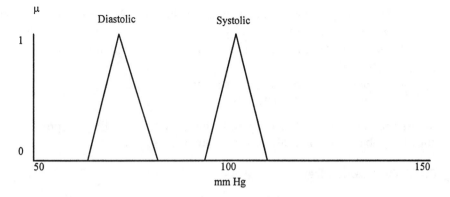

Figure O.1 Membership Functions for Fuzzy Numbers for Two Continuous Variables: Systolic and Diastolic Blood Pressures.

A second useful construct involves the idea of a membership function that indicates normal and abnormal ranges of variables. The membership function assigns a quantifier to a particular numerical value based on a predefined function. An example is given in Figure O.2.

O.2.6 Temporal Data

Early computer-aided decision support systems largely ignored temporal data, although temporal information is very important in diagnostic processes. This is true for the individual patient record in which changes in laboratory tests, physical findings, and medical images can have important implications for identifying disease states and for following the progression of disease processes. The failure to include these important indicators stemmed from the difficulties they posed in both representation and analysis. In fact, even in database design, temporal data pose special representation problems, since they are usually open-ended.

Temporal data can be divided into the following categories, depending on which aspects of the data are important (Hudson and Cohen, 1992):

1. Δ Data: The change in value from the previous recording (example: blood pressure).

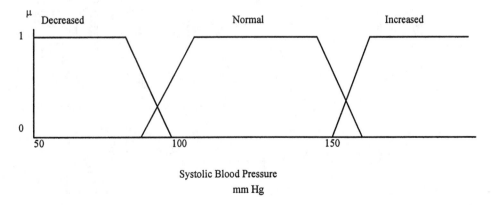

Figure O.2 Membership Function for Ranges of Systolic Blood Pressure.

2. Normalized Δ Data: The change in value relative to the time interval (example: weight gain or loss/month).
3. Duration Data: The duration of time for which the finding persisted (example: fatigue).
4. Sequence Data: A particular sequence of events (example: fever occurring before rash occurring before nausea).

In later chapters, we will investigate techniques for including temporal data in both knowledge-based and neural network systems.

O.2.7 Time Series Data

Time series data occur in a number of contexts in biomedical systems. By far the most common time series that is used for diagnostic purposes in medicine is the electrocardiogram (ECG), an example of which is shown in Figure O.3. The analysis of time series is quite complex; accordingly, only a brief summary will be given here. Time series can be divided into a number of types. The ECG shown in Figure O.3 is a specific type of time series that contains an inherent pattern, known as the QRS complex, associated with each heartbeat. The QRS complex is shown in Figure O.4. The existence of this repeated pattern simplifies the analysis of the time series. By contrast, the electroencephalogram (EEG) which measures brain waves has no inherent, repetitive pattern, as can be seen in Figure O.5. To complicate matters further, both the ECG and EEG are recorded using multiple electrodes, with each lead giving a different pattern. The EEG may use as many as twenty-two leads. Other types of time series data are also useful in determining biological functions, such as hemody-

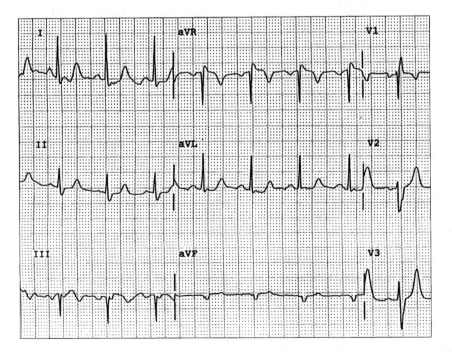

Figure O.3 Example of an Electrocardiogram (ECG).

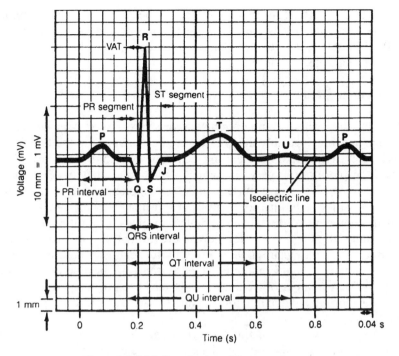

Figure O.4 QRS Complex from Electrocardiogram.

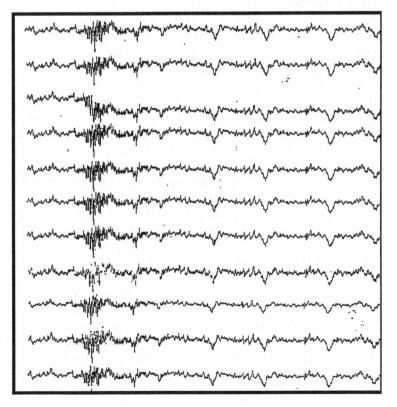

Figure O.5 Example of an Electroencephalogram (EEG).

namic studies. Techniques that have recently been shown to be useful in the analysis of biological time series include wavelet analysis and chaos theory (Cohen et al., 1990). (These techniques are discussed in detail in relation to ECG analysis in Chapters 3 and 18.)

O.2.8 Image Data

One area where computers have scored great success in biomedicine has been medical imaging. Probably the greatest medical advance in the late twentieth century was the development of CT scanning techniques, which in many instances removed the need for exploratory surgery. The same CT techniques that make image reconstruction possible using X rays have subsequently been applied to magnetic resonance imaging, a more sensitive technique for analysis of soft tissue and for metabolic studies. The recent development of digital radiography is replacing traditional methods of storing X-ray film, with direct computer storage providing the ability to transfer images from the office to the physician's home or to remote locations. These systems, denoted PACs (Picture Archiving and Communications System), are becoming more common (Ratib et al., 1992). A number of techniques have also been developed for analysis of images that allow for edge detection, image enhancement, and filtering (Cohen and Hudson, 1988).

Regardless of the imaging technology, all digitized images use the same general format. An image is made up of pixels (picture elements), with the number of pixels per row and the number of rows determining the resolution of the image. For example, an image that is 512×512 has 512 pixels in each row with 512 rows; thus the image contains over 250,000 pixels. This explains why images require so much computer storage! The number of gray levels in a black and white image determines the number of bits per pixel. If 8 bits are used per pixel, 2^8 or 256 gray levels can be represented. For color images, each bit configuration represents a unique color, so the same 256 combinations can represent 256 colors. If the image is three dimensional, the digital representation uses voxels (volume elements) instead of pixels.

Why have computer-imaging techniques succeeded where computerization of other medical information has failed? First, imaging is a well-defined problem. Second, the format of computer images is the same regardless of the technology used to capture the image, whether X rays, ultrasound, magnetic resonance, or nuclear imaging. Thus all images can be stored, manipulated, and transferred by the same methods. Each image, however, uses a large amount of disk space, and transmission requires high bandwidth to achieve acceptable speed. The usefulness of digital imaging is only now becoming a reality because computer hardware advances have made it feasible to manipulate and transfer images at reasonable speeds.

O.3 ORGANIZATION OF THE BOOK

The book is divided into three parts: neural network modeling, artificial intelligence approaches, and alternative approaches to the development of biomedical decision aids. Each chapter contains relevant references to topics covered in that chapter, but the bibliographies are not meant to be exhaustive. The exercises included at the end of each chapter range from straightforward problems designed to ensure an understanding of the basic concepts to more complex exercises that can be developed into projects.

REFERENCES

American Medical Informatics Association. 1996. Proceedings, Fall Symposium.

Ben-Bassat, M., Carlson, R.W., Puri, V.K., Davenport, M.D., Schriver, J.A., Latif, M., Smith, R., Protigal, L., Lipnick, E., and Weil, M. 1980. Pattern-based interactive diagnosis of multiple disorders: The MEDUS system. *IEEE Trans. PAMI* **PAMI-2:** 148–160.

Cohen, M.E., and Hudson, D.L. 1992. Integration of neural network techniques with approximate reasoning techniques in knowledge-based systems. In A. Kandel and G. Langholz, eds., *Hybrid Architectures for Intelligent Systems,* pp. 72–85. Boca Raton, FL: CRC Press.

Cohen, M.E., and Hudson, D.L. 1988. A new class of digital filters for medical imaging. *Engineering in Medicine and Biology,* pp. 359–360. Piscataway, NJ: IEEE.

Cohen, M.E., Hudson, D.L., and Deedwania, P.C. 1985. Pattern recognition analysis of coronary artery disease. In A.H. Levy and B.T. Williams, eds., *American Association for Medical Systems and Informatics,* pp. 262–266.

Cohen, M.E., Hudson, D.L., Moazamipour, H., and Anderson, M.F. 1990. Analysis of hepatic blood flow using chaotic models. In R.A. Miller, ed., *Computer Applications in Medical Care,* vol. 14, pp. 323–327. Washington, DC: IEEE Computer Society Press.

de Dombal, F.T., Leaper, D., Staniland, J., McCann, A., and Horrocks, A. 1972. Computer-aided diagnosis of acute abdominal pain. *Brit. Med. J.* **2:** 9–13.

Fries, J. 1972. Time-oriented patient records and a computer databank. *JAMA* **222(12):** 1536–1542.

Gorry, G.A. 1973. Computer-assisted clinical decision-making. *Method. Inform. Med.* **12:** 45–51.

Greenes, R.A., Pappalardo, A.N., Narble, C.W., and Barnett, G. 1969. Design and implementation of a clinical data management system. *Computers and Biomedical Research* **2:** 469–485.

Hudson, D.L., and Cohen, M.E. 1994. Fuzzy logic in medical expert systems. *IEEE EMBS Magazine* **13(5):** 693–698.

Hudson, D.L., and Cohen, M.E. 1992. The role of temporal data in a neural network for medical decision making. In J.P. Morucci et al., eds., *Engineering in Medicine and Biology,* pp. 1006–1007. Piscataway, NJ: IEEE.

Jackson, P.C. 1974. *Introduction to Artificial Intelligence.* New York: Petrocelli Books.

Kandel, A., and Langholz, G. (eds.). 1992. *Hybrid Architectures for Intelligent Systems.* Boca Raton, FL: CRC Press.

Kulikowski, C.A. 1979. Pattern recognition approach to medical diagnosis. *IEEE Trans. Sys. Sci. Cyber.* **SS6(3):** 173–178.

Miller, P.L. (ed.). 1988. *Selected Topics in Medical Artificial Intelligence.* New York: Springer-Verlag.

Patrick, E., Stelmock, F., and Shen, L. 1974. Review of pattern recognition in medical diagnosis and consulting relative to a new system model. *IEEE Trans. Sys., Man, Cyber* **SMC4(1):** 1–16.

Raeside, D.E., and Chu, W. 1978. An application of pattern recognition to echocardiography. *IEEE Trans. Sys., Man, Cyber* **SMC-8:** 81–86.

Ratib, O., Ligier, Y., Girard, C., et al. 1992. A picture archiving and communication system based on open distributed architecture. *IEEE Engineering in Medicine and Biology* **14:** 1204–1208.

Schultz, J.R. 1976. PROMIS, Problem-oriented medical information system. *Proc. 3rd Illinois Conf. on Medical Information Systems,* pp. 1–14.

Shortliffe, E.H. 1976. *Computer-Based Medical Consultations—MYCIN.* New York: Elsevier/North Holland.

Warner, H.R., Rutherford, B., and Houtchens, B. 1972. A sequential approach to history taking and diagnosis. *Comput. Biomed. Res.* **5:** 256–262.

PART I
NEURAL NETWORKS

1

Foundations
of Neural Networks

1.1 OBJECTIVES OF NEURAL NETWORKS

Neural network research can be divided into two areas of investigation. The first area, the *direct problem,* employs computer and engineering techniques to model the human brain. This type of modeling is used extensively by cognitive scientists (Harley, 1998) and can be useful in a number of domains, including neuropsychiatry (Rialle and Stip, 1994, Ruppin, Reggia, and Horn, 1996), and neurophysiology (Saugstad, 1994). For more detailed coverage of the direct problem, the reader should consult MacGregor (1987) and Aakerlund and Hemmingsen (1998).

The second area, the *inverse problem,* simulates biological structures with the objective of creating computer or engineering systems. The inverse problem is applied extensively in building computer-assisted decision aids used in differential diagnosis, modeling of disease processes, and construction of more complex biomedical models. Part I of this book concentrates mainly on the inverse problem, although the two areas cannot be completely separated since one problem often sheds light on the other.

Neural networks are used to solve problems in which the complete formulation is unknown—that is, no causal model or mathematical representation exists, usually because the problem itself is not completely understood. The neural network uses data to derive patterns that are relevant in differentiating the groups. Neural network models fall into the category of soft computing, as do fuzzy logic approaches, in that solutions are found to approximate problems rather than approximating solutions of exact formulations.

1.1.1 Modeling Biomedical Systems

Historically, numerous modeling techniques have been used, including mathematical approaches and simulation. Some of the early systems were quite successful, especially in the area of drug therapy. Realistic models for most biological systems are still difficult to achieve both because of our limited knowledge and the complexity of these systems. Recent approaches have used chaos theory to address nonlinear dynamics in biological systems. Neural network modeling of biomedical systems comprises the direct problem and has resulted in a number of interesting applications in which neural network models successfully mimic characteristics of human learning as well as providing models of learning disorders. In general, modeling and simulation systems are outside the scope of this book with two exceptions: features of neural networks relevant to modeling and the use of chaos theory in a hybrid system (illustrated in Chapter 18). Modeling using symbolic techniques is considered in Part II of this book.

1.1.2 Establishment of Decision-Making Systems

The use of neural network models as decision aids comprises the inverse problem. These systems have their historical foundations in earlier pattern recognition techniques and limited neural network models.

1.2 BIOLOGICAL FOUNDATIONS OF NEURAL NETWORKS

The motivating factor behind neural network modeling was the structure of biological nervous systems, or biological neural networks. To draw attention to this parallel, neural network models are sometimes referred to as artificial neural networks (ANNs). Although some basics are known about biological nervous systems, a great deal remains unknown.

1.2.1 Structure of the Neuron

Figure 1.1 shows a simple biological cell. A semipermeable membrane that is between 70 and 100 Angstroms in thickness surrounds the cell. In the interior of the cell, components include the nucleus, the mitochondria, and the Golgi bodies. The nucleus

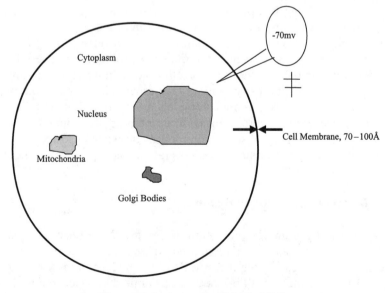

Figure 1.1 Structure of a Biological Cell.

consists of nuclear sap and a nucleoprotein-rich network from which chromosomes and nucleoli arise. A nucleolus contains DNA templates for RNA. The mitochondria produce energy for the cell through cellular respiration. Golgi bodies are involved in the packaging of secretory proteins (Rogers and Kabrisky, 1991).

Figure 1.2 shows a neuron, which is an extension of the simple cell in that two types of appendages have been formed: multiple dendrites and an axon. The dendrites receive input from other neurons, whereas the axon is an output channel to other neurons. Note that a neuron still possesses all the internal features of a regular cell as shown in Figure 1.1. The neuron has important basis characteristics, and it has a number of inputs called *dendrites* and one output called the *axon*. The cell membrane has an electrical resting potential of -70 mV. The resting potential is maintained by pumping positive ions out of the cell. The principal pump is the sodium (Na^+) pump. The main difference between a neuron and an ordinary cell is that the neuron is ex-

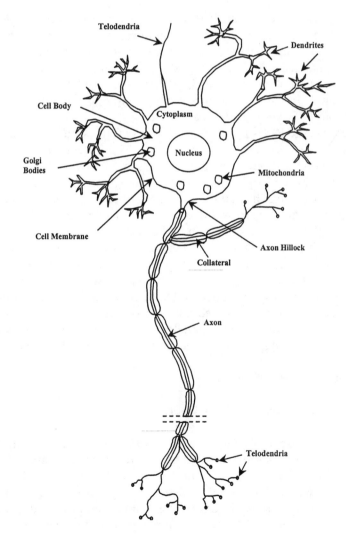

Figure 1.2 Structure of a Neuron.

citable. Because of inputs from the dendrites, the cell may become unable to maintain the -70 mV resting potential, resulting in an action potential that is a pulse transmitted down the axon. Note that the action potential results only after a certain threshold has been exceeded, for example, if the potential is raised above -50 mV. After releasing the pulse, the neuron returns to its resting potential. The action potential causes a release of certain biochemical agents known as *neurotransmitters* that are the means by which messages are transmitted to the dendrites of nearby neurons. These neural transmitters may have either an excitatory or inhibitory effect on neighboring neurons. A number of biochemical transmitters are known, including acetylcholine (usually excitatory), catecholamines, such as dopamine, norepinephrine, and epinephrine, and other amino acid derivatives such as histamine, serotonin, glycine, and γ-aminobutyric acid (GABA). GABA and glycine are two important inhibitory transmitters (Butter, 1968).

1.2.2 Structure of the Central Nervous System

The puzzle of how individual neurons are organized into complex neuronal structures has been the subject of a great deal of research over the years. Santiago Ramón de Cajal was the first to discover the complex interconnection structure in the cerebral cortex summarized in an English translation by DeFelipe and Jones (1988). Along with his associate Camillo Golgi (Golgi, 1886) he produced photographs of the structures by applying dyes that were absorbed differently. For this work, Cajal and Golgi were awarded the 1906 Nobel Prize in medicine.

Later, in the 1930s, Lorente de Nó, one of Cajal's students, examined the types of neurons in the cerebral cortex showing 32 to 34 different types based on shape classification, not on function (Asanuma and Wilson, 1979).

In the 1940s, Hodgkin and Huxley (Hodgkin, 1964; Huxley, 1971) began their well-known work on the giant squid, chosen because of its two very large neurons. Hodgkin and Huxley were awarded the 1963 Nobel Prize for their investigations into threshold, inhibition, and excitation in the giant squid axon.

Next, Hubel and Wiesel (1962) did extensive investigation into the cerebral cortex of the cat. They mapped many complex structures and tracked the path from the optic nerve to the lateral geniculate body to the visual cortex. They found columns of cells in the visual cortex that appeared to be responsible for processing various shapes. In the process, they distinguished between simple, complex, and hypercomplex cells. Their work also emphasized the parallel nature of the visual processing system. Figure 1.3 shows the optical pathways Hubel and Wiesel mapped out.

1.3 EARLY NEURAL MODELS

1.3.1 The McCulloch and Pitts Neuron

In a 1943 paper, McCulloch and Pitts (1943) presented a two-state logical decision element model based on a simplified neuron which they used to compute Boolean functions. They declared that "neural events and the relationship among them can be treated by means of propositional logic" (p. 115). Their artificial neuron performed logical operations on two or more inputs and produced an output if a threshold value was exceeded. This work can be considered the ancestor of artificial neural networks.

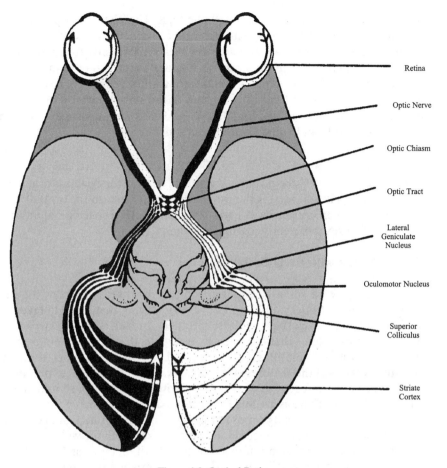

Figure 1.3 Optical Pathways.

1.3.2 Hebbian Learning

In 1949, Donald Hebb (1949) published his approach to learning laws. In his original approach, excitatory neuron coupling weights were increased by a subsequent firing, based on the idea of learning driven by activity. However, weights could only increase. (Many later models were based on this initial work and are discussed in detail in Chapter 5.)

1.3.3 ADALINE

ADALINE, an acronym for ADAptive LINear Element, was developed by Bernard Widrow (Widrow and Stearns, 1985). He used the mathematics of adaptive signal processing to produce the first commercial neural network.

1.3.4 Rosenblatt Perceptron

In the 1950s, Rosenblatt (1962) introduced models of the brain which he called perceptrons. Although his representation of artificial neurons was based on the neuron models of McCulloch and Pitts, he departed from their approach by basing his model on probability theory rather than symbolic logic. The photoperceptron as defined by Rosenblatt responded to optical patterns, and contained a sensory, an association, and a response area (Figure 1.4). The sensory area corresponds to the retinal structure. Each point responds to light in an on/off manner; input is then transmitted to the association area. The connections have three possible weights: 1 (excitatory), -1 (inhibitory), or 0. When a pattern is presented to the sensory area, a unit in the association area becomes active providing its value exceeds a predetermined threshold θ. At time t, the output from the association area is defined as

$$y(t) = \text{sgn} \ \Sigma \ [x_i(t) \ w_i(t) - \theta] \qquad (1.1)$$

where sgn is either $+1$ (for positive argument) or -1 (for negative argument), $x_i(t)$ is the ith input signal, and $w_i(t)$ is the weight of the ith input to the node.

The basic perceptron model was an example of a learning algorithm. Nilsson (1965) summarizes these early learning systems.

1.3.5 Problems with Early Systems

Neural network research experienced a general setback following the publication of a paper by Minsky and Pappert (1969) proving that a single-layer perceptron could not solve the exclusive or (XOR) problem. In fact, single-layer perceptrons can only separate categories that are linearly separable, that is, separable by a hyperplane (in two dimensions, a line). Figure 1.5 shows the XOR problem; c_0 is the category in which the polarity of the features is the same, which should have an output of 0 for the XOR, and c_1 is the category in which the polarity differs, which should have an output of 1 for the XOR. There is no line that can separate these categories. Unfortunately, even though Rosenblatt had proposed the use of multilayer networks to overcome this problem, these criticisms stymied neural network research for well over a decade. The limitation of the current computers in terms of both memory and speed was one reason for the loss of interest in the early neural network research. The problems addressed as examples in the neural network models were fairly simple, with few nodes. The training often took hours to accomplish. Many justifiably felt that these time and

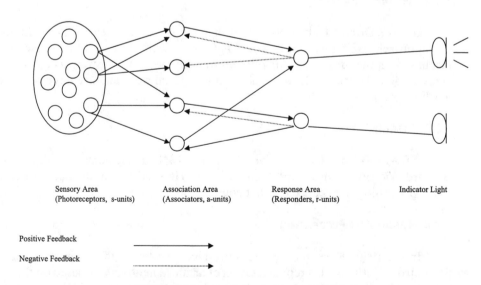

| Sensory Area | Association Area | Response Area | Indicator Light |
| (Photoreceptors, s-units) | (Associators, a-units) | (Responders, r-units) | |

Positive Feedback

Negative Feedback

Figure 1.4 Diagram of Simple Photoperceptron.

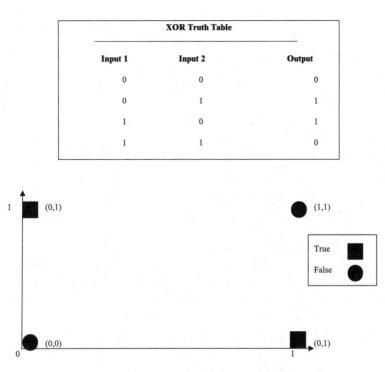

XOR Truth Table		
Input 1	Input 2	Output
0	0	0
0	1	1
1	0	1
1	1	0

Figure 1.5 The Exclusive OR Problem (XOR).

memory considerations made it difficult to tackle practical problems. With the advent of faster and faster hardware with large, inexpensive memory, these worries ceased to be considerations in the new generation of neural network models.

1.4 PRECURSOR TO CURRENT MODELS: PATTERN CLASSIFICATION

Pattern classification (sometimes called pattern recognition) was one of the first methods applied to medical applications and has found applications in diverse areas from electrocardiograms to genetic sorting. (For an historical perspective of pattern recognition, see Chapter 9.)

What is a pattern recognition problem? As an example, consider a group of patients who have come to the emergency room with chest pain. Subsequently, some of these patients are found to have had a myocardial infarction (MI), and others are found to have had angina. The first objective of a pattern classification system is to determine which parameters enabled the medical staff to distinguish between these two diagnoses. This is a two-category problem. The initial phase consists of feature extraction. *Features* are properties of items to be classified that will aid in discriminating between classes.

1.4.1 Feature Extraction

Determining features is the most crucial step in designing a pattern recognition decision aid. In the emergency room example given earlier, we must identify parameters useful in distinguishing between the two classes. Identification of possible features requires domain knowledge or access to domain knowledge relevant to the application. As a simple illustration, suppose we know that patients with MIs in general have low blood pressure, whereas those with angina in general have elevated blood pressure. If we plot the histograms for blood pressure for all patients with either disease, we may get a plot similar to that shown in Figure 1.6. Note the area of overlap between the two groups, so that the groups cannot be completely separated by this one variable. In addition, we know that patients with MIs may have elevated white blood counts, whereas patients with angina have normal white blood counts. If we consider only these two parameters, or features, we have a two-variable problem. We combine these features into a two-dimensional feature vector $\mathbf{x} = (x_1, x_2)$, where x_1 = systolic blood pressure (BP) and x_2 = white blood count (WBC). For the sake of this example, we will consider only systolic blood pressure. In this simple case we can plot x_1 versus x_2. Figure 1.7 shows a sample plot of five cases in each category. The squares represent cases with MI, and the circles represent cases with angina.

The second objective of a pattern classification system is to find a separator that will divide these two classes by placing as many samples into the correct category as possible. The dashed line in Figure 1.7 shows a possible separator with one misclassification. Additional features may result in better classification or a more robust model. The following considerations should be kept in mind:

1. Look for a classification that minimizes error.
   Ideal: all cases classified correctly; if not possible, minimize either the number of errors or the cost of errors.
2. More features may be needed.
   For three features, Figure 1.6 becomes 3-D, for four or more, no picture!

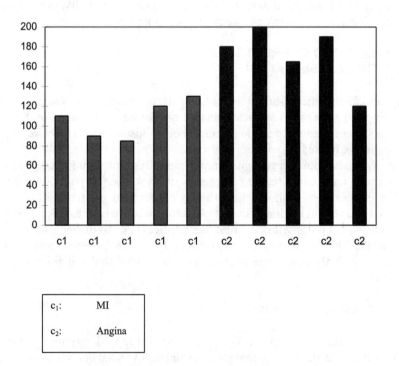

Figure 1.6 Histograms of Systolic Blood Pressures for Myocardial Infarction (MI) and Angina.

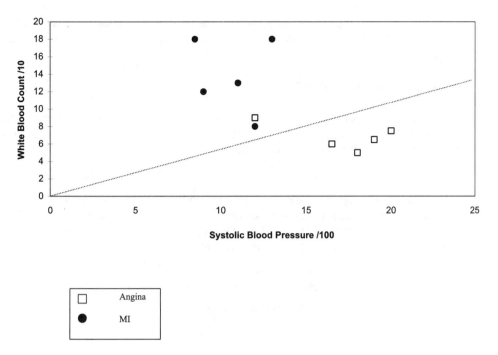

Figure 1.7 Plot of White Blood Count versus Systolic Blood Pressure.

3. More classes may be relevant.
   For example, MI, angina, and congestive heart failure.

The final objective of pattern classification is to use the separator to classify new cases. In this way, the pattern recognition system is used as a decision aid.

1.4.2 Supervised Learning

The preceding classification is an example of supervised learning: data of known classification are used to determine important parameters (components of the feature vector) that contribute to the correct decision. To use supervised learning, a training set must be available for development of the separating vector. A test set is then used to determine the accuracy of the separator. Ideally, the training set and test set should be disjoint.

The question that remains is, How can the separating vector be obtained? In our simple example, we did it geometrically; for data of higher dimensionality, this will not be possible. The separator is determined through a learning algorithm that is the heart of the method. (Learning algorithms will be discussed shortly and in detail in Chapter 6.)

1.4.3 Unsupervised Learning

Unsupervised learning is a much more difficult problem. In this case, data of unknown classification are used. The objective is to try to find patterns in the data that will allow the data to be grouped or clustered according to similar characteristics with the characteristics defined in the feature vector. The main method for accomplishing unsupervised learning is clustering, with a number of variations. (Clustering will be discussed in detail in Chapter 5. Recent approaches also include data mining and genetic algorithms, discussed in Chapter 14.)

1.4.4 Learning Algorithms

The purpose of a learning algorithm is to determine which features are important for a particular decision as well as their relative importance. In most pattern classification systems, a feature vector is defined as

$$\mathbf{x} = (x_1, x_2, \ldots, x_n,) \tag{1.2}$$

where each x_i is a feature and n is the dimensionality of the vector. In classification programs, the objective in the most straightforward two-class problem is to obtain a decision surface that can separate the data. The two-variable equivalent to this is shown in Figure 1.7. For the n-dimensional case, we want the following to hold:

$$D(\mathbf{x}) > 0 \Rightarrow \mathbf{x} \text{ belongs in class 1}$$
$$D(\mathbf{x}) < 0 \Rightarrow \mathbf{x} \text{ belongs in class 2}$$
$$(D(\mathbf{x}) = 0 \text{ is indeterminate})$$

where

$$D(\mathbf{x}) = \sum_{i=1}^{n} = w_i x_i \tag{1.3}$$

or in vector format

$$D(\mathbf{x}) = \mathbf{w} \cdot \mathbf{x} \tag{1.4}$$

In order to find the value for $D(\mathbf{x})$, the values for the two vectors $\mathbf{w}$ and $\mathbf{x}$ must be known. The values for $\mathbf{x}$ are obtained from the data. It is the job of the learning algorithm to determine the values for $\mathbf{w}$. In supervised learning, an additional important piece of information is available: for each $\mathbf{x}$, the class to which it belongs is known.

A general algorithm for supervised learning follows:

Make an initial guess for each component of **w.**
Select a training set of data.
For each vector in the training set:
  Compute D(**x**)
  If D(**x**) *> 0 and* **x** ε *class 1 or* D(**x**) *< 0 and* **x** ε *class 2, do not adjust* **w**
  If D(**x**) *> 0 and* **x** ε *class 2 adjust* **w** *according to rule 1*
  If D(**x**) *< 0 and* **x** ε *class 1 adjust* **w** *according to rule 2*
Until **w** *does not change (or until criterion function is minimized).*

Basically, learning algorithms differ in the definition of rules 1 and 2 in the preceding algorithm and in the determination of the criterion function that determines when the iterative weight adjustment should stop. A number of approaches have been used, including Bayes learning (Chapter 15), perceptrons (Chapter 4), potential functions (Chapter 4), and backpropagation (Chapter 4).

The simple algorithm given above is complicated in practice by a number of factors. The most obvious problem is what to do if **w** does not cease to change, which will happen when it is not possible to correctly classify all samples in the training set. If all samples can be correctly classified, the set is said to be *linearly separable*. If not, the algorithm must terminate on some other condition, which will hopefully ensure that as many samples as possible are classified correctly. This is handled by defining what is known as a *criterion function*. These functions are defined differently depending on the approach taken and will be discussed in detail later in this book.

As an example, consider our two-dimensional problem given earlier. This is a two-category problem. We will consider the presence of MI to be class 1 and the presence of angina to be class 2. Our problem is then defined by the following components:

$$D(\mathbf{x}) = \mathbf{w} \cdot \mathbf{x} = w_1 x_2 + w_2 x_2 \qquad (1.5)$$

where

$$\begin{aligned} x_1: & \quad \text{systolic blood pressure} \\ x_2: & \quad \text{white blood count} \end{aligned}$$

If $D(\mathbf{x}) > 0$, then we will assume that $\mathbf{x}$ belongs to class 1 (MI); if $D(\mathbf{x}) < 0$, we will assume that $\mathbf{x}$ belongs to class 2 (angina); if $D(\mathbf{x}) = 0$, then we can make no determination.

For the purpose of illustration, we will use the perceptron learning rule, defined as

$$w_i(t + 1) = w_i(t) + \eta[d(t) - y(t)]x_i(t) \qquad (1.6)$$

that computes each weight adjustment. The iteration is represented by t, and η is the learning rate, which we will set to 0.01. We define $y(t)$ and $d(t)$ as follows:

$$\begin{aligned} y(t) &= 1 \text{ if } D(\mathbf{x}) > 0 \\ y(t) &= -1 \text{ if } D(\mathbf{x}) < 0 \\ d(t) &= 1 \text{ if vector belongs to class 1} \\ d(t) &= -1 \text{ if vector belongs to class 2} \end{aligned}$$

Table 1.1 contains values for our ten feature vectors. To make our calculations simpler, we can scale the data so that both values are of similar magnitudes. We will divide all WBC values by 1000 and all blood pressure values by 10. We will select the first two vectors of each class, alternating classes, for inclusion in the training set:

$$\begin{aligned} \mathbf{t}_1 &= (11.0, 13.0) & \text{(vector } \mathbf{x}_1, \text{ class 1)} \\ \mathbf{t}_2 &= (18.0, 5.0) & \text{(vector } \mathbf{x}_6, \text{ class 2)} \end{aligned}$$

TABLE 1.1 Feature Vector Values for Differentiation between Myocardial Infarction (MI) and Angina

Feature Vector	Diagnosis	Systolic Blood Pressure	White Blood Count
$\mathbf{x}_1$	MI	110	13,000
$\mathbf{x}_2$	MI	90	12,000
$\mathbf{x}_3$	MI	85	18,000
$\mathbf{x}_4$	MI	120	8,000
$\mathbf{x}_5$	MI	130	18,000
$\mathbf{x}_6$	Angina	180	5,000
$\mathbf{x}_7$	Angina	200	7,500
$\mathbf{x}_8$	Angina	165	6,000
$\mathbf{x}_9$	Angina	190	6,500
$\mathbf{x}_{10}$	Angina	120	9,000

$$\mathbf{t}_3 = (9.0, 12.0) \qquad \text{(vector } \mathbf{x}_2\text{, class 1)}$$
$$\mathbf{t}_4 = (20.0, 7.5) \qquad \text{(vector } \mathbf{x}_7\text{, class 2)}$$

We will make an initial guess for each weight as $w_1 = -0.3$, $w_2 = 1.0$. Initially, we substitute vector $\mathbf{t}_1$ into Eq. (1.5):

$$D(\mathbf{t}_1) = -0.3 \,(11.0) +1.0(13) > 0; \text{therefore } y(t) = 1$$
$\mathbf{t}_1$ belongs to class 1; therefore $d(t) = 1$

Substituting into Eq. (1.6), we see that as the classification is correct, no weight adjustment is made. We then proceed with the second vector substitution, which also results in no weight adjustment as does the third. For the fourth vector

$$D(\mathbf{t}_4) = -0.3(20.0) + 1.0(7.5) > 0, y(t) = 1$$
$\mathbf{t}_4$ belongs to class 2

Therefore, substituting into Eq. (1.6)

$$w_1(1) = -0.3 + 0.01[(-1 - (1)] \, 20.0 = -0.7$$
$$w_2(1) = 1.0 + 0.01[-1 -(1)]7.5 = 0.85$$

The process must then begin again with $\mathbf{t}_1$ and continue until all vectors are classified correctly. After completion of this process, the resulting weights are:

$$w_1 = -0.7$$
$$w_2 = 0.85$$

Our decision surface is

$$D(\mathbf{x}) = -0.7x_1 + 0.85x_2 \tag{1.7}$$

The remainder of the vectors in Table 1.1 will be our test set, which will be used to determine how well our decision surface works. For example, substituting vector $\mathbf{x}_3$ from Table 1.1 in Eq. (1.5):

$$D(\mathbf{x}_3) = -0.7(8.5) + 0.85*(18) > 0, \text{ which is correct since vector } \mathbf{x}_3 \text{ belongs to class 1.}$$

1.5 RESURGENCE OF THE NEURAL NETWORK APPROACH

Neural networks have found a wide range of applications in the last decade (Carpenter and Grossberg, 1988; Sabbatini, 1992; *Computer Magazine,* 1988) and in many cases have replaced knowledge-based approaches that became popular in the 1970s (Davis and Lenat, 1982; Barr and Feigenbaum, 1982). Neural networks permit rapid development of a model through the learning algorithm if sufficient data are available.

Resurgence of the neural network approach began in the late 1970s and early 1980s with the work of Kohonen, Hopfield, Grossberg, and Rummelhart. In the 1970s, Grossberg (1988) developed the adaptive resonance theory (ART) and theories about the functioning of biological nervous systems that Carpenter and Grossberg (1988) later developed into self-organizing neural network architectures. Kohonen (1984) also did pioneering work on self-organizing networks. In the early 1980s, Hopfield and others introduced new approaches based on the early work of Hebb (1949). Rummelhart and his group (Rummelhart and McClelland, 1986) developed the backpropagation method, which became one of the most widely used approaches in neural network design. Hypernet, developed by Cohen and Hudson in the early 1980s (Cohen, Hudson, and Anderson, 1989), extended the potential function approach and in the process introduced the single and multidimensional Cohen orthogonal functions that encompassed the possibility of fractional contribution of nodes. The new approaches developed by these researchers, as well as others, overcame the limitations of the early neural network approaches. These methods, together with the advances made in computer architecture providing faster processing and cheaper memory, made the neural network concept practical. (In Chapters 2 through 5 we will examine in detail the new neural network structures that began in the 1980s, along with biomedical applications for each method.)

1.6 BASIC CONCEPTS

1.6.1 Artificial Neurons

One of the basic ideas behind neural networks is to construct artificial neurons that have the characteristics of actual neurons. Artificial neurons, or nodes as they are often called, receive input from multiple other nodes. These multiple inputs can be considered as dendrites in the biological neuron. Like neurons, the nodes produce one output that can be associated with the axon. In computing the output, the input information is weighted, either positively or negatively. These weights are analogous to the excitatory and inhibitory action of the chemical transmitters in the actual neuron. In neurons, an output results only if a certain threshold voltage is exceeded. This action is sometimes simulated by use of threshold values in the node, although not all models use the threshold approach.

1.6.2 Selection of Input Nodes

In the initial design of a neural network, the number and type of input nodes must be determined. These decisions are based on the nature of the problem. As we will see in the next chapter, nodes may be binary, representing only an on or an off state, or they may accept continuous values. The input nodes must be able to represent all relevant information that is pertinent to the problem. The process of defining input nodes is connected with feature selection in which salient features of the problem under consideration are analyzed. This process is discussed in Chapter 3.

1.6.3 Network Structure

The early neural networks were only two-layer structures. As discussed earlier, this construction greatly limited their usefulness in that only linear problems could be represented. In the second generation of neural networks, new structures were developed which consisted of three or more layers. The most common structure is the three-layer network as illustrated in Figure 1.8. These three layers consist of the input layer, the hidden or interactive layer, and the output layer. Many other network configurations have been used, but in general the three-layer network is capable of addressing all problems which the more complex structures address. The manner in which nodes are connected is different depending on the approach and will be described in detail in later chapters when each method is discussed.

1.6.3.1 Feed-Forward Networks. The methods described in Section 1.4 apply to feed-forward networks. These networks compute weights that are used to determine output from a node that is subsequently fed to the next layer. In the detailed example

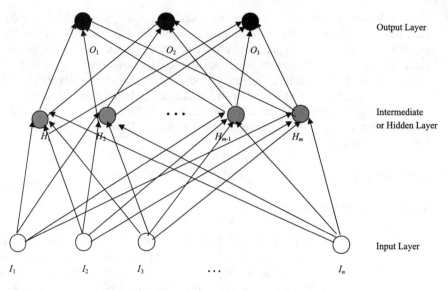

Figure 1.8 Three-Layer Neural Network Structure.

given earlier, the weights determined the impact that the input nodes have on the output, but no information is fed back to the input nodes.

1.6.3.2 Feed-Backward Networks.   The revival of neural networks began in the early 1980s with the work of Hopfield (1982). The Hopfield model was completely different from earlier approaches in that the neurons, or nodes, had two-way connections. Instead of adjusting weights to tune the output of nodes, the network stored patterns that were later used to process unknown input vectors. (The Hopfield net and other feed-backward approaches will be described in detail in Chapter 2.)

1.6.4 Learning Mechanism

We saw an example of a learning algorithm in Section 1.4, with a specific learning rule given by the perceptron learning rule. As we will learn in subsequent chapters, many different learning mechanisms have been tried in neural networks. All have advantages and disadvantages. Some offer strong mathematical foundations, whereas others are more ad hoc. The learning mechanism affects the speed of convergence of the network, and indeed determines whether or not it converges at all. It can also affect the accuracy of the model in classification of unknown cases.

1.6.5 Output

Many neural networks have only one output node. This is not the only possible structure. As we will see in subsequent chapters, it is possible to have multiple output nodes and even output nodes that feed into other types of decision-making strategies, such as symbolic reasoning.

1.7 SUMMARY

In this chapter we have reviewed some of the components of biological nervous systems that are important contributors to the foundations of artificial neural networks. In addition to these biological precursors, the most important technical precursor to neural networks, pattern classification, which was used successfully for many years in design of medical decision-making aids, was summarized. In the subsequent chapters of Part I, we review pattern classification in more depth, along with different types of neural networks and corresponding learning algorithms as well as their uses in biomedical problem solving.

EXERCISES

1. What is the main reason that the neural network approach introduced in the late 1950s was abandoned for over twenty years?
2. In what ways do neural network models correspond to biological nervous systems? Can you list aspects of biological nervous systems that have not been incorporated into neural networks?
3. Explain why the two-layer neural networks of the 1950s and 1960s could not solve the exclusive OR problem.
4. In the example based on Table 1.1, we computed the weighting factors for the first four passes. Complete this calculation, stopping when all four vectors in the training set have been classified correctly. Check to make sure that your weights agree with those given in the text.
5. Substitute the remainder of the vectors in Table 1.1 into Eq. (1.5). How many of them are correctly classified? Does this correspond to the geometrical results in Figure 1.7?
6. Repeat exercise 4, but change the order of the vectors in your training set to x_6, x_1, x_2, x_7. Do you get the same values for w_1 and w_2?
7. If you add a third variable, the linear separator is no longer a line. What is it? What happens for four or more variables? Can the same approach be utilized?
8. Devise an alternative strategy for determining a decision surface if the two groups are not linearly separable.
9. What happens if the classification problem has more than two classes? For example, assume the three possibilities are angina, MI, and congestive heart failure. Is it possible to use a perceptron-type model to solve this problem?
10. Formulate mathematically the perceptron approach for four variables: white blood count, systolic blood pressure, diastolic blood pressure, and pH of the blood.

REFERENCES

Aakerlund, L., and Hemmingsen, R. 1998. Neural networks as models of psychopathology. *Biological Psychiatry* **43(7):** 471–482.

Asanuma, H., and Wilson, V.J. (eds.). 1979. Integration in the nervous system: a symposium in honor of David P.C. Lloyd and Rafael Lorente de No, The Rockefeller University, Tokyo.

Barr, A., and Feigenbaum, E. 1982. *The Handbook of Artificial Intelligence,* vol. 2. Reading, MA: Addison-Wesley.

Butter, C.M. 1968. *Neuropsychology: The Study of Brain and Behavior.* Belmont, CA: Brooks/Cole Publishing Company.

Carpenter, G., and Grossberg, S. 1988. The art of adaptive pattern recognition by a self-organizing network. *Computer* **21:** 152–169.

Cohen, M.E., Hudson, D.L., and Anderson, M.F. 1989. A neural network learning algorithm with medical applications. *SCAMC* **13:** 307–311.

Computer Magazine. 1988. IEEE **21(3).**

Davis, R., and Lenat, D.B. 1982. *Knowledge-Based Systems in Artificial Intelligence.* New York: McGraw-Hill.

DeFelipe, J., and Jones, E.G. (eds.). 1988. *Cajal on the Cerebral Cortex: An Annotated Translation of the Complete Writings*. New York: Oxford University Press.

Golgi, C. 1886. *Sulla fina anatomia degli organi centrali del sistema nervoso*. Milan, Italy: Hoepli.

Grossberg, S. 1988. *Neural Networks and Natural Intelligence*. Cambridge, MA: MIT Press.

Harley, T.A. 1998. Connectionist modeling of the recovery of language functions following brain damage. *Brain and Language* **52(1):** 7–24.

Hebb, D.O. 1949. *The Organization of Behavior*. New York: John Wiley & Sons.

Hodgkin, A.L. 1964. *The Conduction of the Nervous Impulse*. Liverpool, England: Liverpool University Press.

Hopfield, J.J. 1982. Neural networks and physical systems with emergent collective computational abilities. *Proc. Natl. Acad. Sci. USA* **79:** 2554–2558.

Hubel, D.H., and Wiesel, T.N. 1962. Receptive fields, binocular interaction, and functional architecture of the cat visual cortex. *J. Physiology* **160(1):** 106–154.

Hudson, D.L., Cohen, M.E., and Anderson, M.F. 1991. Use of neural network techniques in a medical expert system. *International Journal of Intelligent Systems* **6(2):** 213–223.

Huxley, A.F., and Simmons, R.M. 1971. Proposed mechanism of force generation in striated muscle. *Nature* **233(5321):** 533–538.

Kohonen, T. 1984. *Self-Organization and Associative Memory*. Berlin: Springer-Verlag.

MacGregor, R.J. 1987. *Neural and Brain Modeling*. San Diego: Academic Press.

McCulloch, W.S., and Pitts, W. 1943. A logical calculus of the ideas immanent in neural nets. *Bull. Math. Biophys.* **5:** 115–137.

Minsky, M., and Papert, S. 1969. *Perceptrons: An Introduction to Computational Geometry*. Cambridge, MA: MIT Press.

Nilsson, N.J. 1965. *Learning Machines*. New York: McGraw-Hill.

Rialle, V., and Stip, E. 1994. Cognitive models in psychiatry: from symbolic models to parallel and distributed models (French). *J. of Psychiatry and Neuroscience* **19(3):** 178–192.

Rogers, S.K., and Kabrisky, M. 1991. *An Introduction to Biological and Artificial Neural Networks for Pattern Recognition*. Bellingham, WA: SPIE Optical Engineering Press.

Rosenblatt, F. 1962. *Principles of Neurodynamics*. New York: Spartan Books.

Rummelhart, D.E., and McClelland, J.L. 1986. *Parallel Distributed Processing: Explorations in the Microstructure of Cognition*. Cambridge, MA: MIT Press.

Ruppin, E., Reggia, J.A., and Horn, D. 1996. Pathogenesis of schizophrenic delusions and hallucinations: a neural network model. *Schizophrenia Bulletin* **22(1):** 105–123.

Sabbatini, R.M.E. 1992. Applications of connectionist systems in biomedicine. *MEDINFO*, pp. 418–425. New York: Elsevier.

Saugstad, L.F. 1994. Deviation in cerebral excitability: possible clinical implications. *Int. J. of Psychophysiology* **18(3):** 205–212.

Widrow, B., and Stearns, S.D. 1985. *Adaptive Signal Processing*. Englewood Cliffs, NJ: Prentice-Hall.

2

Classes
of Neural Networks

2.1 BASIC NETWORK PROPERTIES

In the design of neural networks, several aspects are important, notably:

Structure of Networks
    Number of layers
    Connectivity of nodes
Properties of Nodes
    The activation range for each node
    The activation or transfer function
Algorithm Design
    Weight initialization process
    Formula for calculating activation
    Learning method

The examples given in this chapter show some of the variations in these factors.

2.1.1 Terminology

Vectors are denoted in boldface; for example, $\mathbf{x} = (x_1, x_2, \ldots, x_n)$ is a vector with n components. In general, each component of an input vector is represented by one input node. Weights that connect node i to node j are designated by w_{ij}. Matrices are designated by boldface capital letters; for example, $\mathbf{W}$ represents a weight matrix if the dimensions are clear from the context; if not, $\mathbf{W}_{nm}$ designates an n by m matrix.

2.1.2 Structure of Networks

Networks differ in the number of layers that are included. As we saw earlier, the first neural networks had only two layers, and so their capabilities were limited. Most current neural networks consist of three layers: input, hidden, and output. Although some networks may include additional layers, it can be shown that the three-layer network can perform all functions of networks with more layers, but in some cases not as efficiently.

A *fully connected* network means that all nodes are connected to all other nodes. *Feed-forward* networks have connections that point from input nodes to output nodes. *Recurrent networks* have some type of *feedback* connections (from output to hidden layer, for example). If a network is *symmetric,* then reverse connections are equal to forward connections, that is,

$$w_{ij} = w_{ji}.$$

2.1.3 Computational Properties of Nodes

A node is the representation of the biological neuron, and in some publications, the terms *neuron* and *node* are used interchangeably. The activation range of a node indicates the values that it can assume. In some networks, the nodes may be binary with the only allowable values being 0 or 1. In some binary systems, the allowable values are -1 and 1 instead of 0 and 1. This representation is normally termed *bipolar.* An activation level can also be continuous on the unit interval $[0, 1]$ or can assume unrestricted continuous values.

Figure 2.1 shows a typical computational structure for a node in a network. In general, input values are summed in the node. The result may then be adjusted by some offset θ that varies depending on the design of the network. The output is then determined using the adjusted summation as the argument in a function f. (Choices for f are discussed later in this chapter.) The general equation is

$$y = f\left(\sum_{i=1}^{n} (w_i x_i - \theta) \right) \tag{2.1}$$

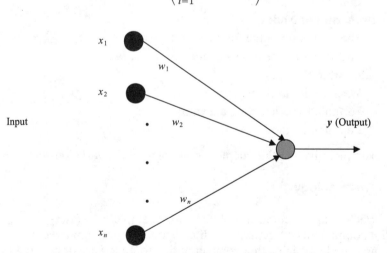

Figure 2.1 Computational Structure of a Node.

where the node has n inputs, w_i is the weight associated with the ith input, θ is the offset or internal threshold value, and f is defined by the algorithm. Some common definitions for f are illustrated in Figure 2.2 (Lau, 1992). Specific examples of the application of these functions are seen in the approaches illustrated in the following sections. These functions are called *activation functions* or *transfer functions.* For some algo-

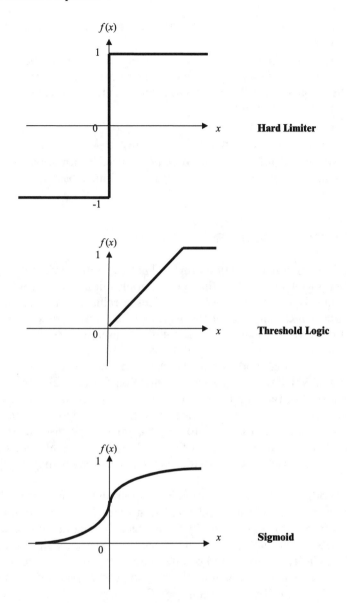

Figure 2.2 Examples of Functional Nonlinearities.

rithms, specific mathematical conditions apply, for example, differentiability. In some instances, linear activation functions are also used.

2.1.4 Algorithm Design

Neural networks can be classified in a number of ways depending on structure, function, or objective. A functional classification given by Fu (1994) divides neural networks into the following categories according to their functional properties.

Classification Models: Classification models assign input data items to two or more categories. These models may use supervised learning in which the categories are known or unsupervised learning in which the categories may not be known.

Association Models: The two types of association models are auto-association, which focuses on the retrieval of an object based on part of the object itself; and hetero-association, which focuses on the retrieval of an object in one set using an object in a different set.

Optimization: The objective of these systems is to find the best solution by minimizing a cost function or other measure.

Self-Organization: This approach organizes information using adaptive learning facilities. It is similar to clustering algorithms, based on unsupervised learning techniques.

2.2 CLASSIFICATION MODELS

The most common application of neural networks in biomedical engineering is in classification problems. We saw this type of application in the previous chapter when we looked at early neural network approaches, specifically the perceptron, as well as other pattern classification approaches. Although the initial perceptron had several limitations that restricted its usefulness, multilayer nonlinear perceptron models have been developed that remove these limitations.

Classification models may be based on neural networks that use supervised learning in which data of known classification are used as a training set to develop a decision surface that can be used later to classify new data items. As will be shown in Chapter 4, there are numerous supervised learning approaches that differ in both theory and application. In addition to the perceptron, supervised learning neural networks include backpropagation, ADALINE (ADAptive LINear Element), potential functions, and min-max networks (which is discussed along with fuzzy approaches in Chapter 16).

Another type of classification model that uses unsupervised learning techniques relies on data for which the classification of each case is unknown. These methods search for patterns in the data by which each case can be classified and are often referred to as clustering. The data are clustered into groups that contain similar cases, in which similarity is determined by one of a variety of measures. Unsupervised learning approaches include Kohonen networks, competitive learning, adaptive resonance theory (ART), and Hebbian learning (see Chapter 5).

Most of the biomedical examples illustrated in this book can be categorized as classification networks, both supervised and unsupervised. Classification networks offer strong techniques for developing decision-making models. These applications are treated in detail in subsequent chapters. In order to give the reader a broad view of the field of neural networks, other types of models and their applications are summarized in the remainder of this chapter.

2.3 ASSOCIATION MODELS

Association models have applications in computer storage problems and communications problems and in general have binary input. These networks can deal with other types of input if it is first converted into a binary format. As mentioned in Chapter 1, many of these networks use a threshold approach.

2.3.1 Hopfield Nets

In 1982, John Hopfield of the California Institute of Technology designed a new type of neural network that was one of the first steps in reviving the neural network methodology that had been essentially dormant for the previous fifteen years (Hopfield and Tank, 1986). The Hopfield network is useful for both auto-association and optimization tasks.

2.3.1.1 Theoretical Basis. The Hopfield net utilizes the concept of surface minimization in physics and consists of a set of interconnected nodes. Each node, or neuron, in the network is binary-valued, traditionally assuming the values of -1 or 1. Each node is connected to every other node but not to itself. The result is $n(n-1)$ connections for n nodes. A diagram of the Hopfield network is shown in Figure 2.3. The main idea is that a single network can store multiple stable states.

In the Hopfield net all weights are symmetric, $w_{ij} = w_{ji}$. The network can assume a set of stable weights so that when a neuron acts on its neighbors the values of the neuron do not change. For a given input pattern, the network can converge to the stable state nearest to that pattern. The network is presented with examples called *probe vectors* that are binary-valued. The vectors in the network that are used for comparison are called *exemplar patterns*.

Output

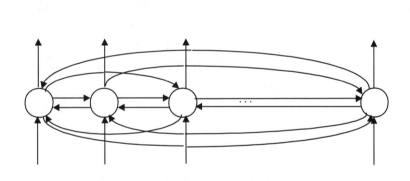

Input

Figure 2.3 Hopfield Network.

Hopfield Algorithm for Auto-Association
Assign Connection Weights

$$w_{ij} = \sum_{s=1}^{m} x_{is}\, x_{js} \qquad\qquad i \neq j \qquad\qquad (2.2)$$

for a network that stores m *patterns, where* w_{ij} *is the connection weight from unit* i *to unit* j *and* x_{is} *is the ith component in the pattern vector (exemplar).*
Initialize
For an input vector x_j

$$\mu_j(0) = x_j$$

where $\mu_j(0)$ is the activation level of unit j *at time* t = 0 *and* x_j *is the* j*th component of the input pattern.*

Iterate until Convergence

At time t

$$\mu_j(t + 1) = F(\sum w_{ij} \mu_j(t)) \qquad (2.3)$$

where

$$F(y) = \begin{bmatrix} 1 & y > 0 \\ -1 & y < 0 \\ \mu_j(t) \ (unchanged) & y = 0 \end{bmatrix}$$

Repeat until the activation levels of nodes remain unchanged with further iterations. The pattern of activation upon equilibrium represents the stored pattern that best matches the unknown pattern. Note that F *is an example of a hard-limited function as illustrated in Figure 2.2.*

EXAMPLE

Consider the following example from Fu (1994):

Use the outer product to construct the initial weight matrix:

$$\mathbf{W} = \sum_i (\mathbf{x}_i{}^T\mathbf{x}_i - I_n) \qquad (2.4)$$

where $\mathbf{x}_i$ is the n-dimensional bipolar vector to be stored and I_n is the nxn identity matrix.

Define three vectors

$$\mathbf{x}_1 = (1, -1, -1)$$
$$\mathbf{x}_2 = (-1, 1, -1)$$
$$\mathbf{x}_3 = (-1, -1, 1)$$

Thus

$$\mathbf{W} = \begin{bmatrix} 0 & -1 & -1 \\ -1 & 0 & -1 \\ -1 & -1 & 0 \end{bmatrix}$$

Then use x_1 as the input vector (also known as the probe vector):

$$F(x_1\mathbf{W}) = F[2, 0, 0] = [1, -1, -1]$$

which is the vector $\mathbf{x}_1$. In other cases, more than one iteration may be necessary.

2.3.2 Other Associative Memory Approaches

The bidirectional associative memory (BAM) (Kosko, 1988; Freeman and Skapura, 1992) can relate an input vector to another vector and can generalize over similar inputs. There are a number of variations on the BAM algorithm, including the ABAM (adaptive bidirectional associative memory), which can accept continuous rather than binary inputs (Kosko, 1987).

2.3.2.1 Theoretical Basis of Bidirectional Associative Memory (BAM). The BAM network associates pairs of vectors such that when vector $\mathbf{a_i}$ is input to the network it recalls vector $\mathbf{b_i}$. The BAM network is shown in Figure 2.4. The backward weight is the transpose of the forward weight, making this a symmetric network.

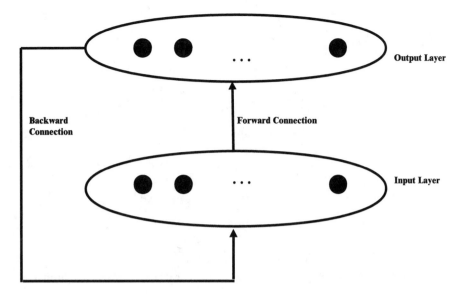

Figure 2.4 The Bidirectional Associative Memory (BAM).

BAM Algorithm
Assign Connection Weights
Forward Weights

$$\mathbf{W} = \sum_{k=1}^{m} \mathbf{x_k}^T \mathbf{y_k} \tag{2.5}$$

for a network that stores m *patterns, where* $\mathbf{W}$ *is the connection weight matrix and patterns* $\mathbf{x_k}$ *and* $\mathbf{y_k}$ *form an association pair.*
Backward Weights

$$w_{ji} = w_{ij}$$

Initialize
For an input vector x_j

$$\mu_j(0) = x_j$$

where $\mu_j(0)$ *is the activation level of unit* j *at time* t $= 0$ *and* x_j *is the jth component of the input pattern.*
Iterate until Convergence
At time t

$$\mu_j(t + 1) = F(\sum w_{ij}\, \mu_j(t)) \tag{2.6}$$

where F *is a hard-limiting function*

$$F(y) = \begin{bmatrix} 1 & y > 0 \\ -1 & y < 0 \\ \mu_j(t) \ (unchanged) & y = 0 \end{bmatrix}$$

(A sigmoid function may be used instead of the hard-limiting function.)
Repeat until the activation levels of nodes remain unchanged with further iterations. The pattern of activation upon equilibrium represents the stored pattern associated with the input pattern.

EXAMPLE

Consider the following example for the six binary vectors:

$$\mathbf{a}_1 = (1\,0\,1\,0\,1) \qquad \mathbf{b}_1 = (1\,1\,1\,0)$$
$$\mathbf{a}_2 = (0\,0\,1\,1\,1) \qquad \mathbf{b}_2 = (1\,1\,0\,1)$$
$$\mathbf{a}_3 = (1\,1\,0\,0\,1) \qquad \mathbf{b}_3 = (1\,1\,0\,0)$$

The bipolar versions of these vectors are:

$$\mathbf{x}_1 = (1\,-1\,1\,-1\,1) \qquad \mathbf{y}_1 = (1\,1\,1\,-1)$$
$$\mathbf{x}_2 = (-1\,-1\,1\,1\,1) \qquad \mathbf{y}_2 = (1\,1\,-1\,1)$$
$$\mathbf{x}_3 = (1\,1\,-1\,-1\,1) \qquad \mathbf{y}_3 = (1\,1\,-1\,-1)$$

The weight matrix is then constructed by

$$w_{ij} = \sum_{k=1}^{m} \mathbf{x}_i^{T}\,\mathbf{y}_j$$

The result produces a 5×4 weight matrix. The construction of the weight matrix is left as an exercise.

2.3.3 Hamming Net

2.3.3.1 Theoretical Basis. A method similar to the Hopfield network that operates on binary input and has applications in communication theory is the Hamming network (Lau, 1992). This network uses the optimum minimum error classifier for this situation that selects the minimum Hamming distance. The Hamming distance is the number of bits in the input that do not match the exemplar. For example, given the two vectors:

$$\mathbf{x}_1{:} = (0, 1, 1, 1, 0, 0, 1)$$
$$\mathbf{x}_2{:} = (0, 1, 0, 1, 0, 0, 1)$$

the Hamming distance between the two is 1. A diagram of the Hamming net is shown in Figure 2.5.

Hamming Algorithm

Assign Connection Weights

$$w_{ij} = x_{is}/2 \qquad \theta_j = n/2$$
$$1 \le j \le n, 1 \le j \le m$$

In the upper subset

$$w_{ij} = 1, \qquad k = 1$$
$$-\varepsilon \qquad k \ne 1 \quad \varepsilon < 1/m$$

for a network that stores m *patterns, where* w_{ij} *is the connection weight from unit* I *to unit j and* θ_j *is the threshold for that node.* x_{is} *is the ith component in the pattern vector* $\mathbf{x}_s$. *All thresholds in the upper quadrant are zero.*

Initialize

For an input vector x_j

$$\mu_j(0) = F\left(\sum_{i=1}^{n} w_{ij}\,x_i - \theta_j\right) \tag{2.7}$$

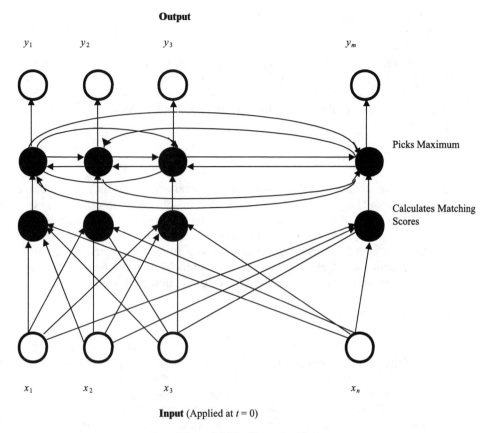

Figure 2.5 The Hamming Net.

where $\mu_j(0)$ is the output (or activation) level of unit j in the upper subnet at time 0, x_i is the ith component of the input pattern, and F is the threshold logic nonlinearity from Figure 2.2.

Iterate until Convergence

At time t

$$\mu_j(t + 1) = F(\mu_j(t) - \varepsilon \sum \mu_k(t))$$
$$k \neq j \qquad\qquad (2.8)$$
$$1 \leq k, j \leq m$$

This process is repeated until convergence when the output of only one node is positive.

2.3.4 Applications of Association Models

As mentioned earlier, the initial application of association models was computer storage. These models have also been used in communications involving data transfers. In auto-associative procedures, an input vector that is like a sample vector **a** will recall the stored vector **a** and will also recall itself. The auto-associative approach is seen in the generation of the weight matrix that is derived from exemplar vectors multiplied by their transposes. In auto-association as illustrated above in the Hopfield net, a memory can be completed or corrected upon retrieval by self-association if given a partial or corrupted input. The Hopfield net suffers from a number of problems, including a tendency to converge to local minima and limited network capacity. The BAM approach is similar to the Hopfield net, but unlike the Hopfield net, the BAM network generates matrices that are not necessarily square.

The Hamming net is an example of a maximum likelihood classifier. It implements the optimum random minimum error classifier when bit errors are random and independent; thus its performance is always as good as or better than the Hopfield net when used as an optimizer. (Minimum error classification methods are discussed in Chapter 4.)

2.4 OPTIMIZATION MODELS

Neural networks are useful for solving optimization problems that cannot easily be solved by algorithmic means. An optimization problem consists of finding the best solution given a set of constraints. The variables are encoded as input vectors, and the constraints are represented by weights connecting the nodes, which may be positive or negative. An energy function is compared to a function derived from problem constraints in order to adjust the weights. The Hopfield net, discussed earlier as an autoassociative network, can also be used for optimization problems.

2.4.1 Hopfield Net

The Hopfield algorithm must be modified slightly when used as an optimization method. The energy function of the Hopfield net is a Lyapunov function, which becomes smaller for any change in the state of the network until a stable state is reached. A Lyapunov function exists for all feedback networks and provides a characteristic that is equivalent to energy, hence the name "energy function." In the energy model, any stable state represents a potential well. An input vector represents an initial condition that will lead to the selection of a potential well (Chester, 1993).

Hopfield Algorithm for Optimization
The Hopfield algorithm is modified in the following manner for optimization problems:
Assign Connection Weights
Determine an energy function E_C based on the constraints of the problem.
Compare the function with the energy function of the Hopfield net based on:

$$E_H = -\tfrac{1}{2}\sum_j\sum_i w_{ij}\,\mu_i\,\mu_j - \sum_i I_i\,\mu_i + \sum_i \theta_i\,\mu_i \qquad (2.9)$$

which is a Lyapunov function, discussed below. E_H is the network energy, I_i is the external input to node i, and θ_i is the threshold for node i.
Initialize
$\mu_j(0)$ = small randomized value
Iterate until Convergence
At time t

$$\mu_j(t+1) = F(\sum w_{ij}\,\mu_j(t) + I_i) \qquad (2.10)$$

where

$$F(y) = \begin{cases} 1 & y > \theta_i \\ -1 & y < \theta_i \\ \mu_j(t)\ \textit{(unchanged)} & y = \theta_i \end{cases}$$

Repeat until the activation levels of nodes remain unchanged with further itera-
tions. The pattern of activations represents the optimized solution.

EXAMPLE

Hopfield and Tank (1985) applied the Hopfield net to the traveling salesman problem (TSP). An n-city TSP requires an array of n^2 nodes. Each row in the matrix represents a single city, and each column represents the order in which that city is visited. A five-city visit for cities A, B, C, D, E in which the order of the visits was C, A, E, D, B is represented by

	1	2	3	4	5
A	0	1	0	0	0
B	0	0	0	0	1
C	1	0	0	0	0
D	0	0	0	1	0
E	0	0	1	0	0

Hopfield and Tank designed an energy function that restricted the network into one active neuron for each column and each row that was also proportional to the sum of the distances between cities. The general idea is to minimize the sum of the distances. For the ten-city case, for which there are more than 180,000 paths, the network chose one of the two shortest possible paths. However, the approach breaks down if the number of cities exceeds 30.

The Hopfield net has stability problems that are better addressed by Boltzmann machines.

2.4.2 Boltzmann Machines

In Boltzmann machines, local minima are avoided by adding some randomness to the energy function. The binary states of the neurons are updated by stochastic means.

2.4.2.1 Theoretical Basis.

The basis for this approach was molecular physics in which the Boltzmann distribution provides the probability density function for the kinetic energy of particles in a gas of absolute temperature T. The probability that any given particle has an energy between E and $E + \Delta E$ is proportional to $e^{-E/kT}dE$ where k is the Boltzmann constant. The assumption (Hinton and Sejnowski, 1986) is that in a fully connect Hopfield-type binary network (states 0 and 1) the kth neuron has a probability p_k of being in the on state (activation is 1), where

$$p_k = 1/(1 + e^{-\Delta E/kT}) \tag{2.11}$$

where ΔE_k is the energy gap between the on and off states of the neuron and T is analogous to the system temperature. The network's global energy is

$$\sum_{i<j} w_{ij}\, x_i x_j \tag{2.12}$$

where x_i is the ith binary nodal signal and w_{ij} is the weight connection from node i to node j. At thermal equilibrium, the probability of each state is constant and corresponds to the Boltzmann distribution

$$P_A/P_B = e^{-(E_A - E_B)/T} \tag{2.13}$$

with the probability of the ratio of any two states depending on the difference in energy.

Boltzmann Algorithm

Assign Connection Weights

Same as Hopfield optimization net

Initialize
Select an initial temperature.
Iterate until Convergence
Calculate the probability that unit i *is active:*

$$P_i = 1/(1 + e^{-\Delta E_i/T}) \tag{2.14}$$

where ΔE_i *is the total input energy received by unit* i.
The weights are calculated by

$$\Delta w_{ij} = \varepsilon \, (P_{ij}^+ - P_{ij}^-) \tag{2.15}$$

Repeat until thermal equilibrium is achieved. The pattern of activation represents the optimized solution.

2.4.3 Applications of Optimization Models

As we saw in the example of the traveling salesman problem, optimization methods can be used in problems that cannot be solved using the algorithmic approach. Applications in this category include problems that are described by means of constraints for which a unique solution does not exist. In general, they involve tradeoffs among the variables to achieve the best overall solution in terms of an optimization function. The objective in the traveling salesman problem was to minimize the distance. In a problem involving the development of a medical protocol, the objective may be to minimize patient risk. (Additional optimization approaches will be discussed in Chapter 5.)

2.5 SELF-ORGANIZATION MODELS

Self-organization models are networks that can organize themselves without knowing the correct classification of input patterns and thus fall into the category of unsupervised learning. Some examples of self-organization models are Kohonen networks, competitive learning, Hebbian learning, and adaptive resonance theory (ART). These systems are discussed in detail in Chapter 5 as examples of unsupervised learning.

In 1981 Kohonen (1988) demonstrated the feasibility of the concept that systems could organize data without being taught. Since that time, a number of extensions to the initial concept have evolved. Figure 2.6 shows a two-layer network with *n* input nodes (corresponding to the dimensionality of the input vectors) and *m* output nodes corresponding to the *m* decision regions. Every input node is connected to every output node. The connections from input node *i* to output node *j* is w_{ij}. The information can be arranged in an *n* by *m* matrix in which each row represents input nodes and columns represent output nodes. The matrix elements are the corresponding weights. The *i*th column in the matrix represents the set of synaptic input weights leading to the *i*th output node.

Initial weights are chosen randomly. The organization process begins with the determination of the similarity of an input vector to representation of each category. A number of methods exist. A distance measure, such as the Euclidean distance, can be computed between the input vector and the other vectors for each of the *m* output nodes. Alternatively, the dot product could be used. A winner among the vectors represented by the columns in the matrix is selected according to the calculation showing to which vector the input is most similar.

Assume we are using the dot product. Each node computes the dot product of its weight vector and the input vector

$$\mathbf{n}_i = \mathbf{x} \, \mathbf{w}_i \tag{2.16}$$

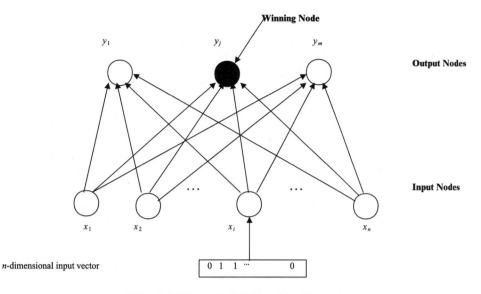

Figure 2.6 Kohonen's Self-Organizing Network.

where $\mathbf{n}_i$ is the activation of unit I, $\mathbf{x}$ is the input vector, and $\mathbf{w}_i$ is the weight vector for unit i, the ith column of the matrix. In matrix notation

$$\mathbf{N} = \mathbf{XW} \tag{2.17}$$

Only the node with the maximum activation (the largest dot product) will produce an output (equal to 1). This process is similar to the k-means clustering algorithm (see Chapter 5). The network learns by adjusting weights according to

$$\mathbf{w}(t + 1) = \mathbf{w}(t) + \eta(\mathbf{x} - \mathbf{w}(t)) \tag{2.18}$$

where η is the learning rate. Kohonen learning makes the winning weight vector closer to the input vector.

Other self-organization models have been developed by a number of researchers including Carpenter and Grossberg (1986). The work by Hebb (1949) forms the basis for this type of learning. Chapter 5 presents additional algorithms pertaining to these approaches, along with biomedical applications.

There are many applications of self-organization models in biomedicine, including problems involving data analysis when nothing is known about either the number of categories present or the correct classification of each case, or both. (These topics are addressed in detail in Chapter 5.)

2.6 RADIAL BASIS FUNCTIONS (RBF)

Radial basis functions (RBF) utilize a combination of supervised and unsupervised learning techniques (Moody and Darken, 1989). The network consists of an input layer, a hidden layer, and an output layer as shown in Figure 2.7.

2.6.1 Theoretical Basis

Learning in the hidden layer is unsupervised with methods such as k-means clustering (Duda and Hart, 1973). Learning in the output layer is supervised and uses a least mean squares type of algorithm (see Chapter 4). After an initial solution is found, it is optimized through a supervised learning method.

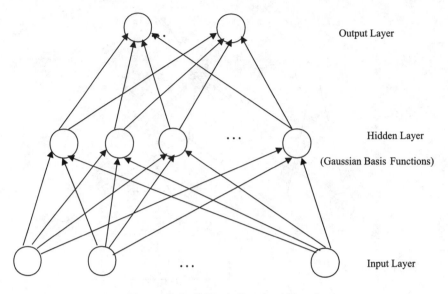

Output Layer

Hidden Layer

(Gaussian Basis Functions)

Input Layer

Figure 2.7 Radial Basis Function Network.

Each unit in the hidden layer has a localized receptive field usually represented by a Gaussian function:

$$\mu_i = \exp[-(\mathbf{x} - \mathbf{w}_i)\cdot(\mathbf{x} - \mathbf{w}_i)/2\sigma_i^2] \qquad (2.19)$$

where $\mathbf{x}$ is the input vector, $\mathbf{w}_i$ is the weight vector for hidden unit i, and σ_i^2 is the normalization factor. The activation level of the output unit is

$$\mu_j = w_{ij}\mu_i \qquad (2.20)$$

where $\mathbf{w}_{ij}$ is the weight from hidden unit i to output unit j.

Radial Basis (RBF) Algorithm

Assign Connection Weights

Output layer weights assigned to small random numbers.

Initialize

Hidden layer weights determined through clustering.

Iterate until Convergence

For the output layer

$$w_{ij}(t + 1) = w_{ij}(t) + \Delta w_{ij} \qquad (2.21)$$

where

$$\Delta w_{ij} = \eta \; \delta_i \mu_j$$

where η is the learning rate, and

$$\delta_i = T_i - \mu_i$$

where T_i is the target output activation and μ_i is the actual output activation at unit i.

Repeat until convergence.

2.6.2 Applications of Radial Basis Functions

The radial basis approach can be used for modeling and classification, and it is also useful in dimensionality reduction. An application to neurobiological data is given in Poggio and Girosi (1990).

2.7 SUMMARY

We have seen examples of the major categories of neural networks: classification, association, optimization, self-organization, and radial basis functions, along with corresponding learning algorithms. The most relevant of these for the design of computer-assisted support systems in biomedicine are classification and self-organization networks. The other techniques discussed here have, however, been used in biomedical problems. The researcher needs to keep an open mind regarding the availability of all these techniques to permit the development of innovative approaches to computer-assisted support systems.

EXERCISES

1. For the diagram in Figure 2.1, assume that you have the following input to the node with the weights indicated:

Input values:	1	−1	−1	1	1
Weights:	.5	.3	.2	.1	.1

   The internal threshold value is .2. Compute the output value for each of the functions given in Figure 2.2.
2. Re-do the example for the associative Hopfield net given in the text but replace the bipolar vectors with binary vectors (e.g., $\mathbf{x}_1 = (0\ 0\ 1)$). Does this change the outcome? Do you need to adjust the functions in Figure 2.2?
3. For the BAM algorithm, compute the weight vector from the information given in the text. What is the result when you present the vectors $\mathbf{a}_1$ and $\mathbf{b}_1$?
4. Set up the problem definition for a traveling salesman problem with three cities. Design an energy function that meets the specified requirements.
5. What is the major difference between Boltzmann machines and the other optimization models? What types of problems are better suited to Boltzmann machines?
6. Self-organization models rely on unsupervised learning. Give a detailed example of a biomedical problem that would best be solved by an unsupervised learning approach. Define input variables for this application.

REFERENCES

Carpenter, G.A., and Grossberg, S. 1986. Neural dynamics of category learning and recognition: Attention, memory consolidation, and amnesia. In J. Davis, R. Newburgh, E. Wegman, eds., *Brain Structure, Learning, and Memory*. AAAS Symposium Series.

Chester, M. 1993. *Neural Networks, A Tutorial*. Englewood Cliffs, NJ: Prentice-Hall.

Duda, R.O., and Hart, P.E. 1973. *Pattern Classification and Scene Analysis*. New York: John Wiley & Sons.

Freeman, J.A., and Skapura, J.A. 1992. *Neural Networks, Algorithms, Applications, and Programming Techniques*. Reading, MA: Addison-Wesley.

Fu, L.M. 1994. *Neural Networks in Computer Intelligence.* New York: McGraw-Hill.

Hebb, D.O. 1949. *The Organization of Behavior.* New York: John Wiley & Sons.

Hinton, G.E., and Sejnowski, T.J. 1986. Learning and relearning in Boltzmann machines. *Parallel Distributed Processing: Explorations in the Microstructure of Cognition,* Vol. 1. Cambridge, MA: MIT Press.

Hopfield, J.J., and Tank, D.W. 1986. Computing with neural circuits: A model. *Science* **233:** 625–633.

Hopfield, J.J., and Tank, D.W. 1985. Neural computation of decisions in optimization problems. *Biological Cybernetics* **52:** 141–152.

Kohonen, T. 1988. *Self-Organization and Associative Memory.* New York: Springer-Verlag.

Kosko, B. 1988. Bidirectional associative memories. *IEEE Trans. SMC* **18(1):** 49–60.

Kosko, B. 1987. Adaptive bidirectional associative memories. *Applied Optics* **26:** 4947–4960.

Lau, C. 1992. *Neural Networks, Theoretical Foundations and Analysis.* New York: IEEE Press.

Moody, J., and Darken, C.J. 1989. Fast learning in networks of locally-tuned processing elements. *Neural Computation* **1(2):** 281–294.

Poggio, T., and Girosi, F. 1990. Networks for approximation and learning. *Proc. IEEE* **78(9):** 1481–1497.

Classification Networks
and Learning

3.1 NETWORK STRUCTURE

In this chapter, we will discuss neural network classification systems in which data vectors are to be assigned to categories based on their values. The system may divide data into two categories or multiple categories.

3.1.1 Layer Definition

For the purpose of the discussion, we will make a number of simplifying assumptions and will use vector notation to represent feature vectors and nodes in each layer. We will assume a three-layer network.

3.1.2 Input Layer

The input layer consists of n nodes, $n_1, n_2, \ldots, n_n$, where each node represents each input variable in a 1-to-1 mapping. This is not the only possible configuration. For example, if binary nodes are used, several may be required to represent each variable. We will, however, assume the straightforward 1-to-1 mapping here.

3.1.3 Hidden Layer

The hidden, or interactive layer, consists of interaction of nodes from the input layer. The learning algorithm determines the exact configuration. For purposes of this discussion we will assume m nodes, $i_1, i_2, \ldots, i_m$.

3.1.4 Output Layer

The output layer represents the classification phase. If it is a two-category problem, the output layer will have two nodes. Another possibility is to have one output node that fires if the condition is present and does not fire if it is not present. For mul-

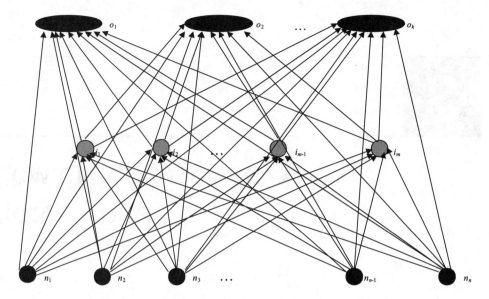

Figure 3.1 Three-Layer Classification Neural Network.

tiple category problems, more output nodes are required. The output nodes will be designated $o_1, o_2, \ldots, o_k$. In the case of the possibility of concurrent diseases, more than one of the output nodes may fire. For networks designed for differential diagnosis, relative strengths of the firings may be considered. Figure 3.1 shows a neural network with this general configuration.

3.2 FEATURE SELECTION

Feature extraction is a process through which input variables are selected for the design of a neural network. Feature selection is the same regardless of whether the learning is supervised or unsupervised. Feature extraction represents the first step in the process.

3.2.1 Types of Variables

First, it must be determined what type of variables can be represented in the nodes in the input layer. As we saw in the last chapter, some networks accept only binary input. Although any number can be represented as a binary number, this is not an efficient way to design a system if most variables are in fact continuous.

3.2.2 Feature Vectors

A feature vector **x** consists of n components, denoted $x_1, x_2, \ldots, x_n$. Each x_i represents a variable that is relevant to the classification problem.

An example of a feature vector for the classification of exercise testing data useful for determining presence of coronary artery disease is:

x_1: Resting systolic blood pressure
x_2: Resting diastolic blood pressure
x_3: Resting heart rate

x_4: Maximum ST depression

x_5: Heart rate at end of test

x_6: Systolic blood pressure at end of test

x_7: Diastolic blood pressure at end of test

In this example, the first three variables assume integer values, the fourth assumes continuous values, and the last three are Δ variables that represent changes over time. The ST depression is a variation of the normal electrocardiogram (ECG) pattern. (Refer to Figure O.4.)

The important aspect of feature extraction is to enumerate all possible variables that may be useful in the classification process. If features are included which turn out to be unimportant, their weights will approach zero in the learning process. Thus it is better to err on the side of including too many variables. The number of variables that are feasible to include is limited, however, by the amount of data available for training, for roughly ten cases are needed for every variable that is included.

The variables shown in the preceding example are all clinical parameters. Many other possibilities exist, such as patient history, family history, and imaging and time series data, including ECG. These last two categories are discussed in the next two subsections. Some variables may be categorical. In most learning algorithms, categorical variables must be ordered. For example, if the categorical variable represents type of heart medication, there will be no inherent ordering from bad to good, lesser to greater, and so on. However, this information may be used if each medication is included as a separate binary variable that indicates whether or not the patient takes that medication. In general, this approach must be used for all nonordered categorical variables.

3.2.3 Image Data

Image data present additional difficulties. Some of the classic problems in pattern recognition have dealt with the recognition and classification of images. Feature extraction in images consists of identifying some aspect of an image that allows it to be recognized. In complex images, this phase can be quite involved. A large body of literature exists in this area (Duda and Hart, 1973), but the problem remains partially unsolved. For medical images, many approaches have been tried (Vannier, Yates, and Whitestone, 1992). For analysis of some images, for example, images of the head, symmetry is often a useful feature, with asymmetrical findings indicators of disease. Figure 3.2 shows a CT (computed tomography) scan of the head of a patient with a possible tumor. Notice the asymmetry in the image. Other potentially useful features are changes in gray levels, areas with irregular borders, and changes from previous images of the same patient. As in all feature extraction, the selection of image features will be influenced by the goal of the classification system.

3.2.4 Time Series Data

Time series data can be considered in two categories: those with built-in patterns (e.g., ECGs) and those without built-in patterns (e.g., EEGs). Automatic analysis of ECGs is largely dependent on variations from the normal QRS complex previously illustrated in Figure O.4 in the Overview. In the preceding example, the maximum ST depression is a feature extracted from the QRS complex of the ECG (Cohen, Hudson, and Deedwania, 1985). Other aspects of the ECG, such as heart rate and R-R interval fluctuations, may also be important features, as we will see in Chapter 18 in the chaotic analysis of the ECG (Cohen, Hudson, and Deedwania, 1996).

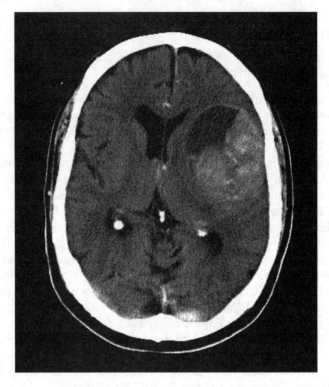

Figure 3.2 CT Scan of Head of Patient with Tumor.

For time series without patterns, feature extraction becomes even more difficult. In the EEG, spikes are important for determining brain activity. Both the frequency of occurrence and the magnitude of spikes may represent important clues. Additional complications with EEGs is the large number of channels recorded (up to 22), resulting in very large data sets. Work is continuing on the development of techniques for EEG analysis (Freeman, 1987; Kalayci and Ozdamar, 1995; Leuchter et al., 1993; Mpitsos et al., 1988; Petit et al., 1993; Pritchard et al., 1994; Woyshville and Calabrese, 1994).

3.2.4.1   Chaotic Analysis of Time Series.   Chaos theory, a new area of research that has developed in the last twenty years, has been shown to be especially promising in the field of cardiology. Chaotic analysis provides a new way of looking at nonlinear time series data that in general result in systems with intractable mathematical solutions. Chaotic analysis has been shown to be useful in the analysis of ECGs (Chialvo and Jalife, 1987; Goldberger, 1989) and, to a more limited extent, in the analysis of EEGs (Freeman, 1987). It is also useful in other medical time series, such as hemodynamic studies (Cohen, Hudson, and Anderson, 1993).

From the point of view of decision-making systems, the contribution of chaos theory is a measure of either the presence or absence of chaos in a system or of the degree of chaos present. There are two approaches to chaotic analysis: *graphical* and *numerical*. Graphical techniques include strange attractors, Poincaré plots, and second-order difference plots. Numerical techniques include the fractal dimension, the Lyapunov exponent, and central tendency measure. In Chapter 18, we discuss second-order difference plots and central tendency measure in terms of a specific hybrid system.

3.2.4.2 Graphical Measures of Chaos

POINCARÉ PLOTS.   A Poincaré plot is obtained from a time series by taking the value of the time series at time n and plotting it against the value at $(n - 1)$. In general, nonchaotic systems will have points clustered close together, whereas chaotic systems will have more dispersed points.

SECOND-ORDER DIFFERENCE PLOTS.   A second-order difference plot is similar to a Poincaré plot except that $a_{n+2} - a_{n+1}$ is plotted versus $a_{n+1} - a_n$. This results in a plot that is centered around the origin as shown in Figure 3.3. Again, the relative dispersion of points is the relative measure of chaos. This plot is used in computing the central tendency measure.

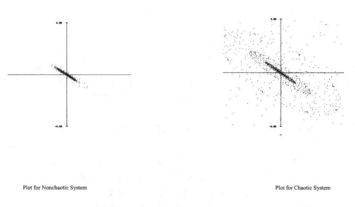

Plot for Nonchaotic System   Plot for Chaotic System

Figure 3.3 Second-Order Difference Plots.

STRANGE ATTRACTORS.   Strange attractors, first described by Ruelle and Takens (1971), are another method for describing chaotic systems. A strange attractor is shown in Figure 3.4. The basic idea is that a phase state is created in which the state of the process is represented by a point. The strange attractor then charts this point through time. Other types of attractors, fixed points and limit cycles, have been used in physics for some time.

Figure 3.4 A Strange Attractor.

3.2.4.3 Numerical Measures of Chaos

FRACTAL DIMENSION.   The fractal dimension gives a measure of the degree of irregularity, or the efficiency of the object in the amount of space that it occupies. For example, a one-dimensional line occupies no space. But the outline of a Kock curve that has infinite crowding into a finite space occupies more space than a line but less than a two-dimensional form (Gleick, 1987). Mandelbrot (1977) developed a method of calculating the fractal dimension.

LYAPUNOV EXPONENT. The Lyapunov exponent provides a method for measuring the effects of stretching, contracting, and folding in the phase space of an attractor, which gives a picture of properties that lead to stability or instability (Gleick, 1987).

CENTRAL TENDENCY MEASURE. The central tendency measure (CTM) measures the degree to which points are clustered around the origin in second-order difference plots. It is computed by

$$n = \left[\sum_{i=1}^{t-2} \delta\,(d_i)\right]/(t-2) \tag{3.1}$$

where

$$\delta(d_i) = \begin{array}{l} 1 \text{ if } [(a_{i+2} - a_{i+1})^2 + (a_{i+1} - a_i)^2]^{.5} < r \\ 0 \text{ otherwise} \end{array}$$

where t is the total number of points in the time series and r is a radius selected by the user depending on the radius of dispersion of the points. A practical example of this approach is shown in Chapter 18.

The use of measures of chaos in decision-making systems presupposes that these measures are different in the diseased state than in the normal state, or that they differ from one disease to another. Experimental evidence can lend support to these conjectures. In the case of the ECG, there is mounting evidence that this is in fact the case and that these measures can be effective in diagnostic problems (Cohen, Hudson, and Deedwania, 1996). Numerical measures of chaos can be used directly as input to neural network models as one or more parameters in the decision-making process. For the graphical measures, some method of comparison must be established.

3.2.5 Issues of Dimensionality

As we saw in Chapter 1, when we discussed linearly separable models in two dimensions, the classes were separated by a line that would generalize to a plane in three dimensions. After three dimensions, we can no longer visualize the class separation, but the mathematical concepts generalize, with *hyperplanes* separating classes in higher dimensions. As we will see in the next chapter, many interesting problems are not linearly separable but may be separated with higher-order equations. These surfaces in n-dimensional space are called *hypersurfaces*. By taking an equation of high enough order, any two classes can be separated. However, this decision surface will not be useful in classifying new data sets as it is *overdetermined*. When nonlinear equations are used, care must be taken to avoid the generation of overdetermined decision surfaces.

Decision surfaces will be represented by $D(\mathbf{x})$ where $\mathbf{x}$ is an n-dimensional vector. If $n = 2$ and $D(\mathbf{x})$ is linear, then

$$D(\mathbf{x}) = w_1 x_1 + w_2 x_2 = \mathbf{w} \cdot \mathbf{x} \tag{3.2}$$

For general n, the linear equation becomes

$$D(\mathbf{x}) = \sum_{i=1}^{n} w_i x_i = \mathbf{w} \cdot \mathbf{x} \tag{3.3}$$

which is the equation of a hyperplane. In the next chapter we will see a number of ways of generating equations for nonlinear $D(\mathbf{x})$.

With the increase in the number of variables, and thus the increase in the dimensionality, more cases are needed to train the system. In some approaches, attempts are made to reduce the dimensionality by eliminating or combining variables. If a system of high dimensionality is trained on too few sample cases, the result is a model that produces poor results when new cases are introduced.

3.3 TYPES OF LEARNING

The basic types of learning undertaken with neural networks are supervised and unsupervised. We have seen some examples of each. In the next chapter, we will present details on a number of supervised approaches, with unsupervised approaches treated in Chapter 5. In the following subsection, we introduce basic concepts that are common to all approaches. Other nonneural network approaches also use supervised and unsupervised learning, including pattern recognition (Chapter 1), genetic algorithms (Chapter 14), Bayesian learning, and discriminant analysis (Chapter 15).

3.3.1 Supervised Learning

Supervised learning is also called *learning with a teacher*. The network must be presented with data for which the correct classification is known.

Assume that we define our feature vector, as above, with seven components, and that the objective is to determine from these seven data items whether or not the patient has coronary artery disease (CAD). We make the following definition:

If $D(\mathbf{x}) > 0$, the patient has CAD   (class 1)
If $D(\mathbf{x}) < 0$, the patient does not have CAD   (class 2)
If $D(\mathbf{x}) = 0$, no decision can be made

Assume we have a training set of thirty-five cases, the first two of which are:

$\mathbf{x}^1 = (130, 100, 98, 2.8, 102, 131, 102)$ $\mathbf{x}^1$ is in class 1 (CAD)
$\mathbf{x}^2 = (120, 77, 72, 0.0, 110, 160, 90)$ $\mathbf{x}^2$ is in class 2 (No CAD)

If we consider the simple linearly separable case, the objective of supervised learning is to determine the w_i's in Eq. (3.2). This is a straightforward procedure since we know the following:

1. The values for all x_i's for each vector in the training set
2. The range of appropriate values for $D(\mathbf{x})$ for each vector in the training set

Thus the only unknowns are the w_i's. Remember, however, that we do not have actual values of $D(\mathbf{x})$, but only boundary conditions. The task of the learning algorithm is to iteratively adjust the w_i's until all vectors in the training set are correctly classified. (Methods by which this process can be accomplished are discussed in Chapter 4.)

In most situations, especially in biomedical applications, the classes will not be linearly separable and higher-order functions must be used.

3.3.1.1   Selection of Training and Test Sets.   Generally, a training set is selected randomly from the available data vectors. In order to produce a reliable separation, a number of factors must be considered:

1. The training set must be representative of the data set.
2. The training set must be large enough.
3. The training set must not contain vectors that are contradictory, that is, vectors with identical components that belong to different classes.

Problems with training of neural networks include:

1. Different weights may be obtained from different training sets.
2. Different weights may be obtained by altering the order in which the vectors in the training set are presented to the learning algorithm.

A separate set of vectors should be used to test the accuracy of the model once it is obtained. A number of measures can be used to determine accuracy:

Sensitivity = # classified correctly as positive/# of true positives
Specificity = # classified correctly as negative/# of true negatives
Accuracy = # correctly classified/total number

For example, assume we are trying to classify patients into presence or absence of CAD, and we have the following distribution in our test sets:

Number of patients with CAD:	56
Number of patients without CAD:	63
Number of patients with CAD classified correctly:	51
Number of patients without CAD classified correctly:	60

We obtain the following measures of accuracy:

Sensitivity = 51/56 = 0.91
Specificity = 60/63 = 0.95
Accuracy = 111/119 = 0.93

In classification problems, if the training set is changed to improve sensitivity, it is often at the expense of specificity, and vice versa, as a shift in the decision surface may improve the classification in one category at the expense of the other. Often ROCs (receiver-operator curves) are used to analyze the balance between sensitivity and specificity. An ROC curve is shown in Figure 3.5. The y-axis is sensitivity, and the x-axis is $1 -$ specificity. The goal is to try to find a combination that is as close as possible to the upper left-hand corner of the graph.

3.3.1.2 Selection of Learning Algorithm. Selecting an appropriate learning algorithm depends on the nature of the problem and the type of data involved. Although many learning algorithms may produce results, remember that there is no one answer in defining classification functions. Some factors to consider are:

1. Convergence properties
2. Stability
3. Accuracy in classifying new cases
4. Ability to interpret results

In the next chapter, we will compare these factors in a number of different learning algorithms.

3.3.2 Unsupervised Learning

In unsupervised learning, also called *learning without a teacher,* we do not have the advantage of having data of known classification. We often do not even know how many categories exist. The general idea behind unsupervised learning is to find a mea-

Sample Sensitivities and Specificities			
	Sensitivity	**Specificity**	**1-Specificity**
x^1	0.91	0.95	0.05
x^2	0.99	0.80	0.20
x^3	0.93	0.93	0.07
x^4	0.87	0.99	0.01
x^5	0.00	1.00	0.00
x^6	1.00	0.00	1.00

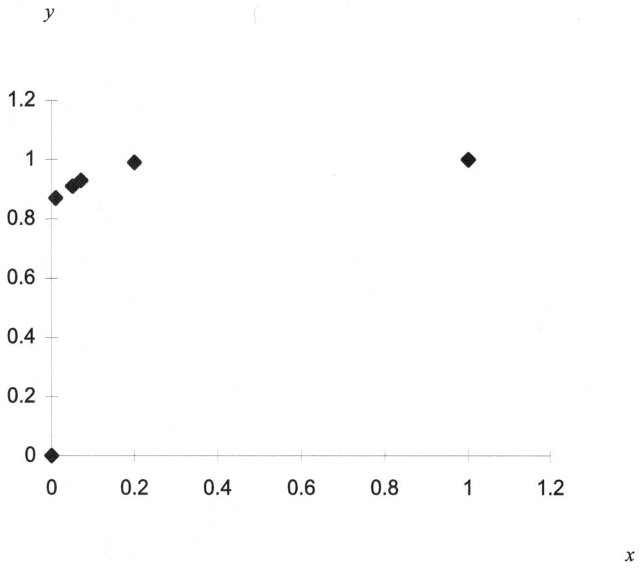

Figure 3.5 ROC Curve, x: $(1 - \text{specificity})$, y: sensitivity.

sure of similarity that can be used to determine which pattern vectors are "closest" to other pattern vectors; hence the name "clustering" is often used as the data will tend to group in natural clusters. This phenomenon is easy to observe in two dimensions by simply plotting the data points to determine if natural clusters are found. It is even possible in three dimensions if good graphical displays are available. However, for higher dimensions, an algorithm must be used to detect the multidimensional clusters.

Consider as an example our two-category problem of presence or absence of CAD, but for simplicity we will assume we have only the following two variables available from the exercise treadmill test (ETT): maximum ST depression in millimeters (ST) and change in systolic blood pressure from the beginning to the end of the test (ΔBP). The values are given in Table 3.1. These data are plotted in Figure 3.6. We can identify two clusters visually. If we did not have the visual aid, that is, if this were a higher dimensional space, what distance measure, also known as metric, would we use? The most straightforward is the Euclidean distance

$$d(\mathbf{x}, \mathbf{y}) = [(x_1 - y_1)^2 + (x_2 - y_2)^2]^{1/2} \tag{3.4}$$

Table 3.1 Two-Dimensional Vectors for
Identification of CAD

Vector	ST Depression	ΔBP
x^1	2.5	5
x^2	0.0	25
x^3	0.5	30
x^4	2.0	10
x^5	1.5	−5
x^6	1.5	35
x^7	0.0	50
x^8	3.0	10

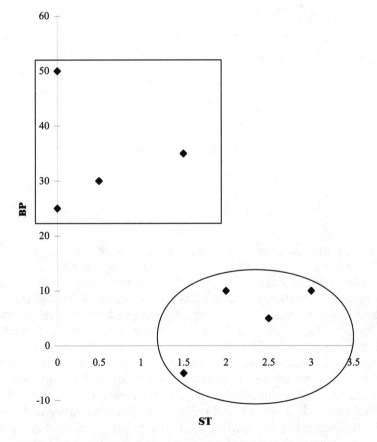

Figure 3.6 Plot of Change in Systolic Blood Pressure (BP) versus Maximum
ST Depression (ST).

where **x** and **y** are two-dimensional vectors. Several other distance measures could be used, including the following:

City Block

$$d(\mathbf{x}, \mathbf{y}) = |x_1 - y_1| + |x_2 - y_2| \tag{3.5}$$

Maximum Value

$$d(\mathbf{x}, \mathbf{y}) = \max \{|x_1 - y_1|, |x_2 - y_2|\} \tag{3.6}$$

We already saw a metric for binary vectors in Chapter 2, the Hamming distance.
A metric must satisfy the following:

1. $d(\mathbf{x}, \mathbf{y}) \geq 0$ and $d(\mathbf{x}, \mathbf{y}) = 0$ if and only if $\mathbf{x} = \mathbf{y}$ (positivity)
2. $d(\mathbf{x}, \mathbf{y}) = d(\mathbf{y}, \mathbf{x})$ (symmetry)
3. $d(\mathbf{x}, \mathbf{y}) + d(\mathbf{y}, \mathbf{z}) \geq d(\mathbf{x}, \mathbf{z})$ (triangle inequality)

These definitions are easily extended to vectors of any dimension. In Chapter 5, we will analyze a number of approaches that use these and other metrics and that also use different approaches for classifying data.

The choice of a suitable metric is not always straightforward. Some metrics are better suited to the data set than others. For example, the Euclidean distance gives the shortest geometrical distance between two points, the city block distance gives the distance between two points following a right-angle-only path, and the maximum value distance measures the distance between the two vector components that are furthest removed from each other. Another factor to consider is that scaling of the data can result in entirely different clusters than the original data set.

3.3.3 Causal Models

Causal models imply that a cause and effect relationship is used in the reasoning process. In Part II of this book we will discuss artificial intelligence approaches which use causal reasoning. In general, neural network models do not use causal reasoning as relationships between variables, and outcomes are learned by associating certain values of variables with outcomes. These relationships do not tell us anything about cause and effect. However, the discovery of association between ranges of values and outcomes can lend clues for further investigation.

3.4 INTERPRETATION OF OUTPUT

What type of output do we expect from a classification neural network? The primary output is the assignment of the input vector to the correct classification. However, it may be possible to learn more than this from the process. The weights associated with the input nodes indicate the strength of the contribution of the variable toward the classification decision. In networks with all nodes interconnected, it is difficult to interpret these weights. With some algorithms, the weight interpretation is much more straightforward. This is one of the issues we will investigate in Chapters 4 and 7.

3.5 SUMMARY

We have seen the importance of feature extraction in the development of classification networks for use as input to both supervised and unsupervised algorithms. In biomedical problems, it is particularly important to include all data types, especially nontextual data such as images and time series. Supervised learning, in which the correct classification of the data sets is known, is the most widely used approach for the development of classification systems. In some cases, however, correct classification for training data is not available, and unsupervised learning is the only option available. In either approach, two phases are involved in neural network development: the training phase and the testing phase. Only after the completion of these two steps can the model be used for classification.

EXERCISES

1. For the seven variables given in the example for diagnosis of CAD, given the information that the importance of these parameters is how they change during the ETT, how could the number of variables be reduced? Give a list of the reduced variable set.

2. Compute the Euclidean distance between x^1 and x^2 and x^1 and x^3 from Table 3.1. Do the same calculations for the city block metric and the maximum value metric. For the given data set, which of these metrics appears to make the most sense?

3. Using the graph in Figure 3.4 based on the data in Table 3.1, assuming there should be two categories, write down the vectors that belong to each category. Is there any way to tell which group is the CAD group?

4. Using your classification from exercise 3, divide the eight data vectors into a training set and a test set. Can you determine a linear $D(x)$ based on the training set that will separate all vectors in the training set? Does it classify all data in the test set correctly?

5. Is it possible to change the continuous variables in Table 3.1 into binary variables? If so, how? Do you think the classification would work as well with binary variables?

6. Show that the Euclidean distance, the city block distance, and the maximum value distance meet the conditions for metrics. Does the Hamming distance also fulfill these requirements?

REFERENCES

Chialvo, R., and Jalife, J. 1987. Non-linear dynamics of cardiac excitation and impulse propagation. *Nature* **330:** 749–752.

Cohen, M.E., Hudson, D.L. and Anderson, M.F. 1993. Blood flow data exhibit chaotic properties. *International Journal of Microcomputer Applications* **12(3):** 37–40.

Cohen, M.E., Hudson, D.L., and Deedwania, P.C. 1996. Application of continuous chaotic modeling to signal analysis. *EMBS Magazine* **15(5):** 97–102.

Cohen, M.E., Hudson, D.L., and Deedwania, P.C. 1985. Pattern recognition analysis of coronary artery disease. In A.H. Levy and B.T. Williams, eds., *American Association for Medical Systems and Informatics,* pp. 262–266.

Duda, R.O., and Hart, P.E. 1973. *Pattern Classification and Scene Analysis.* New York: John Wiley & Sons.

Freeman, W.J. 1987. Simulation of chaotic EEG patterns with a dynamic model of the olfactory system. *Biological Cybernetics* **56:** 139–150.

Gleick, J. 1987. *Chaos, Making a New Science.* New York: Penguin Books.

Goldberger, A.L. 1989. Cardiac chaos. *Science* **243(2987):** 1419.

Kalayci, T., and Ozdamar, O. 1995. Wavelet preprocessing for automated neural network detection of EEG spikes. *IEEE EMBS Magazine,* March/April **14(2):** 160–166.

Leuchter, A.F., Cook, I.A., Newton, T.F., Dunkin, J., Walter, D.O., Rosenberg-Thompson, S., Lachenbruch, P.A., and Weiner, H. 1993. Regional differences in brain electrical activity in dementia: use of spectral power and spectral ratio measures. *Electroencephalography and Clinical Neurophysiology,* December **87(6):** 385–393.

Mandelbrot, B. 1977. *The Fractal Nature of Geometry.* New York: W.H. Freeman.

Mpitsos, G.J., Burton, R.M., Jr., Creech, H.C., and Soinila, S.O. 1988. Evidence for chaos in spike trains of neurons that generate rhythmic motor patterns. *Brain Research Bulletin* **21:** 529–538.

Petit, D., Lorrain, D., Gauthier, S., and Montplaisir, J. 1993. Regional spectral analysis of the REM sleep EEG in mild to moderate Alzheimer's disease. *Neurobiology of Aging,* March–April **14(2):** 141–145.

Pritchard, W.S., Duke, D.W., Coburn, K.L., Moore, N.C., Tucker, K.A., Jann, W.S., and Hostetler, R.M. 1994. EEG-based, neural-net predictive classification of Alzheimer's disease versus control subjects is augmented by non-linear EEG measures. *Electroencephalography and Clinical Neurophysiology* **91(2):** 118–130.

Ruelle, D., and Takens, F. 1971. On the nature of turbulence. *Communications in Mathematical Physics* **20:** 167–192.

Vannier, M.W., Yates, R.E., and Whitestone, J.J. (eds.). 1992. *Electronic Imaging of the Human Body.* Wright Paterson Air Force Base, Ohio: CSERIAC.

Woyshville, M.J., and Calabrese, J.R. 1994. Quantification of occipital EEG changes in Alzheimer's disease utilizing a new metric: the fractal dimension. *Biological Psychiatry* **35(6):** 381–387.

4

Supervised Learning

4.1 DECISION SURFACES

In Chapter 1 we discussed pattern recognition and the idea of decision surfaces and discriminant functions. The basic idea in supervised learning from a mathematical point of view is to separate a set of n-dimensional vectors into m classes using a decision surface or discriminant function. In supervised learning, we know the classification of the data, so the objective is to find a function that will classify the data correctly. We will need to consider a number of subcategories of discriminant functions.

The most straightforward case is the division of n-dimensional vectors into two categories by means of a single discriminant function. The simplest function is linear. Sets of vectors that can be successfully separated by a linear discriminant function are said to be *linearly separable*. Define a discriminant function $D(\mathbf{x})$ where $\mathbf{x}$ is an n-dimensional vector and $\mathbf{w}$ is an n-dimensional weight vector. Then:

$$D(\mathbf{x}) = w_0 + w_1 x_1 + w_2 x_2 + \ldots + w_n x_n = w_0 + \sum_{i=1}^{n} w_i x_i = w_0 + \mathbf{w}^T \mathbf{x} \qquad (4.1)$$

where

$$D(\mathbf{x}) = \begin{bmatrix} > 0 & \text{if } \mathbf{x} \, \varepsilon \text{ class 1} \\ < 0 & \text{if } \mathbf{x} \, \varepsilon \text{ class 2} \end{bmatrix}$$

Since the comparison is made to zero, the constant w_0 is not relevant and will be omitted in some of the following discussions. All boldface, lowercase letters are assumed to be column vectors; thus $\mathbf{x}$ in Eq. (4.1) is a column vector with n components, $\mathbf{w}^T$ is a row vector, and the result of the multiplication $\mathbf{w}^T\mathbf{x}$ gives a scalar value for $D(\mathbf{x})$, which is a function of the n-dimensional vector $\mathbf{x} = [x_1, \ldots, x_n]$.

In the training phase, we know the values of the components of all vectors $\mathbf{x}$ and we know the classification for each vector $\mathbf{x}$. The only components we do not know are the values for $\mathbf{w}$. It is the task of the learning algorithm to determine these values.

4.2 TWO-CATEGORY SEPARATION, LINEARLY SEPARABLE SETS

4.2.1 Fisher's Linear Discriminant

One of the first methods for constructing decision functions by using supervised learning was Fisher's Linear Discriminant (Duda and Hart, 1973). This is a statistical procedure that requires the definition of a criterion function $J(\mathbf{w})$ which must be maximized. The concept of a criterion function will be repeated in many of the methods we will see later in this chapter. The idea behind the discriminant function is to project the n-dimensional samples onto a line $y = \mathbf{w}^T\mathbf{x}$, as illustrated in Figure 4.1. The samples from the two classes will be mixed together. The orientation of the line is then changed in an attempt to separate the sample into the proper categories. The decision surface, $D(\mathbf{x})$, is a line that is perpendicular to the projected line that divides the classes. The mathematical formulation requires the following definitions:

$$\text{Sample Mean } \mathbf{m}_i = (1/k_i)\sum_{\mathbf{x}\varepsilon X_i} \mathbf{x} \tag{4.2}$$

$$\text{Projected Mean } m_i = -(1/k_i)\sum_{y\varepsilon Y_i} y = (1/k_i)\sum_{\mathbf{x}\varepsilon X_i} \mathbf{w}^T\mathbf{x} = \mathbf{w}^T\mathbf{m}_i \tag{4.3}$$

where X_i is the set of all vectors in class i and k_i is the number of samples in class i. Thus

$$|m_1 - m_2| = \mathbf{w}^T|(\mathbf{m}_1 - \mathbf{m}_2)| \tag{4.4}$$

The scatter for projected samples in class i is defined as:

$$s_i^2 = \sum_{y\varepsilon Y_i} (y - m_i)^2 \tag{4.5}$$

The Fisher Linear Discriminant is that linear function $\mathbf{w}^T\mathbf{x}$ for which the criterion function $J(\mathbf{w})$ is maximum where

$$J(\mathbf{w}) = |m_1 - m_2|^2/(s_1^2 + s_2^2) \tag{4.6}$$

The objective is to obtain J as a function of $\mathbf{w}$.

The scatter matrices are defined as:

Scatter Matrix S_i

$$S_i = \sum_{\mathbf{x}\varepsilon X_i} (\mathbf{x} - \mathbf{m}_i)(\mathbf{x} - \mathbf{m}_i)^T \tag{4.7}$$

Within Class Scatter S_w

$$S_w = S_1 + S_2 \tag{4.8}$$

Between Class Scatter S_B

$$S_B = (\mathbf{m}_1 - \mathbf{m}_2)(\mathbf{m}_1 - \mathbf{m}_2)^T \tag{4.9}$$

Then

$$s_i = \sum_{\mathbf{x}\varepsilon X_i} (\mathbf{w}^T\mathbf{x} - \mathbf{w}^T\mathbf{m}_i)^2 = \mathbf{w}^T S_i \mathbf{w} \tag{4.10}$$

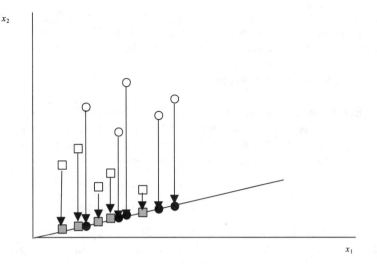

Linear Discriminant Which Does Not Separate Samples

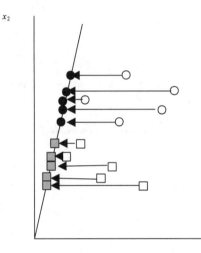

Linear Discriminant Which Does Separate Samples

Figure 4.1 Projection of N-Dimensional Points to One Dimension.

The criterion function can be written as

$$J(\mathbf{w}) = \mathbf{w}^T S_B \mathbf{w} / (\mathbf{w}^T S_w \mathbf{w}) \tag{4.11}$$

This is the Rayleigh quotient of mathematical physics. The weight vector $\mathbf{w}$ is obtained by solving for the eigenvalues:

$$\mathbf{w} = S_w^{-1}(\mathbf{m}_1 - \mathbf{m}_2) \tag{4.12}$$

This produces the Fisher Linear Discriminant, which is the linear function with the maximum ratio of between-class scatter to within-class scatter.

Additional details on linear discriminants can be found in Duda and Hart (1973). Other types of discriminant functions are discussed in Section 4.2.4 of this chapter.

Note that for methods that do not project vectors onto a line, but operate in the dimension of the feature vector, the decision surface $D(\mathbf{x})$ will not be a line but a hyperplane. If the decision surface is nonlinear, the function will be a hypersurface.

4.2.2 Gradient Descent Procedures

Before discussing specific methods, we will restate the problem in a slightly different manner. Recall that our objective for vectors in the training set is to classify all samples correctly by finding a set of weights that produce an appropriate decision equation. Thus we want to solve the inequalities

$$\begin{aligned} \mathbf{w}^T\mathbf{x} > 0 \qquad &\text{if } \mathbf{x} \ \varepsilon \text{ class } 1 \\ \mathbf{w}^T\mathbf{x} < 0 \qquad &\text{if } \mathbf{x} \ \varepsilon \text{ class } 2 \end{aligned} \qquad (4.13)$$

We can simplify this statement if we normalize the vectors by replacing all vectors in class 2 by their negatives. The problem is then to solve the set of inequalities:

$$\mathbf{w}^T\mathbf{x} > 0 \qquad \text{for all } \mathbf{x} \text{ in the training set} \qquad (4.14)$$

One method of proceeding is through the use of gradient descent procedures (Duda and Hart, 1973). The gradient descent procedure minimizes a criterion function $J(W)$ where W is a solution matrix.

Gradient Descent Algorithm
Assign arbitrary values to W_1 the initial weight matrix.
Compute $\nabla J(W_1)$, the gradient, which gives the direction of steepest descent.
At step k + 1, *adjust the weights according to*

$$W_{k+1} = W_k - \rho_k \, \nabla J(W_k) \text{ where } \rho_k \text{ is a scale factor} \qquad (4.15)$$

Repeat until a minimum is found.

In the next section we will see that the perceptron algorithm is similar to the gradient descent algorithm.

4.2.3 Perceptron Algorithm

The perceptron algorithm follows the same approach as the gradient descent procedure except that the criterion function is different (Rosenblatt, 1962; Nilsson 1965). The perceptron criterion function is:

$$J(\mathbf{w}) = \sum_{y \varepsilon Y} (-\mathbf{w}^T\mathbf{y}) \qquad (4.16)$$

where $J(\mathbf{w})$ is the set of samples misclassified by $\mathbf{w}$. Weight adjustments at the $k + 1$ step are made by the following:

$$\mathbf{w}_{k+1} = \mathbf{w}_k + \rho_k \sum_{y \varepsilon Y} \mathbf{y} \qquad (4.17)$$

A special case of the perceptron is the fixed increment rule:

$$\begin{aligned} \rho_k &= 1, \mathbf{w}_1 \text{ is arbitary} \\ \mathbf{w}_{k+1} &= \mathbf{w}_k + \mathbf{y}_k. \end{aligned} \qquad (4.18)$$

In the variable increment rule, ρ_k can be adjusted.

4.2.4 Relaxation Procedures

A modification of the gradient descent procedure is the relaxation procedure (Motzkin and Schoenbert, 1954). We define

$$J(\mathbf{w}) = \sum_{\mathbf{y}\varepsilon Y} (\mathbf{w}^T\mathbf{y})^2 \tag{4.19}$$

where J is again the set of misclassified samples.

Relaxation Algorithm

Select the initial weights w_1 arbitrarily.

Adjust weights at step k + 1 *according to*

$$\mathbf{w}_{k+1} = \mathbf{w}_k + \rho_k \sum_{\mathbf{y}\varepsilon Y} (\mathbf{b}-\mathbf{w}^T\mathbf{y})\mathbf{y}/(\|\mathbf{y}\|)^2 \tag{4.20}$$

where $\mathbf{w}^T\mathbf{y} \geq \mathbf{b}$ *for all samples.*

The vector **b** in the preceding algorithm is a boundary that provides a cushion to prevent the decision surface from coming too close to the edge of the decision region; that is, no samples are allowed to fall within a distance **b** of the decision surface.

4.2.5 Potential Functions

The idea behind potential functions comes from the study of electricity (Aizerman, Braverman, and Rozonoer, 1964; Tou, 1974; Young and Calvert, 1974). The basic concept is that each vector $\mathbf{x}_i$ is thought of as a point in space where an electrical charge q_i could be placed. The charge will be positive if $\mathbf{x}_i$ is in class 1 and negative if $\mathbf{x}_i$ is in class 2. The resultant electrostatic potential represents a decision surface. The potential due to n charges is

$$D(\mathbf{x}) = q_iK(\mathbf{x}, \mathbf{x}_i) \tag{4.21}$$

The potential function $K(\mathbf{x}, \mathbf{x}_i)$ of physics varies inversely with $\|\mathbf{x} - \mathbf{x}_i\|$, the Euclidean distance; however, other functions are also suitable. See Figure 4.2 for examples. The most suitable choices are maximum at $\mathbf{x} = \mathbf{x}_i$ and decrease as $\|\mathbf{x} - \mathbf{x}_i\|$ approaches infinity. The corrected decision function is:

$$D'(\mathbf{x}) = \begin{bmatrix} D(\mathbf{x}) + K(\mathbf{x}, \mathbf{x}_k) \text{ if } \mathbf{x}_k \text{ is in class 1 and } D(\mathbf{x}_k) < 0 \\ D(\mathbf{x}) - K(\mathbf{x}, \mathbf{x}_k) \text{ if } \mathbf{x}_k \text{ is in class 2 and } D(\mathbf{x}_k) > 0 \\ D(\mathbf{x}) \text{ otherwise} \end{bmatrix} \tag{4.22}$$

The actual algorithm is similar to the perceptron algorithm. The similarity to the fixed increment rule is seen through the following representation (Duda and Hart, 1973):

If $K(\mathbf{x}, \mathbf{x}_k)$ can be represented by the expansion

$$K(\mathbf{x}, \mathbf{x}_k) = \sum_{i=1}^{n} y_i(\mathbf{x})\, y_i(\mathbf{x}_k) = \mathbf{y}_k^T\mathbf{y} \tag{4.23}$$

where $\mathbf{y} = \mathbf{y}(\mathbf{x})$ and $\mathbf{y}_k = \mathbf{y}(\mathbf{x}_k)$ and n is the dimension of the vector. Substituting into Eq. (4.21)

$$D(\mathbf{x}) = \mathbf{w}^T\mathbf{y}, \text{ where} \tag{4.24}$$

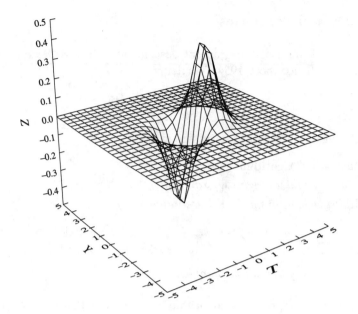

Figure 4.2 Positive and Negative Potential Functions.

$$\mathbf{w} = \sum_{i=1}^{n} q_i \mathbf{y}_i \tag{4.25}$$

The weight adjustments to go from $D(\mathbf{x})$ to $D'(\mathbf{x})$ are then

$$\mathbf{w}' = \begin{bmatrix} \mathbf{w} + \mathbf{y}_k \text{ if } \mathbf{y}_k \text{ is in class 1 and } \mathbf{w}^T \mathbf{y}_k < 0 \\ \mathbf{w} - \mathbf{y}_k \text{ if } \mathbf{y}_k \text{ is in class 2 and } \mathbf{w}^T \mathbf{y}_k > 0 \\ \mathbf{w} \text{ otherwise} \end{bmatrix} \tag{4.26}$$

4.3 NONLINEARLY SEPARABLE SETS

In many cases, it is not possible to find a linear decision function $D(\mathbf{x})$ that can successfully categorize all vectors. If this happens, there are two alternatives:

1. Find a nonlinear function that will separate the functions.
2. Settle for a decision surface that misclassifies some of the vectors.

4.3.1 Nonlinear Discriminant Functions

The most straightforward generalization is from the linear discriminant function to the quadratic:

$$D(\mathbf{x}) = w_0 + \sum w_i x_i + \sum\sum w_{ij} x_i x_j \tag{4.27}$$

In the more general form:

$$D(\mathbf{x}) = \sum w_i y_i(\mathbf{x}) = \mathbf{w}^T \mathbf{y} \tag{4.28}$$

where $\mathbf{w}$ is an n-dimensional weight vector and $y_i(\mathbf{x})$ is a set of functions of $\mathbf{x}$.
As an example, consider the quadratic discriminant

$$D(\mathbf{x}) = w_1 + w_2 x + w_3 x^2 \tag{4.29}$$

$$y = \begin{bmatrix} 1 \\ x \\ x^2 \end{bmatrix} \qquad \mathbf{w}^T = [w_1 \ w_2 \ w_3] \qquad (4.30)$$

4.3.2 Hypernet, A Nonlinear Potential Function Algorithm

The method used in Hypernet is a modification of the potential function approach to pattern recognition (Cohen et al., 1986). Rather than using the Euclidean distance formula, the potential function is used:

$$P(\mathbf{x}, \mathbf{x}_k) = \sum_{i=1}^{\infty} \lambda_i \ \Phi_i(\mathbf{x}) \ \Phi_i(\mathbf{x}_k) \qquad (4.31)$$

for $k = 1, 2, 3 \ldots$, where $\Phi_i(\mathbf{x})$ are orthonormal functions and λ_i are nonzero real numbers. The orthogonal functions of mathematical physics may be used as potential functions (Young, 1974). P_i is computed by substituting the values from the first feature vector for case 1, x_1. Subsequent values for P_k are then computed by

$$P_k = P_{k-1} + r_k P(\mathbf{x}, \mathbf{x}_k) \text{ where} \qquad (4.32)$$

$$r_k = \begin{bmatrix} 1 & \text{If } P_i < 0 \text{ and class 1} \\ -1 & \text{If } P_i > 0 \text{ and class 2} \\ 0 & \text{If } P_i > 0 \text{ and class 1 or } P_i < 0 \text{ and class 2} \end{bmatrix} \qquad (4.33)$$

The orthonormal functions can in fact be replaced by orthogonal functions, since multiplication by a normalizing factor does not affect the final relative outcome. The functions used in Hypernet are chosen from the set of multidimensional orthogonal functions developed by Cohen, represented by the general class (Cohen et al., 1986):

$$C_n(x_1, \ldots, x_m) = \frac{m!}{n!(m-n)!} + \sum_{k=1}^{n} \frac{(-1)^k(m-k)!}{(n-k)!(m-n)!} \sum_{i_k=k}^{m} \sum_{i_{k-1}=k-1}^{i_k-1} \cdots \sum_{i_2=2}^{i_3-1} \sum_{i_1=1}^{i_2-1}$$

$$\sum_{p=1}^{k} \frac{x_i^{a(n,i_p)}[a(n,i_p) + v_{ip}]}{v_{ip}} \qquad (4.34)$$

where m is the dimensionality of the data, $a_i, i = 1, \ldots, k$ are parameters that may be arbitrarily selected, A is the normalization constant, and $v_i, i = 1, \ldots, m$ are assigned values corresponding to the components of the first feature vector. Note that while high-order equations can be obtained using this method, in general only linear and second-order terms are used to prevent overfitting of the decision surface (a subject that will be discussed in Chapter 6).

Hypernet Algorithm
Read in values for input nodes;
Compute value P$_1$.
Until no changes
    Compute P$_i$
    IF P$_i$ > 0 *and class 1, no change*
    IF P$_i$ < 0 *and class 2, no change*
    IF P$_i$ > 0 *and class 2, or* P$_i$ < 0 *and class 1, then adjust* P$_i$ *using Eqs. (4.32) and (4.33)*
Output decision hypersurface equation with weighting factors, D(**x**) = P$_i$(**x**).

4.3.3 Categorization of Nonlinearly Separable Sets

4.3.3.1 Minimum Squared Error Procedures (MSE). Minimum squared error procedures use all samples instead of only the misclassified samples (Duda and Hart, 1973). The method works if the set is not linearly separable but does not necessarily produce a separating surface if they are separable. The objective is to solve the set of equations

$$\mathbf{w}^T\mathbf{y}_i = \mathbf{b}_i \qquad (4.35)$$

where $\mathbf{b}_i$ are arbitrary positive constants. This set of linear equations can be represented by an $m \times n$ matrix:

$$Y = \begin{bmatrix} \mathbf{y}_1^T \\ \mathbf{y}_2^T \\ \cdot \\ \cdot \\ \cdot \\ \mathbf{y}_m^T \end{bmatrix} \qquad (4.36)$$

where each $\mathbf{y}$ is an n-dimensional vector, $\mathbf{b}$ is an n-dimensional constant vector, and there are m samples. We then get the matrix equation

$$Y\mathbf{w} = \mathbf{b}, \quad \text{or} \qquad (4.37)$$

$$\mathbf{w} = Y^{-1}\mathbf{b} \qquad (4.38)$$

using the pseudoinverse

$$Y^\dagger = (Y^TY)^{-1}Y^T \qquad (4.39)$$

However, Y is rectangular with more equations than unknowns (i.e., $\mathbf{w}$ is overdetermined) so no unique solution exists. The method thus attempts to minimize the error

$$E = Y\mathbf{w} - \mathbf{b} \qquad (4.40)$$

The criterion function is

$$J(\mathbf{w}) = \|Y\mathbf{w} - \mathbf{b}\| = \sum(\mathbf{w}^T\mathbf{y}_i - \mathbf{b}_i)^2 \qquad (4.41)$$

The gradient is

$$\nabla J(\mathbf{w}) = \sum_{i=1}^{n} 2(\mathbf{w}^T\mathbf{y} - \mathbf{b}_i)\mathbf{y}_i = 2Y^T(Y\mathbf{w} - \mathbf{b}_i) = 0 \qquad (4.42)$$

With the proper choice of **b**, this method is related to the Fisher Linear Discriminant. Other MSE procedures include the Widrow–Hoff procedure (Widrow and Hoff, 1960) and the stochastic approximation (Yau and Schumpert, 1968).

4.3.3.2 Ho–Kashyap Procedure. The Ho–Kashyap procedure also works for nonseparable sets, but it has the advantage of producing a separating vector if separable (Ho and Kashyap, 1966).

If the sets are linearly separable, there exist **w** and **b** such that

$$Y\mathbf{w} = \mathbf{b} > 0. \qquad (4.43)$$

The criterion function is defined as

$$J(\mathbf{w}, \mathbf{b}) = \|Y\mathbf{w} - \mathbf{b}\|^2 \tag{4.44}$$

The criterion function is minimized subject to gradient descent

$$J_\mathbf{w} = 2Y^T(Y\mathbf{w} - \mathbf{b}) \tag{4.45}$$

$$J_b = -2(Y\mathbf{w} - \mathbf{b}) \tag{4.46}$$

Ho–Kashyap Algorithm
Choose arbitrary $\mathbf{b}_1 > 0$

$\mathbf{b}_{k+1} = \mathbf{b}_k + 2\rho\mathbf{e}_k^+$ *where* $\tag{4.47}$

$\mathbf{e}_k = Y\mathbf{w}_k - \mathbf{b}_k \tag{4.48}$

$\mathbf{e}_k^+ = \frac{1}{2}(\mathbf{e}_k + |\mathbf{e}_k|) \tag{4.49}$

$\mathbf{w}_k = Y^\dagger\mathbf{b}_k$ *where* $Y^\dagger$ *is defined in Eq. (4.39).* $\tag{4.50}$

The nonseparable case can also be configured as a linear programming problem (McKinsey, 1952).

4.4 MULTIPLE CATEGORY CLASSIFICATION PROBLEMS

In some problems, separating vectors into two categories is insufficient. The goal is to consider three or more categories. If this is the case, the preceding model must be expanded. Again there are two choices:

1. Break the multicategory problem into a series of two-category problems.
2. Construct a more complex mathematical structure for the decision function.

4.4.1 Extension of Fisher Discriminant

The basic idea of the Fisher Linear Discriminant for projecting n-dimensional samples onto a line can be extended to project n-dimensional space into $c - 1$ dimensions where $n \geq c$. The description given in Section 4.2.1 can be generalized as follows:

$$S_W = \sum_{i=1}^{c} S_i \tag{4.51}$$

where S_i is defined in Eq. (4.7). The generalization for S_B as given by Duda and Hart (1973) is

$$S_B = \sum_{i=1}^{c} n_i(\mathbf{m}_i - \mathbf{m})(\mathbf{m}_i - \mathbf{m}) \tag{4.52}$$

where m is the total mean vector. Then

$$S_T = S_W + S_B \tag{4.53}$$

We wind up with $c - 1$ discriminant functions

$$y_i = \mathbf{w}_i^T\mathbf{x} \tag{4.54}$$

The entire projection can be written as a matrix equation

$$\mathbf{y} = W^T\mathbf{x} \tag{4.55}$$

4.4.2 Kesler Construction

Another method of constructing multicategory discriminant functions is the Kesler Construction. The following definitions are used, assuming there are c categories with vectors of dimension n:

$$D_i(\mathbf{x}) = \mathbf{w}_i{}^T\mathbf{y}, \qquad i = 1, \ldots, c \qquad (4.56)$$

Vector $\mathbf{x}$ is assigned to class i if $D_i(\mathbf{x}) > D_j(\mathbf{x})$ for all $i \neq j$, that is, $\mathbf{w}_i{}^T\mathbf{y}_k > \mathbf{w}_j{}^T\mathbf{y}_k$, where we are assuming $\mathbf{y}$ is a function of $\mathbf{x}$ as in Eq. (4.28).
Rewriting

$$\mathbf{w}_i{}^T\mathbf{y}_k - \mathbf{w}_j{}^T\mathbf{y}_k > 0 \qquad (4.57)$$

The following $c - 1$ samples each of dimension $(c \cdot n)$ must be classified correctly:

$$\begin{bmatrix} \mathbf{w}_1 \\ \mathbf{w}_2 \\ \mathbf{w}_3 \\ \cdot \\ \cdot \\ \cdot \\ \mathbf{w}_c \end{bmatrix}^T \cdot \begin{bmatrix} \mathbf{y} & \mathbf{y} & & \mathbf{y} \\ -\mathbf{y} & 0 & & 0 \\ 0 & -\mathbf{y} & \cdots & 0 \\ \cdot & \cdot & & \cdot \\ \cdot & \cdot & & \cdot \\ \cdot & \cdot & & \cdot \\ 0 & 0 & & -\mathbf{y} \end{bmatrix} > 0 \qquad (4.58)$$

Consider the following illustration of this method. Assume we have a three-category problem, with the following vectors in each class (with Y_i representing the set of vectors in class i):

$$Y_1 = \{\mathbf{y}_{11} = (1, 2, 1), \mathbf{y}_{12} = (1, 1, 4)\}$$
$$Y_2 = \{\mathbf{y}_{21} = (1, -1, -1), \mathbf{y}_{22} = (1, -3, -1)\}$$
$$Y_3 = \{\mathbf{y}_{31} = (1, -1, -1), \mathbf{y}_{32} = (1, -3, -1)\}$$

Assume $\mathbf{w}_1(0) = \mathbf{w}_2(0) = \mathbf{w}_3(0) = (0, 0, 0)$ are the initial weights for each category. (Note that the number in parentheses indicates the ith adjustment in the weight vectors.) Thus we have three decision functions, $g_1, g_2,$ and g_3. Each feature vector has three components. The goal is to find the g_i's so that all vectors are classified correctly. We set up the first member of the sequence

$$\begin{bmatrix} \mathbf{y}_{11} \\ -\mathbf{y}_{11} \\ \mathbf{0} \end{bmatrix}$$

and compute the g_i's:

$$g_1 = \mathbf{w}_1{}^T\mathbf{y}_{11} = (0\ 0\ 0)\,(1\ 2\ 1)^T = 0$$
$$g_2 = \mathbf{w}_2{}^T\mathbf{y}_{11} = (0\ 0\ 0)\,(1\ 2\ 1)^T = 0$$

This is an incorrect result, because g_1 is not greater than g_2, that is, $g_1 - g_2 = \mathbf{w}_1{}^T\mathbf{y}_{11} - \mathbf{w}_2{}^T\mathbf{y}_{11} < 0$.
Compute adjusted weight vectors:

$$\mathbf{w}_1(1) = \mathbf{w}_1(0) + \mathbf{y}_{11} = (1\ 2\ 1)$$
$$\mathbf{w}_2(1) = \mathbf{w}_2(0) - \mathbf{y}_{11} = (-1\ -2\ -1)$$
$$\mathbf{w}_3(1) = \mathbf{w}_3(0) = (0\ 0\ 0)$$

Consider the second member of the sequence:

$$\begin{bmatrix} \mathbf{y}_{11} \\ \mathbf{0} \\ -\mathbf{y}_{11} \end{bmatrix}$$

$$g_1 = \mathbf{a}_1(1)^T \mathbf{y}^{11} = (1\ 2\ 1)\ (1\ 2\ 1)^T = 6$$

$$g_3 = (0\ 0\ 0)\ (1\ 2\ 1)^T = 0$$

This is a correct result as $g_1 > g_3$.
Compute new set of weights:

$$\mathbf{w}_1(2) = \mathbf{w}_1(1) = (1\ 2\ 1)$$
$$\mathbf{w}_2(2) = \mathbf{w}_2(1) = (-1\ -2\ -1)$$
$$\mathbf{w}_3(2) = \mathbf{w}_3(1) = (0\ 0\ 0)$$

The next member of the sequence is:

$$\begin{bmatrix} \mathbf{y}_{12} \\ -\mathbf{y}_{12} \\ 0 \end{bmatrix}$$

The completion of this problem is left as an exercise.

4.4.3 Backpropagation

Backpropagation (Rummelhart, McClelland, and PDP Research Group, 1986) is a type of nonlinear gradient descent procedure. It can be used for multicategory classification. The objective is to minimize the error criterion

$$J = (1/2)[\Sigma(T_i - D_i)^2] \tag{4.59}$$

where T_i is the target result for decision i and D_i is the current value.

Backpropagation Algorithm
Initialize
   Set all weights $\mathbf{w}$ *and* ω *and thresholds* θ *and* φ *to small random numbers.*
   Compute activation levels:

$$D(\mathbf{x}) = F(\Sigma(\omega\ \mathbf{y}(\mathbf{x},\ \theta) - \varphi))\ \text{where} \tag{4.60}$$

$$\mathbf{y} = F(\Sigma(\mathbf{w}(\mathbf{x} - \theta))\ and \tag{4.61}$$

$$F(\alpha) = 1/(1\text{-}exp(-\alpha)) \tag{4.62}$$

   Adjust weights according to

$$\mathbf{w}_{k+1} = \mathbf{w}_k + \eta\delta(\mathbf{x}) \tag{4.63}$$

$$\omega_{k+1} = \omega_k + \eta\xi(\mathbf{y}) \tag{4.64}$$

   where

$$\delta_i(\mathbf{x}) = x_i(1 - x_i)\ \delta^T\mathbf{w} \tag{4.65}$$

$$\xi_j(\mathbf{y}) = D_j(\mathbf{y})\ (1 - D_j(\mathbf{y}))\ (T_j - D_j(\mathbf{y})) \tag{4.66}$$

η *is the learning rate.*

4.5 RELATIONSHIP TO NEURAL NETWORK MODELS

In this chapter, we have discussed supervised learning techniques but have not mentioned neural networks. What is the connection? The first neural network, and the first supervised learning algorithm, was the perceptron algorithm described earlier. In its linear form, a two-layer neural network represents the perceptron algorithm, as did the original neural networks in the 1950s. In fact, the linear approaches discussed here are equivalent to the two-layer networks with all their inherent drawbacks. The nonlinear approaches, however, overcome these problems, as do the multilayer networks. Many of the approaches described have been used in neural network learning, including gradient descent procedures (backpropagation) and potential functions (Hypernet). As an example, consider backpropagation, which was described earlier in terms of a multicategory nonlinear learning algorithm. When stated in neural network terminology, we have the following algorithmic form, similar to the neural network algorithms presented in Chapter 2 (Fu, 1994):

Assign Connection Weights
Set all w_{ij} and threshold values θ_i to small random values.

$1 \leq i \leq n, 1 \leq j \leq m$

Initialize
The activation of an input layer node is set to the instance presented to the network. For the hidden and output layers, the activation is

$$O_j = F\left(\sum_{i=1}^{n} w_{ij} (O_i - \theta_j)\right) \qquad (4.67)$$

where w_{ij} is the weight from an input unit O_i, θ_j is the node threshold, and F is a sigmoid function.

$$F(\alpha) = 1/(1 - exp(-\alpha)). \qquad (4.68)$$

Iterate Until Convergence
At time t

$$w_{ji}(t + 1) = w_{ji}(t) + \Delta w_{jj} \qquad (4.69)$$

$$\Delta w_{jj} = \eta \delta_j O_i \qquad (4.70)$$

$$\delta_j = O_j(1 - O_j)(T_j - O_j) \text{ for output units} \qquad (4.71)$$

$$\delta_j = O_j(1 - O_j) \sum_k \delta_k w_{kj} \text{ for hidden units} \qquad (4.72)$$

where δ_k is the error gradient at unit k *to which a connection is made from hidden unit* j.
η is the learning rate $(0 < \eta < 1)$
This process is repeated until convergence in terms of the selected error criterion.

What, then, constitutes a neural network model? Neural network algorithms are based on some aspect of the biological nervous system, with nodes representing the activity of individual neural firings and connections representing the biological neural network structure. These structures lead to the mathematical formulations in which the learning methods described here can be used. A diagram of the backpropagation three-layer network is shown in Figure 4.3.

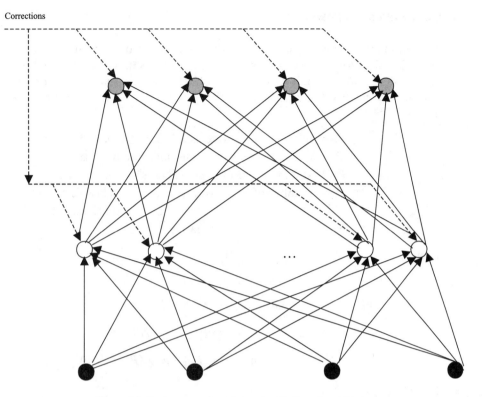

Corrections

Figure 4.3 Backpropagation Network with Four Input Nodes.

Historically, research in neural networks has inspired work in learning algorithms. For example, Rosenblatt's original work in the photoperceptron (Rosenblatt, 1962) is directly related to the Parzen window approach (discussed in Chapter 15), which is also closely aligned with potential functions.

4.6 COMPARISON OF METHODS

4.6.1 Convergence and Stability

Some of the methods we have described have convergence proofs, such as the perceptron algorithms, whereas others converge only under specified circumstances. Some of the descent learning algorithms may converge to local minima rather than absolute minima. Some algorithms, such as backpropagation, may result in chaos or oscillatory behavior and may fail to converge. Note in Eq. (4.71) the presence of the logistic equation $Aa_n(1 - a_n)$, which can produce chaotic solutions depending on the value of A. Chapter 8 will discuss convergence and stability for the methods described above in more detail.

4.6.2 Training Time

Training time depends on the algorithm, the network structure, the number of input nodes, and the number of categories. Methods such as backpropagation may have very long training times compared to other methods, such as the potential function approach. Lengthy training time is less of a problem than convergence or stability considerations, especially now as computer speeds have greatly increased and will apparently continue to do so.

4.6.3 Predictive Power

In biomedical applications, the predictive power of a result is of utmost importance. The decision surface generated by the methods described must be tested on an independent data set to determine their effectiveness in reaching accurate decisions. Four measures are often used in medical applications to measure accuracy and predictive power:

P_C = number of positive cases correctly classified
P_I = number of positive cases incorrectly classified
P_T = Total number of positive cases
N_C = number of negative cases correctly classified
N_I = number of negative cases incorrectly classified
N_T = Total number of negative cases

Then

$$\text{Sensitivity} = P_C/P_T \tag{4.73}$$

$$\text{Specificity} = N_C/N_T \tag{4.74}$$

$$\text{Positive predictive value} = P_T/(P_C + N_I) \tag{4.75}$$

$$\text{Accuracy} = (P_C + N_C)/(P_T + N_T) \tag{4.76}$$

4.7 APPLICATIONS

In the last decade, neural networks have been applied to numerous medical problems. An example is shown using the Hypernet neural network.

4.7.1 Single-Category Classification

Many medical decision-making problems rely on multiple parameters. The neural network approach is useful not only in combining parameters but also in assigning weights to each parameter that indicate their relative importance.

As an example, consider the analysis of exercise treadmill testing (ETT) (Cohen, Hudson, and Deedwania, 1985). Parameters that are typically recorded are shown in Table 4.1. In addition to recorded parameters, computed parameters have previously been found to be useful. These include:

Change in blood pressure from beginning to end of test

Change in heart rate from beginning to end of test

Product of heart rate and systolic blood pressure at end of test (double product)

Initially, we will consider this to be a two-category problem: presence or absence of coronary artery disease (CAD). The results of the cardiac catheterization are used to determine the correct classification: 0 vessel disease will be class 1, and 1, 2, or 3 vessel disease will be class 2. Data of known classification are divided into a training set and a test set. After training, the neural network determined that the following parameters should be used in the decision surface:

x_1 = maximum ST depression
x_2 = percentage change in heart rate from beginning to end of test

TABLE 4.1 Parameters Pertaining to Diagnosis of
Coronary Artery Disease (CAD)

Identification number
Age
Date of cardiac catheterization
Results of cardiac catheterization (0, 1, 2, or 3
 diseased vessels)
Date of ETT resting heart rate
Resting blood pressure
Resting ECG results (normal, abnormal)
Time of angina
Heart rate at time of angina
Blood pressure at time of angina
Time of 1 mm ST depression
Heart rate at time of 1 mm ST depression
Blood pressure at time of 1 mm ST depression
Maximum ST depression
Total duration of ETT
Heart rate at end of ETT
Blood pressure at end of ETT
Total duration of chest pain
Total duration of ST depression
Reason for stopping ETT

---

x_3 = percentage change in blood pressure from beginning to end of test
x_4 = double product

The neural network diagram for this example is shown in Figure 4.4. Although this figure is similar to the backpropagation network, in the hidden layer only two nodes at a time interact whereas in the backpropagation network all nodes are connected. Also, there are direct connections from the input to the output layer in Hypernet.

4.7.2 Multicategory Classification

In reality, the problem described here is a four-category classification problem, with the following categories:

class 0:	No CAD
class 1:	1-vessel disease
class 2:	2-vessel disease
class 3:	3-vessel disease

The approach taken by Hypernet is to develop separate decision surfaces for each decision. The classifications of interest are the following:

0 vs. 1
0 vs. 2
0 vs. 3
1 vs. 3

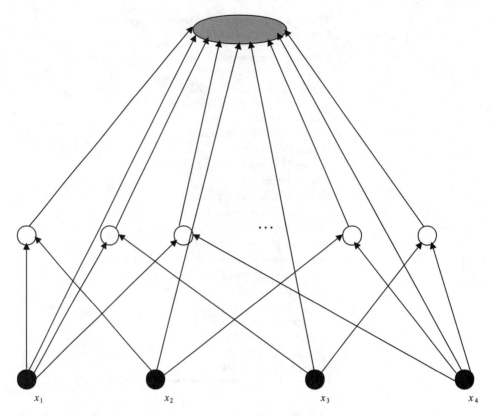

Figure 4.4 Classification of Coronary Artery Disease Using Hypernet.

The remaining combinations, 1 vs. 2 and 2 vs. 3, are omitted because of the difficulty in distinguishing these cases clinically. The four preceding parameters are again selected during the training phase. Evaluation of this model produces measures of sensitivity, specificity, and predictive value as described earlier. For example, for the 0 vs. 3 case results are shown in Table 4.2.

From these values, we can calculate the following:

$$\text{Sensitivity} = 38/41 = 0.93$$
$$\text{Specificity} = 7/8 = 0.88$$
$$\text{Accuracy} = 45/49 = 0.92$$
$$\text{Positive Predictive Value} = 41/39 = 1.05$$

The decision surface that was generated by Hypernet for the 0 vs. 3 problem is:

$$D(\mathbf{x}) = -6.3 + 3.7x_1 + 4.1x_2 + 7.3x_3 + 4.7x_4$$
$$- 17.4x_3x_4 + 8.9x_2x_4 + 1.1x_1x_4 + 7.1x_1x_3 - 0.9x_2x_3 \quad (4.77)$$

TABLE 4.2   CAD Results for No Disease versus 3-Vessel Disease

	Correctly Classified	Incorrectly Classified	Total
Class 1 (0 vessel disease)	7	1	8
Class 2 (3 vessel disease)	38	3	41
Total	45	4	49

4.7.3 Reduction of Nodes

As seen in the preceding examples, the number of contributing features has been significantly reduced. There are a number of reasons for limiting the number of input nodes. A rule of thumb is that for each node in the network, between five and ten instances are required for weight training. It is therefore important not to include more nodes than the available data set can reliably train. In addition, the greater the number of nodes, the longer the training time, and the more likely it is that there may be convergence or stability problems with some algorithms. There are a number of processes by which node reduction can be accomplished which will be discussed in Chapter 6. Hypernet uses a combination of expert opinion and statistical significance to obtain the initial set of nodes. It then uses threshold pruning for further reduction.

4.8 SUMMARY

An interesting illustration of the application of neural networks to a problem in biomedical engineering is given by Sepulveda, Granat, and Cliquet (1997) for the development of adaptive control of gait swing by neuromuscular electrical stimulation (NMES). The subject had full mobility in all limbs but had a completely paralyzed left leg with some sensation. Input variables came from two electrogoniometers, and output consisted of variations in pulse width (PW). In the training phase, stimulation PWs were preset to different values until a few good swing cycles were observed. Goniometer and corresponding stimulation variations were presented as learning targets to the neural network. Backpropagation was used for training with a learning rate for the output layer of 1.1 when the number of bad outputs exceeded one-third of the total target outputs. The learning rate for the middle layer was set to half of this rate. The resulting network was shown to be useful in gait control. In addition, the network itself was easily adaptable to any number of stimulation channels and biomechanical sensors simply by adding or subtracting neurons.

Chen et al. (1995) illustrate another interesting application of the backpropagation method in identifying gastric contractions using surface electrodes. A principal component feed-forward neural network was used by Sveinsson et al. (1997) to analyze event-related potentials from ECGs of male schizophrenic patients compared to normal volunteers. Principal component analysis is a method for reducing the number of features.

A 1992 article by Sabbatini lists over 100 applications of neural networks in medicine and biology. These applications continue to abound. Good sources of biomedical applications of neural networks can be found in *IEEE Transactions on Pattern Analysis and Machine Intelligence, IEEE Transactions on Neural Networks, IEEE Engineering in Medicine and Biology* Magazine, *Computers in Biomedical Research,* as well as in numerous conference proceedings such as IEEE Engineering in Medicine and Biology Society, Artificial Neural Networks in Engineering (ANNIE), the Biomedical Engineering Society, and MEDINFO.

EXERCISES

1. Given the following vectors, compute the scatter matrices for the Fisher Linear Discriminant:

Class 1: $\mathbf{x}_1^T = [2,4]$ $\mathbf{x}_2^T = [1,-3]$
Class 2: $\mathbf{x}_1^T = [-1,3]$ $\mathbf{x}_1^T = [-3,2]$

2. Are the vectors in problem 1 linearly separable? Justify your answer graphically.

3. For the vectors in problem 1, classify the samples using the perceptron algorithm with $\rho = 0.5$ and $\mathbf{w}_0^T = [1\ 1]$. (The weight vector should converge within two iterations.)

4. Complete the Kesler construction calculations for the example given in Section 4.4.2. Verify that your decision function separates the vectors.

5. Given the two class problem with the following sample vectors:

$$X_1 = \{(3,5), (4,2)\} \qquad X_2 = \{(-2,-3), (-3,-4)\}$$

   a. Set up the set Y to be used for the two-category fixed increment rule.
   b. Using an initial guess of $w_1 = (1\ 0\ 0)$, find a separating weight vector.
   c. Write an equation for the decision surface.

6. Given the set of variables collected for the example in Section 4.7, how would you go about reducing this number before beginning the training process? Consider eliminating irrelevant and redundant variables and combining variables.

7. Comparing Figures 4.3 and 4.4, the neural network structures for backpropagation, and Hypernet, what are the major differences in structure? How do these differences affect the development of the decision surface? What effect do they have on the interpretation of results?

REFERENCES

Aizerman, M.A., Braverman, E.M., and Rozonoer, L.I. 1964. Theoretical foundations of the potential function method in pattern recognition learning. *Automation and Remote Control*, **25:** 821–837.

Chen, J.D.Z., Lin, Z., Wu, Q., and McCallum, R.W. 1995. Non-invasive identification of gastric contractions from surface electrogastrogram using backpropagation neural networks. *Med. Eng. Phys.* **17(3):** 219–225.

Cohen, M.E., Hudson, D.L., and Deedwania, P.C. 1985. Pattern recognition analysis of coronary artery disease. In A.H. Levy and B.T. Williams, eds., *American Association for Medical Systems and Informatics,* pp. 262–266.

Cohen, M.E., Hudson, D.L., Touya, J.J., and Deedwania, P.C. 1986. A new multidimensional polynomial approach to medical pattern recognition problems, in R. Salamon, B. Blum, and M. Jorgensen, eds., *MEDINFO 86,* pp. 614–618.

Duda, R.O., and Hart, P.E. 1973. *Pattern Classification and Scene Analysis.* New York: Wiley-Interscience.

Fu, L.M. 1994. *Neural Networks in Computer Intelligence.* New York: McGraw-Hill.

Ho, Y-C., and Kashyap, R.L. 1965. An algorithm for linear inequalities and its applications. *IEEE Trans. Elec. Comp.* **EC-14:** 1501–1514.

McKinsey, J.C.C. 1952. *Introduction to the Theory of Games.* New York: McGraw-Hill.

Motzkin, T.S., and Schoenbert, I.J. 1954. The relaxation method for linear inequalities. *Canadian J. of Mathematics* **6:** 393–404.

Nilsson, N.J. 1965. *Learning Machines: Foundations of Trainable Pattern-Classifying Systems.* New York: McGraw-Hill.

Rosenblatt, F. 1962. *Principles of Neurodynamics: Perceptrons and the Theory of Brain Mechanisms.* Washington, D.C.: Spartan Books.

Rummelhart, D.E., McClelland, J.L. and the PDP Research Group. 1986. *Parallel Distributed Processing,* Vols. 1 and 2. Cambridge, MA: MIT Press.

Sabbatini, R.M.E. 1992. Applications of connectionist systems in biomedicine. In Lun, K.C., Degoulet, P., Piemme, T.E., and Rienhoff, O., eds., *MEDINFO 92,* pp. 418–425. New York: Elsevier.

Sepulveda, F., Granat, M.H., and Cliquet, A. 1997. Two artificial neural systems for generation of gait swing by means of neuromuscular electrical stimulation. *Med. Engr. Phys.* **19(1):** 21–28.

Sveinsson, J.R., Benediktsson, J.A., Stefansson, S.B., and Davidsson, K. 1997. Parallel principal component neural networks for classification of event-related potential waveforms. *Med. Engr., Phys.* **19(1):** 15–20.

Tou, J.T. 1974. *Pattern Recognition Principles.* Reading, MA: Addison-Wesley.

Widrow, B., and Hoff, M.E. 1960. Adaptive switching circuits. *IRE WESCON Conv. Record* **Part 4:** 96–104.

Yau, S.S., and Schumpert, J.M. 1968. Design of pattern classifiers with the updating property using stochastic approximation techniques. *IEEE Trans. Comp.* **C-17:** 861–872.

Young, T.Y., and Calvert, T.W. 1974. *Classification, Estimation, and Pattern Recognition.* New York: Elsevier.

5

Unsupervised Learning

5.1 BACKGROUND

Unsupervised learning is much more difficult than supervised learning because not only do we not know the correct classification of our data sets, but we often do not even know how many categories we should have. The first unsupervised learning approach was *clustering,* a method developed approximately forty years ago.

5.2 CLUSTERING

5.2.1 Basic Isodata

In the following discussion, we will assume that we have a c-category problem where the value for c is known (i.e., we know how many categories exist) and that we have m samples to classify. For now, we also assume that the samples are one dimensional. The most straightforward approach to assigning samples to the proper category is the Basic Isodata Procedure.

Basic Isodata Algorithm
Choose some initial values for the means $\mu_1, \ldots, \mu_c$.
Classify the m samples by assigning them to the class of the closest mean.
Re-compute the means as the average of the samples in the class.
Repeat until no mean changes value.

EXAMPLE: $c = 2, \mu_1 = -2, \mu_2 = -1$ Samples = $\{-2, -1, 3\}$
Pass 1
   -2 belongs to class 1
   -1 belongs to class 2
   3 belongs to class 2
   $\mu_1 = -2, \mu_2 = 1$

Pass 2
  −2 belongs to class 1
  −1 belongs to class 1
  3 belongs to class 2
  $\mu_1 = -1.5, \mu_2 = 3$
Pass 3
  −2 belongs to class 1
  −1 belongs to class 1
  3 belongs to class 2
  $\mu_1 = -1.5, \mu_2 = 3$ (no change in means)

5.2.2 Similarity Measures

The objective of the similarity measure approach is to try to find natural groupings. We will now assume that $\mathbf{x}$ is an n-dimensional column vector. One similarity measure is the normalized inner product

$$s(\mathbf{x}, \mathbf{x'}) = \mathbf{x}^T\mathbf{x'}/(\|\mathbf{x}\|\ \|\mathbf{x'}\|) \tag{5.1}$$

where $s(\mathbf{x}, \mathbf{x'})$ is invariant to rotation and dilation but is not invariant to translation or linear transformations. If the vectors are binary-valued, then $\mathbf{x}^T\mathbf{x'}$ represents the number of attributes shared by $\mathbf{x}$ and $\mathbf{x'}$, and $\|\mathbf{x}\|\ \|\mathbf{x'}\|$ is the geometric mean of the number of attributes possessed by $\mathbf{x}$ and $\mathbf{x'}$ since $\|\mathbf{x}\|\ \|\mathbf{x'}\| = (\mathbf{x}^T\mathbf{x}\ \mathbf{x'}^T\mathbf{x'})^{1/2}$.

For example, if $\mathbf{x}^T = (1\ 0\ 0\ 1\ 1)$ and $\mathbf{x'}^T = (1\ 1\ 0\ 1\ 0)$, then $\mathbf{x}^T\mathbf{x'} = 2$ and $\|\mathbf{x}\|\ \|\mathbf{x'}\| = 3$. Other similarity measures include:

Fraction of Shared Attributes

$$s(\mathbf{x}, \mathbf{x'}) = \mathbf{x}^T\mathbf{x'}/n \qquad \text{where } n \text{ is the dimension of the vector} \tag{5.2}$$

Ratio of Shared Attributes to Number Possessed by $\mathbf{x}$ or $\mathbf{x'}$ (Tanimoto Coefficient)

$$s(\mathbf{x}, \mathbf{x'}) = \mathbf{x}^T\mathbf{x'}/(\mathbf{x}^T\mathbf{x} + \mathbf{x'}^T\mathbf{x'} - \mathbf{x}^T\mathbf{x'}) \tag{5.3}$$

5.2.3 Criterion Functions

Criterion functions measure the quality of the partition of the data. The objective is to find a partition that extremizes a criterion function (i.e., either maximizes or minimizes). We have previously seen criterion functions in Chapter 4 in conjunction with supervised learning.

5.2.3.1 Sum of Squared Error Criteria. The objective of the sum of squared error criteria is to minimize J, the criterion function. We make the following definitions:

$$k_i = \text{number of samples to be classified in the set } X_i$$
$$\mathbf{m}_i = (1/k_i)\sum_{\mathbf{x}\varepsilon X_i} \mathbf{x}_i \tag{5.4}$$

$$J = \sum_{i=1}^{c}\sum_{\mathbf{x}\varepsilon X_i} \|\mathbf{x} - \mathbf{m}_i\|^2 \tag{5.5}$$

This approach measures the variance from the center of the cluster represented by the current mean. It works well on compact clusters. If there is a large difference in the number of samples in each cluster, a partition that splits a large cluster is favored over one that leaves it intact. This problem is made worse by the presence of outliers.

5.2.3.2   Minimum Error Criteria.   This approach is similar to the sum of squared error criteria but with a different criteria function:

$$J = 1/2 \sum_{i=1}^{c} k_i \, s_i \tag{5.6}$$

$$\text{where } s_i = (1/k_i^2) \sum_{\mathbf{x} \varepsilon X_i} \sum_{\mathbf{x'} \varepsilon X_i} \|\mathbf{x} - \mathbf{x'}\|^2 \tag{5.7}$$

5.2.3.3   Scattering Criteria.   In Chapter 4, we defined the scatter matrix in Eq. (4.7). We can similarly define the scatter matrix for the ith cluster

$$S_i = \sum_{\mathbf{x} \varepsilon X_i} (\mathbf{x} - \mathbf{m}_i)(\mathbf{x} - \mathbf{m}_i)^T \tag{5.8}$$

We can define the within-cluster scatter S_w and the between-cluster scatter S_B according to Eqs. (4.8) and (4.9). The total scatter is

$$S_T = S_W + S_B \tag{5.9}$$

We can then define two criteria:

Determinant Criterion

$$J = |S_W| \tag{5.10}$$

Invariant Criterion

This criterion is invariant to linear transformations:

$$tr \, S_W^{-1} S_B = \sum_{i=1}^{n} \lambda_i \tag{5.11}$$

where λ_i are the eigenvalues of $S_W^{-1} S_B$, tr is the trace (sum of diagonal elements), and n is the dimensionality of the vectors.

5.2.3.4   Iterative Optimization.   Any of the above criteria can be used in an iterative optimization procedure.

Iterative Optimization Algorithm
   Select a criterion function.
   Find sets that extremize criterion function (solve by exhaustive enumeration).
      (Note: There are c^n/c ways of partitioning n elements into c subsets!)
Alternate Algorithm
   Select a criterion function.
   Find a reasonable initial partition.
   Move samples if the move will improve the value of the criterion function.

How does this approach compare to the Basic Isodata Algorithm discussed earlier? Basic Isodata waits until all m samples have been reclassified before updating. Iterative optimization updates after each sample. The latter is more susceptible to local minima.

5.2.4 Hierarchical Clustering

Hierarchical clustering uses m samples and starts with c clusters. A sequence of partitions are made:

1. m clusters, 1 sample/cluster
2. m-1 clusters

    .

    .

    .

n. 1 cluster, n samples

At level k, $c = m - k + 1$.

At some level, every two samples will be in the same cluster. If two samples are together at level k, they will remain together at higher levels. There are two methods: *agglomerative* (bottom-up) starts with m singletons, and *divisive* (top-down) starts with 1 cluster.

> **Basic Agglomerative Clustering Algorithm**
> *Initialize: Let ξ = n, and $X = \{x_i\}$ i = 1, . . ., m.*
> *If ξ = c stop.*
> *Find nearest pair of distinct clusters, say X_i and X_j.*
> *Merge X_i and X_j, delete X_j, decrement ξ by one.*
> *Repeat.*

The procedure terminates when the specified number of clusters has been obtained.

5.2.5 Metrics

In the above procedure, it is necessary to determine distances between clusters. We will first consider distance measures in two dimensions. To qualify as a distance measure, or metric, between two points, the following must hold:

$$d(x, y) > 0 \text{ and } d(x, y) = 0 \text{ if and only if } x = y \qquad \text{(positivity)} \qquad (5.12)$$

$$d(x, y) = d(y, x) \qquad \text{(symmetry)} \qquad (5.13)$$

$$d(x, y) + d(y, z) \geq d(x, z) \qquad \text{(triangle inequality)} \qquad (5.14)$$

The most common distance measure is the Euclidean distance:

$$d(x, y) = [(x_1 - y_1)^2 + (x_2 - y_2)^2]^{0.5} \qquad (5.15)$$

Other common distance measures are the city block distance, also known as the absolute value metric:

$$d(x, y) = |x_1 - y_1| + |x_2 - y_2| \qquad (5.16)$$

and the maximum value metric:

$$d(x, y) = \max \; \{|x_1 - y_1|, |x_2 - y_2|\} \tag{5.17}$$

These metrics can be generalized to higher dimensions.

Some measures that are commonly used to determine the distance between clusters are:

$$D_{\min}(X_i, X_j) = \min_{\mathbf{x} \varepsilon X_i, \mathbf{x} \varepsilon X_j} \|\mathbf{x} - \mathbf{x'}\| \tag{5.18}$$

$$D_{\max}(X_i, X_j) = \max_{\mathbf{x} \varepsilon X_i, \mathbf{x} \varepsilon X_j} \|\mathbf{x} - \mathbf{x'}\| \tag{5.19}$$

$$D_{\text{avg}}(X_i, X_j) = (1/n_i n_j) \sum_{\mathbf{x} \varepsilon X_i} \sum_{\mathbf{x} \varepsilon X_j} \|\mathbf{x} - \mathbf{x'}\| \tag{5.20}$$

$$D_{\text{mean}}(X_i, X_j) = \|\mathbf{m}_i - \mathbf{m}_j\| \tag{5.21}$$

where $\| \; \|$ indicates the Euclidean distance. One of the best-known clustering algorithms, nearest neighbor, uses $D_{\min}$ as a distance measure. In terms of graph theory terminology, the algorithm produces a minimal spanning tree by making an edge between the nearest pair of nodes. The furthest neighbor algorithm uses $D_{\max}$ and adds edges between every pair of nodes in the new cluster. The diameter of a cluster is the largest distance between a pair of points. Both of these approaches are very sensitive to outliers. D_{avg} and D_{mean} can be used as compromises. Figure 5.1 shows the classification of the same data sets using nearest and furthest neighbor algorithms.

Statistical nearest neighbor methods are discussed in Chapter 15. A number of fuzzy clustering techniques have also been developed. These will be discussed in Chapter 16.

For detailed treatment of the topics in Section 5.2, see Duda and Hart, 1973; Tou, 1974; Young and Calvert, 1974.

5.3 KOHONEN NETWORKS AND COMPETITIVE LEARNING

Kohonen developed the self-organizing feature map in 1981 and demonstrated how it could be implemented as a neural network (Kohonen, 1988, 1990; Lau, 1992). The Kohonen network is shown in Figure 5.2. It consists of n input nodes that represent an n-dimensional binary input vector. The network has c output nodes that represent c decision regions. Every input node is connected to every output node. The objective is to group input vectors into c classes. The weight vector $\mathbf{w}_j$, $j = 1, \ldots, n$ represents the weights associated with the input vector's connection to node j; thus each $\mathbf{w}_j$ has n components. If these column vectors are arranged in a matrix, we have an n by c matrix for all the weights in the network.

The algorithm performs clustering using a similarity measure on a winner-take-all basis. The node with the largest value is the winner. Only this node will generate an output of 1. All other nodes generate an output of 0.

Initially, the weights are chosen randomly. The idea of selecting a winning node was first introduced by Carpenter and Grossberg (1987) in their work on competitive learning. Although there is only one winning node, the weights of neighboring nodes are also modified. The output of each node acts in an inhibitory fashion on other nodes but is excitatory in its own area. This moderation of competition is called *lateral inhibition,* a concept that derives from biological neural networks. The algorithm is similar to the k-means clustering algorithm discussed in Chapter 16 as an example of the minimum squared error approach.

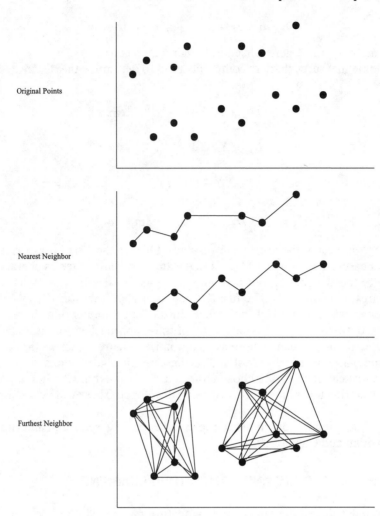

Original Points

Nearest Neighbor

Furthest Neighbor

Figure 5.1 Nearest and Furthest Neighbor Clustering.

Since the winner's weight generates the largest dot product, its weight vector is closest to the input vector. The learning process makes the winning node even more similar to the input pattern. The network uses single-pass learning rather than multi-pass feedback. After the training phase, the network operates by finding the winning node but does not modify the weights.

Kohonen Competitive Learning Algorithm

Initialization

Initialize weights to small random values.

Activation

The value for output node n_i is computed by

$$\mathbf{n}_i = \mathbf{w}_i^T\mathbf{x}. \tag{5.22}$$

This represents the similarity or distance if both the weight vector and the input vector are normalized, usually to unit length. In matrix form:

$$N = WX \tag{5.23}$$

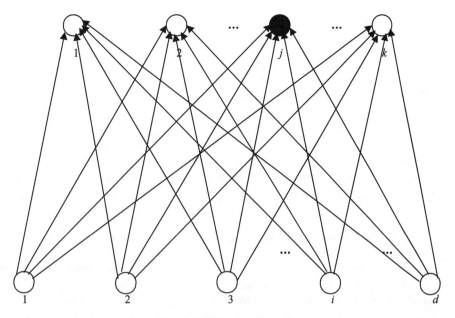

Figure 5.2 Kohonen Network.

Weight Training

The winning node adjusts its weights according to:

$$\mathbf{w}_{k+1} = \mathbf{w}_k + \eta(\mathbf{x} - \mathbf{w}_k) \text{ where } \eta \text{ is the learning rate.} \qquad (5.24)$$

The Kohonen network is an example of competitive learning. One important aspect of competitive learning is how to divide the input space into disjoint subspaces to associate each input vector with the subspace to which it belongs. Learning vector quantization methods use competitive learning to find decision surfaces but in a supervised learning approach.

5.4 HEBBIAN LEARNING

Hebb (1949) attempted to explain how the brain functioned on a cellular level. The essence of Hebb's law is that if two neurons fire simultaneously, the connection between them is strengthened. Thus Hebbian learning (Kosko, 1986) is also called correlation learning. If we consider w_{ij} to be the weight for the connection between neurons i and j, then the weight adjustment at interval k will be:

$$w_{ij}(k+1) = a_i a_j \qquad (5.25)$$

where a_l is the activation level, or value, of node l at time k. Hebbian learning only uses excitatory influences among neurons. It does not use any inhibitory influences. Thus synapses only strengthen, which can lead to stability problems.

The linear association network associates pairs of vectors $(\mathbf{x}_i, \mathbf{y}_i)$ so that if $\mathbf{x}_i$ is the input, $\mathbf{y}_i$ will be the result. If a vector close to $\mathbf{x}_i$ is presented, then a vector close to $\mathbf{y}_i$ will be the result. The computation is straightforward:

$$\mathbf{y}_i = \mathbf{w}_i^T \mathbf{x}_i \qquad (5.26)$$

The learning rule in Eq. (5.25) can be used to associate a new pair:

$$\mathbf{w}(k+1) = \mathbf{x}_i^T \mathbf{y}_i. \qquad (5.27)$$

For m pairs of vectors

$$\mathbf{w} = \sum_{i=1}^{m} \mathbf{x}_i{}^T \mathbf{y}_i \tag{5.28}$$

If $x_1, \ldots, x_m$ are orthonormal, then

$$\mathbf{x}_i{}^T \mathbf{x}_i = \begin{bmatrix} 1 & \text{if } i = j \\ 0 & \text{otherwise} \end{bmatrix} \tag{5.29}$$

Thus $\mathbf{x}_i$ can be transformed into $\mathbf{y}_i$ without error. If the space is n-dimensional, the maximum number of associations is n. If they are not orthonormal, an error will result in trying to retrieve $\mathbf{y}_i$ from $\mathbf{x}_i$.

5.5 ADAPTIVE RESONANCE THEORY (ART)

As noted earlier, Carpenter and Grossberg (1988) developed adaptive resonance theory. The original ART network accepted only binary input. Later, ART2 was developed, which also accepted continuous-valued input. The general algorithm will be discussed in terms of the original ART, also known as ART1. The ART network is basically a two-layer network as shown in Figure 5.3. It is, however, much more complex than it appears. The network has two phases: recognition and comparison. There are bottom-up synapses, represented by b_{ij}, the component of the weight vector connecting input node i to output node j. In addition, there are top-down synapses where t_{ij} is the component of the weight vector which connects output node i to input node j. The number of input nodes corresponds to the dimension of the input vector (Chester, 1993).

Each node in the bottom layer receives three inputs: the input value (x_i), the signal from the upper layer mediated by t_{ij}, and a logic signal from G_1. The network works on a *two-thirds* rule: at least two of the three inputs must be positive for the node to be activated. The G_1 gate works as follows. When an input vector $\mathbf{x}$ is introduced, the presence of a single 1 bit in x activates the OR gate in G_1. The NOR gate in G_1 is true because there are not yet any signals coming from the top layer. Thus the ith node will be triggered if and only if $x_i = 1$. Thus x will pass through the bottom layer unchanged, and b will be identical to x. In the recognition phase, the network operates using a winner-take-all strategy, where the winning node has the bottom-up weight vector closest to the input vector as determined by the dot product. (In the first cycle, a random selection determines the winner.) To moderate the winner-take-all strategy, in the comparison phase the network uses a vigilance test:

$$\sum_i x_i \, t_{ij} / \sum_i x_i > \rho \tag{5.30}$$

where ρ is the vigilance parameter, $0 \le \rho \le 1$. For binary values, the numerator is the number of attributes possessed by both vectors and the denominator is the number of attributes in the input vector. If the vigilance test fails, the network will continue to search for another output neuron whose weight vectors best match the input vector. If all neurons fail, a new neuron will be added. When a winner is confirmed, the G_2 circuit is set to 0. At this point, the weights are modified. The top-down weights are computed using a logical AND ($\wedge$) operation:

$$t_{ij}(k + 1) = x_i \wedge t_{ij}(k) \tag{5.31}$$

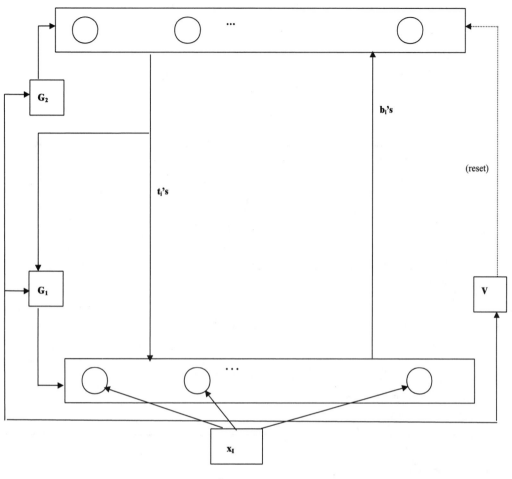

Figure 5.3 Adaptive Resonance Theory (ART1) Network.

The bottom-up synapses are based on a weighted version of the AND operation:

$$b_{ij}(k+1) = x_i \wedge t_{ij}(k)/[(L-1) + \sum x_i t_{ij}(k)] \tag{5.32}$$

where L is a user-selected constant (typically equal to 2) (Fu, 1994).

ART1 Algorithm

Initialization

 $t_{ij}(0) = 1$

 $b_{ij}(0) = L/(L-1+d)$

 where d *is the number of input units.*

Activation

 Activation of input nodes is determined by the input vector.

 Activation of the output nodes is:

$$O_j = F_w[\mathbf{b}^T\mathbf{x}] \tag{5.33}$$

where $F_w(x) = $ $\begin{array}{l} 1 \\ 0 \end{array}$ $\begin{bmatrix} \textit{if } x = max_i(I_i) \\ \textit{otherwise (the winner-take-all strategy)} \end{bmatrix}$

Vigilance test

If O_j *is the winner, compute*

$$\sum_i x_i \, t_{ij} / \sum_i x_i > \rho$$

If the vigilance test is passed, update weights; otherwise set $O_j = 0$, *disable* O_j, *and repeat. If all output nodes have been disabled, add a new output unit.*

Weight Training

$$t_{ij}(k + 1) = t_{ij}(k) \, x_i \qquad\qquad (5.34)$$

$$b_{ij}(k + 1) = L t_{ij}(k) \, x_i / [(L - 1) + \Sigma x_i t_{ij}(k)] \qquad\qquad (5.35)$$

EXAMPLE

For the six-dimensional vector **x**

$$\mathbf{x} = (1, 0, 0, 0, 1, 1)$$

Assume that O_j is the winning node and

$$t_j = (1, 1, 0, 0, 0, 1)$$

The weight vector is changed to

$$t_j = (1, 0, 0, 0, 0, 1)$$

5.6 APPLICATIONS

All of the networks discussed here and in Chapter 4 have strengths and weaknesses, and some are better suited to one application type. (These issues will be discussed in detail in Chapter 7.) In the remainder of this chapter we will look at some general uses for unsupervised learning and provide references to some specific biomedical examples.

5.6.1 Dimensionality Reduction

Because we live in three-dimensional space, we cannot visualize data sets in excess of three dimensions. One application of clustering techniques is to reduce the dimensionality of data to two or three dimensions so that it can be visualized.

5.6.1.1 Minimization of Criteria Functions. Assume that we have the following set of n-dimensional samples, $\mathbf{x}^1, \ldots, \mathbf{x}^m$ and we wish to generate a set of k-dimensional samples $\mathbf{y}^1, \ldots, \mathbf{y}^m$ where $k < n$. We then define the following distance measures

   δ_{ij}: distance between x_i and x_j

   d_{ij}: distance between y_i and y_j

The objective is to make these distance measures as close as possible for all i, j. We can accomplish this by utilizing one of the following criteria:

$$J_E = (1/\sum_{i<j} \delta_{ij}^2) \sum_{i<j} (d_{ij} - \delta_{ij})^2 \tag{5.36}$$

$$J_{FF} = \sum_{i<j} [(d_{ij} - \delta_{ij})^2/\delta_{ij}] \tag{5.37}$$

$$J_{EF} = (1/\sum_{i<j} \delta_{ij}^2) \sum_{i<j} (d_{ij} - \delta_{ij})^2/\delta_{ij} \tag{5.38}$$

The gradient descent method is then used to minimize the chosen error criteria.

5.6.1.2 Clustering and Dimensionality Reduction. This method is a modification of hierarchical clustering. The $n \times n$ matrix of distances is replaced by a $d \times d$ correlation matrix $\mathbf{R} = [\rho_{ij}]$ with $d < n$ where

$$\rho_{ij} = \sigma_{ij}/(\sigma_{ii}\sigma_{jj})^{1/2} \tag{5.39}$$

where σ_{ij} is the covariance.
Note that

$$\rho_{ij} = \begin{bmatrix} 0 \text{ if uncorrelated} \\ 1 \text{ if correlated} \end{bmatrix}$$

Features are then merged if ρ_{ij} is large. The following is the algorithm:

Hierarchical Dimensionality Reduction (Duda and Hart, 1973)
Initialize: Let d_t = n, *the original dimensionality of the sample vectors.*
If d_t = d, *stop* (d *is the desired dimensionality*).
Compute correlation matrix, find most correlated pair of clusters, f_i *and* f_j.
Merge f_i, f_j.
Delete $f_j, d_t = d_t - 1$.
Repeat.

5.6.2 Biomedical Applications

Under what circumstances would unsupervised learning be useful in biomedical applications? One area where clustering appears to be a natural approach is classification of cell types. An interesting new application of self-organization is a global classification of all currently known protein sequences (Linial et al., 1997). Every protein sequence is partitioned into segments of 50 amino acid residues and a distance is calculated between each pair of segments. The space of segments is embedded into Euclidean space. The procedure uses a self-organized hierarchical clustering algorithm. Another recent example employs a Kohonen network for ventricular tachycardia source localization that uses body surface potential maps (Simelius et al., 1997). The objective is to obtain localization for different types of ventricular tachycardia.

5.6.3 Diagnosis of CAD as a Clustering Problem

Consider the problem from Chapter 4 for diagnosis of coronary artery disease. Assume that we have the same data set but that we do not know the correct classification of any of the cases. We will use the same four parameters:

x_1 = maximum ST depression
x_2 = percentage change in heart rate from beginning to end of test

x_3 = percentage change in blood pressure from beginning to end of test

x_4 = double product

We therefore have a set of four-dimensional vectors of unknown classification. We also assume that we do not know the correct number of categories. The objective is to determine four-dimensional clusters for the data set. As the dimension is greater than three, visual inspection is of no use, so one of the algorithms described in this chapter must be used. If we wish to apply hierarchical clustering, a distance measure must be defined. A sample vector for this problem is:

$$\mathbf{x}^1 = (1.5, 0.2, -0.05, 11000)$$

First, for most distance measures, each parameter should be in the same range to prevent one component from assuming undue importance. One method of ensuring equal ranges is to normalize each vector by dividing by the largest occurrence of each variable over the entire data set. For example, assume we have the following maximum values for the data set:

$$\text{Max}(x_1) = 2.5$$
$$\text{Max}(x_2) = 0.5$$
$$\text{Max}(x_3) = 0.45$$
$$\text{Max}(x_4) = 32,000$$

The normalized vector is then:

$$\mathbf{x}^1 = (0.60, 0.40, -0.11, 0.34)$$

Hierarchical clustering can be examined at each stage to see if the clusters seem to make clinical sense. In the absence of a gold standard for diagnosis, such as cardiac catheterization, the clustering approach may be the only strategy available.

5.6.4 Other Biomedical Applications

An interesting application of clustering using the nearest neighbor rule is given in Bonato et al. (1995). The objective was to improve the identification of late potentials (LP) in patients affected by greater arrhythmogenic right ventricular disease (GARVD). Previous methods using spectral mapping of the ECG based on Fourier analysis suffered from poor reproducibility, a consequence of improper localization of the QRS segments. A new filtering method was used to increase the reliability of normality factors, which were then grouped using cluster analysis, greatly improving sensitivity results.

Another study compared the performance of three supervised learning approaches and one unsupervised learning approach on analysis of EMG interference patterns (Abel et al., 1996). The supervised learning techniques were backpropagation, radial basis network, and learning vector quantization. The unsupervised technique was a self-organizing feature map. The supervised learning approaches performed better overall than the unsupervised learning. Is this result one you would expect?

A new unsupervised learning algorithm, the prototype distribution map (PDM), is based on the self-organizing map (SOM) procedure (Boyanov and Hadjitodorov, 1997). This method has been applied to acoustic analysis of pathological voices caused by laryngeal diseases. The PDM operates on the already formed SOM. It is used to reduce dimensionality by eliminating less significant neurons. In the classification stage, the objective is to eliminate the most serious error: classification of an individual with laryngeal disease as normal. Four preliminary classifications and scores are combined: PDM classifier, K-NN classifier, LDA (linear discriminant analysis) classifier, and classical SOM. The final decision is made by:

1. If at least two classification methods accept a sample as a member of the disease class and the combined weights exceed 0.5, then the sample is accepted.
2. If only one method accepts the sample or the weights are less than 0.5, the sample is rejected.

The following parameters are used as features:

Deviations in the pitch period
Deviations in the amplitudes of pitch pulses
Degree of unvoiceness
Stability of "To" generation
Degree of dissimilarity of shape of pulse pitches
Harmonics-to-noise ratio
Low-to-high energy ratio
Noise-to-harmonics ratio
Ratio of energy concentrated in the pitch impulse in cepstra to total cepstral energy

The accuracy of this approach exceeded 90% percent.

5.7 SUMMARY

Unsupervised learning can be used when little is known about the data set. It only requires a set of input vectors. Because of this lack of information, care must be taken in interpreting the output. First, if the number of categories is unknown, some means of deciding the appropriate number of clusters must be defined. One method is through the use of criterion functions. In any case, the results must be viewed in terms of the application to determine if they make sense and can be interpreted in terms of the problem. Unsupervised learning can be used as a first step in the investigating possible patterns in the data as a data mining technique that can be followed by more studies involving supervised learning or statistical analysis.

EXERCISES

1. For the following two-class clustering problem, use the city block distance and the initial cluster centers of (0, 0) for class 1 and (5, 3) for class 2. The data set to be grouped is

$$x_1 = (1, 0)$$
$$x_2 = (0, 3)$$
$$x_3 = (5, 5)$$

Compute two passes of the Isodata procedure on the above data. Give the cluster centers after the two passes, and indicate if the procedure needs to be repeated.

2. Given the feature vectors:

$X_1 = \{(2, 1), (1, 4)\}$ (class 1)
$X_2 = \{(-1, -1), (-3, -1)\}$ (class 2)
$X_3 = \{(1, -5), (2, -3)\}$ (class 3)

(a) Compute the mean of each class

(b) Using the mean as a prototype, classify the sample $(1, -1)$ by the nearest neighbor algorithm using each of the following metrics:

    i. Euclidean

    ii. City block

    iii. Maximum coordinate

3. Write the multidimensional generalizations for the Euclidean, city block, and maximum coordinate metrics. Show that your definitions meet the three conditions necessary for a metric.

4. (a) Describe a biomedical application that would be suitable for solution by a Kohonen network.

   (b) Could an ART network also be used for solution of this problem? Explain.

5. Assume you have the following input parameters for your network:

x_1 = blood pressure

x_2 = heart rate

x_3 = white blood count

x_4 = potassium level

x_5 = cholesterol level

If you run a dimensionality reduction algorithm that combines variables x_1 and x_2 (i.e., x_2 is deleted), how does this affect interpretation of the output?

REFERENCES

Abel, E.W., Zacharia, P.C., Forster, A., and Farrow, T.L. 1996. Neural network analysis of the EMG interference pattern. *Med. Eng. Phys.* **18(1):** 12–17.

Bonato, P., Bettini, R., Speranza, G., Furlanello, F., and Antolini, R. 1995. Improved late potential analysis in frequency domain. *Med. Eng. Phys.* **17(3):** 232–238.

Boyanov, B., and Hadjitodorov, S. 1997. Acoustic analysis of pathological voices. *EMBS Magazine* **16(4):** 74–82.

Carpenter, G.A., and Grossberg, S. 1988. The ART of adaptive pattern recognition by a self-organizing neural network. *Computer* **21(3):** 77–88.

Carpenter, G.A., and Grossberg, S. 1987. A massively parallel architecture for a self-organizing neural pattern recognition machine. *Computer, Vision, Graphics, and Image Processing* **37:** 54–115.

Chester, M. 1993. *Neural Networks, A Tutorial.* Englewood Cliffs, NJ: Prentice-Hall.

Duda, R.O., and Hart, P.E. 1973. *Pattern Classification and Scene Analysis.* New York: Wiley-Interscience.

Fu, L.M. 1994. *Neural Networks in Computer Intelligence.* New York: McGraw-Hill.

Hebb, D. 1949. *The Organization of Behavior.* New York: John Wiley & Sons.

Kohonen, T. 1990. The self-organizing map. *Proc. IEEE* **78(9):** 1464–1480.

Kohonen, T. 1988. *Self-Organization and Associative Memory.* New York: Springer-Verlag.

Kosko, B.M. 1986. Differential Hebbian learning. *Proc. American Institute of Physics: Neural Networks for Computing* 277–282.

Lau, C. (ed.). 1992. *Neural Networks, Theoretical Foundations and Analysis.* Piscataway, NJ: IEEE Press.

Linial, M., Linial, N., Tishby, N., and Yona, G. 1997. Global self-organization of all known protein sequences reveals inherent biological signatures. *J. of Molecular Biology* **238(2):** 539–556.

Rogers, S.K., and Kabrisky, M. 1991. *An Introduction to Biological and Artificial Neural Networks for Pattern Recognition.* Bellingham, WA: SPIE Optical Engineering Press.

Similius, K., Reinhardt, L., Nenonen, J., Jierala, J., Toivonen, L., and Katila, T. 1997. Self-organizing maps in arrhythmia localization from body surface potential mapping. *IEEE, EMBS* **19:** 62–64.

Tou, J.T. 1974. *Pattern Recognition Principles.* Reading, MA: Addison-Wesley.

Young, T.Y., and Calvert, T.W. 1974. *Classification, Estimation, and Pattern Recognition.* New York: Elsevier.

6

Design Issues

6.1 INTRODUCTION

For each specific application for which neural network modeling seems appropriate, a number of factors need to be considered in the design of the network, including

> Objective of the model
> Information Sources
> Type of input data
> Requirements of output
> Availability of data

6.1.1 Objective of the Model

If the model is a diagnostic model, is the purpose to find a model that will correctly classify new cases, or to determine which parameters can aid in differentiating among classes, or both? The type of network may affect your ability to obtain the required information. The impact of network design on output is discussed later in this chapter in conjunction with implications of network structure and choice of learning algorithm.

6.1.2 Information Sources

In some situations, it may be better to use a knowledge-based approach. Both knowledge-based and data-driven approaches have advantages and disadvantages. Some problems lend themselves better to one than the other. Before choosing a methodology, one should closely examine an application to locate the bulk of the information useful for decision making and determine the amount of effort that will be required for the full development of the information base. Figure 6.1 illustrates areas that should be considered before choosing a methodology. If a database exists or can be created with an acceptable amount of additional effort, then the neural network ap-

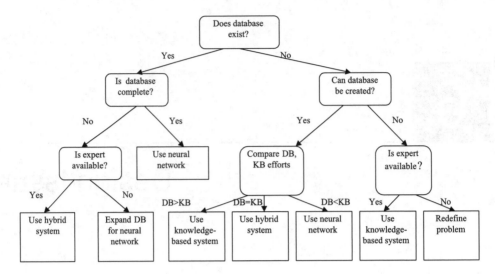

Figure 6.1 Choosing a Methodology.

proach is appropriate. If most decision-making information is in the form of expert opinion, then the knowledge-based approach is more appropriate. (Knowledge-based approaches are discussed in Part II.) If a combination of data-derived and expert-derived information is available, a hybrid method should be considered. (Hybrid systems are discussed in Chapters 17 and 18.)

6.2 INPUT DATA TYPES

6.2.1 Extracting Information from the Medical Record

Figure 6.2 shows one page from a typical medical record. Some patients, especially the elderly and those with chronic diseases, may have multiple volumes, with each volume containing 100 pages or more. Although many hospital information systems have some portions of the medical record in digital form, the handwritten medical record continues to exist in some form in most hospitals, clinics, and physician's offices. The handwritten format introduces a number of problems, including:

Location of pertinent items, such as previous test results

Comparison of new information with previous history

Missing information

Illegible information

Information with multiple interpretations

Because of these problems, the first step in most medical research problems is to devise a data collection sheet that includes only the information relevant to the current decision. The process of completing these data collection sheets, which usually includes information from the written record as well as computerized results, can pose challenging problems in itself.

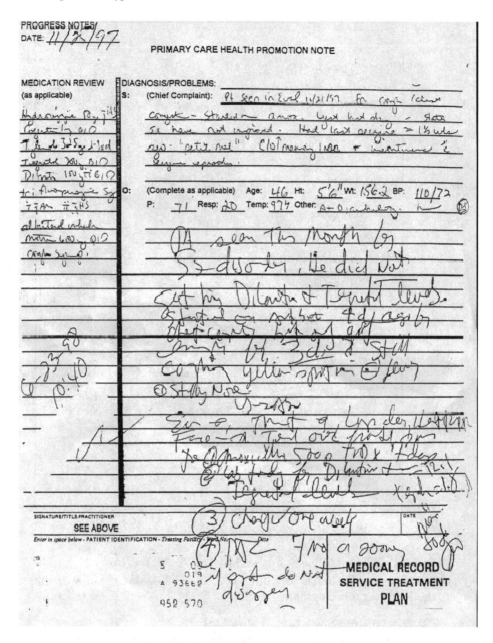

Figure 6.2 Sample Sheet from Medical Record.

6.2.2 Using Information from Data Collection Sheets

Figure 6.3 shows a data collection form for the investigation of cardiac problems. This is an actual form that has been used to evaluate diagnostic factors in coronary artery disease and congestive heart failure. The goal is to convert this information into a form that can be used by the neural network. As we have seen in previous chapters, some neural networks accept only binary input, whereas others accept continuous vari-

ID Number	*(Integer)*
Age	*(Integer)*
Sex	*(Binary)*
Hx of bypass	*(Binary)*
Hx of MI	*(Binary)*
Presence of symptoms (Increased, Decreased, Stable)	*(Categorical)*
Dyspnea	*(Binary)*
Orthopnea	*(Binary)*
PND	*(Binary)*
Duration of Symptoms	*(Continuous)*
Physical Findings	
Resting Heart Rate	*(Continuous)*
Edema	*(Binary)*
Rales	*(Binary)*
Gallup	*(Binary)*
Mitroregurgitation	*(Binary)*
Functional Impairment (NYHA)	*Categorical)*
LV Ejection Fraction	*(Continuous)*
Echo	*(Subjective)*
ETT Data	*(Binary)*
Resting Heart Rate	*(Continuous)*
Resting Blood Pressure	*(Continuous)*
Time of Maximum ST Depression	*(Continuous)*
Time of Angina	*(Continuous)*
Total Exercise Time	*(Continuous)*
Heart Rate at End of Test	*(Continuous)*
Blood Pressure at End of Test	*(Continuous)*
Reason for Stopping ETT	*(Subjective)*
Holter Data	*(Subjective)*
Electrolytes	
Na	*(Continuous)*
K	*(Continuous)*
Mg	*(Continuous)*
BUN	*(Continuous)*
Cr	*(Continuous)*
Drugs	
Digitalis	*(Binary)*
Diuretic	*(Binary)*
ACE Inhibitor	*(Binary)*
Vasodilators	*(Binary)*
Anti-arrhythmic	*(Binary)*
URI/Viral Syndrome	*(Binary)*

Figure 6.3 Data Collection Form for Patients with Heart Disease.

ables as input, or a combination of the two. Decision making in biomedicine may utilize the following types of input:

Binary (y/n, present/absent, true/false, 0/1)

Continuous (laboratory values, blood pressure, heart rate, etc.)

Categorical (stable, improved, diminished; drug use categories such as beta blockers, calcium channel blockers, anti-inflammatory)

Fuzzy (ranges of test values, partial presence of symptoms)

For a particular problem, only a subset of these variables may be present. When selecting an approach, the application must be examined to determine suitable data types. Different problems that arise are discussed using Figure 6.3 as an example.

6.2.2.1 Coding Multiple Responses.
Note that "Electrolytes" has multiple listings. In fact, each of the entries—Na, K, and so on—contains a continuous variable so that this item requires five nodes in the network for its representation. Possible im-

plementations include direct continuous input, binary nodes that indicate if the value is in the normal range, a categorical variable that indicates if the value is low, normal, or high, or fuzzy variable that indicates the degree to which the value is normal. The choice of the best representation depends not only on the data items but also on the decision to which the data items contribute.

6.2.2.2 *Ordering Categorical Data.* Consider "Presence of symptoms" in which the form indicates that either increased, decreased, or stable should be entered for each of the three symptoms listed. In order for most learning algorithms to make use of categorical data, it must be ordered, that is, arranged from worst to best or vice versa. The easiest solution is to code the entries as decreased: 1, stable: 2, increased: 3, or some equivalent designation.

6.2.2.3 *Changing Categorical Data into Binary Data.* Consider the entry in the data collection form for drugs. How should this information be utilized? Under drugs, a list of categories is given, and for some patients, drugs from multiple categories will be used. How is this information to be represented? The most straightforward approach is to define a binary variable for each category, with a 0 for "not using" and a 1 for "using."

6.2.2.4 *Considering the Use of Fuzzy Input Data.* Earlier we mentioned that the electrolytic values could be considered as fuzzy numbers. If this option is chosen, a neural network model that can process this type of information must be used. Typically, fuzzy input data are represented as triangular numbers that indicate the degree of precision for the value (Bezdek, 1987). For example, potassium (K) may have a normal range of 3.5 to 5.5 that would be represented by a trapezoidal membership function. The triangular function representing actual patient values would depend on the degree of precision of the test (see Figure 6.4). (For computational methods associated with fuzzy data, see Chapter 16.)

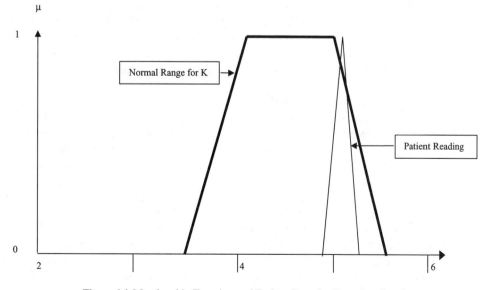

Figure 6.4 Membership Function and Patient Data for Potassium Level.

6.2.2.5 Missing Data. Missing data is one of the major problems in establishing decision models in the health sciences, especially in retrospective studies where chart review is the chief source of information. In prospective studies with established protocols for data collection, this problem can be reduced but never completely eliminated. Several approaches can be used to deal with missing values:

Remove the cases.
Enter the minimum value.
Enter the maximum value.
Enter the average value.

The first option ensures the integrity of the data, but if the number of variables is high and the number of missing values is also high, this approach will not be practical. The choice of whether to use the minimum, maximum, or average value depends on the variable and its potential clinical significance. For example, if blood pressure is the missing value, putting on a minimum or maximum value would indicate a pathological condition; thus, the average would be preferable.

Note the entry "Holter data" on the collection sheet. This entry indicates only if the Holter showed irregularities, with the irregularity listed. Again we have the same choices of listing binary input (normal, abnormal) or each arrhythmia as a separate binary node (present/absent). For more sophisticated means of dealing with time series data such as Holter data, see the following section as well as Chapter 18 (Cohen and Hudson, 1998).

6.2.3 Time Series Data

Time series data are important in clinical decision making, especially in cardiology through the use of the ECG. Many automated systems are in general use for analysis of ECGs (McLaughlin et al., 1996). These systems generally report the presence and types of arrhythmias. Usually, the presence of specific types of arrhythmias is indicative of different cardiac disorders. The Holter tape is an extended version of the ECG and is recorded via a device that the patient wears over a twenty-four hour or forty-eight hour period. While it offers the advantage of recording the ECG under conditions of normal activity, it also records over 100,000 points of data in a twenty-four hour period. New work has indicated that the pattern of the R-R intervals (time between heartbeats) is useful information in diagnosing specific cardiac conditions.

Summary measures are used to provide information regarding the presence or absence of chaos that may be indicative of disease. It is difficult to verify the presence of chaos in experimental models. In the evaluation of time series data collected experimentally, possible approaches for determining the presence of chaos are the Lyapunov exponent, the fractal dimension (Eberhart, 1989), and the central tendency measure (see Chapter 3). The Lyapunov exponent and the fractal dimension are used to determine the presence or absence of chaos in the system. The central tendency measure is used differently in that it indicates the degree of chaos in the system. (The incorporation of these measures is treated in Chapters 3 and 18.)

Interpretation of data from biosensors falls under the category of time series analysis and has the added complication of multiple-channel output. In addition to data overload, other problems include determination of the proper sampling rate to keep data points to a minimum without loss of crucial information. For online monitoring systems, interpretation must be accomplished in real time. If a neural network model is used for decision making, this requirement will limit execution time.

6.2.4 Image Data

In the collection sheet, also notice the entry "Echo," which is for echocardiography information extracted from imaging of the heart through ultrasound (Salmasi and Nicolaides, 1989). This information can determine enlargement of the heart and other physical abnormalities. In the medical record, summary information is often provided, and it must then be coded.

6.3 STRUCTURE OF NETWORKS

The network structure may vary depending on the application, although some general guidelines are not application-dependent.

6.3.1 Number of Layers

As we saw earlier, the two-layer networks have theoretical limitations and cannot solve certain problems, notably the *exclusive OR* problem. In general, it can be shown that a three-layer network can perform any task that a network with more layers can perform. Sometimes, however, use of more layers makes problems conceptually simpler. For example, in the Hypernet algorithm, if fractional contributions of nodes are used, one hidden layer can represent fractional contributions while another can represent integral contributions.

6.3.2 Connectivity

The function of a network depends not only on the number of its layers but also on its connectivity. We have seen examples of fully connected networks in which every node is connected to every other node such as backpropagation, and we have also examined partly connected networks such as Hypernet. The connectivity will affect the size of the training set as well as the interpretation of the output.

6.4 IMPLICATIONS OF NETWORK STRUCTURES

6.4.1 Classification Potential

In order to examine the effects of number of layers and degree of connectivity, we will use the simple examples of networks in Figure 6.5. All networks have three input nodes and one output node. The network in part (a) is a fully connected feedforward two-layer network. Part (b) is a partially connected three-layer network, and (c) is a fully connected three-layer network.

For part (a), we will assume that the activation of a node is computed according to the following:

$$N = \sum_{i=1}^{n} w_i x_i \tag{6.1}$$

where x_i is the input from node i and w_i is the weight of the connection. Then:

$$N = w_1 x_1 + w_2 x_2 + w_3 x_3 \tag{6.2}$$

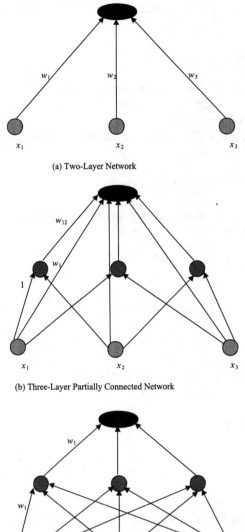

(a) Two-Layer Network

(b) Three-Layer Partially Connected Network

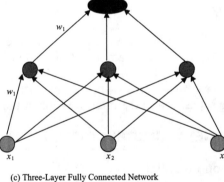

(c) Three-Layer Fully Connected Network

Figure 6.5 Network Structures.

In other words, this is a linear network that will only separate linearly separable sets.
For (*b*), all weights are indicated by the connection to the output node:

$$N = w_1x_1 + w_2x_2 + w_3x_3 + w_{12}x_1x_2 + w_{13}x_1x_3 + w_{23}x_2x_3 \qquad (6.3)$$

This is a nonlinear network that contains direct contribution of linear terms as in Eq.
(6.1) and interaction terms—that is, multiplication of each input node times all other
input nodes. Thus the hidden layer performs the multiplication operations. The nodes
contribute equally to the interaction; that is, the weights from level 1 to level 2 are all
equal to one.

For (*c*) it is more difficult to write the corresponding equation, because all input
nodes combine at level 2, which are then combined again at the output level. Note that

there are no direct connections from input layer to output layer. For the kth node of the hidden layer we have

$$N_{hk} = w_{k1}x_1 + w_{k2}x_2 + w_{k3}x_3 \tag{6.4}$$

Note that this is only one node in the hidden layer. All the x_i's will also be used in the other nodes in the hidden layer. For the output layer

$$N_o = \omega[N_{h1}] + \mu[N_{h2}] + \rho[N_{h3}] \tag{6.5}$$

Any data set can be separated if the order of the equation is high enough—that is, it has enough curves. In practice, it is dangerous to use a high-order equation as a decision surface because of the problem of overfitting (Hudson, Cohen, and Anderson, 1991). Although the equation separates the given data set, it will be too fine-tuned to work well on new cases.

6.4.2 Training

6.4.2.1 Number of Cases Required.
The network structure has an impact on the number of cases required for adequate training. A general rule of thumb is that between five and ten cases are needed for each node in the network. Thus the network in Figure 6.5a would require at least twenty cases, whereas the networks in Figures 6.5b and c would require at least thirty-five cases. Acquiring a sufficient number of cases can be difficult, especially if a large number of input nodes are used. In addition, the size of the training set is often reduced because of missing values. Appropriate cases must also be selected for the specific problem under analysis as seen in the following example. The exact number of cases for adequate training is difficult to determine, for it depends on the degree of separation of classes as well as the differences in the data vectors themselves. If new cases are added to a training set and the weights in the decision surface do not change or change only slightly, this is a good indication that adequate training has occurred.

EXAMPLE

As a practical illustration of what typically happens with data sets, consider the following actual example (Hudson et al., 1992). In an attempt to refine the parameters important in determining prognosis, 1756 cases of melanoma were examined from the melanoma clinic at the University of California at San Francisco (UCSF in 1990), established by the late M. S. Blois, M.D. The UCSF Clinic is one of the largest melanoma treatment centers in the United States and has been in operation for almost thirty years.

Each patient case contained several hundred parameters, but for the purposes of this analysis, 109 were considered useful. The data were distributed as follows:

Total number of cases:	1756
Stage 1 cases:	1567
Cases eliminated:	
Acral-lentiginous and mucosal (unusual types of melanoma)	53
Missing values	143
Remaining cases	1371

The goal of the model was to compare parameters for those who survived melanoma and those who died. Thus the remaining 1371 cases were grouped as follows:

Group 1 (surviving)	1177
Group 2 (died from melanoma)	167
Group 3 (died from other causes)	27

In order to make a valid comparison, group 1a was formed, which consisted of those surviving after five years, with no stage 3 symptoms. This group contained 304 patients. The rationale for selecting this group was that five-year survival is the usual criterion for a cancer "cure." However, at the five-year point the patient must be cancer-free. The model was then established using group 1a and group 2:

Group 1a (surviving > 5 years, no stage 3 symptoms)	304
Group 2 (died from melanoma)	167

Thus with a data set consisting of 1756 cases, only 471 were suitable for inclusion owing to the restrictions of the problem.

6.4.3 Reduction in Number of Nodes

If the number of cases that can be used for training is limited, then the number of network nodes must be limited to a size that can be supported by the data. This can be accomplished in two ways: (1) reduce the number of input nodes, or (2) reduce the connectivity of the network.

Input nodes are selected in a number of ways:

Each available data item is used as an input node.

Nodes are selected through expert consultation or historical data.

Nodes are selected through statistical significance.

Nodes are pruned when weights drop below a certain threshold value.

All except the first alternative permits adjustment of the number of input nodes.

6.4.3.1 Expert Intervention. In some cases, experts in the field may determine that some of the nodes are not relevant to the decision at hand. For instance, it may be known that age is not a factor in the diagnosis of certain diseases. This method can be effective in limiting the number of nodes but runs the risk of eliminating information that is falsely believed to be irrelevant.

6.4.3.2 Statistical Significance. A method such as analysis of variance can be run to determine p-values indicating whether each variable is significant in the discrimination process. This method can provide a basis for selecting nodes with the lowest p-values, but again, it runs the risk of omitting important variables. Actually, nodes with low significance may make an important contribution when combined with other variables.

6.4.3.3 Threshold Pruning. The learning algorithm may drop nodes when their weight drops below a certain threshold, that is, when the weight gets close to zero. The major problem with this approach is that in iterative training, weights may drop to small values after a number of iterations only to increase again after subsequent iterations.

6.4.3.4 Other Techniques.

Other techniques for node reduction include elimination of nodes that are highly correlated with other nodes; combination of data items; and focusing decisions so that fewer nodes are relevant.

An example of highly correlated variables is the presence of arrhythmias and the occurrence at PVCs on ECG analysis. Since the second is a more specific finding, the first can be omitted. An example of combination of data items is seen in the following. Refer to Figure 6.2 for ETT (Exercise Treadmill Testing) data. Although the heart rate and systolic blood pressure are entered at the beginning and end of the test, the important aspect is the change in each reading. Thus these four variables can be reduced to two—change in heart rate and change in systolic blood pressure. (Hudson, Cohen, and Deedwania, 1993). An example of a focused decision would be to limit a decision to the presence or absence of a specific cardiac disorder such as angina rather than a general determination of type of heart disease.

6.4.4 Output

How does the network structure affect the output? The effect depends on the purpose of the network. In some classification models, the sole objective is to find the correct classification of a case presented to the network in a black-box manner. Thus the only output considered is the classification of the case. If this is the desired result, then the network structure directly affects the output only in the number of possible output nodes. As we will see later (Chapter 16), use of fuzzy neural networks makes it possible to have membership in multiple classes (Ruspini, 1969; Archer and Wang, 1991). This is also true in some extended Bayesian systems introduced by Patrick and discussed in Chapter 15 (Patrick and Fattu, 1984).

In other cases, especially in biomedical applications, not only is the classification important, but so are the parameters that led to the conclusion. In fact, as in the melanoma decision given earlier, determining the contributing factors was the primary objective of the model. If this is the case, then the network structure greatly influences the interpretation of the contribution of the input parameters. Obviously, a linear network as shown in Figure 6.5a is the easiest to interpret but has the least power for classification. The network in Figure 6.5c is extremely difficult to interpret, whereas Figure 6.5b offers a compromise between classification power and interpretive power.

6.5 CHOICE OF LEARNING ALGORITHM

The learning algorithm determines the network structure; thus once the desired structure of the network has been determined, the choices of learning algorithms will be automatically limited. The aspects of the network design which are intertwined with the learning algorithm are type of input nodes (binary, continuous, fuzzy, etc.); and connectivity. Additional aspects of the learning algorithm that must be considered are convergence and stability. For some algorithms, it is possible to show theoretically that the algorithm will converge under specified conditions. For others, the conditions under which it will not converge can also be specified. A summary of convergence properties for some of the learning algorithms that have been discussed earlier will be given in Chapter 7 (Duda and Hart, 1973; Fu, 1994; Chester, 1993).

Some learning algorithms may not be stable under some conditions. These algorithms may decay into oscillatory or chaotic conditions and either fail to produce a solution or, worse, produce a meaningless solution. For these algorithms, in order to ensure stability, certain limiting, or boundary, conditions must be specified. Often this is difficult when experimental data are used; therefore these algorithms work well for artificially generated well-behaved data sets but not for experimental data. Comparisons using different approaches are given in Chapter 8 (Maxwell et al., 1986).

6.6 SUMMARY

It is not possible to determine the best approach to decision making under all conditions. This choice is dependent on the type of application, the type of decision-support information that is available (specifically if it is expert-based or data-based), the input parameters, and the type of results required. Analysis of these parameters in advance of choosing a methodology not only saves time but also increases the chances of developing a useful decision-support system.

EXERCISES

1. From viewing the medical record in Figure 6.2:
   (a) What aspects would be the most difficult to computerize?
   (b) What do you see as the chief advantages of the computerized medical record?
   (c) How would the computerized medical record affect the following?
      Patient care
      Emergency services
      Medical costs
2. For the data set in Figure 6.3, identify other possible data types for each entry. If it is possible to formulate the data structure for an item in multiple ways, give all possibilities.
3. In the melanoma example in Section 6.3.2.2,
   (a) What is the goal of the neural network model?
   (b) Why was it necessary to form Group 1a instead of using Group 1 directly?
4. Devise a set of four three-dimensional feature vectors that cannot be separated by the network in Figure 6.5a but can be separated by the network in Figure 6.5b. Give the separating vector for part (b).

REFERENCES

Archer, N.P., and Wang, S. 1991. Fuzzy set representation of neural network classification boundaries. *IEEE Trans. Sys., Man, Cyber* **21(4):** 735–742.

Bezdek, J.C. 1987. Some non-standard clustering algorithms. *NATO ASI Series G14.* New York: Springer-Verlag.

Chester, M. 1993. *Neural Networks: A Tutorial.* Englewood Cliffs, NJ: Prentice-Hall.

Cohen, M.E., and Hudson, D.L. 1999. Chaos and Time Series Analysis. *Encyclopedia of Electrical and Electronics Engineering.* New York: John Wiley & Sons.

Duda, R.O., and Hart, P.E. 1973. *Pattern Classification and Scene Analysis.* New York: Wiley-Interscience.

Eberhart, R.C. 1989. Chaos theory for the biomedical engineer. *IEEE Engineering in Medicine and Biology Magazine* September, 41–45.

Fu, L.M. 1994. *Neural Networks in Computer Intelligence.* New York: McGraw-Hill.

Hudson, D.L., Cohen, M.E., and Anderson, M.F. 1991. Use of neural network techniques in a medical expert system. *International Journal of Intelligent Systems* **6(2):** 213–223.

Hudson, D.L., Cohen, M.E., Banda, P.W., and Blois, M.S. 1992. Medical diagnosis and treatment plans derived from a hybrid expert system. In A. Kandel and G. Langholz, eds., *Hybrid Architectures for Intelligent Systems,* pp. 329–344. Boca Raton, FL: CRC Press.

Hudson, D.L., Cohen, M.E., and Deedwania, P.C. 1993. A neural network for symbolic processing. In A.Y.J. Szeto, and R.M. Rangayyan, eds., *Engineering in Medicine and Biology,* pp. 248–249. Piscataway, NJ: IEEE.

McLaughlin, S.C., Chishti, P., Aitchison, T.C., and Macfarlane, P.W. 1996. Techniques for improving overall consistency of serial ECG analysis. *J. of Electrocardiology* **29**(Suppl.): 41–45.

Maxwell, T., Giles, C.L., Lee, Y.C., and Chen, H.H. 1986. Nonlinear dynamics in artificial neural networks. *American Institute of Physics, SPIE* 299–304.

Patrick, E.A., and Fattu, J.M. 1984. Mutually exclusive categories statistically dependent during concept formation. *Computer Applications in Medical Care* **8:** 100–106.

Ruspini, E. 1969. A new approach to fuzzy clustering. *Information and Control* **15:** 22–32.

Salmasi, A.M., and Nicolaides, A.N. (eds.). 1989. *Cardiovascular Applications of Doppler Ultrasound.* Edinburgh: Churchill Livingstone.

7

Comparative Analysis

7.1 INTRODUCTION

It is easy to become confused when confronted by the numerous approaches available for the design of neural networks. Unfortunately, there is no straightforward universal approach for choosing the best methodology. Several factors affect the choice, including the form of the available data, particularly whether or not the data are of known classifications; the number of classes into which the data are to be divided; the amount of available data; and the number of parameters involved.

7.2 INPUT DATA CONSIDERATIONS

How does one choose a neural network approach? Making the final choice depends on the answer to a number of questions.

Is your data of known classification?
What type of input variables do you have (binary, categorical, continuous, etc.)?
Approximately how many input variables do you have?
How many cases are available for training? for validation?
Do you know how many classification categories are involved? If so, how many?
What do you know about the structure of the data?

It should be clear from your data set whether you are looking at a supervised (known classification) or an unsupervised (unknown classification) learning problem. Once this distinction has been made, methods within each category can be compared. Figure 7.1 gives a graphical summary of the types of decisions that must be made when choosing an algorithm. The remainder of this chapter provides a summary of the methods studied in Chapter 4 (supervised learning) and Chapter 5 (unsupervised learning), along with more details regarding the advantages and disadvantages of each approach.

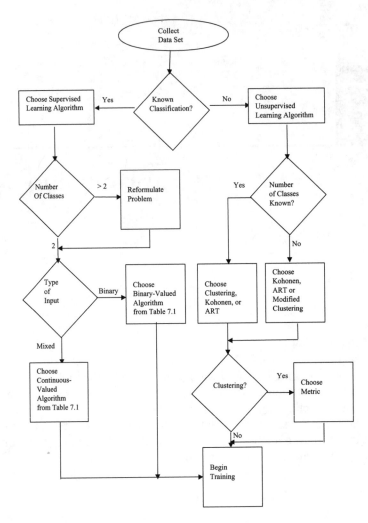

Figure 7.1 Choosing an Approach.

7.3 SUPERVISED LEARNING ALGORITHMS

The learning algorithm determines what a network can do. However, each learning algorithm may behave differently depending on the nature of the data. It is useful to compare methods by considering the following:

Type of input data

Ability to handle nonlinearly separable data

Assurance of obtaining separation on data which is separable

Stability of decision surface

In Chapter 4, we looked at a number of supervised learning techniques that have some features in common (Chester, 1993; Fu, 1994; Widrow, 1990). These are reviewed here, and their capabilities are summarized.

7.3.1 Gradient Descent Procedures

In Chapter 4 we discussed a number of gradient descent learning algorithms that differ both in their criterion function and in the manner in which weights are adjusted. As you will recall, the general approach is to find a solution to the set of linear inequalities

$$\mathbf{w}^T\mathbf{y} > 0 \tag{7.1}$$

by minimizing a criterion function $J(\mathbf{w})$, where $\mathbf{w}$ is an n-dimensional weight vector and $\mathbf{y}$ is an n-dimensional feature vector. The weight at the $k + 1$ point in time is defined by

$$\mathbf{w}_{k+1} = \mathbf{w}_k - \rho\nabla J(\mathbf{w}_k) \tag{7.2}$$

where ∇ is the gradient. The scale factor ρ is the learning rate and must be carefully chosen. If it is too small, convergence will be slow; if it is too large, it may cause the process to diverge.

A subset of gradient descent procedures, minimum squared error procedures do not attempt to solve inequalities, but rather seek a solution to the equation

$$\mathbf{w}^T\mathbf{y}_i = b_i \tag{7.3}$$

where the b_i's are arbitrary positive constants. Matrix notation is used to represent the resulting simultaneous equations.

A summary of linear gradient descent properties is given in Table 7.1, based on Duda and Hart (1973). $\mathbf{y}^k$ indicates the k sample that is to be classified. Note that some of these approaches work only with linearly separable sets. Another major difference is seen in minimum squared error approaches in that they use all samples, not just those that are misclassified. These are practical considerations when choosing an algorithm. In general, it is not possible to know in advance if the training set will be linearly separable. It is thus safer to use a minimum squared error procedure. However, caution must be used. Although these approaches in general work for nonseparable sets, they do not necessarily produce a separating surface for sets that are separable and may not converge at all in some cases. The linear perceptron, of which the fixed increment algorithm is a special case, has been shown to have severe limitations in the solution of some problems, in particular the exclusive OR (Gorry, 1973). These shortcomings can be remedied by using nonlinear versions of the perceptron or similar algorithms (see Chapter 4).

7.3.2 Extensions to Nonlinear Decision Functions

The following generalization of the perceptron algorithm extends its ability to separate nonlinearly separable sets. The decision function is

$$D(\mathbf{x}) = \sum w_i y_i(\mathbf{x}) = \mathbf{w}^T\mathbf{y} \tag{7.4}$$

where $\mathbf{w}$ is an n-dimensional weight vector and $y_i(\mathbf{x})$ is a set of arbitrary functions of $\mathbf{x}$. Similar extensions can be made for other descent algorithms. In terms of network structure, the original perceptron was a two-layer network, and the generalization is a

TABLE 7.1 Gradient Descent Procedures

Name	Criterion	Descent Algorithm	Properties
Fixed Increment	$J = \sum(-\mathbf{w}^T\mathbf{y})$ $\mathbf{w}^T\mathbf{y} \leq 0$	$\mathbf{w}_{k+1} = \mathbf{w}_k + \mathbf{y}^k$ $\mathbf{w}_k^T\mathbf{y}^k \leq 0$	Finite convergence if linearly separable, does not converge if nonseparable
Variable Increment	$J = \sum -(\mathbf{w}^T\mathbf{y} - b)$ $\mathbf{w}^T\mathbf{y} \leq b$	$\mathbf{w}_{k+1} = \mathbf{w}_k + \rho_k\mathbf{y}^k$ $\mathbf{w}_k^T\mathbf{y}^k \leq b$	Convergence if linearly separable to solution, does not converge if nonseparable
Relaxation	$J = \sum -(\mathbf{w}^T\mathbf{y} - b)^2/\|\mathbf{y}\|^2$ $\mathbf{w}^T\mathbf{y} \leq b$	$\mathbf{w}_{k+1} = \mathbf{w}_k + \rho\dfrac{[(b - \mathbf{w}_k^T\mathbf{y}^k)\mathbf{y}^k]}{\|\mathbf{y}^k\|^2}$ $\mathbf{w}_k^T\mathbf{y}^k \leq b$	Convergence if linearly separable to solution, does not converge if nonseparable
Widrow-Hoff	$J = \sum -(\mathbf{w}^T\mathbf{y} - b)^2$	$\mathbf{w}_{k+1} = \mathbf{w}_k + \rho_k(b_k - \mathbf{w}_k^T\mathbf{y}^k)\mathbf{y}^k$	Tends toward solution
Pseudoinverse	$J = \|\mathbf{Y}\mathbf{w} - \mathbf{b}\|^2$	$\mathbf{w} = \mathbf{Y}^\dagger\mathbf{b}$	Yields solution in all cases, does not necessarily produce separating vector
Ho-Kashyap	$J = \|\mathbf{Y}\mathbf{w} - \mathbf{b}\|^2$	$\mathbf{b}_{k+1} = \mathbf{b}_k + \rho(\mathbf{e}_k + |\mathbf{e}_k|)$ $\mathbf{e}_k = \mathbf{Y}\mathbf{w}_k - \mathbf{b}_k,\ \mathbf{w}_k = \mathbf{Y}^\dagger\mathbf{b}_k\ 1$	Yields solution in all cases, finds solution if nearly separable
Linear Programming	$J = \sum -(\mathbf{w}^T\mathbf{y}_i - b_i)^2$ $\mathbf{w}^T\mathbf{y}_i \leq b_i$	Simplex Algorithm	Finite convergence to solution whether or not separable
Backpropagation	$J = (1/2)[\sum (\mathbf{T}_i - \mathbf{D}_i)^2]$	$\mathbf{w}_{k+1} = \mathbf{w}_k + \eta\delta(\mathbf{x})$ $\omega_{k+1} = \omega_k + \eta\xi(\mathbf{y})$	May converge to local minima, works with nonseparable sets
Potential Functions	$J = \sum(-\mathbf{w}^T\mathbf{y})$ $\mathbf{w}^T\mathbf{y} \leq 0$	$\mathbf{w}_{k+1} = \mathbf{w}_k + \mathbf{y}^k$ $\mathbf{w}_k^T\mathbf{y}^k \leq 0$	Finite convergence to solution whether or not separable

three-layer network. Generally, three-layer networks will work on data sets that are not linearly separable (Gibson and Cowan, 1990).

7.3.3 Extensions to Multiple Categories

In Chapter 4, two methods were given for extending these algorithms to multi-category problems: (1) Kesler's construction, and (2) c two-category problems, where c is the number of classes. In either case, the amount of calculation increases dramatically and requires sufficient cases in each category for proper training. In neural network representations, two-category problems either have one output node that fires for class 1 and does not fire for class 2, or two output nodes where node i fires for class i. The second construction is easy to generalize to multiple categories with the addition of more output nodes. Mathematically, however, the addition of more output nodes has the same implication for increased calculation and larger training sets as the methods discussed earlier. Figure 7.2 illustrates these two approaches.

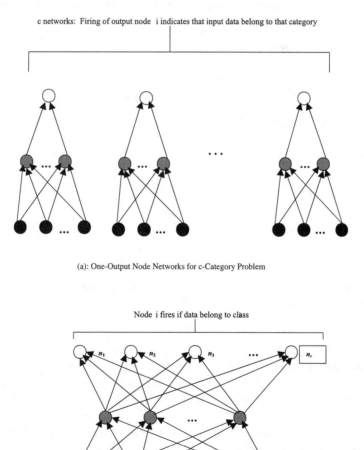

c networks: Firing of output node i indicates that input data belong to that category

(a): One-Output Node Networks for c-Category Problem

Node i fires if data belong to class

(b): Multiple-Output Node Networks

Figure 7.2 Neural Network Structures for Multiple Category Classification.

7.4 UNSUPERVISED LEARNING

Unsupervised learning is a much more difficult problem because it is not always possible to determine if a correct solution has been found. The methods described in Chapter 5 all work well within certain constraints but may also encounter major difficulties. These difficulties are discussed in two categories: clustering algorithms and self-organizing networks.

7.4.1 Clustering Methods

7.4.1.1 Choice of Method.   Most of the methods used in clustering employ iterative optimization (Duda and Hart, 1973). Like all hill-climbing procedures, these methods can be shown to result in local optimization, which may or may not be global. As is the case with supervised learning, if the order of the samples is changed (i.e., the starting point is different), a different solution may be found.

The difference in clustering measures is basically the choice of the distance measure or metric. Following are commonly used metrics along with the clustering algorithm associated with them:

Nearest Neighbor

$$D_{\min}(X_i, X_j) = \min_{\mathbf{x}\varepsilon X_i \mathbf{x'}\varepsilon X_j} \|\mathbf{x} - \mathbf{x'}\| \tag{7.5}$$

Furthest Neighbor

$$D_{\max}(X_i, X_j) = \max_{\mathbf{x}\varepsilon X_i \mathbf{x'}\varepsilon X_j} \|\mathbf{x} - \mathbf{x'}\| \tag{7.6}$$

Compromises

$$D_{\mathrm{avg}}(X_i, X_j) = (1/n_i n_j) \sum_{\mathbf{x}\varepsilon X_i} \sum_{\mathbf{x'}\varepsilon X_j} \|\mathbf{x} - \mathbf{x'}\| \tag{7.7}$$

$$D_{\mathrm{mean}}(X_i, X_j) = \|\mathbf{m}_i - \mathbf{m}_j\| \tag{7.8}$$

D_{avg} can also be used in place of a similarity measure when the similarity between mean vectors cannot be defined. (For examples of the uses of these measures, see Chapter 5.)

7.4.1.2 Choice of Distance Measure.   If clustering is viewed as grouping items in geometrical terms as we do with similarity measures, then the choice of the distance measure, or metric, has some impact. If the Euclidean distance is used, the results are invariant to translations and rotations (i.e., the space is isotropic). However, it is not invariant to linear transformations or any other transformation that distorts distance relationships. If the distance itself has no meaning in the data set, then this is not a problem. For example, if the data are ordered categorical, such as symptoms (0: improved, 1: no change, 2: worsened), then it is the order and not the distance between the categories that matters. If the data are continuous physical exam readings such as heart rate, a distortion of the distance, for example, between a heart rate of 92 and a heart rate of 96, may give more weight to the difference than the clinical situation would warrant. To avoid this problem with other data sets, the data can be scaled in advance so that all features have zero mean and unit variance. (These methods are discussed further in Chapter 15 when we consider probabilistic approaches.) The normalization method may not be useful if the magnitude of the variable is important for determining subclasses, which is often an important consideration in clustering. For example, an enzyme level that exceeds a certain threshold may be indicative of the occurrence of a myocardial infarction and should be grouped accordingly.

7.4.1.3   Limitations.   In most of the methods discussed in Chapter 5, it was assumed that the number of clusters was known in advance. For unknown data sets, this is usually not the case. The only methods appropriate in this case are variations that try a different number of clusters and then compare results. This is often a difficult task inasmuch as the correct classifications of the data are unknown. Typically, the method starts with one cluster, then goes to two, four, and so on, in a procedure similar to hierarchical clustering.

7.4.2 Self-Organization Networks

7.4.2.1   Kohonen Networks.   The Kohonen network (Kohonen, 1990) is an alternative method to hierarchical clustering for performing clustering through the winner-take-all paradigm. The competitive learning algorithm seeks a local minimum using the criterion

$$J = 1/2 \sum \left\| \mathbf{w}_k - \mathbf{x}_p \right\|$$

where $\mathbf{w}_k$ is the center of the winning cluster corresponding to neuron k, $\mathbf{x}_p$ is the presented input pattern, and $\| \ \|$ is the Euclidean distance (Fu, 1994). As such, it has the same limitations discussed under descent procedures.

7.4.2.2   ART Networks.   The ART networks (Carpenter and Grossberg, 1987) are also examples of competitive learning. As you will recall, the initial ART network accepted only binary input, but this restriction was removed in the ART2 network that accepts continuous input. The ART networks are resonating networks in that weights are passed in both directions between the input and output layers. The theoretical bases for resonating networks are quite complex. The system designer has little control over assignment of patterns to categories. The system is more sensitive to noisy data than clustering methods, including the Kohonen network (Chester, 1993).

7.5 NETWORK STRUCTURES

7.5.1 Number of Categories

In most problems, the number of possible categories is known. Most of the algorithms we have discussed assume this knowledge. In most biomedical applications, the number of classes is known. Some classes, such as the ART network, add categories as necessary. In problems such as spatiotemporal pattern recognition, it is useful to have networks that can determine the number of classes required.

7.5.2 Connectivity

The connectivity of a network can affect its performance. For networks that are completely connected, the mathematical description of the network becomes quite complex, as does the interpretation of how each input node contributes to the final decision. The backpropagation network (Rummelhart, McClelland, and PDP, 1986) is an example of a network that is fully connected between adjacent layers but does not have connections that jump from layer 1 to layer 3, for example. In general, the user does not have control over the level of connectivity as the algorithm determines the connectivity.

7.6 INTERPRETATION OF RESULTS

When choosing an algorithm, it is important to determine the desired result at the outset. There are a number of possibilities, which are often different for supervised and unsupervised learning.

7.6.1 Supervised Learning

The three phases of the supervised learning process are training, evaluation, and classification.

7.6.1.1 Training.   The objectives of training are
1. To find a model that correctly classifies all or most of the cases in the training set.
2. To determine which parameters are important in the model.
3. To determine the relative importance of each parameter.

The first objective is present in virtually all supervised learning approaches. In some cases, this may be the only objective. If so, the model is viewed in a black-box fashion with the assumption that the user is interested only in the result, not in the process that led to the result. If this is the case, the only consideration in selecting an algorithm is its effectiveness in obtaining a reliable separation of the data.

In most approaches, the parameters that are in the final model can be identified. These may or may not be the same parameters with which the training process started, for many algorithms perform pruning of input nodes when the weights attached to these nodes drop below a certain value.

If part of the objective of the training process is to identify the relative contributions of input nodes to the output decision, then more attention must be paid to the choice of algorithm. For fully connected networks, one obtains a matrix of weights that is extremely difficult to interpret. Partially connected networks provide more direct interpretation of results. To determine relative weights, the data must be scaled before training. (Scaling is discussed in Section 7.6.3.) For example, consider a network with three input nodes and four nodes in the hidden layer in a fully connected network, as illustrated in Figure 7.3. Assume that the weight between node i in the input layer and node j in the hidden layer is w_{ij} and that the weight from node j in the hidden layer to node k in the output layer is ω_{jk}. If we wish to determine the impact of input node i on output node k, we have the following weights to interpret: $w_{i1}, w_{i2}, w_{i3}, w_{i4}, \omega_{1k}, \omega_{2k}, \omega_{3k}, \omega_{4k}$.

7.6.1.2 Evaluation.   Once training has been completed, the accuracy of the model must be tested on a different data set, the test set. Although this is part of the classification phase, the objective is not to classify data, for the proper classification is already known, but to compare the classification obtained by the model to the known classification. The objective of this phase is to determine the effectiveness of the model,

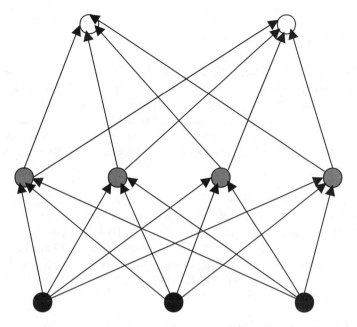

Figure 7.3 Fully Connected Network with Three Input Nodes.

which may be measured in terms of sensitivity, specificity, accuracy, and predictive power. (For an example, see Chapter 5.)

7.6.1.3 Classification.   Use of the model for true classification is seen in the classification of new data for which the prior classification is unknown. At this point, the user is relying on the accuracy and ability to generalize the network to perform effectively on new cases. Its success in accomplishing accurate classification depends not only on the algorithm but also on the data on which it was trained and tested. In multicategory problems (i.e., more than two categories), the objective may be to establish a differential diagnosis list. A case may be classified as belonging to more than one category, which can be accomplished by the following:

1. If the network has multiple output nodes, more than one may fire for a particular case.
2. If the problem is formulated as c problems where each problem is to determine membership or nonmembership (e.g., presence or absence of disease), membership may be found to hold in more than one subcase.

All the multiple results would then be considered as possible outcomes. In Chapter 16, we will see that fuzzy methods can attach a degree of membership to each category, thus providing additional information for differential diagnosis.

7.6.2 Unsupervised Learning

We can consider the same three phases in unsupervised learning, although the goal in each case may be slightly different.

7.6.2.1 Training.   The objectives of training in unsupervised learning include
1. Determination of natural clustering of data into groups or clusters.
2. Determination of number of significant clusters.

3. Development of maps that provide insight into data relationships.
4. Dimensionality reduction.

7.6.2.2 Evaluation. The evaluation of unsupervised learning models is extremely difficult because the correct outcome is unknown. One approach is to break data into two sets through a random process and to run the algorithm separately on each set. Results can then be compared to see if similar models have been established. In some cases, some knowledge regarding the general nature of the data may be known, which can be used to ascertain whether the model seems reasonable.

7.6.2.3 Classification. Once a model has been established, new cases can be classified. As an example, consider a clustering problem in which a model with three clusters was produced. A new data vector can then be classified using the similarity measure or metric used in establishing the model. The new sample will be assigned to the cluster to which it is most similar. As we will see in Chapter 16, fuzzy clustering algorithms assign a degree of membership to each new vector in each cluster. This is a useful approach for problems such as differential diagnosis.

7.6.3 Data Scaling and Normalization

To compare the weights attached to input nodes relative to one another, the input variables must be in the same range. Looking at an earlier example, consider these two vectors:

$$\mathbf{x}^1 = (130,100,98,2.8,102,131,102) \qquad \mathbf{x}^1 \text{ is in class 1}$$
$$\mathbf{x}^2 = (120,77,72,0.0,110,160,90) \qquad \mathbf{x}^2 \text{ is in class 2}$$

Clearly, these are not comparable ranges. The most common solution is to normalize the data to values between 0 and 1 or -1 and 1 by dividing by the largest value possible for each variable.

7.6.4 Dependence on Training Data

One major limitation of all learning approaches is that the training is done on a specified set of cases that must represent a similar population to the one on which it is to be used. Thus, if the network was trained on the detection of heart disease in a military hospital, the result may not be applicable to a public hospital because the demographics do not correspond in terms of age, gender, physical condition, and other important factors.

7.7 SUMMARY

Choosing an appropriate modeling technique is a complex process involving the evaluation of a number of factors. In some cases, it may be useful to try two or more methodologies and compare results, although this will obviously require additional time and effort. The best measure of a model is its performance on a test set, keeping in mind that its performance on new cases will depend on the similarity of the sample population to the training population.

EXERCISES

1. What is the first step in establishing a neural network model?

2. List three ways in which data can be obtained for use in a medical decision-making system. For each method, how can you ensure the reliability of the data?

3. Describe the relationship among the following procedures for finding discriminant functions:
   (a) Descent algorithm
   (b) Fixed increment algorithm
   (c) Perceptron algorithm
   (d) Minimum squared error algorithm
   (e) Ho–Kashyap Algorithm

4. Give an example of a clustering problem that would best utilize each of the following:
   (a) Minimum distance metric
   (b) Maximum distance metric
   (c) Average distance metric

5. Can the perceptron algorithm be used for problems in differential diagnosis? Explain.

6. How can you be sure that the data set that was used for training a network will be suitable in a new environment? What factors must be considered?

REFERENCES

Carpenter, G.A., and Grossberg, S. 1987. A massively parallel architecture for a self-organizing neural pattern recognition machine. *Computer, Vision, Graphics, and Image Processing* **37:** 54–115.

Chester, M. 1993. *Neural Networks, A Tutorial.* Englewood Cliffs, NJ: Prentice-Hall.

Duda, R.O., and Hart, P.E. 1973. *Pattern Classification and Scene Analysis.* New York: Wiley-Interscience.

Freeman, J.A., and Skapura, D.M. 1992. *Neural Networks: Algorithms, Applications, and Programming Techniques.* Reading, MA: Addison-Wesley.

Fu, L.M. 1994. *Neural Networks in Computer Intelligence.* New York: McGraw-Hill.

Gibson, G.J., and Cowan, C.F.N. 1990. On the decision regions of multilayer perceptrons. *Proc. IEEE* **78(10):** 1590–1594.

Gorry, G.A. 1973. Computer-assisted clinical decision-making. *Method. Inform. Med.* **12:** 45–51.

Kohonen, T. 1990. The self-organizing map. *Proc. IEEE* **78(9):** 1464–1480.

Lau, C. 1992. *Neural Networks: Theoretical Foundations and Analysis.* New York: IEEE Press.

Rummelhart, D.E., McClelland, J.L., and the PDP Research Group. 1986. *Parallel Distributed Processing,* vols. 1 and 2. Cambridge, MA: MIT Press.

Widrow, B. 1990. 30 years of adaptive neural networks: Perceptron, Madaline, Backpropagation. *Proc. IIII* **78(9):** 1415–1442.

8

Validation and Evaluation

8.1 INTRODUCTION

Two separate issues are involved in testing neural networks as decision-support systems for biomedical applications. First, the technical performance of the chosen algorithm must be assured, and second, the performance of the algorithm on the specific application must be evaluated. A neural network classification model is made up of two components: the learning algorithm and the training data. A fault in either component can cause the system to fail to achieve its goal. When evaluating and validating a neural network model, we assess three aspects of the system:

1. The integrity of the data alone
2. The technical performance of the learning algorithm
3. The performance of the learning algorithm in conjunction with the training data

The next three sections in this chapter will focus in turn on these three issues.

8.2 DATA CHECKING

8.2.1 Verification of Accuracy of Data for Training

A number of sources of information may be used to establish biomedical decision-support systems. These include chart review, databases, and prospective studies. Each has its own difficulties, as we will see.

8.2.1.1 Chart Review. The advantage of chart review is that all medical institutions already have rooms full of data. This is also one of its disadvantages: Unless the patient records are computerized, it is a major chore to extract data from medical records. Major complications include searching through multiple page records for the information, interpreting what is written (often deciphering what is written!), and dealing with missing information. The researcher is restricted to the information that has been recorded which differs from patient to patient and from visit to visit, and may not include all parameters that would be useful to include in the model. In fact, the major step in going from paper records to computerized records is the format of the medical record. This problem remains thirty years after the first attempts to revise it and produce an electronic medical record.

If you are lucky enough to work with a medical facility with computerized medical records, some of the problems mentioned earlier will still remain, including missing information. If the format of the electronic record is standardized, it should remove some of the difficulties with information differing from one patient and one visit to another. However, it still may not contain all relevant information.

8.2.1.2 Databases. Databases may be local or from outside sources such as Internet databases, or a combination of the two. Databases have major advantages over medical records in that the data items are already organized and in digital format. Combination of databases that were collected at different sites is difficult due to inconsistencies in the variables recorded. In addition, the criteria for certain items may differ from one institution to another. For example, in one study a coronary artery may be considered blocked if it is 70 percent occluded, whereas another may use 75 percent as the cutoff.

8.2.1.3 Prospective Studies. The prospective study is the best method for collecting data, for the researcher has control over what is collected and who collects it. Both are major factors in maintaining consistency, which is necessary because many aspects of biomedicine require interpretation. The data collection sheet in Figure 6.3 illustrates this point. Note that although some items, such as test results, are straightforward numerical values, many others, such as presence of symptoms, are not. The major drawback to prospective studies is the time it takes to acquire sufficient data, especially in areas where followup information is needed.

8.2.2 Appropriateness of Data for Training

The following factors need to be considered when selecting a training set:

Is the data representative of the population you wish to study?
Are there as few missing values as possible?
Has the accuracy of the data been verified as far as possible?
Does the data need to be scaled?
Are there approximately ten cases per node in the network?

In addition, for supervised algorithms, the following must be verified:

Is the data set consistent? That is, are there any identical vectors with different classifications?
Are there sufficient cases in each classification category?
Is a reliable gold standard available for determining correct classification?

It is important to remember that your model is built using the data in the training set and will only be as good as the data.

8.2.3 Use of Gold Standards in Supervised Learning

A significant problem in supervised learning is the determination of the correct classification. In general, a so-called gold standard is used for diagnosis. For example, the gold standard for determining coronary artery disease is cardiac catheterization. Not all patients, however, will have had cardiac catheterization, for it is an invasive procedure and poses risk to the patient. If this test has not been done, the diagnosis may be determined by other less reliable means. Thus the network is often trained on an assumed diagnosis. As another example, if the objective of a model is to determine which parameters should be included in the decision to perform surgery on patients with carcinoma of the lung, the data classification will represent what was actually done, not what should have been done. This type of problem can be alleviated to some degree by using followup data to determine if the correct decision was made, but there is no certain way of making this determination.

8.3 VALIDATION OF LEARNING ALGORITHM

8.3.1 Technical Integrity of Algorithm

If you are using a purchased algorithm, it has likely been tested thoroughly. However, you should not rely on this, but should do your own testing on a trial set of data to see if the algorithm behaves as expected. If you have written the algorithm yourself, this testing must be more extensive.

8.3.2 Appropriateness of Algorithm for Given Application

8.3.2.1 Theoretical Considerations. In Chapter 7, we discussed choosing an algorithm that is appropriate for your application. Some considerations to remember include:

Select an algorithm that is appropriate for the type of input data in your application.

Make sure that the algorithm does not produce a network with more nodes than your data can support.

Determine if the algorithm produces output that you can interpret in terms of your problem definition.

Consider the stability and convergence properties of the algorithm.

8.3.2.2 Practical Considerations. The training time required by the algorithm may be a consideration. However, in general, as the training is done only once, even if the training time is long it is not a severe limitation. Training algorithms that have a high number of iterations may have problems of error propagation especially if they involve addition and subtraction of large numbers.

8.3.2.3 Comparison to Other Approaches. In an ideal world, it is beneficial to develop models using more than one approach. This involves a commitment of time, both human and computer. The traditional method for evaluating software involves benchmarking. When benchmarking systems, a specified set of criteria are established in advance and the algorithms are compared according to these criteria. Some possible items to include when benchmarking neural network algorithms are:

Training time
Number of iterations required
Convergence of algorithm
Stability of solution if additional vectors are added to training set
Stability of solution if order of training vectors is changed
Accuracy of results

8.4 EVALUATION OF PERFORMANCE

8.4.1 Supervised Learning Algorithms

Once your input data has been selected and verified to the greatest degree possible and the integrity of the algorithm has been established, it is time to test the two together. Once the training has been done, evaluation must be done on a separate set of data, the test set.

8.4.1.1 Performance of Algorithm on Test Set. The performance of the algorithm on the test set is the primary method of evaluation. It is important to use measures such as sensitivity and specificity to test the accuracy by category as well as the overall accuracy. It is possible to obtain very high accuracy in one category at the expense of the other. In medical problems, the goal is usually to balance the two. In some applications, however, it is better to err on the side of obtaining false positives rather than obtaining false negatives. The converse can also be true.

8.4.1.2 Relevance of Contributing Parameters. In addition to the classification results, it is important to look at the contributing parameters. Do they make sense from a medical point of view? It is difficult to convince medical professionals to accept a model that includes parameters that appear to be irrelevant to the problem. On the other hand, sometimes new relationships can be discovered through this process. Another danger is a model that does not contain a parameter that historically has been believed to be important. In some cases, it turns out that the model is correct, and the long-held belief is not.

8.4.1.3 Comparison to Other Methods. Can your results be compared to other methods? This is always possible but may be time-consuming. Often, as statistical analysis is the accepted method of analyzing medical data, it is useful to compare results with traditional statistical methods. Classification results can be compared with results from discriminant analysis. The significance of contributing parameters can be compared with t-tests or analysis of variance, depending on whether the data are continuous or discrete.

Your results can also be compared to historical data through literature searching or consultation with experts. Remember that you cannot assume that the model is incorrect because it differs from historical belief. A model is most useful if it contains something new. The new information will not, and should not, be accepted without additional verification.

8.4.2 Unsupervised Learning

As mentioned earlier, it is very difficult to evaluate unsupervised learning results. There are a few approaches, however:

See if the model makes sense from a medical standpoint.

Verify that the distance between clusters or groupings is large enough.

Compare the outcome to historical results.

Determine if the clusters are representative of a disease or condition.

8.4.2.1 Applicability to Other Data Sets. Once having gone to the trouble of collecting data, implementing an algorithm, and developing a model, one would hope that the model would be applicable to other data sets. In practice, one must be very careful. The following must be considered:

Is the other data set demographically similar?

Does it contain most of the same parameters used in your model?

Can you verify the accuracy of the data?

Do you know the criteria used when the data were collected, especially on subjective questions?

If the answer is yes to all of these questions, it may be possible to use the model directly to classify new cases. Remember, there are three phases:

1. Training
2. Testing
3. Classification

There are a number of options for the new data:

Classify new data using old model (begins with step 3).

Test new data using old model (begins with step 2).

Re-train model on new data and compare results with previous model (begins with step 1).

Combine new data and old data in the same training set (begins with step 1).

If you use the new data set for supervised training, make certain that the gold standard for determining the correct classification is the same in both models.

EXAMPLE

Consider the following case study for determining the prognostic factors in congestive heart failure (CHF) (Hudson et al., 1997). We had previously described a neural network model for prognostic factors in congestive heart failure (CHF) (Hudson, Cohen, and Deedwania, 1996). The initial model was based on a sample of 100 CHF patients: 50 surviving and 50 deceased. The data collection sheet is shown in Figure 6.3. The learning algorithm used was Hypernet (Cohen and Hudson, 1992). The variables identified in the initial model were:

Symptom status (decreased, stable, increased)

Blood urea/nitrogen concentration (BUN), orthopnea (y/n)

Dyspnea at rest (y/n)

Heart rate

Edema (y/n)

Functional impairment (levels 1–3)

Proxysmal nocturnal dyspnea (PND), (y/n)

The second study included 450 additional patients who had been treated for CHF and were followed between 1992 and 1996. The parameters from the original model were used with the new expanded data set to test stability. The model was retrained using data from both studies but was limited to the parameters identified in the first study.

Table 8.1 shows the results for the second study. Table 8.2 shows the comparison of sensitivity and specificity with the original study. Note that both the sensitivity and specificity dropped in the second study. Although the data were collected at the same institution using the same criteria, a different student intern completed the data collection form for the second study. Other possible reasons for the difference may be due to natural variations. An additional possibility is that the original data set was not large enough for complete training. The exact reason for the difference may be resolved through additional analysis. In some cases, no definitive answer can be found.

Table 8.1 Classification Results for Expanded Data Set

	Correctly Classified	Incorrectly Classified
Group 1 (surviving)	198	87
Group 2 (deceased)	121	44
Total	319	131

Table 8.2 Comparison Between First and Second Data Set

	Sensitivity	Specificity	Accuracy
Initial Model	79%	80%	79%
Expanded Model	70%	73%	71%

8.5 SUMMARY

In the development of medical decision-making aids, through the use of neural networks or other methods, accuracy is of extreme importance because the decisions impact the health of individuals. Hence it is more important in the medical field than in most other fields to test the model as thoroughly as possible. In the real world, it is nearly impossible to achieve 100 percent accuracy, a goal that physicians would like to achieve. Bear in mind that human decision making also cannot ensure 100 percent accuracy. The best that we can hope for is a careful analysis of possible sources of error.

EXERCISES

1. Using the medical record excerpt in Figure 6.2, devise a data collection sheet that would extract information relevant to the record. If you think you will need certain information but cannot find it on the record, include it on the sheet.
2. Give a copy of your data collection sheet and Figure 6.2 to two people and ask them to fill in the information on the sheet. Compare the results.
3. Does the order in which training vectors are presented to a learning algorithm affect the results? Why or why not?
4. Can you think of an empirical method for determining if your network has been trained using an adequate data set?
5. Give an example in which it would be better to have false positives than false negatives. Give another example in which it would be better to have false negatives.

6. What is the most time-consuming part of establishing a neural network algorithm? Justify your answer.

REFERENCES

Cohen, M.E., and Hudson, D.L. 1992. Integration of neural network techniques with approximate reasoning techniques in knowledge-based systems. In A. Kandel and G. Langholz, eds., *Hybrid Architectures for Intelligent Systems,* pp. 72–85. Boca Raton, FL: CRC Press.

Hudson, D.L., Cohen, M.E., and Deedwania, P.C. 1996. A neural network model for analysis of prognostic factors in congestive heart failure. *Journal, American College of Cardiology* **27(2):** 358A.

Hudson, D.L., Cohen, M.E., Gul, K.M., and Deedwania, P.C. 1997. Clinical usefulness of a neural network model for evaluation of prognostic factors in CHF in predicting mortality. *Journal, American College of Cardiology* **29(2):**35A.

PART II
ARTIFICIAL INTELLIGENCE

9

Foundations of Computer-Assisted Decision Making

9.1 MOTIVATION FOR COMPUTER-ASSISTED DECISION MAKING

The objective of computer-assisted medical decision making is to allow the medical professional to use the computer as a tool in the decision process. The decision-making field is a broad one and encompasses several different approaches. Six general subdivisions exist (Shortliffe, Buchanan, and Geigenbaum):

Databases
Mathematical modeling and simulation
Pattern recognition
Bayesian analysis
Decision theory
Symbolic reasoning

Figure 9.1 shows these subdivisions with areas of overlap and subdivisions. In this chapter, these topics are discussed in terms of biomedical decision making, although the techniques are general and can be used in any application.

9.2 DATABASES AND MEDICAL RECORDS

Table 9.1 shows the development of medical databases over a thirty-year period. Examples for each decade are described here.

9.2.1 The First Decade (1970–1980)

One problem inherent in any approach to decision making in medicine is the form of the medical record. Medical records include diverse components: quantitative test results, time series data such as ECGs and EEGs, medical images from a variety of

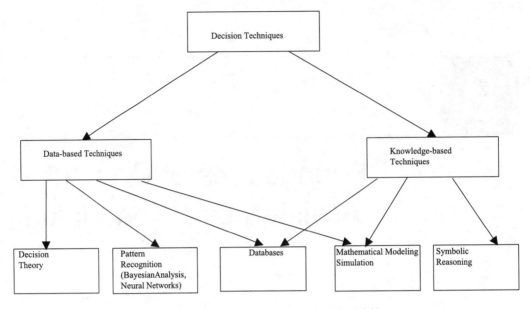

Figure 9.1 Approaches to Automated Decision-Making.

sources, and handwritten notes. For the past three decades, attempts have been made to organize these diverse data into a format that can be readily automated.

Early work in developing the computerized medical record was done by Greenes et al. in 1970 at Massachusetts General Hospital. This work resulted in the COSTAR system, which was organized as a hierarchical database, and became the forerunner of MUMPS (Massachusetts General Hospital Utility Multi-Programming System), which is both an operating system and a computer language. MUMPS was used to create the Veterans Affairs Medical Information System (DHCP), which is still in use.

PROMIS (problem-oriented medical information system) (Schultz, 1976; Walton, Holland, and Wolfe, 1978), developed at the University of Vermont in 1968,

TABLE 9.1   Medical Database Developments

Decade 1: 1970–1980	Decade 2: 1980–1990
Patient Record Structures	Differential Diagnosis
Hierarchical Database	RECONSIDER
National Library of Medicine	DXplain
COSTAR	**Decade 3: 1990–Present**
Frames	Online Databases
PROMIS	National Library of Medicine
MEDUS/A	Radiological Databases
Time-Oriented Record	CHORUS
ARAMIS	Human Genome Project
Disease Databases	Electronic Transfer of Patient Data
Oncology	
Rheumatology	
Retrieval Structures	
Query Languages	
MEDIQ	
Decision Support	
HELP	

was directed toward the problem of logical organization of medical data, as well as toward feedback on medical action. The approach includes acquiring a database on each individual, with a list of problems identified. A plan of action is then developed for each problem. Medical information is structured in units called *frames*, with the frames organized in a network structure. The system contains two databases: the individual patient data and the medical knowledge base. A four-phase plan is utilized: (1) the starting point is the database from which a problem list is formulated; (2) from the problem list, initial plans are made for each problem; (3) progress notes are also recorded; and (4) the database is used to devise a medical plan of action.

The ARAMIS system (McShane and Fries, 1979; Fries, 1972; Wiederhold, Fries, and Weyl, 1975), originally developed at Stanford in the 1970s for data on arthritis, built on some of the ideas incorporated in PROMIS. It also introduced the important concept of the time-oriented data record (TOD) in order to display the patient's progress and to permit the development of causal relationships. TOD consists of two distinct files: the main file of patient records, which has one record for each patient visit; and a transposed file, in which each parameter becomes a separate record, hence emphasizing the change of the parameter over time. A three-dimensional array structure is obtained when all patient data are incorporated into a series of standardized forms completed by the physician at each visit. The system utilizes several retrieval programs that provide statistical analysis and graphical display with scattergrams and histograms. There is also a program for clinical consultation. The idea of a most valuable variable (MVV) is used. The variable that contributes the most information is selected, and using this variable, the researcher analyzes the data. This variable is then discarded, and the procedure is repeated using the remaining variables.

The HELP program of Warner, Olmsted, and Rutherford (1972), also developed in the 1970s, was a medical decision-support system. It provides access to raw data, as well as all currently relevant decisions previously made on the patient. Five types of data are considered:

COD data such as blood pressure and ECG parameters

COM data consisting of comments

BIN binary data from the patient history consisting of presence or absence of conditions

ADD data that refers to another decision

OLD data that refers to previous decisions

Another medical database management system, MEDUS/A, was developed by Miller at Harvard beginning in 1977 (Miller and Strong, 1978). The data are organized in frames similar to the PROMIS system. MEDUS/A uses a modified hierarchical approach to structure the database. Patient data are subdivided into problems, which are further subdivided into evaluations. A query language, called MEDIQ, provides the user interfaces. The objective of the system is to develop a data management tool, not a tool of analysis.

An early attempt to organize a tumor registry database was begun by Cabral and Wi-Huang (1978) at the University of Illinois. The data are decomposed into subsets of structured files. The database consists of an incidence file containing a small set of data on every tumor known to the system and two patient files. The patient data are divided into confidential and nonconfidential files. A hypothetical tree structure is created for the data on each patient, with semantic pointers used to indicate the location of data relevant to the case. At about the same time Blum and Lenhard (1978) developed an oncology information system for hospital use. The database consisted of different classes of files: *patient files* organized by history number, diagnosis, or protocol; *locator files* organized by patient name; *dictionary files* for laboratory results; and *system files*. The key patient files included the abstract file which provided a summary of the disease, the census file with dates of admission and related information, the patient clinical data file, request files which contained requests for printed output, and preformatted files with plots and flow diagrams.

Recurring themes in these approaches were the requirement of retaining physician notes, the necessity of tracking values that change over time, and the recognition of two distinct classes of information: patient data and medical knowledge data. They also pointed to shared problems. The database approach is effective only if large amounts of data are collected, which requires cooperation among many groups working in the same field. Problems include the occurrence of missing values and, at the time, the problem of storing and accessing large amounts of information.

9.2.2 The Second Decade (1980–1990)

RECONSIDER, authored by M.S. Blois et al. (1983) of the University of California at San Francisco, is a prompting aid that suggests diseases for inclusion in the differential diagnosis. Among its advantages are its breadth of coverage (3262 diseases are currently represented in it), its simplicity (which makes its operation readily comprehensible to the user-physician), and its rapid response. It is specifically intended as an aid to memory, a feature in which computers are frequently superior to humans, and not as a substitute for human inference or judgment, where at the present they may not perform as well. The database for RECONSIDER was taken from Current Medical Information and Terminology (CMIT) data (Gordon, 1971).

A system similar to RECONSIDER, DXplain was begun with the support of the American Medical Association (Barnett et al., 1987). Originally available through AMA/NET, it is now accessible via the World Wide Web (Elhanan, Socratous, and Cimino, 1996). Another commercial medical program that employs database retrieval, Iliad, uses frame-based structures (see Chapter 10). It also uses Bayesian and cluster analysis to arrive at consultative decisions (Lincoln et al., 1988).

9.2.3 Current Approaches to Medical Databases

Currently, database development tools are available on personal computers. Through expanded memory size and large disk storage capacity, it is quite feasible to develop useful medical databases using PC technology.

The greatest current advance in access to data is the Internet. Numerous medical databases exist which are available to Internet users, including medical imaging databases. This technology presents new challenges in maintaining confidentiality and in ascertaining the accuracy of information that has been collected.

An extremely useful database is MEDLINE, which provides access to the medical literature either through the Internet or on CD-ROM. In addition, a growing number of databases exist on the Internet which can be freely accessed, including chemical abstracts, conference papers, dissertation abstracts, federal research in progress, pharmaceutical abstracts, science citation index, and social science citation index. The National Library of Medicine (NLM) maintains a number of bibliographic databases including AVLINE, BIOETHICSLINE, CANCERLIT, CATLINE, HEALTH,

HISTLINE, HSTAR, POPLINE, and TOXLINE and factual databases including CHEMID, DENTALPROJ, PDQ, and TOXNET.

Another active area of database creation is radiology (Martinez et al., 1995). These databases in general contain archived images representing healthy and diseased conditions of various body systems. For example, a system called CHORUS (Collaborative Hypertext of Radiology) was developed to facilitate collaboration among physicians (Kahn, 1995). It consists of a computer-based radiology handbook developed and published electronically via the World Wide Web on the Internet. This system allows physicians without computer expertise to read documents, contribute knowledge, and critically review the handbook's content by using a simple, graphical user interface from virtually any type of computer system.

The most extensive biomedical database project is the Human Genome Project. Much effort continues to be directed toward selecting methods for representing the complex data structures involved. This project has already proven to be extremely useful in locating new genetic markers for disease and will continue to be an area of active research in the foreseeable future. A number of approaches have been used, including the introduction of an object-oriented conceptual model (Hearne et al., 1994) and work on locus mapping (Guidi and Roderick, 1993). Access to the human genome database is available through the World Wide Web.

Problems in implementing computerized medical records remain to this day. Most of these problems now center around compliance in recording data in a specified format, including the limitation of handwritten notes, compatibility among different recording systems, and privacy issues related to electronic transfer of medical records. Specific database designs are discussed in the next chapter.

9.3 MATHEMATICAL MODELING AND SIMULATION

In some specialized cases, biological processes can be represented by mathematical equations. This type of modeling has been in existence for some time and does not necessarily involve the use of a computer. However, some equations can be evaluated with the aid of a computer that could not otherwise be evaluated, or only with great difficulty. Simulation involves the representation of a process on the computer and may or may not involve actual mathematical modeling.

One area where mathematical formulation is possible is in the administration of drugs, where dosage can be based on body weight and certain metabolic factors. Jelliffe, Buell, and Kalabe (1972) developed an early program to aid in the dosage of digoxin, a drug that is toxic at high levels. The model used body weight as the primary determining factor. The program was implemented on a time-sharing system that could be dialed by a physician seeking advice; this was a fairly revolutionary idea for its time. Another computer-aided drug dosage system by Shiner, also in 1972, utilized tests that check drug levels in the blood. The level of toxicity of the drug was determined by statistical analysis. A later program by Peck et al. (1973) was also developed to determine optimal digoxin levels. The method involved checking digoxin levels and attempting to keep them within safe bounds by altering the dosage.

An early consultation program developed by Bleich (1972) provided information on acid-base disorders. It checked blood levels of sodium, potassium, and sugar, along with other constituents. The program was used chiefly as a teaching aid. Also in 1972, Lincoln developed a simulation model for leukemia chemotherapy. The system consisted of four levels of abstraction: parameter identification, functional organization that showed the relationship among parameters, a teaching model, and a patient-specific model.

Bouckaert (1977) developed a model of the endocrine system based on Boolean matrices. In a Boolean matrix, the values are restricted to 1 and 0 indicating the presence or absence of a parameter. The system was simplified to represent only a two-organ system.

Peddicord (1977) developed a computational model of the cerebellar cortex and peripheral muscle based on physiological data from the cat. He begins with a mathematical model of a single neuron and develops a model of the cerebellar loop. The result is a discrete space, continuous time (DSCT) representation.

A 1976 paper by Walker proposes a framework for automatic model construction. The framework consists of a representation in which causal models can be written, an algorithm for constructing a general causal model from empirical data, and an algorithm that uses a causal particular hypothesis. The fundamental problem addressed is the representation of knowledge.

Simulation models continue to be applied to problems that can be restricted to systems for which enough information is available. Recent work in nonlinear dynamics points to problems in representing systems that may be chaotic (Eberhart, 1989; Skinner et al., 1992; Guarini and Onofri, 1993). Many recent models have been developed, especially in cardiology, based on principles of chaos theory (Goldberger, 1989). The normal sinus rhythm of the heart is seen to be a chaotic function that at times shows reduced variability, which may be representative of heart disease (Lipsitz and Goldberger, 1992; Garfinkel et al., 1992). Debate arose regarding whether chaos represents the healthy or the diseased state. In our work (Cohen et al., 1994) we have shown that the normal heart can also be chaotic. It is a matter of the degree of chaos that differentiates the diseased heart from the normal. Application of chaos theory to analysis of electrocardiograms shows promise for development of diagnosis models (Cohen, Hudson, and Deedwania, 1996). In neurology, similar patterns are seen in the electroencephalogram; only here the underlying processes are understood to a lesser degree (Hoppensteadt, 1989; Freeman, 1987; Olsen, Truty, and Schaffer, 1988). Chaotic patterns have also been established in the firing of motor neurons (Mpitsos et al., 1988). A number of studies have illustrated chaotic patterns in disease epidemics (Freeman, 1987), one of the early areas of chaotic investigation. (Chaotic analysis is discussed in Chapter 17.)

In some areas, modeling can provide very accurate results. Unfortunately, most physical processes are too complicated to yield realistic mathematical representations at this stage of our knowledge. Problems approached using this methodology are highly structured and cannot deal with circumstances not anticipated in the model.

9.4 PATTERN RECOGNITION

Pattern recognition was one of the first methods used in medical applications and has found wide applications in diverse areas, from electrocardiogram to genetic sorting problems. Pattern recognition itself encompasses a variety of approaches. A common method of classification is known as discriminant analysis, discussed briefly in Chapter 1 with additional details in Chapter 15. Another method of classification utilizes Bayes' Rule (see Chapter 15). Other pattern recognition techniques include parameter estimation and supervised learning, which involve estimating parameters of known statistical distributions, using the normal distribution, and nonparametric, unsupervised learning techniques such as Parzen windows and k-nearest neighbor estimation and other clustering techniques. Duda and Hart (1973) and Young and Calbert (1974) provide detailed analyses of early pattern recognition techniques.

In 1969, Kulikowski used a pattern recognition approach to diagnosis of hyperthyroidism (Kulikowski, 1970). He used a sequential diagnostic procedure, determining at each stage the likelihood of the presence of the disease. A new set of variables, or features, was used at each stage, and all variables were used to make the diagnosis. Thresholds for the features were used to separate patients into three categories: those who did not have the disease, those where doubt remained, and those who probably did have the disease. In the second case, one of several tests was recommended.

A major problem associated with the pattern recognition approach is the selection of features that will yield good discrimination. A second problem arises when the number of features, or the dimensionality, becomes too large. It then becomes advantageous to select a set of principal features that lie in a subspace of much smaller dimensionality but still yield good discrimination.

A 1974 summary of pattern recognition in medical diagnosis was compiled by Patrick, Stelmock, and Shen (1974) and contains over 120 references. Patrick lists the principal components of pattern recognition systems, which include feature extraction and various decision-making strategies, including Bayesian discriminant analysis, loss functions, nearest-neighbor rules, and clustering techniques.

One common application of pattern recognition has been the analysis of time series data, such as electrocardiography and electroencephalography. A second important area is image analysis. A paper by Raeside and Chu (1978) describes an application to echocardiography, a type of ultrasound imaging. The authors attempted classification by similarity measures and found the results to be poor; they then turned to Fourier analysis. The first step in the procedure was again feature extraction. The classification methods considered were k-nearest neighbor, Bayes' Rule, and nonparametric statistical classification in which the parameters were ascertained from the data. It was found that while these three classification methods gave roughly equivalent results, the Fourier analysis yielded much better results than the similarity measure approach.

In the 1980s, more complex pattern recognition systems were developed, including Patrick's extension of Bayes' Theorem to permit multicategory classification (Patrick and Fattu, 1989). Other approaches include potential function approaches to pattern recognition (Duda and Hart, 1973; Cohen, 1985). (More details on this approach have been given in Chapter 4.)

Pattern recognition methods have yielded very good results in a variety of applications, and many of these systems are in practical use today. However, the pattern recognition approach presents several inherent problems. Deciding which features should be selected to yield good discrimination is a difficult question and must be approached anew with each application. Often the number of features becomes large, leading to difficulties of dimensionality, which in turn requires a larger number of samples to provide valid statistical results. Verification of resulting classifications is also difficult. Final difficulties arise in the violation of independence assumptions. In addition, mutual exclusiveness and exhaustiveness of categories frequently do not apply in real-world situations.

9.5 BAYESIAN ANALYSIS

9.5.1 Early Bayesian Systems

In 1972, Warner, Rutherford, and Houtchens developed a strategy for patient history taking and diagnosis based on Bayesian analysis. A matrix of probabilities was used in which each row represents a diagnosis and each column represents a question to be asked of the patient. Each element in the matrix is a number indicating the likelihood that a patient having the disease of that row should answer yes to the question of that column. Bayes' Rule is used to compute P_{D_i}, the probability of having the ith disease, with $A_i = D_i$ and $B = Q_j$ where P_{D_i} is the probability of having the ith disease and P_{Q_j} is the probability that a patient with the ith disease will answer yes to the jth question. The purpose was to direct the questioning process in the appropriate direction and avoid asking unnecessary questions.

A system developed by de Dombal from 1972 to 1974 described diagnosis of abdominal pain using the Bayesian approach (de Dombal et al., 1972, 1974). The probabilities used were compiled from a large patient population. Seven diagnoses were possible: appendicitis, diverticular disease, perforated duodenal ulcer, nonspecific abdominal pain, cholecystitis, small bowel obstruction, and pancreatitis. The work emphasizes the computer as a tool in helping the physician make the diagnosis. The computer was found to arrive at accurate diagnoses in 91.5 percent of the cases, whereas the accuracy of the senior clinicians was 81.2 percent. As an interesting sidelight, the clinicians improved considerably during the study, having apparently benefited from the computer feedback information.

In most practical situations, the assumptions of conditional independence usually do not hold. Nor is the assumption of mutual exclusiveness and exhaustiveness of disease categories usually valid. In addition, relevant conditional probabilities may not be stable over time and are dependent on the population from which they are drawn. Because of these considerations, Bayes' Rule must be applied with care.

9.5.2 Bayesian Belief Networks

Bayesian formulations can be generalized to produce Bayesian belief networks (Szolovits, 1995). The basic goal of these networks is to deal with uncertainties in diagnostic clue assessment while still considering the dependencies between elements in the reasoning sequence (Montironi, Bartels, and Hamilton, 1996). They have also been applied to radiological diagnosis (Haddawy, Kahn, and Butarbutar, 1994). In addition, attempts have been made to convert a rule-based system to a belief network (Korver and Lucas, 1993).

9.6 DECISION THEORY

Decision theory is a broad category of which Bayesian analysis is a part. Any attempt to make choices on an automated basis can be considered part of this field. Decision trees or networks are often used to enumerate all possible events, with each event represented by a node in the tree or network. The path chosen may be determined by the user or by a statistical decision. Usually, probabilities are not used directly but are weighted according to the risk or cost involved in each possible path.

Markovian analysis is a technique often used in decision theory. A Markov process is one in which the current state is dependent only on the previous state and the transition function. Markovian processes may be time-dependent or may be considered to be in equilibrium. Markovian analysis is treated in detail in Kleinrock (1975).

In a 1973 paper, Gorry described a system based on decision theory. His system consisted of a Phase I and Phase II program. The Phase I program considers tests for which the risk or cost is negligible, so that the benefit can be measured completely in terms of the amount of information to be gained. In Phase II, the inference function determines new information, and the question selection function determines which is the best question to ask next. In Phase II, the program balances expected risk against expected benefit and selects the treatment with maximal expected value. A second matrix contains probabilities of complications.

A 1976 paper by Gheorghe uses a Markovian decision model applied to respiratory disease. The advantage of the Markovian approach is that it gives a dynamic view, with the patient's condition represented as a state. Gheorghe identifies the three stages of diagnosis as taking measurements, reaching a conclusion as to the state of the process, and making a decision regarding a course of action to follow. The current state is assumed to depend only on the immediate past transition and the current state of knowledge about the system, thus making the process Markovian. The model can be represented as time-dependent, resulting in a continuous Markov process, but in practice it is usually considered to be steady state. The Markovian model is expanded to include AND/OR gates.

Some major difficulties arise in attempting to assign numerical values to intangibles, such as discomfort and time in the hospital. Overlapping or coincidental diseases generally are not well handled by these techniques. Attempts to incorporate time parameters into these systems also cause major complications.

9.7 SYMBOLIC REASONING TECHNIQUES

Development of knowledge-based expert systems is divided into early systems and second-generation systems (see Table 9.2).

9.7.1 Early Expert Systems

Artificial intelligence techniques have been under development since the advent of computers. In early artificial intelligence approaches, programs rely on qualitative judgments of heuristics rather than numerical calculation. Among the techniques are

TABLE 9.2 Historical Development of Knowledge-Based Systems

Early Systems	Second-Generation Systems
Causal Nets	Deep Causal Systems
Neuronal Muscle Control	Heart Failure (Long)
Rule-Based Models	MDX
MYCIN	IDM
MEDICO	Reasoning with Uncertainty
HEADMED	Fuzzy Logic
PUFF	Adlassnig
EMERGE	Esogbue
Rule-Based Shells	Anderson
EMYCIN	Approximate Reasoning
EXPERT	EMERGE
Frames	Other Techniques
Taking the present illness	Bayesian Belief Networks
Simulation	Dempster-Shafer
Kidney Disease	Hybrid Systems
Data-based Rule Deduction	
RX	
Theorem Proving	
Drug Interactions	
Combined Data, Knowledge-Based	
INTERNIST	

methods of knowledge representation, heuristic search, natural language understanding, and inexact reasoning. These methods are summarized in Winston (1977).

Pople and Werner (1972) did early work in modeling neuronal muscle control activities. Their system utilized an inferential processor that analyzed data and proposed hypotheses. The data were arranged in a causal net, and the program was written in LISP.

In 1973, Gorry recommended a change to a new methodology and found that his previous programs could not handle the complexities that arise in actual situations, such as interactions among multiple diseases. He came to the following conclusions:

1. Gross knowledge coupled with a large number of experimental facts and mini-decision procedures seems to form the basis of clinical judgment.
2. Knowledge used by experts is both factual and procedural.
3. Knowledge is associated with certainty factors.
4. A large part of this knowledge is not specifiable a priori.
5. Experts seem to be able to recall all knowledge on the subject.

The new prototype that Gorry proposed would utilize a simple language that would allow experts to give advice to the program. He cited the following areas for investigation:

1. Concept identification
2. Language development
3. Explanation

These areas subsequently have been researched by many workers.

MYCIN, developed by Shortliffe in the mid-1970s, was a highly successful system for diagnosing infections and prescribing antimicrobial therapy (Shortliffe, 1973, 1975, 1976). It was the first rule-based system in medicine and derived from earlier work by Buchanan, Sutherland, and Feigenbaum (1969) on DENDRAL, a rule-based system for chemical synthesis. The basic information structure of these systems is the production rule, described by Davis and King (1975) in detail. All of MYCIN's knowledge was contained in these rules, which consist of premises and conclusions. Each conclusion also contained a certainty factor, indicating the degree of confidence in that conclusion. The system had several interesting features. It had a good English interface, it was able to understand questions asked in ordinary English, as long as they were restricted to a specified subset of English; and it could recognize misspellings. The program could also answer questions regarding its own conclusions. Upon being queried, it would supply the line of reasoning followed in reaching a conclusion, and it would cite the rules that had been invoked. The program could also accept new rules entered by the user. The order of searching the rules was not predetermined; rather, it relied on the information provided for each individual case to ascertain its path. The MYCIN system contained approximately 200 inference rules. Use of the rules produced a depth-first search of an AND/OR goal tree, similar to PLANNER (Winston, 1977). The maximum number of rules for a single subgoal was approximately 30. Meta rules were used to suggest strategies.

An outgrowth of MYCIN, EMYCIN was developed as a management system for Stanford's oncology clinic. The goal of EMYCIN was to set up an expert system shell that could be adapted to any application.

Pauker et al. (1976) and Szolovits and Pauker (1976) presented a different approach to analyzing the present illness. The program contained four components. (1) The patient-specific data comprised the computer's knowledge about the patient. (2) A supervisory program selected questions, sought and applied relevant advice, and generated and tested hypotheses. (3) A short-term memory allowed patient data to interact with general medical knowledge. (4) Finally, an associative, long-term memory was organized in frames that represented clinical states, physiologic states, or diseases. The frames were casually linked in a network. The decision strategy employed problem-solving techniques for searching the network.

Another rule-based system developed in 1976 was MEDICO (Walser and McCormick, 1976). It consisted of a knowledge base with long- and short-term memories, a rule interpreter, and a program that maintained the knowledge base. The long-term memory had two divisions: episodic memory which contained information about particular patients and events, and systemic memory which contained general knowledge about diseases, tests, and treatments. The knowledge was contained in inference rules. An inference rule has a set E of propositions and a proposition H that is the hypothesis to be verified. E is a support for H if it triggers H. For example, E is often a pathological condition that represents evidence for H, where H is a possible diagnosis. Each rule also has a strength measure indicating how far the supports go toward confirming the hypothesis. The short-term memory contains propositional descriptions of current clinical events as state models. The rule interpreter applies rules and switches between parts of the knowledge base.

Wiener and Vinaver (1977) described a computer simulation of medical reasoning applied to kidney disease based on medical logic. The object was to indicate possible diseases on the basis of patient history, physical examination, and routine diagnostic tests, and then to branch to specific investigations for more definite diagnoses. Classification among six diseases was attempted. Three stages were defined: the suspected, the probable, and the diagnosed. Each stage was confirmed or rejected on the basis of present observations and previously confirmed inference.

A major difficulty with rule-based systems is acquiring sufficient and reliable rules. The normal procedure is to interview experts in the field. In 1978, Blum and Wiederhold proposed a system, RX, for deducing rules from a medical database, ARAMIS. Since that time, a number of other researchers have followed this path.

Automated theorem-proving was another artificial intelligence approach applied to biomedical data. In 1978, Darvis presented such a system for analyzing drug interactions. The knowledge was represented by means of Horn formulas, which can represent a conclusion with multiple premises. The theorem prover in this system uses pattern matching to find a conclusion that matches input data.

In the same year, Weiss et al. (1978) developed a causal association network for glaucoma, CASNET. A loop-free network was used to describe causal relationships among variables. Multiple causes and effects are possible. A node in the network represents a pathophysical state, and an edge represents the causal connection. A pathway from the starting node to the terminal node gives a complete disease process. Progression along a pathway indicates increasing seriousness. The network is defined by the quadruple (S,F,X,N), where

S = set of starting states (no antecedent causes)

F = set of final states (no effects)

X = mapping between states (causal relationships)

N = total number of states

Certainty measures are used to represent confidence that a certain state exists. Transitions between states are given weights, and statistical likelihood measures are used to determine the optimal transition.

In 1980, the techniques from CASNET were applied to a program for diagnosis and treatment of rheumatic disease. The researchers used an expert system shell, EX-PERT, which like EMYCIN, is used to construct new consultative programs. EXPERT was also applied to the construction of knowledge bases in endocrinology, clinical pathology, neuro-ophthalmology, and internal medicine (U.S. Department of Health, 1980). In addition, a psychopharmacological adviser called HEADMED was developed at the University of Texas at Galveston for dealing with psychiatric drugs (U.S. Department of Health, 1980). It was rule-based and recommended drug use for individual patients. It followed the logic scheme laid out by MYCIN.

Also in 1980, the first expert system to be put into clinical use for pulmonary function and ventilation management was PUFF (U.S. Department of Health, 1980). First tested at Pacific Medical Center in San Francisco, it contained approximately 250 decision-making rules to interpret pulmonary function indications. Another segment of the program, VM, was used to provide advice concerning intensive care patients supported by ventilators.

INTERNIST, an ambitious project to design a decision-support system for all of internal medicine, was undertaken by Miller, Pople, and Myers (1982). It combined database information with knowledge-based information to give consultative advice on a broad range of diseases. INTERIST-I was superseded by QMR (Miller, Masarie, and Myers, 1986), which uses the consultative portion with the DXplain database. QMR covers 600 diseases.

9.7.2 Second-Generation Expert Systems

Thus, by the 1980s, numerous medical expert systems had been designed and implemented, but only one, PUFF, was in actual clinical use. A number of problems remained with this approach, which in the late 1970s had virtually replaced the pattern recognition approach to computer-assisted decision making. Construction of the knowledge base was time-consuming and required interaction between the designer of the expert system and domain experts in the application area. Often communications problems arose. Once the knowledge base was developed, it required updating as new information became known. One of the major strengths of the knowledge-based approach was the separation of the reasoning process, handled by the inference engine, from the domain knowledge. In theory, this allowed the application to be changed by simple replacement of the knowledge base without altering the program. This rarely happened, as each inference engine was tuned toward specific features of its initial application.

Another common thread in these early systems was the recognition of the role of uncertainty in medical decision making. MYCIN dealt with uncertainty by including certainty factors that indicated the degree of confidence that an implication was correct. As it turns out, uncertainty in reasoning is much more complex and arises in many parts of the expert system, including patient data and the knowledge base. Criticisms were also raised regarding the production rule format, which generated rules known as heuristics. It was argued that this was not really the way the people reasoned and that what was needed were more causal and deep reasoning models rather than ad hoc rules. In the 1980s, researchers attempted to address some of these issues. The systems are often referred to as second-generation expert systems.

9.7.2.1 Causal Systems.   A new approach to expert system development involved the use of deep reasoning as opposed to heuristic reasoning. Deep models are more objective in that they model the structure and function of the system. Deep models are also called *causal models* because they apply cause and effect reasoning. Not all causal models, however, are deep models. An example of a causal model that is not deep would be a relationship such as "angina causes elevated blood pressure." Although this is a causal relationship, it is not based on the mechanisms of the disease. Deep causal models not only involve relationships between diagnosis and symptoms, but also describe the behavior of the modeled system. For a discussion of causal and deep reasoning, see Torasso and Console (1989).

CASNET, as described earlier, is an example of a causal system that does not utilize deep reasoning. It probably represents the earliest attempt to design a causal system. In the early 1980s, Reggia, Nau, and Wang (1983) proposed another causal model that established causal relationship between findings and diagnostic possibilities.

In biomedical applications, it is very difficult to develop deep causal knowledge because of the complexity of biological systems. Basically, a causal model is represented by states of a system and relationships among the states, as we saw in CASNET. The relationship differ depending on the system. (For a discussion of causal models and deep reasoning, see Chapter 10.)

In 1981, Patil described a system, ABEL, which combined heuristic reasoning and deep reasoning and had three levels of knowledge representation: pathophysiological, intermediate, and clinical. The clinical level is represented using heuristic knowledge. In 1983, Long developed a causal system for treatment of heart failure in which temporal data were an important component in the causal relationships. MDX (Chandrasekaran and Mittal, 1983) also uses causal knowledge but not directly in the reasoning process. IDM (Fink, Lusth, and Duran, 1985) uses causal knowledge for cases, which could not be solved using heuristic knowledge.

A paper by Miller (1987) surveys causal approaches in artificial intelligence systems that use qualitative causal models as opposed to quantitative causal models (i.e., mathematical models). A study by Jang (1994) combines association-based reasoning and causal reasoning in the same system. A recent approach uses a fuzzy state space approach to medical diagnosis (Bellamy, 1997) in an attempt to incorporate uncertainty into the model.

9.7.2.2 Reasoning with Uncertainty.   The development of knowledge-based expert systems in medicine began about a decade after Zadeh's introduction of fuzzy logic (Zadeh, 1965) with the MYCIN system. Although MYCIN did not use fuzzy logic directly, one of its major components was certainty factors, an early recognition of the major role that uncertainty plays in medical decision making. In the two decades since the introduction of MYCIN, knowledge-based medical expert systems have abounded. Virtually all of these systems have made some attempt to deal with uncertainty, with some using fuzzy logic directly. Numerous other approaches to approximate reasoning have also been employed, along with other methods that are more ad hoc in nature.

One of the earliest medical expert systems to use fuzzy logic was developed by Adlassnig (1980) in which he applied theoretical principles from fuzzy logic to a diagnostic problem. Anderson et al. (1982) designed another very early fuzzy medical expert system. Esogbue and Elder (1983) also employed fuzzy logic techniques to develop a fuzzy mathematical model for medical diagnosis. EMERGE (Hudson and Cohen, 1988) used techniques from approximate reasoning in a knowledge-based system for emergency room admissions of patients with chest pain. This system was begun in the late 1970s with a modified production rule format and was updated to include approximate reasoning methods in the mid-1980s. EMERGE can also be used as an expert system shell for the development of other applications. Another expert system shell that could handle both exact and inexact reasoning was developed by Leung, Wong, and Lam (1988). Sanchez (1989) analyzed fuzzy inference in detail in a case study.

Another popular approach uses the idea of a possibility measure rather than a probability measure, introduced by Dubois and Prade (1980) and illustrated in a medical application by Vila and Delgado (1983). A later use of possibility theory to develop an expert system for the analysis of evoked potentials combines possibility theory with heuristic rules (Brai, Vibert, and Koutlidis, 1994).

In the 1990s, approaches to reasoning with uncertainty continue to abound. Bayesian Belief Networks are used for this purpose, along with the statistical-based Dempster-Shafer approach. Recent biomedical applications of fuzzy set theory and fuzzy logic include a system for diagnosis of coronary artery disease (Ciox, Shin, and Goodenday, 1991) and MEDUSA, a fuzzy expert system for the diagnosis of abdominal pain (Fathi-Torbaghan, 1994).

Fuzzy logic had been applied successfully in many commercial devices. Hess (1995) discusses the idea of applying this technology to medical devices and Rau et al. (1995) examine potential applications of fuzzy control in medicine.

9.7.2.3 Hybrid Systems.   Recently, many researchers have abandoned the idea of one technology in favor of a combination of approaches. The number of these combined systems, denoted hybrid systems, have grown in the last few years (Kandel and Langholz, 1992; Cohen, 1992).

9.8 SUMMARY

Beginning in the 1970s, symbolic techniques replaced pattern classification as the dominant method for developing biomedical computer-assisted decision-support systems. For the next decade, the majority of new systems were developed using symbolic techniques. This trend began to change in the mid-1980s with the resurgence of the neural network approach, spurred by the development of new theoretical approaches and increased computing power. However, both of these methodologies remain important tools, with the choice dependent on the nature of the problem and the sources of domain knowledge available to tackle the problem. In some cases, combination of the two methods into a hybrid system affords an opportunity to take advantage of all sources of domain knowledge.

EXERCISES

1. If you were designing a computer-assisted decision-support system for determining the presence of diabetes, which of the above approaches would you use? Why? What kinds of parameters would you need to include?
2. For which of the approaches discussed in this chapter would it be easiest to maintain a system that is up to date? Explain.
3. Find an article that has appeared in the literature within the last year and categorize it into one of the six areas given.
4. Assume you are designing a new medical device for monitoring patient status. Which

approach would you take? For this application, what are the most important factors to consider?

5. Which of the above approaches would be able to handle nontextual data such as electrocardiograms and medical images? Justify your answer.

REFERENCES

Adlassnig, K.P. 1980. A fuzzy logical model of computer-assisted medical diagnosis. *Math. Inform. Med.* **19(3):** 141–148.

Anderson, J., Bandler, W., Kohout, L.J., and Trayner, C. 1982. The design of a fuzzy medical expert system. In M.M. Gupta, A. Kandel, W. Bandler, and J.B. Kiszha, eds., *Approximate Reasoning in Expert Systems,* pp. 689–703. North Holland: Elsevier Science Publishers.

Barnett, C.O., Cimino, J.J., Hupp, J.A., and Hofer, E.P. 1987. DXplain, an evolving diagnostic decision-support system. *JAMA* **258(1):** 67–74.

Bellamy, J.E. 1997. Medical diagnosis, diagnostic spaces, and fuzzy systems. *J. Amer. Veterinary Medical Association* **210(3):** 390–396.

Ben-Bassat, M., Carlson, R.W., Puri, V.K., Davenport, M.D., Schriver, J.A., Latif, M., Smith, R., Protigal, L. Lipnick, E., and Weil, M. 1980. Pattern-based interactive diagnosis of multiple disorders: The MEDUS system. *IEEE Trans. PAMI* **PAMI-2:** 148–160.

Bleich, H. 1972. Computer-based consultations: Acid-base disorders. *Amer. J. of Medicine* **53:** 285–291.

Blois, M.S., Sherertz, D.D., Kim, H., Tuttle, M.S., Erlbaum, M., Harrison, P., and Yamashita, D. 1983. RECONSIDER, an experimental diagnostic prompting program. *Proc. of ACP Computer Workshop,* pp. 7–28.

Blum, B., and Lenhard, R.E., Jr. 1978. Privacy and security in an oncology information system. *SCAMC* **2:** 500–508. Washington, DC: IEEE.

Blum, R., and Wiederhold, G. 1978. Inferring knowledge from clinical data banks utilizing techniques from artificial intelligence. *IEEE Conf. on Medical Appl.* **2:** 303–307.

Bouckaert, A., and Thiry, S. 1977. Physiopathological inference by computer. *Int. J. Biomed. Comput.* **8:** 85–94.

Brai, A., Vibert, J.F., and Koutlidis, R. 1994. An expert system for the analysis and interpretation of evoked potentials based on fuzzy classification: application to brainstem auditory evoked potentials. *Computers and Biomedical Research* **27(5):** 351–366.

Buchanan, B., Sutherland, G., and Feigenbaum, E. 1969. Heuristic DENDRAL: A program for generating explanatory hypotheses in organic chemistry. *Machine Intelligence,* vol. 4. New York: American Elsevier.

Cabral, R., and Wy-Huang Cheng. 1978. An integrated database system for managing medical information: A tumor registry application. *IEEE Conf. on Medical Appl.* **2:** 298–302.

Chandrasekaran, B., and Mittal, S. 1983. Deep versus compiled knowledge approaches to diagnostic problem-solving. *Int. J. Man-Machine Studies* **19:** 425–436.

Ciox, K.J., Shin, I., and Goodenday, L.S. 1991. Using fuzzy sets to diagnose coronary artery disease. *Computer,* pp. 57–63.

Cohen, M.E., Hudson, D.L., and Deedwania, P.C. 1985. Pattern recognition analysis of coronary artery disease. In A.H. Levy, B.T. Williams, eds., *Amer. Assoc. for Medical Systems and Informatics,* pp, 262–266.

Cohen, M.E., and Hudson, D.L. 1992. Integration of neural network techniques with approximate reasoning techniques in knowledge-based systems. In A. Kandel and G. Langholz, eds., *Hybrid Architectures for Intelligent Systems,* pp. 72–85. Boca Raton, FL: CRC Press.

Cohen, M.E., Hudson, D.L., Anderson, M.F., and Deedwania, P.C. 1994. Continuous chaotic modeling with applications to biological systems. *Intelligent Engineering Systems Through Artificial Neural Networks* **4:** 825–830.

Cohen, M.E., Hudson, D.L., and Deedwania, P.C. 1996. Application of continuous chaotic modeling to signal analysis. *EMBS Magazine* **15(5):** 97–102.

Darvis, R., Futo, I., and Szeredi, P. 1978. Logic-based program system for predicting drug interactions. *Int. J. Biomed. Comput.* **9:** 259–272.

Davis, R., and King, J. 1975. An overview of production systems. *Stanford Artificial Intelligence Laboratory, Memo AIM-271, Computer Science Dept. Report* #STAN-CS-75-524, pp. 1–38.

de Dombal, F.T., Leaper, D., Staniland, J.R., McCann, A.P., and Horrocks, J.C. 1972. Computer-aided diagnosis of acute abdominal pain. *Brit. Med. J.* **21(5804):** 9–13.

de Dombal, F.T., Leaper, D., Horrocks, J., Staniland, J., and McCann, A., 1974, Human and computer-aided diagnosis of abdominal pain. *Brit. Med. J.* **1:** 376–380.

Dubois, D., and Prade, H. 1980. *Fuzzy Sets and Systems: Theory and Applications,* vol. 144. Orlando: Academic Press.

Duda, R.O., and Hart, P.E. 1973. *Pattern Classification and Scene Analysis.* New York: John Wiley and Sons.

Eberhart, R.C. 1989. Chaos theory for the biomedical engineer. *IEEE Engineering in Medicine and Biology Magazine.* September: 41–45.

Elhanan, G., Socratous, S.A., and Cimino, J.J. 1996. Integrating DXplain into a clinical information system using the World Wide Web. *Proc. AMIA Fall Symposium,* 348–352.

Esogbue, A.O., and Elder, R.C. 1983. Measurement and valuation of a fuzzy mathematical model for medical diagnosis. *Fuzzy Sets and Systems* **10:** 223–242.

Fathi-Torbahgan, M., and Meyer, D. 1994. MEDUSA: a fuzzy expert system for medical diagnosis of acute abdominal pain. *Methods of Information in Medicine* **33(5):** 522–529.

Fink, P., Lusth, J., and Duran, J. 1985. A general expert system design for diagnostic problem solving. *IEEE Trans. PAMI* **PAMI-7:** 553–560.

Freeman, W.J. 1987. Simulation of chaotic EEG patterns with a dynamic model of the olfactory system. *Biological Cybernetics* **56:** 139–150.

Fries, J. 1972. Time-oriented patient records and a computer databank. *JAMA* **222(12):** 1536–1542.

Garfinkel, A., Spano, M.L., Ditto, W.L., and Weiss, J.N. 1992. Controlling cardiac chaos. *Science* **257:**1230–1235.

Gheorghe, A.V. 1976. A Markovian decision model for clinical diagnosis and treatment applied to the respiratory system. *Trans. IEEE Sys., Man, Cyber.* **SMC-6 (9):** 595–605.

Goldberger, A.L. 1989. Cardiac chaos. *Science* **243(4987):** 1419.

Gordon, B. (ed.) 1971. *Current Medical Information and Terminology,* 4th ed. Chicago: American Medical Association.

Gorry, G.A. 1973. Computer-assisted clinical decision-making. *Method. Inform. Med.* **12:** 45–51.

Gorry G.A., Kassirer, P., Essig, and Schwartz, W. 1973. Decision analysis as the basis for computer-aided management of acute renal failure. *Amer. J. Med.* **12:** 472–484.

Greenes, R.A., Barnett, G.O., Klein, S.W., Robbins, A., and Prior, R.E. 1970. Retrieval and review of medical data by physician-computer interaction. *New England J. Med.* **282:** 307–315.

Greenes, R. A., Pappalardo, A.N., Narble, C.W., and Barnett, G. 1969. Design and implementation of a clinical data management system. *Computers and Biomedical Research* **2:** 469–485.

Guarini, G., and Onofri, E. 1993. Complexity and predictability in internal medicine. *Recenti Progresi in Medicina* **84(10):** 691–697.

Guidi, J.N., and Roderick, T.H. 1993. Inference of order in genetic systems. *ISMB* **1:** 163–171.

Haddawy, P., Kahn, C.E., Jr., and Butarbutar, M. 1994. A Bayesian network model for radiological diagnosis and procedure selection: work-up of suspected gallbladder disease. *Medical Physics* **21(7):** 1185–1192.

Hearne, C., Cui, Z., Parsons, S., and Hajnal, S. 1994. Prototyping a genetics deductive database. *ISMB* **2:** 170–178.

Hess, J. 1995. Fuzzy logic and medical device technology. *Med. Device Technol.* **6(8):** 37–46.

Hoppensteadt, F.C. 1989. Intermittent chaos, self-organization, and learning from synchronous synaptic activity in model neuron networks. *Proc. National Academy of Sciences USA* **86:** 2991–2995.

Hudson, D.L., and Cohen, M.E. 1988. An approach to management of uncertainty in a medical expert system. *International Journal of Intelligent Systems* **3(1):** 45–58.

Jang, Y. 1994. A hybrid system for diagnosing multiple disorders. *Proc. AMIA* 454–460.

Jelliffe, R., Buell, J., and Kalabe, R. 1972. Reduction of digitalis toxicity by computer-assisted glycoside dosage regimens. *Ann. Intern. Med.* **77:** 881–906.

Kahn, C.E., Jr. 1995. CHORUS: a computer-based radiology handbook for international collaboration via the World Wide Web. *Radiographics* **15(4):** 963–970.

Kandel, A., and Langholz, G. (eds.). 1992. *Hybrid Architectures for Intelligent Systems.* Boca Raton, FL: CRC Press.

Kleinrock, L. 1975. *Queueing Systems,* vol. 1., pp. 26–52. New York: John Wiley & Sons.

Korver, M., and Lucas, P.J. 1993. Converting a rule-based expert system to a belief network, *Medical Informatics* **18(3):** 219–241.

Kulikowski, C.A. 1970. Pattern recognition approach to medical diagnosis. *IEEE Trans. Sys. Sci. Cyber.* **SS6(3):** 173–178.

Leung, K.S., Wong, F.W., and Lam, W. 1988. The development of an expert computer system on medical consultation. *Int. J. of Bio-Medical Computing* **23(3,4):** 265–278.

Lincoln, M.J., Turner, C., Hesse, B., and Miller, R. 1988. A comparison of clustered knowledge structures in Iliad and Quick Medical Reference. *SCAMC12,* pp. 131–135. New York: IEEE Computer Society Press.

Lincoln, T.L. 1972. The clinical significance of simulation and modeling in leukemia chemotherapy. *AFIPS* 1139–1143.

Lipsitz, L.A., and Goldberger, A.L. 1992. Loss of complexity and aging. *Journal of the American Medical Association* **267(13):** 1806–1809.

Long, W. 1983. Reasoning about state from causation and time in a medical domain. *Proc. AAAI,* pp. 251–254. Washington, DC.

McShane, D., and Fries, J. 1979. TOD: a software system for the ARAMIS databank. *Computer* **12(11):** 34–40.

Martinez, R., Chimiak, W., Kim, J., and Alsafadi, Y. 1995. The rural and global medical informatics consortium and network for radiology services. *Computers in Biology and Medicine* **25(2):** 85–106.

Miller, P., and Strong, R. 1978. Clinical care and research using MEDUS/A, a medically oriented data base management system. *IEEE Conf. on Medical Applications* **2:** 288–297.

Miller, R.A., Masarie, F.E., and Myers, J.D. 1986. Quick medical reference for diagnostic assistance. *MD Computing* **3:** 34–38.

Miller, R.A., Pople, H.E., and Myers, J.D. 1982. INTERNIST-I, an experimental computer-based diagnostic consultant for general internal medicine. *N. Engl. J. Med.* **307:** 468–476.

Miller, P.L., and Fisher, P.R. 1987. Causal models in medical artificial intelligence. W.W. Stead, ed., *Proc. Computer Applications in Medical Care,* pp. 17–22. New York: IEEE Computer Society Press.

Montironi, R., Bartels, P.H., and Hamilton, D. 1996. Atypical adenomatous hyperplasia (adenosis) of the prostate: development of a Bayesian belief network for its distinction from well-differentiated adenocarcinoma. *Human Pathology* **27(4):** 396–407.

Mpitsos, G.J., Burton, Jr., R.M., Creech, H.C., and Soinila, S.O. 1988. Evidence for chaos in spike trains of neurons that generate rhythmic motor patterns. *Brain Research Bulletin* **21:** 529–538.

Olsen, L.F., Truty, G.L., and Schaffer, W.M. 1988. Oscillations and chaos in epidemics: A nonlinear dynamic study of six childhood diseases in Copenhagen, Denmark. *Theoretical Population Biology* **33:** 244–270.

Patil, R. 1981. Causal representation of patient illness for electrolyte and acid-base diagnosis. *MIT/LCS/TR-267.*

Patrick, E., Stelmock, F., and Shen, L. 1974. Review of pattern recognition in medical diagnosis and consulting relative to a new system model. *IEEE Trans. Sys., Man, Cyber* **SMC4(1):** 1–16.

Patrick, E.A., and Fattu, J.M. 1989. *Artificial Intelligence with Statistical Pattern Recognition.* Englewood Cliffs, NJ: Prentice-Hall.

Pauker, S.G., Gorry, G.A., Kassirer, J., and Schwartz, W. 1976. Towards the simulation of clinical cognition: Taking a present illness by computer. *Amer. J. Med.* **60:** 981–996.

Peck, C.C., Shiner, L., Carrol, M., Martin, M., Combs, D., and Melmon, D. 1973. Computer-assisted digoxin therapy. *New Eng. J. Med.* **289:** 441–446.

Peddicord, R.G. 1977. A computational model of cerebellar cortex and peripheral muscle, *Int. Biomed. Comput.* **8:** 217–238.

Pople, H., and Werner, G. 1972. An information processing approach to theory formation in biomedical research. *AFIPS* 1125–1138.

Raeside, D.E., and Chu, W. 1978. An application of pattern recognition to echocardiography. *IEEE Trans. Sys., Man, Cyber* **SMC-8:** 81–86.

Rau, G., Becker, K., Kaurmann, R., and Zimmermann, H.J. 1995. Fuzzy logic and control: principal approach and potential applications in medicine. *Artificial Organs* **19(1):** 105–112.

Reggia, J.A., Nau, D.S., and Wang, P.Y. 1983. Diagnostic expert systems based on a set covering model. *Int. J. Man Machine Studies* **19:** 437–460.

Sanchez, E., and Bartolin, R. 1989. Fuzzy inference and medical diagnosis, a case study. *Proceedings, First Annual Meeting, Biomedical Fuzzy Systems Association,* pp. 1–18.

Schultz, J.R. 1976. PROMIS, problem-oriented medical information system. *Proc. 3rd Illinois Conf. on Medical Information Systems,* pp. 1–14.

Shea, G. 1978. An analysis of Bayes' procedure for diagnosing multistage disease. *Comp. Biomed. Res.* **11:** 65–75.

Sheiner, L.B., Rosenberg, B., and Melmon, K. 1972. Computer-aided drug dosage, *AFIPS* 1093–1099.

Shortliffe, E.H. 1976. *Computer-Based Medical Consultations—MYCIN.* New York: Elsevier/North Holland.

Shortliffe, E.H., Axline, S., Buchanan, B., Marigan, R., and Cohen, S. 1973. An artificial intelligence program to advise physicians regarding antimicrobial therapy. *Comput. Biomed. Res.* **6:** 544–560.

Shortliffe, E.H., Buchanan, B., and Geigenbaum, E. 1979. Knowledge engineering for medical decision-making: A review of computer-based clinical decision aids. *Proc. IEEE* **67(9):** 1207–1224.

Shortliffe, E.H., Davis, R., Axline, S.G., Buchanan, B.G., Green, C.C., and Cohen, S.N. 1975. Computer-based consultations in clinical therapeutics: Explanation and rule acquisition capabilities of the MYCIN system. *Comput. Biomed. Res.* **8:** 303–320.

Skinner, J.E., Molnar, M., Vybinal, T., and Mitra, M., 1992. Application of chaos theory to biology and medicine. *Integrative Physiology and Behavioral Science* **27(1):** 39–53.

Szolovits, P. 1995. Uncertainty and decisions in medical informatics. *Methods of Information in Medicine* **34(1–2):** 111–121.

Szolovits, P., and Pauker, S. 1979. Computers and clinical decision making: Whether, how and for whom? *Proc. IEEE* **67(9):** 1224–1226.

Szolovits, P., and Pauker, S. 1976. Research on a medical consultation. *Proc. 3rd Illinois Conf. on Medical Information Systems,* pp. 299–320.

Torasso, P., and Console, L. 1989. *Diagnostic Program Solving: Combining Heuristic, Approximate, and Causal Reasoning.* New York: Van Nostrand Reinhold.

United States Department of Health. 1980. *Report on Artificial Intelligence in Medicine.*

Vila, M.A., and Delgado, M. 1983. On medical diagnosis using possibility measures. *Fuzzy Sets and Systems* **10:** 211–222.

Walker, A. 1976. A framework for model construction and model-based deduction in systems with causal loops. *Proc. 3rd Illinois Conf. on Medical Information Systems,* pp. 121–151.

Walser, R., and McCormick, B. 1976. Organization of clinical knowledge in MEDICO. *Proc. 3rd Illinois Conf. on Medical Information Systems,* pp. 159–175.

Walton, P., Holland, R., and Wolf, L. 1979. Medical Guidance and PROMIS. *Computer* **12(11):** 19–27.

Warner, H.R., Olmsted, C., and Rutherford, B. 1972. HELP—A program for medical decision-making. *Comput. Biomed. Res.* **5:** 65–74.

Warner, H.R., Rutherford, B., and Houtchens, B. 1972. A sequential approach to history taking and diagnosis. *Comput. Biomed. Res.* **5:** 256–262.

Weiss, S.M., Kulikowski, C., Amanel, S., and Safir, A. 1978. A model-based method for computer-aided medical decision making. *Artificial Intelligence* **11:** 145–172.

Wiederhold, G., Fries, J., and Weyl, S. 1975. Structured organization of clinical data bases. *AFIPS* **44:** 479–485.

Wiener, F., and Vinaver, J. 1977. Computer simulation of medical reasoning in the assessment of kidney disease. *Int. J. Biomed. Comput.* **8(3):** 203–216.

Winston, P.H. 1977. *Artificial Intelligence.* Reading, MA: Addison-Wesley.

Young, T.Y., and Calvert, T.W. 1974. *Classification, Estimation, and Pattern Recognition.* New York: American Elsevier Publishing Company.

Zadeh, L.A. 1965. *Fuzzy Sets, Information and Control* **8:** 338–353.

10

Knowledge Representation

In this chapter, we discuss general types of knowledge representations that are useful in decision-support systems. For each approach, a brief background will be provided, followed by details of the structure of the representation. The approaches are illustrated with biomedical examples.

10.1 PRODUCTION RULES

10.1.1 General Structure

Production rules were the first knowledge representation used in so-called expert systems. The first example was DENDRAL (Buchanan, Sutherland, and Feigenbaum, 1969), a program that gave advice in chemical synthesis. DENDRAL was soon followed by MYCIN (Shortliffe, 1976), the first medical expert system to use a knowledge-based approach.

Production rule systems contain a situation recognition part and an action part (Winston, 1977). The production can be thought of as a situation–action pair in which the first part is a list of items to watch for and the second is a list of things to do. Another way to look at the situation is in terms of inference structures: "If this condition holds, then this action is appropriate" (Barr and Feigenbaum, 1981). The initial concept of a production rule can be represented as:

IF   Condition A AND Condition B AND Condition C . . .
THEN Action α

The condition part of the rule can have several components that are ANDed together. For example, a rule from the MYCIN (Shortliffe, 1976) system is:

IF   The site of the culture is one of those sites that are normally sterile
       AND
       The portal of entry of the organism is the same as the site of a prior organism with
       the same identity as this current organism

THEN There is further suggestive evidence (0.3) that each of them is a prior organism with the same identity as this current organism

This type of inference is said to be in conjunctive form.

How, then, does the system work? An attempt is made to confirm the conditions. If all the conditions are found to be true, then the rule fires, and the conclusion is invoked. The computer algorithm that handles these functions is referred to as the *inference engine*. The process has essentially three phases: matching, conflict resolution, and action. However, in this process a number of complicating factors arise, which we shall now examine.

10.1.2 Methods of Confirming Conditions

10.1.2.1 Matching. As seen in the preceding example, matching case data with rules can be complex. In the MYCIN system, the general procedure was to ask the user questions that were directed at confirming conditions. Thus the inference engine collects information for the case under consideration from questioning the user. Part of a typical run from MYCIN is given below, with the user response preceded by ** (Shortliffe, 1976):

> From what site was the specimen for CULTURE-1 taken?
> **BLODD
=BLOOD
> How many days ago was this blood culture (CULTURE-1) obtained?
> **2
> I will refer to the first offending organism from this blood culture (CULTURE-1) as:
> . . . . .ORGANISM-1>>>>>
> Enter the identity (genus) of ORGANISM-1:
> **UNK
> Staining characteristics of ORGANISM 1 (gram):
> WHAT IS THE STAIN OF ORGANISM-1?
> Expected responses are: ACIDFAST GRAMPOS GRAMNEG
> Enter HELP for list of user options.
> **GRAMNEG
> IS ORGANISM-1 a rod or coccus (Etc.):
> **ROD

This excerpt points to a number of issues that arise in the use of production rules.

10.1.2.1.1 NATURAL LANGUAGE PROCESSING.   MYCIN allows the user to enter English words, such as BLOOD and GRAMNEG. However, general natural language processing is not required here. The allowable responses are self-limiting, which we see explicitly in the list provided for possible staining responses. Also, the system can recognize minor misspellings, such as BLODD for BLOOD, a process that is again simplified by the restriction of possible responses. There are expert systems that do more extensive natural language processing, but in general, because of the restriction of knowledge-based systems to domain-specific applications, the language will be a subset of the natural language. For more details on natural language processing, refer to Barr and Feigenbaum (1981).

10.1.2.1.2 PARTIAL MATCHING.   In the questioning process, information is accumulated, which is then matched with the information in the conditions. In the example given here, either the condition is matched or it is not. As we will see later, because of the complexity of medical data, it is possible to have partial substantiation of con-

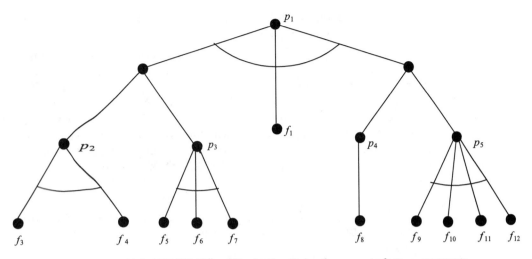

Figure 10.1 AND/OR Tree of Production Rules. f_i represents facts, p_i represents productions, AND nodes are marked with an arc.

ing productions. For example, consider the following example which corresponds to part of the AND/OR tree in Figure 10.1:

EXAMPLE: Production Rules

Rule p_1
IF		Possible MI
AND		Shock
AND		Abnormal mental status
THEN		Admit to CCU

Rule p_2
IF		Pain is unremitting
AND		Pain is excruciating
THEN		Possible MI

Rule p_4
| IF | | BP < 100/60 |
| THEN | | Shock |

Patient Facts
f_1: **A**bnormal mental status
f_3: **P**ain unremitting
f_4: **P**ain excruciating
f_8: **B**P 80/40

Then the result will be the confirmation of rule p_1.

Looking at production rule systems in this manner has limited usefulness because many other factors come into play. Yet it can give an idea as to whether the search is broad and shallow or narrow and deep.

General rule searching strategies fall into two categories: forward-chaining and backward-chaining. In forward-chaining, the system works from known facts to deduced facts. In backward-chaining, a conclusion is hypothesized, and the system uses the production rules to work backward to obtain facts to support the conclusion. If the idea is to determine all that can be deduced from a set of facts, as in differential diag-

ditions, or degrees to which the conditions exist. Systems that allow this type of par
fuzzy matching will be discussed in Chapter 16.

10.1.2.1.3 DATA-DRIVEN APPROACHES. As an alternative to questioning
rule-based system can be data-driven. By this we mean that the user can enter inf
mation pertaining to the case, and the inference engine will then attempt to match 1
information with conditions in the production rules. If some of the conditions
matched, the program may then ask the user additional questions to fully substanti
the conditions. However, a primary difference with the data-driven approach is that
data entered determines the starting point for the rule search. We will see an exam
of a data-driven system, EMERGE, in Section 10.1.4. Data-driven searching strateg
will be discussed in Chapter 12.

10.1.2.2 Conflict Resolution. Data on the specific case is matched with
conditions in the rules. Two major problem areas are:

1. In what order should the rules be searched?
2. What if more than one rule is confirmed or substantiated?

We will discuss the first problem in the following section. With regard to the seco
question, some strategies include (Winston, 1977):

All production rules are arranged in one long list. The first matching product
is the one used. The others are ignored.

The matching production with the toughest requirements is the one used wh
toughest means the longest list of constraining premise or situation elements

The matching production most recently used is used again.

Some aspects of the total situation are considered more important. Producti
matching high-priority situation elements are privileged.

A number of other approaches to conflict resolution among substantiated ru
have been tried (Barr and Feigenbaum, 1981):

The highest priority rule, in which priority is determined by the system desig
The most specific rule, that is, the one with the most detailed condition part.
The rule that refers to the element most recently added to the context.
A new rule, that is, a rule-binding instantiation that has not occurred previou
An arbitrary rule.
Not to choose, explore all applicable rules.

Usually, the objective of the expert system will determine the conflict resoluti
strategy. If the objective is to establish a differential diagnosis, then all substantia
rules are considered.

10.1.3 Rule Searching Strategies

If production rules are of the conjunctive form, like those we saw earlier, then 1
searching of the rules can be thought of as an AND/OR tree. The conditions of a s
gle rule represent an AND node, and the combination of this rule with other rules re
resents OR nodes. The OR conditions are also referred to as disjunctions. Figure 10
shows an AND/OR tree of production rules, with f_i presenting facts and p_i represer

nosis, then the system must run forward. If, on the other hand, the objective is to verify or dispute a specific conclusion, the backward-chaining is more appropriate.

As we have already seen, these are not the only possibilities. In some systems, the response to one rule may determine the next rule that is fired. For instance, the action portion of one rule may match the condition portion of another rule. Many systems also contain meta rules, which are production rules that address the general strategy of the inference process and alter the order in which the rules are searched. More details regarding inference engines and searching strategies will be given in Chapter 12.

10.1.4 Expanded Production Rule Systems

Production rule structure can be expanded in a number of directions. Both the left-hand side (conditions) and the right-hand side (action) of production rules have been extended. Here we consider an example from the EMERGE system (Hudson and Cohen, 1988), which allows additional structures in the left-hand side.

Instead of restricting conditions to the conjunctive form, three forms are allowed: conjunctive (AND), disjunctive (OR), and COUNT n, in which COUNT requires n conditions out of a list of m to be substantiated. We can represent these conditions, denoted standard conditions (SC), as follows:

$$SC_i(m, m) \equiv AND$$
$$SC_i(1, m) \equiv OR$$
$$SC_i(n, m) \equiv COUNT\ n,\ 1 < n < m$$

where m is the number of conditions in a production rule and i is the number of the SC. $SC_i(n, m)$ assumes the value to be true or false, depending on whether or not the standard conditions hold. Examples from the EMERGE chest pain rule base include:

$SC_1(1, 5)$
  ANY OF
    Abnormal mental status
    Cold, clammy skin
    Gray, cyanotic skin
    Weak peripheral pulses
    Urinary output < 30 cc/hr
$SC_{15}(2, 3)$
  2 of 3
    Sweating
    Nausea
    Dizziness
$SC_{29}(2, 2)$
  ALL OF
    Pain excruciating
    Pain unremitting

Thus we see that the SC function includes AND and OR, and introduces the new logical construct COUNT n. These constructs are then combined into rules such as the following:

Rule 10 (CF 0.9)
IF   ALL OF
        Blood Pressure $< 100/60$
        SC_1
THEN patient should be admitted to the CCU

This rule therefore results in a conjunctive combination of a single finding with a disjunction of five findings.

10.1.5 Certainty Factors

In the examples from the MYCIN and EMERGE rule bases, we see that both include a certainty factor. Certainty factors were an early recognition of the necessity of dealing with uncertain information in medical decision-support systems. The certainty factors for these two systems were used differently. Each will be described briefly.

In MYCIN (Shortliffe, 1976), each production rule includes what is termed a certainty factor, with a value between 0 and 1, inclusive. The certainty factors are combined using the AND/OR tree description discussed earlier. At AND nodes, the smallest certainty factor on the conditions branches is multiplied by the certainty factor for that rule. The result is then passed upward in the tree. At OR nodes, the certainty factors on the branches reinforce each other. For one branch, the overall certainty is the certainty factor (CF) associated with that branch. The remaining distance to total certainty is $(1 - CF_1)$. For a second branch, these factors are multiplied and subtracted, that is, $(1 - CF_1 \times CF_2)$.

Similar certainty factors are used in EMERGE, although the derivation is somewhat different. Computation of the certainty factor is derived from decision trees established during a major project called Criteria Mapping (Greenfield et al., 1977; Hudson, 1983). The goal of the project was to develop flow diagrams for the purpose of evaluating emergency room procedures. These flow diagrams were subsequently used to develop the EMERGE knowledge base.

In the EMERGE system, three responses are possible—yes, no, and ?—the last response indicating that no information is available regarding that item. A sample tree for the situation when all information is known is shown in Figure 10.2. In this case, the certainty of an admissible disease is read from the end of a branch, with no calculation required. For example, a patient with atrial fibrillation with no history who is not in shock and who shows the atrial fibrillation resolved on the second ECG would have a certainty factor of 0.2. Note that spanning the tree may include the substantiation of several rules. If only some of the information is known, the certainty of an admissible disease must be calculated. The values for branches that are known to have affirmative responses are changed to 1.0, whereas those that are known to have negative responses are changed to 0.0. The certainty factor for each branch is calculated by multiplying all values along that branch. An overall certainty factor must then be calculated for all possible branches. The following definitions are used:

CF = 1 (admissible disease)
CF = 0 (not an admissible disease)
CF_1 and $CF_2 = CF_1*CF_2$ (multiplication)
NOT (CF) = 1 − CF (not admissible = 1 − admissible)

A consistent logical OR can be defined by applying deMorgan's laws:

$$CF_1 \ OR \ CF_2 = CF_1 + CF_1 - CF_1*CF_2$$

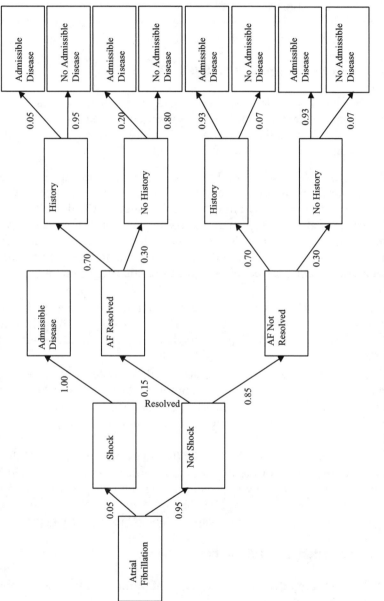

Figure 10.2 EMERGE Scoring with Complete Information.

Figure 10.3 shows a tree for a patient with atrial fibrillation who is not in shock, with the atrial fibrillation resolved on the second ECG but with no information pertaining to the patient's history. There are only two reachable admissible disease nodes. For the first admissible branch, the multiplication yields 0.035; the second yields 0.06. The resulting overall certainty factor is $0.035 + 0.06 - 0.035*0.06 = 0.0929$.

These ad hoc approaches deal with some aspects of uncertain information, but the general concept is quite complex. More inclusive methods for reasoning with uncertain information are discussed in Chapter 16.

10.1.6 Advantages of Production Systems

At the time knowledge-based systems using production rules were introduced, developers claimed that this method possessed advantages over other methods currently in use that were either algorithmic or data-based pattern recognition systems. These advantages included the following:

Modularity: The knowledge base was separate from the inference engine. In other words, in theory, a general inference engine could be developed which would function with any knowledge base, whether the domain was diagnosis of the cause of abdominal pain or oil prospecting. This is not the case with algorithmic programs where the algorithm is developed for the specific project at hand. It is also true, however, of pattern classification and neural network systems, in which new models are developed using the same algorithm by replacing the database.

Uniform knowledge structure: The production rule format provided a uniform structure into which many applications could easily fit. This uniformity of structure made it possible to change knowledge bases without changing the inference engine.

Human-like reasoning: As the rules for these systems were developed in conjunction with one or more experts in the problem domain, the systems gave the appearance of reasoning in the same manner as humans. The situation was modeled as a set of IF–THEN rules that are familiar to everyone from elementary logic.

Explanation capabilities: Because of the rule structure and the ability of the program to keep track of the rule searching order, explanations could be provided for each consultation by regurgitating the rules that had fired. Thus the result seemed to have the force of logic behind it, unlike pattern classification systems in which recommended classifications seemed to appear by magic.

10.1.7 Disadvantages of Production Systems

Although these advantages advanced the artificial intelligence approach, there were also a number of disadvantages.

Difficulty of following flow: It is difficult to follow the flow of rule invocation since in most systems it changes for every run as the data presented cause the path through the rules to alter. For this reason, it is also difficult to completely debug production systems with large numbers of rules.

Inefficient: Production system substantiation is not an efficient process from a computer standpoint owing to the high level of symbolic, as opposed to numeric,

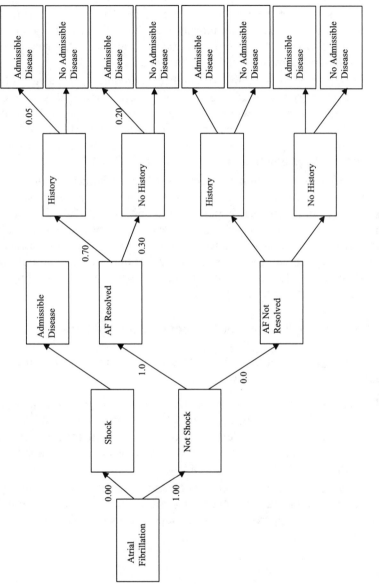

Figure 10.3 EMERGE Scoring with Incomplete Information.

processing. In addition, symbolic information requires additional storage. As computers have become faster with larger memory capacities, these factors are no longer as significant.

Knowledge base development: Probably the most serious drawback to the knowledge-based approach is difficulty in developing the knowledge base. In general, the system designer must communicate at great lengths with one or more experts in order to develop the required rules. This process is fraught with difficulties. There are often communication problems across disciplines, different experts may seriously disagree on specific rules, and once the rule base is complete it must be updated to include new knowledge.

Domain specificity: Although the inference engine may theoretically be general, in practice most inference engines are geared to take advantage of certain aspects of the domain knowledge. Thus the process of changing the knowledge base is not completely straightforward. The domain specificity of the knowledge base makes the development of each new application a new project subject to the difficulties we have mentioned.

Restrictions in production format: The original production rule format was presented to experts as the structure into which the knowledge should be placed. This suggestion forced the expert to think in terms of IF–THEN conjunctions, although in reality this may not be the way decisions are reached. Many systems have expanded this structure to incorporate more types of logical constructs, but it is still very difficult to determine the actual human decision-making process. As we shall see in Chapter 16, fuzzy logic and approximate reasoning may play significant roles in our thinking processes.

10.1.8 Areas of Applications of Production Rule Systems

In what areas does it make sense to use the production rule format? Some general guidelines include the following:

Applications with a body of factual information rather than a unified well-understood theory: For example, a problem in mechanics is suited to an algorithmic structure since the underlying principles are well known. A problem in prognosis of heart failure is better suited to a knowledge-based approach because a sufficiently detailed model is not available.

Processes represented as a set of independent actions rather than dependent subprocesses: The production rule format allows actions to be taken independently. The algorithmic approach combines dependent subprocesses into a model of the whole.

10.2 FRAMES

10.2.1 General Structure

The term *frame* was introduced in 1975 by Minsky. The basic idea was that when a person enters a situation, he or she already has considerable knowledge about the situation that has been gained through previous experience. The objective of the frame was to provide a structure that would contain general information that could then be adjusted to fit the particular situation. Consider the following example for patient monitoring in the operating room (OR):

```
OR Monitoring Frame
     Specialization of:          Monitoring
     Types: Range:               (electrophysiological monitoring, blood gas monitoring,
                                     OR monitoring . . .)
     Physical characteristics    (body weight, height, age)
     Surgery                     (abdominal, chest, plastic)
```

The general frame is then specialized for specific instances:

```
John Smith Monitoring Frame
     Specialization of:          OR Monitoring Frame
     Physical characteristics:   (185, 70, 67)
     Surgery                     (abdominal)
```

10.2.2 Inheritance

The specific frame inherits properties from the more general frame, but more of the slots are filled in with additional information. It was felt that this structure more closely resembled human information processing in that one does not start from scratch on each new problem but rather employs examples of similar situations that have been previously encountered. Subframes inherit characteristics of more general frames. Slots in frames may also be filled in with default values. Default and inherited values are easy methods for filling in slots since they do not require reasoning processes. If neither of these methods is appropriate, slots may be filled in by means of slot-specific heuristics (Barr and Feigenbaum, 1981). Another method is the use of triggers that are invoked when the value of a slot is found or changed. These triggers implement procedures that are data-driven. This triggering mechanism has been used in frame-based medical decision aids (Szolovitz, Hawkinson, and Martin, 1977; Aikins, 1979). It is a useful approach in ruling out specific diagnoses and thus can be used in systems that provide differential diagnoses lists. In this process, specific symptoms or other facts invoke triggers.

This idea of inheritance was a precursor to object-oriented programming and databases that will be discussed in more detail in the next section. The frame is essentially equivalent to an object in the object-oriented approach. Although the idea of frames is intuitively pleasing, it turns out that it is quite difficult to reason with information structured in this way.

10.2.3 Example of a Frame-Based Decision-Support System

An example of frame-based information is the HELP systems (Bouhaddou, Haug, and Warner, 1987). A HELP frame can represent the selection algorithm of a query to the patient database. The HELP frames support complex queries involving data from multiple sources and can also be used for Bayesian calculations. A method

```
TITLE:     Lung consolidation
TYPE:             Interpretation
FINDINGS:
a.         Coarse crackles (rales)
b.         Bronchial breath sounds
c.         Egophony (E-a changes)
d.         Increased vocal fremitus
e.         Dullness to percussion
f.         Whisper pectoriloquy
g.         CSR - lung infiltrate with alveolar  pattern and air
bronchograms


True if g or if (a and b) and (c or d or e or f)
```

Figure 10.4 Clustered Frame with Boolean Decision Logic (Lincoln et al., 1988).

for reasoning with frame information is seen in HELP (Yu et al., 1988) with a similar approach in Iliad, a commercial decision-support system. The system uses clustered frames with Boolean decision logic and Bayesian frames that combine several clustered frames. Examples are shown in Figures 10.4 and 10.5 (Lincoln et al., 1988).

TITLE:	Pneumonia		Disease	No disease
TYPE:	probability			
a priori (prevalence): .025				
FINDINGS:			Disease	No disease
a.	@7.141.112	Lung consolidation	.99	.07
b.	@7.149.117	Signs of systemic infection	.90	.20
c.	@7.141.113	Pleuritic chest pain	.25	.02
	else			
	Pleural effusion		.05	.01
d.	7.141.119 Hypoxemia		.40	.10
e.	Dyspnea		.40	.10
f.	Cough with sputum		.90	.15
	else			
g.	Cough		.90	.25

Figure 10.5 Bayesian Frame with Several Clustered Frames (Lincoln et al., 1988).

10.3 DATABASES

A distinction is made here between databases and knowledge bases. In general, databases contain information in raw form, that is, textual information. Textual information includes all of the data types discussed in the Overview. Even image databases contain images that are represented as numbers in the form of pixels or voxels. Knowledge bases, on the other hand, contain symbolic information that shows relationships among variables, such as the rules and frames discussed earlier. As data files become larger and more complex, efficient means for organizing them become crucial. The primary physical structure of computer storage traditionally consisted of records, made up of fields, and files made up of records. Although this is an efficient storage mechanism, it is not efficient for retrieval purposes. The organization of databases is viewed from a logical perspective for retrieval purposes rather than from a physical storage perspective. Typically, three types of relationships occur among entities in databases: one-to-one (a patient has one social security number), one-to-many (a physician has many patients), and many-to-many (a patient has multiple tests, and each test is ordered for multiple patients), although higher order relationships are possible.

Traditional database structures included hierarchical structures in which fields in the top level referred to additional databases at lower levels. Figure 10.6 shows a hierarchical database. A more efficient approach is the relational structure described in the following section.

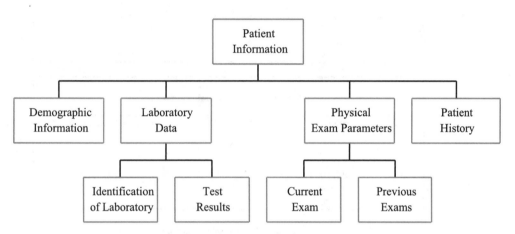

Figure 10.6 Example of a Hierarchical Database Design.

10.3.1 Relational Databases

Many modern databases are relational, including the UNIX-based INGRES and the Microsoft Access database. Relational databases consist of entities and relationships, both of which are represented by tables. There is a firm mathematical basis to the relational structure. A number of definitions are required (Date, 1977):

Definition: Given a collection of sets $D_1, D_2, \ldots, D_n$, R is a relation on those n sets if it is a set of ordered n-tuples $< d_1, d_2, \ldots, d_n >$ such that d_i belongs to D_i. $D_1, \ldots$ are the domains of R. n is the degree.

Figure 10.7 shows sample relations. The rows in the figure are the tuples, and the columns are the attributes. There is no ordering among tuples and usually no ordering among sets. Some columns may have the same domains as other columns. The number of tuples is the cardinality. The relation is normalized if every value in the relation is atomic (nondecomposable). Comparing to the traditional field/record/file physical storage, we find that the attribute is a field, the tuple is a record, and the relation is a file.

Each relation must have a key that uniquely distinguishes a tuple. More than one attribute may be used as a key. In the patient information relation, the Ptinfo is the unique identifier. In the example given, the patient name would also be a unique identifier. There are two rules pertaining to the interpretation of keys:

Patient Information Relation (Ptinfo)

PtID	PtName	DOB	DateAdmitted
4352	J. Smith	7/1/33	9/15/96
2289	M. Leeds	2/13/46	10/2/96
7701	S. Jones	11/24/56	9/30/96
8813	D. Jay	4/3/29	8/25/96
2222	G. Street	1/1/50	10/3/96
9128	L. Love	5/18/12	7/31/96

Physician Information Relation (Phyinfo)

PhyID	PhyName	Hospital
11531	W. Holly	County General
92038	K. Klein	Glenhaven
53950	A. Wall	County General

Patient/Physician Relation (Ptphy)

PhyID	PtID	Days_in_Hospital
11531	2289	3
11531	4352	9
11531	9128	1
53950	7701	12
53950	2222	7
92038	8813	2

Figure 10.7 Sample Relations.

Integrity Rule 1 (entity integrity):
No component of a primary key value may be null.

Integrity Rule 2 (foreign key):
Definition: A given domain may be designated as primary iff $\exists$ some single-attribute primary key defined on that domain.

Let D be a primary domain, and let R_1 be a relation with an attribute A defined on D. Then, each value of A in R must be either (a) null or (b) equal to V, where V is the primary key value in R_2 with the primary key defined in D.

The second rule is the basis for the relationship among tuples. For example, in Figure 10.7, the physicians are linked with the patients through the patient ID key that appears in the tuples of the patient relation and the physician relation.

The *extension* of a given relation is the set of values appearing in the relation at any given instant. The *intention* of a given relation is specified in the relational scheme (type of variable). The intention defines all possible extensions. It has two parts:

Naming structure: relation name plus name of attributes

Integrity constraints:

Key constraints: primary keys, alternate keys

Referential constraints: foreign keys

A recent addition to the concept of a relational database is that of a distributed database where components are on different computers in the same location or at any location. With the advent of the Internet and improved data communications, this type of database will undoubtedly become more common. A recent application is outlined in Marrs et al. (1993).

10.3.2 Query Languages

Databases present an efficient means for data organization as well as for data retrieval. Data retrieval is accomplished through the use of a query language. In general, each database package (INGRES, Access, etc.) has its own query language. An example of a query is: "Find the names of all physicians and a list of their patients who spent more than 5 days in the hospital after 9/1/96." Note that this query must use all three relations in our example. The result is:

Physicians	Patients
W. Holly	J. Smith
A. Wall	S. Jones, G. Street

Query operations are governed by relational algebra, which allows the development of nonprocedural high-level query languages. One common query language, Structured Query Language (SQL), is used in a number of database programs, including Microsoft Access. A query language allows the user to retrieve stored information based on logical constructs. SQL contains commands such as the following:

```
SELECT . . . FROM
```

A use of SQL for the above example is

```
SELECT PtName FROM Ptinfo WHERE DateAdmitted > 9/1/96.
```

This query selects all patients admitted after 9/1/96 from the patient information table. The WHERE can contain any combinations of ANDs, ORs, and NOTs.

Other commands include COUNT (number of values), SUM (sum of values), AVERAGE, MAX, and MIN.

10.3.3 Object-Oriented Databases

Relational databases offer an approach for efficient organization and retrieval of data. However, this approach does not use semantic information of the type we saw in production rules and frames. By semantic information we mean knowledge about the domain being modeled. In short, databases contain large bodies of data and little knowledge, whereas expert systems contain large knowledge bases and small amounts of data (Barsalou, 1988). Object-oriented databases attempt to combine the two.

The object-oriented approach has the following advantages (Barsalou, 1988; Stefik and Bobrow, 1986; Wiederhold, 1986):

1. The paradigm supports the distinction between conceptual entities and instances of those entities. After retrieval, links to related information are maintained.
2. Objects combine the properties of procedures and data. The current state is

captured through the instances, and behavior is represented by the entity's methods that are triggered by message sending.

3. Class hierarchies allow the inheritance of properties from general classes to more specific entities, as we saw in the frame paradigm.

The object-oriented approach is accomplished by including a structure such as a frame as an entity in the database along with the relations we saw above (if a relational structure is used). Information for filling frames can be generated by collapsing information from multiple tables from several relationships. Frames can also be included in hierarchically structured databases. ONCOCIN (Kahn et al., 1985) uses an object-oriented database, which includes temporal components, a subject discussed later in this chapter.

10.4 PREDICATE CALCULUS AND SEMANTIC NETS

Predicate calculus is a formal approach for translating statements in natural language into mathematical representations for the purpose of automated logical reasoning. A complete treatment of predicate calculus can be found in Nilsson (1971).

10.4.1 Syntax

The syntax is composed of an alphabet of symbols and definitions of expressions that can be constructed from the symbols.

Alphabet
Punctuation marks: , ( )
Logical symbols: $\sim$ (NOT), $\Rightarrow$ (IMPLIES), $\wedge$ (AND), $\vee$ (OR)
n-adic functions: f_i^n
f_i^0 are constants also denoted: a, b, c, . . .
n-adic predicates: p_i^n

Expressions
Terms
    Each constant is a term.
    Functions of terms are terms.
Atomic functions
    Propositions are atomic formulas.
    Propositions of atomic terms are atomic formulas.
Well-formed formulas (wffs)
    An atomic formula is a wff.
Negation of a wff is a wff.

The value of a wff has a value of true (T) or false (F). Its value is determined recursively from its component parts. Quantifiers can be defined to simplify statements. The two basic quantifiers are the universal quantifier $\forall$ and the existential quantifier $\exists$. Statements are put into *clause form* through a series of manipulations that produce statements which contain only predicates along with the operations $\wedge$ and $\vee$, with the understanding that all variables are universally quantified.

10.4.2 Method of Proof

The idea behind showing that some wff W is a logical consequence of a given set of wffs S is a demonstration that W follows from S, which is the same as showing that no interpretation satisfies the union of S and $\sim W$. Therefore, the approach is to show that $S \cup \sim W$ is unsatisfiable. The method by which we proceed is through the use of a semantic tree.

10.4.3 Semantic Trees

A semantic tree is a binary tree in which a branch to the left represents a value of T and a branch to the right represents a value of F. The complete tree contains all possible paths that may satisfy a set of clauses. The objective is to show that there is no path that will satisfy the set. Along a certain path, it is possible to determine that the path cannot satisfy the clauses without proceeding further. The node in the tree at which this occurs is called a failure node, and the tree can be terminated at that point.

To clarify this procedure, consider the following example of unsatisfiable clauses due to Nilsson (1971):

$P(x) \vee Q(y)$
$\sim P(a)$
$\sim Q(b)$

Figure 10.8 shows the semantic tree with failure nodes for this example. Following the tree to the left, the value of F for $P(a)$ does not satisfy the set of clauses, so this node becomes a failure node. Verification of the other failure nodes is left as an exercise.

10.4.4 Semantic Interpretation

Now can the above be used to reason in the biomedical domain? Consider the following example. If we have the rule

IF Blood Pressure $< 100/60$ THEN Shock is present

Symbolically, this can be written
$$P(x) \Rightarrow Q(y)$$
where $P(x)$ is the function $(x < 100/60)$, x represents blood pressure, and $Q(y)$ is the function (shock) where y assumes the value 0 (false) or 1 (true).
If we then have the data
$$BP = 80/40$$
We have an instance $P(a)$ where $a = 80/40$.
We then must put this information into clause form.
$P(x) \Rightarrow Q(y)$ can be written as $\sim P(x) \vee Q(y)$ so our set of clauses is
$\sim P(x) \vee Q(y)$
$P(a)$

10.4.5 Applications

It is possible to use predicate calculus and deductive reasoning for biomedical systems that are relatively well-defined. One example is to expand SNOMED III (Systematized Nomenclature of Medicine) for representation of coding schemes to include

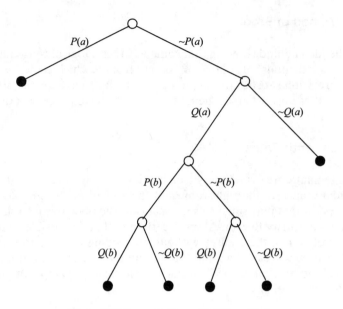

Figure 10.8 Semantic Tree with Failure Nodes.

conceptual-graph formalisms which will permit the codes to be used in relational data models or in other formal systems such as first-order predicate calculus (Campbell and Musen, 1992). A second application involves mapping for digestions by restriction enzymes to find solution sets. The approach uses predicate calculus as well as constraint methods of solution (Dix and Yee, 1994).

10.5 TEMPORAL DATA REPRESENTATIONS

10.5.1 Knowledge-Based Systems

In production systems, time-dependent diagnostic possibilities are included in the standard production rule format. For example, in the EMERGE system (Hudson and Cohen, 1988), there are a number of rules such as

```
IF      SC₃₃(1,2)
        SC₃₄(2,2)
        Dependent rales
        Not (proved old)
THEN Admit
where
        SC₃₃(1,2)  OR
                   Pain diffuse and precordial
                   Dyspnea
        SC₃₄(2,2)  AND
                   > 45 years old
                   Symptoms > 20 minutes
```

This rule specifies a definite time period for the persistence of symptoms. It also refers to patient history with the statement "proved old," which indicates an indefinite time frame for a previous occurrence of the event.

There are also references with an indefinite time duration:

IF   Atrial fibrillation
        BP $< 100/60$
        SC_1
        Continuing chest pain
        Heart rate > 120
THEN Admit

where SC_1 is defined in Section 10.1. The duration for continuing chest pain is unclear.

In the knowledge-based system approach, the person interacting with the system must deal with temporal variables by finding the information. Thus temporal variables do not become a problem of data representation. This is not the case in data-based systems such as neural networks, which require temporal information to be recorded in the data in a usable format.

10.5.2 Data-Based Systems

The time-oriented data model (Wiederhold, 1975) discussed earlier has been used as the foundation for many databases. Information is stored as $<$ attribute, time, value $>$ tuples. Laboratory data, physical findings, and therapeutic interventions can all be represented as these temporal points. The major focus is to record the time of these *point events*. However, diagnosis often depends on more complex trends that cannot be adequately represented in this manner. A taxonomy of temporal classes was developed in Cousins, Kahn, and Frisse, 1989 which comprised *simple events*, *complex events*, and *intervals*. Simple events are analogous to the $<$ attribute, time, value $>$ tuple. Complex events represent point events that contain an interval of uncertainty. Events with no significant temporal duration are called *atomic events*. Point events are atomic and may occur before, during, or after other points. Intervals contain both points and subintervals. Figure 10.9 shows these types of events in the chest pain rule base.

10.6 SUMMARY

The choice of knowledge representation is dependent on the type of information that is available as well as on the reasoning methodology. Using production rules as the basis for representation requires that appropriate knowledge also be available regarding the reasoning process. The use of predicate calculus and semantic nets requires that the problem be well-defined. Database representations, on the other hand, provide an efficient means of storing and retrieving data without including any higher-order reasoning. The frame and object-oriented approaches are partial compromises between the knowledge-based production rule approach and the database approach.

EXERCISES

1. In standard production rule systems, rules are in conjunctive form. What does this mean? Give an example from an application of your choice. If you were making a decision regarding the subject that you chose for your example, would you reason in this way? If not, what reasoning process would you use?

2. In the EMERGE system, in addition to conjunctions, disjunctions are allowed. Add a rule to your application from exercise 1 that is in disjunctive form. If both types of

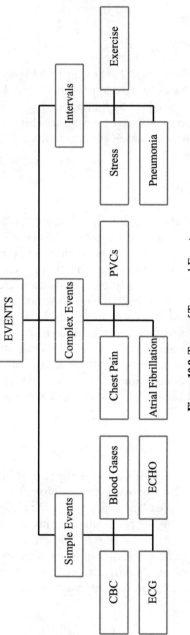

Figure 10.9 Types of Temporal Events.

rules are used, will the rule base contain more or fewer rules? Can you rewrite your rule using one or more rules in conjunctive form?

3. What happens to the AND/OR tree illustrated in Figure 10.1 if you allow disjunctive production rules? Draw an example.

4. What is the role of the certainty factor in the MYCIN system? The certainty factor indicates the degree of certainty in what part of the reasoning process? Is the same true in the EMERGE system?

5. For computation of the certainty factor in the EMERGE system, what would be the certainty factor for a patient with the following findings: atrial fibrillation, no shock, atrial fibrillation not resolved on the second ECG, previous history of atrial fibrillation. What if there is no information regarding previous history? (Refer to Figures 10.2 and 10.3.)

6. List three advantages of production rules.

7. What does the property of inheritance mean in regards to frame-based knowledge? Does the frame structure facilitate the development of reasoning processes? Why or why not?

8. For the following, illustrate the structure for a hierarchical database and for a relational database: medical image database that includes digital radiographs, MRI, CT, ultrasound, and SPECT images for patients from three hospitals. Information also includes referring physician, radiologist who reads the scan, demographics and history information for the patients, and contact information for the referring physician.

9. Explain the common thread between frames and object-oriented databases. Can you restructure the database from exercise 8 as an object-oriented database?

10. Explain the reason for the failure nodes in Figure 10.8.

11. List as many different ways that you can think of in which temporal information is used in the medical record.

REFERENCES

Aikins, J.S. 1979. Prototypes and production rules: An approach to knowledge representations for hypothesis formation. *International Joint Conference on Artificial Intelligence* (*IJCAI*) **6:** 1–3.

Barr, A., and Feigenbaum, E.A. 1981. *The handbook of artificial intelligence.* Vol. 1. Reading, MA: Addison-Wesley.

Barsalou, T. 1988. An object-oriented architecture for biomedical expert database systems. *Society for Computer Applications in Medical Care* (*SCAMC*) (IEEE Computer Society Press): 572–578.

Bouhaddou, O., Haug, P.H., and Warner, H.R., 1987. Use of the HELP clinical database to build and test medical knowledge, *SCAMC* **11** (IEEE Computer Society Press): 64–67.

Buchanan, B., Sutherland, G., and Feigenbaum, E. 1969. Heuristic DENDRAL: A program for generating explanatory hypotheses in organic chemistry, *Machine Intelligence,* **4.** New York: American Elsevier.

Campbell, K.E., and Musen, M.A. 1992. Representation of clinical data using SNOMED III and conceptual graphs. *SCAMC* **16:** 354–358.

Cousins, S.B., Kahn, M.G., and Frisse, M.E. 1989. The display and manipulation of temporal information. *SCAMC* **13** (IEEE Computer Society Press): 76–80.

Date, C.J. 1977. *An introduction to database systems.* 2nd ed. Reading, MA: Addison-Wesley.

Dix, T.I., and Yee, C.N. 1994. A restriction mapping engine using constraint logic programming. *Intelligent Systems for Molecular Biology* (*ISMB*) **2:** 112–120.

Greenfield, S., Nadler, M., Morgan, M., and Shine, K. 1977. The clinical management of chest pain in an emergency department: Quality assessment by criteria mapping. *Medical Care* **15:** 898–905.

Hudson, D.L. 1983. Use of certainty factors to determine emergency room priorities. *American Association for Medical Systems and Information* **2:** 240–244.

Hudson, D.L., and Cohen, M.E. 1988. An approach to management of uncertainty in an expert system. *International Journal of Intelligent Systems* **3(1):** 45–58.

Kahn, M.G., Ferguson, J.C., Shortliffe, E.H., and Fagen, L.M. 1985. Representation and use of temporal information in ONCONIN. *SCAMC* **9** (IEEE Computer Society Press): 172–176.

Lincoln, M., Turner, C., Hesse, B., and Miller, R. 1988. A comparison of clustered knowledge structures in Iliad and in Quick Medical Reference. *SCAMC* **12** (IEEE Computer Society Press): 131–135.

Marrs, K.A., Steib, S.A., Abrams, C.A., and Kahn, M.G. 1993. Unifying heterogeneous distributed clinical data in a relational database. *Proceedings, SCAMC* **17:** 644–648.

Minsky, M. 1975. A framework for representing knowledge. In P. Winston, ed., *The psychology of human vision,* pp. 211–277. New York: McGraw-Hill.

Nilsson, N.J. 1971. *Problem-solving methods in artificial intelligence.* New York: McGraw-Hill.

Shortliffe, E.H. 1976. *Computer-based medical consultations—MYCIN.* New York: Elsevier/ North Holland.

Stefik, M., and Bobrow, D.G. 1986. Object-oriented programming: themes and variations. *AI Magazine* **6(4):** 40–52.

Szolovitz, P., Hawkinson, L.B., and Martin, W.A. 1977. An overview of OWL, a language for knowledge representation, Rep. No. TM-86. *Laboratory for Computer Science,* Cambridge, MA: MIT.

Wiederhold, G. 1986. Views, objects, and databases. *Computer* **19 (12):** 37–44.

Wiederhold, G., Fries, J., and Weyl, S. 1975. Structured organization of clinical data bases. *AFIPS* **44:** 479–485.

Winston, P.H. 1977. *Artificial intelligence.* Reading, MA: Addison-Wesley.

Yu, H., Haug, P.J., Lincoln, M.J., Rutner, C., and Warner, H.R. 1988. Clustered knowledge representation, increasing the reliability of computerized expert systems. *SCAMC* **12** (IEEE Computer Society Press): 126–130.

11

Knowledge Acquisition

11.1 INTRODUCTION

The knowledge-based expert system is based on the premise that the inference engine and the knowledge base are separate entities, which allows the same inference engine to be used for multiple applications. One of the major problems associated with the knowledge-based system is the development of the knowledge base itself. The name itself comes from the fact that expert input is used in the knowledge base. In early systems, a person called a *knowledge engineer* solicited input directly from domain experts. This procedure has evolved to include derivation from examples and from databases. These approaches are discussed in the following sections.

11.2 EXPERT INPUT

11.2.1 Acquisition for a New System

11.2.1.1 Use of Existing Material. In early work on the EMERGE system (described in detail in Chapter 18), the knowledge base was in terms of rules whose antecedents could be one of three forms: conjunctions, disjunctions, and confirmation of a specified number in a list (i.e., three out of five). The original knowledge base was derived from flowcharts called criteria maps, which had been developed over a number of years with the goal of evaluating the appropriateness of treatment in the emergency room (Greenfield et al., 1977). A portion of the criteria map for chest pain is shown in Figure 11.1. If the answer to a question is yes, the flow goes to the right; otherwise it proceeds down to the next box. This format is ideal for establishing rules in the specified three formats (Hudson and Estrin, 1984). Three rules that correspond to the boxes numbered 1, 2, and 3 are:

Rule 1
    IF   **ALL OF**
                ANY OF
                     Pain diffuse and precordial

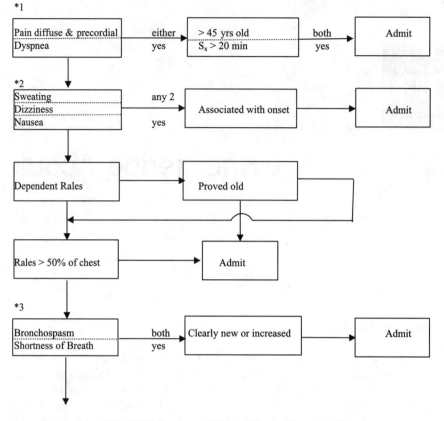

Figure 11.1 Portion of Criteria Map for Chest Pain.

                 Dyspnea
            >45 years old
            Symptoms > 20 minutes
     THEN Patient should be admitted
Rule 2
    IF   **ALL OF**
                 ANY 2 OF
                     Sweating
                     Nausea
                     Dizziness
             Associated with onset
     THEN Patient should be admitted
Rule 3
    IF   **ALL OF**
             Bronchospasm
             Shortness of breath
             Clearly new or increased
     THEN Patient should be admitted

Figure 11.2 illustrates the process for rule base development in the EMERGE system. Often, written sources can be found which can be used as a basis for establishing the rule base, which can then be completed through expert input.

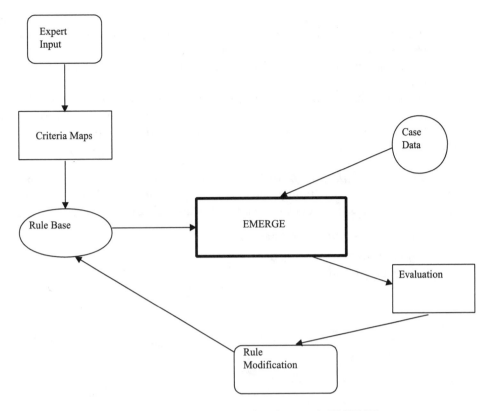

Figure 11.2 Knowledge Base Development in EMERGE.

11.2.1.2 Techniques for Knowledge Elicitation. The idea of eliciting information from experts is not as straightforward as it sounds. First, the person collecting
the information, sometimes called the knowledge engineer, must know the type of information that is required. In other words, one cannot go to a cardiologist and say: "Tell
me about coronary artery disease." The questioning must be focused. A better initial
approach is, "How do you make decisions regarding the presence of coronary artery
disease?" Usually more specific questioning is needed. For a particular condition,
symptoms may be sought. The knowledge engineer must be careful, however. If he or
she asks questions in a prespecified format, the expert will fit his answers into this format and may exclude some of the actual decision-making process.

An anecdote may help to illustrate this point. After the EMERGE system had
been in operation for some time, it was decided to include techniques for approximate
reasoning (Hudson and Cohen, 1988). In particular, instead of the three binary logic
constructions that had been used, the antecedents were to be weighted according to
relative degree of importance, and instead of entering a yes/no in response to presence
of symptoms, a degree of presence was to be indicated. Reluctantly, we approached the
cardiologist with this idea, assuming that he would not be eager to have to enter a degree of presence. We were surprised to learn that the medical residents were in fact
trained to record a value between 1 and 10 in order to indicate the degree of severity
of chest pain. He had never mentioned this because he responded to our conception of
the knowledge structure as being binary. This illustrates the importance of not constraining questioning to a presupposed structure that excludes information actually

used in the human decision process. There is a fine line between guiding the expert's response into a format that can be built into the automated system and altering the expert process so that it will fit. Complete communication between a knowledge engineer and a domain expert is very difficult if there is no overlap of knowledge between the two.

Another inherent problem is whether or not we actually know how we make decisions. When pressed on this point, most people will come up with a description, but it may not represent the actual process. Figure 11.3 illustrates the process for expert elicitation of knowledge.

11.2.1.3 *Dealing with Multiple Experts.* Problems can arise when multiple experts are contacted. Although most experts agree on general points, there may be specific serious disagreements. Potential problems include:

Different conditions for diagnosis
Different treatment strategies
Contradictory rules

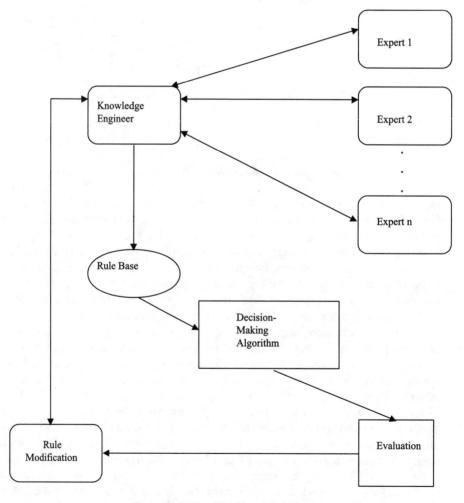

Figure 11.3 Acquiring Expert Information.

If more than two experts are used, consensus building can be employed to remove inconsistencies.

11.2.1.4   Consistency.   For a knowledge-based system to function properly, the knowledge base must be consistent. This requirement seems obvious, and on the surface it appears that the creation of a consistent knowledge base is straightforward. However, a number of complications can arise:

> In large knowledge bases, it becomes difficult to determine if contradictory information is included.
>
> Due to rule chaining, combinations of some sequences may reach conclusions that are inconsistent with other sequences.

The second of these is very difficult to detect. The sequence of rule generation is dependent both on the case data and the searching strategy. With complex knowledge bases, the number of possible sequences grows exponentially, making complete debugging difficult, if not impossible. Searching strategies are treated in more detail in Chapter 12.

11.2.1.5   Completeness.   A major proviso of expert systems is that they function properly only in the domain for which they are designed. Thus, if a patient presents to the emergency room complaining of chest pain, a program such as EMERGE that is designed to evaluate different types of chest pain can perform well on most cases but would miss a diagnosis of mental illness that may have led to perceived chest pain. Determining the boundaries in which an expert system is competent is not always straightforward. However, every effort must be made to adequately cover the area for which the program claims competence.

11.2.2 Updating of Information

Expert systems in biomedicine must be continually updated as knowledge in the field changes and expands. This process is usually done in connection with domain experts to determine which new information is worthy of inclusion. Evaluation of literature is not always easy, for many studies produce conflicting results. The new field of evidence-based medicine (Sackett et al., 1997) has much to contribute to both the development and update of expert system knowledge bases.

In updating a knowledge base, the method of eliciting knowledge remains important. Consider the following example from Teiresias (Davis, 1982). Rather than asking the expert "What should I know about bacteremia?" it is much better to phrase the question in the following format:

> Here is a case history for which you claim the performance program incorrectly deduced the presence of pseudomonas. Here is how it reached its conclusions, and here are all the facts of the case. Now, what is it that you know that the performance program doesn't, which allows you to avoid making that mistake?

This type of questioned focusing is likely to elicit much more information.

The Teiresias system was designed to aid in the task of knowledge base development (Davis and Buchanan, 1977). The human expert communicates via Teiresias with the performance program, which in this case is MYCIN (Shortliffe, 1976). The expert must state advice in terms that the system understands and must evaluate the system's performance and assign credit or blame to individual rules. The system also provides a means for including strategic information for problem solving in terms of meta-rules, a subject discussed in Section 11.4.

11.3 LEARNED KNOWLEDGE

Because of the problems illustrated in the preceding sections, many researchers have sought alternatives to expert input. One common approach is learning through examples. In Part I of this book we have focused on learning in the context of neural networks and pattern classification. In Cohen and Feigenbaum (1982) the history of learning in artificial intelligence research is summarized. The learning techniques we have seen so far are one aspect of this research. In the following, we provide summaries of the other approaches. The three types of learning to be discussed, as outlined in Cohen and Feigenbaum (1982), are rote learning, learning by being told (advice-taking), and learning from examples (induction).

11.3.1 Rote Learning

Rote learning is simply storing information that has been told to the system. Early game-playing programs, such as Samuel's (1959) checkers program, are examples of rote learning. Traditional expert-supplied rules that comprise domain-specific knowledge bases are also a form of rote learning. Much of human learning is also of the rote fashion. It can be argued that a certain amount of rote learning must occur before higher levels of learning are possible. Rote learning systems require knowledge organization and searching strategies (a topic to be discussed in Chapter 12).

11.3.2 Learning by Being Told

How does advice-taking differ from rote learning? In a computer system, high-level information must be processed and represented in a suitable form. This process is called *operationalization*. The process involves such activities as deducing the consequences of actions, filling in details, and asking for more advice. EMYCIN (Davis and Buchanan, 1976), an offshoot of the MYCIN system (Shortliffe, 1976), was designed to help develop new knowledge bases. The system assisted a domain expert in carrying out the five steps summarized in Hayes–Roth, Klahr, and Mostow (1980): request, interpret, operationalize, integrate, and evaluate.

11.3.3 Learning from Examples

11.3.3.1   Pattern Classification and Neural Networks.   The supervised and unsupervised learning techniques discussed in Section 11.1 rely on learning from examples. For these algorithms, the examples are in numeric format. In artificial intelligence systems, the emphasis is usually on nonnumeric examples.

11.3.3.2   Learning Single Concepts.   One example given by Winston (1977) is the learning of the concept of an arch through use of semantic nets (discussed in Chapter 10). The program is presented with examples of arches as well as near misses. These are illustrated in Figure 11.4. The idea is for the computer to learn that an arch consists of two standing blocks that support a third block lying on its side. The first challenge is the knowledge representation. The method Winston chose is networks of linked con-

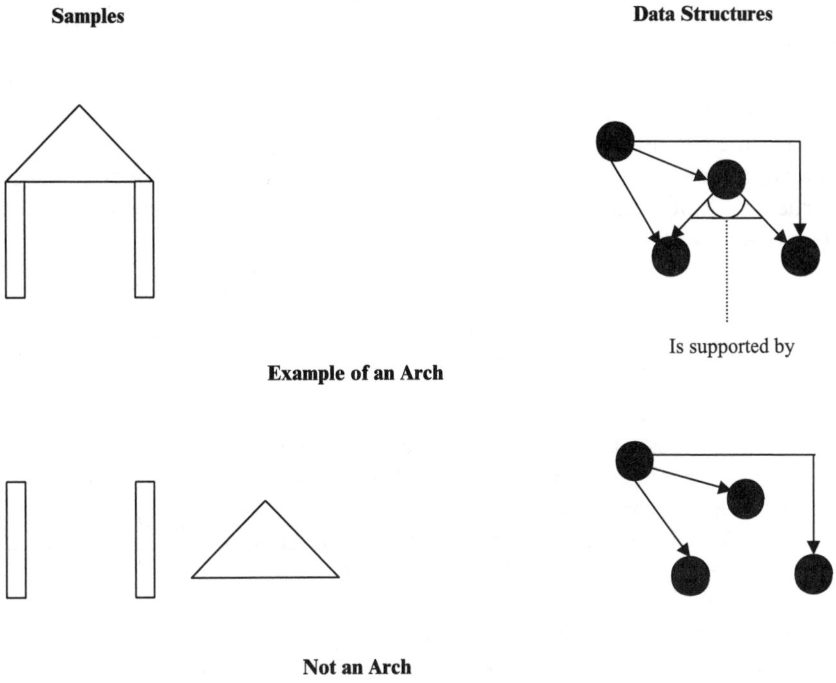

Samples   **Data Structures**

Example of an Arch

Is supported by

Not an Arch

Figure 11.4 Learning a Simple Concept.

cepts. The initial example is represented by the network adjacent to it in Figure 11.4. Winston's learning algorithm is the following:

> *Initialize:*
> *Concept description corresponds to the first positive example.*
> *Repeat until all examples have been examined:*
> *Convert the next example into a semantic network description.*
> *Match the current example with the concept description.*
> *Annotate the graph indicating nodes and links that do not match.*
> *Use the annotated skeleton to modify the concept description.*
> *If the current example is a:*
> *Positive instance, modify the concept description.*
> *Negative instance, add a necessary condition to the concept description.*

This example points out two important ideas in using nonnumeric data: proper representation and concept formation. In the next section, we will discuss concept formation in a more complex problem.

11.3.3.3 Learning Multiple Concepts. As mentioned in Chapter 9, DEN-DRAL (Buchanan, Sutherland, and Feigenbaum, 1969) was one of the first rule-based systems. Its focus was chemical synthesis. An outgrowth of this system, Meta-DEN-DRAL (Buchanan and Mitchell, 1978), discovers rules about the operation of a mass spectrometer, an instrument that produces a spectrum which is a histogram of the number of fragments (intensity) plotted against their mass-to-charge ratio. A sample

spectrogram is shown in Figure 11.5. The molecular structure of a compound can be determined through analysis of the spectrum. Heuristic DENDRAL was designed to accomplish this analysis automatically and produce a set of cleavage rules for each possible structure. The simulated spectra are compared to the actual spectrum to
determine the most likely structure of the unknown sample. Meta-DENDRAL is the
learning segment of Heuristic DENDRAL. Its role is to discover cleavage rules for a
structural family. In order to solve this problem, the following are given (Cohen and
Feigenbaum, 1982):

A representation language for describing molecular structure.

A training set of known molecules for a given structural family, comprising their
structures and mass spectra.

The objective is to find the cleavage rules.

The representation language corresponds to ball and stick molecular models, a
diagram of which is shown in Figure 11.6a. These models are represented by an undirected graph shown in Figure 11.6b in which nodes represent molecules and edges represent bonds. Hydrogen atoms are excluded. Each atom has four features:

1. Atom type
2. Number of nonhydrogen neighbors
3. Number of hydrogen atoms bonded to the atom
4. Number of double bonds

The bond environment makes up the left-hand portion of the rule. The action portion
of the rule specifies that the designated bond will cleave in the mass spectrometer. The
left-hand side is matched with the structure that is undergoing electron bombardment

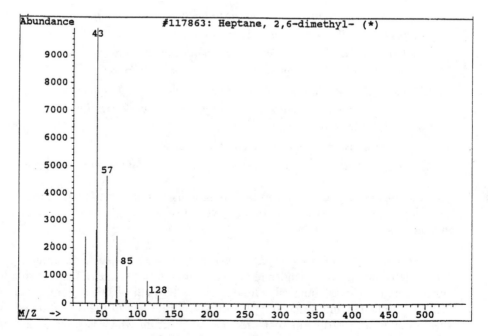

Figure 11.5 Sample Mass Spectrogram.

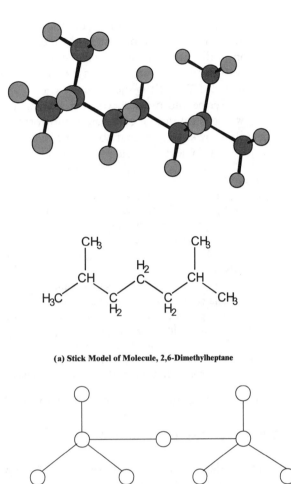

(a) Stick Model of Molecule, 2,6-Dimethylheptane

Figure 11.6 Molecular Knowledge Representation.

(b) Undirected Graph Representation

in the mass spectrometer. If the left-hand side is matched, the right-hand side indicates that the bond designated with an asterisk will break.

The training instances must be converted into specific points in the rule space. The program must hypothesize which bonds were broken in order to produce the given spectrum. In order to do this, it uses the half-order theory of mass spectrometry in which one fragmentation slices the molecule into two pieces, then one of these pieces is again split, and so forth. A number of specific rules are used in this process (Cohen and Feigenbaum, 1982). The process results in a simulated spectrum that is compared to the observed spectrum. If these match, a causal relationship is inferred. The search strategies of Meta-DENDRAL will be discussed in Chapter 12.

11.4 META-KNOWLEDGE

Meta-knowledge is a higher level knowledge than domain knowledge. It is the knowledge that the system has regarding the handling of the domain knowledge. Most expert systems utilize some form of meta-knowledge, which can be defined as knowledge about the objects or data representations. For example, a central theme of Teiresias is exploration of the use of meta-knowledge. In short, meta-knowledge is the representation in the program of knowledge about the program itself, including how much it knows and how it reasons. It uses the same knowledge representation format as the domain knowledge. Thus the domain knowledge contains object-level representations that describe the outside world with which the program deals, and the meta-level knowledge that describes the internal world of the program, which can be considered its self-knowledge. Comparison of these two types of knowledge can be seen in a meta-rule and an object level rule from MYCIN (Barr and Feigenbaum, 1982):

Meta-Rule 001
IF   1) The infection is a pelvic-abscess, and
          2) There are rules that mention in their premise Enterobacteriaceae, and
          3) There are rules that mention in their premise gram positive rods,
THEN There is suggestive evidence (0.4) that rules dealing with Enterobacteriaceae should be
          evoked before those dealing with gram positive rods.
MYCIN Rule 095
IF   The site of the culture is blood and
          The gram stain is positive and
          The portal of entry is gastrointestinal tract and
          [A-the abdomen is the locus of infection or
          B-the pelvis is the locus of infection]
Then   There is strongly suggestive evidence that
          Enterobacteriaceae is the class of organisms for which therapy should cover.

The rule-searching scheme for MYCIN is discussed in Chapter 12.

11.5 KNOWLEDGE BASE MAINTENANCE

Knowledge base maintenance is as important as the initial establishment of the knowledge base, especially in fields where knowledge is rapidly expanding. Some of the same issues that were discussed in knowledge base development apply here.

11.5.1 Assuring Accuracy

Unlike neural network and pattern classification algorithms that are based on data, knowledge-based systems are based on rules, frames, or other structures that represent expert input. Verifying the accuracy of knowledge bases, as opposed to databases, raises a different set of issues. These issues are addressed in detail in Chapter 13.

11.5.1.1 Permission to Change Knowledge Base.   The Teiresias system allows experts to review and modify the domain knowledge base. The ability to do so raises questions about who is allowed to perform modifications. In general, the expert system user is not permitted to alter the database even if he or she disagrees with it. Every time the knowledge base is changed, the process of evaluation must be repeated.

11.5.1.2 Verifying Sources of Information.   When using expert sources of input, much of the information relies on the expertise of the expert. Usually, expert systems are based on the opinions of multiple experts and hence are in a sense self-regulating. However, care must be taken in the selection of experts. In many fields, different subgroups exist who view the domain differently. If all experts are chosen from the same subgroup, then the knowledge-based system will incorporate the bias of the subgroup. Sometimes this is the intention of the system, but it is important for the user to be aware of potential limitations.

11.5.2 Maintaining Consistency

As new rules are added, maintaining consistency among the rules becomes a problem. When a new rule is added, its consistency must be checked with the entire knowledge base. For systems with hundreds of rules, this can become a formidable task.

Chapter 13 addresses these issues in more detail along with some practical methods for handling them.

11.6 SUMMARY

Knowledge acquisition in knowledge-based systems remains a challenge. It requires communication between the system developer and the domain expert, and it is often hindered by lack of common knowledge between the two. Other complications arise when two or more domain experts disagree. In addition to knowledge elicitation, other techniques for knowledge base development include the use of learning techniques. These may be used alone or in conjunction with expert input.

EXERCISES

1. Using the criteria map in Figure 11.1, derive two additional rules.
2. Assume that you wish to expand on the information shown in the criteria map. Devise three questions you would ask a domain expert that could lead to information to be included in the rule base.
3. What is the major difference between learning in knowledge-based systems and neural network learning? Is there any possibility for combining the two? Explain.
4. What do the arches learning problem and Meta-DENDRAL have in common?
5. Knowledge representation is a key component in knowledge-based systems. How does knowledge representation affect the reasoning process? How does the reasoning process affect knowledge representation?
6. Explain in your own words the meaning of meta-knowledge. Are alternatives available to using meta-knowledge in the reasoning process of knowledge-based systems? Is meta-knowledge completely separate from domain knowledge? Explain.

REFERENCES

Barr, A., and Feigenbaum, E.A. 1982. *The handbook of artificial intelligence,* Vol. 2. Los Altos, CA: William Kaufmann.

Buchanan, B., Sutherland, G., and Feigenbaum, E. 1969. Heuristic DENDRAL: A program for generating explanatory hypotheses in organic chemistry. In *Machine Intelligence* **4.** New York: American Elsevier.

Buchanan, B.G., and Mitchell, T.M. 1978. Model-directed learning of production rules. In D.A. Waterman and F. Hayes-Roth, eds., *Pattern-directed inference systems,* pp. 297–312. New York: Academic Press.

Cohen, P.R., and Feigenbaum, E.A. 1982. *The handbook of artificial intelligence.* Vol. 3. Los Altos, CA: William Kaufman.

Davis, R. 1982. *Knowledge-based systems in artifical intelligence.* New York: McGraw-Hill.

Davis, R., and Buchanan, B. 1977. Meta-level knowledge: Overview and applications. *IJCAI* **5:** 920–928.

Greenfield, S., Nadler, M., Morgan, M., and Shine, K. 1977. The clinical investigation and management of chest pain in an emergency department: Quality assessment by criteria mapping. *Medical Care* **83:** 761–770.

Hayes-Roth, R., Klahr, P., and Mostow, D. 1981. Advice-taking and knowledge refinement: An iterative view of skill acquisition. In J.R. Anderson, ed., *Cognitive Skills and Their Acquisition,* pp. 231–253. Hillsdale, NJ: Lawrence Erlbaum.

Hudson, D.L., and Estrin, T. 1984. Derivation of rule-based knowledge from established medical outlines. *Computers in Biology and Medicine* **14(1):** 3–13.

Hudson, D.L., and Cohen, M.E. 1988. An approach to management of uncertainty in a medical expert system. *International Journal of Intelligent Systems* **3(1):** 45–58.

Sackett, D.L., Richardson, W.S., Rosenberg, W., and Haynes, R.B. 1997. *Evidence-based medicine.* New York: Churchill Livingstone.

Samuel, A. 1959. Some studies in machine learning using the game of checkers. *IBM Journal of Research Development* **3(3):** 211–229.

Shortliffe, E. 1976. *Computer-based medical consultations—MYCIN.* New York: American Elsevier.

Winston, P.N. 1977. *Artificial intelligence.* Reading, MA: Addison-Wesley

12

Reasoning Methodologies

12.1 INTRODUCTION

This chapter provides an overview of the reasoning methodologies utilized in knowledge-based systems. The most straightforward of these methods is exhaustive search, one of the early techniques of artificial intelligence. Other methods include directed search, rule base searching, inference engines, and automated deduction. In the next section, representation methods are discussed, followed by outlines of different reasoning strategies.

12.2 PROBLEM REPRESENTATIONS

Searching was a major component of early research in artificial intelligence and remains an important technique in the implementation of systems that require the intelligent retrieval and analysis of information. There are a number of good textbooks outlining searching methodology, including Nilsson (1971), Barr and Feigenbaum (1981), and Davis (1982).

12.2.1 Graphs and Trees

The most general data structure in terms of searching algorithms is the graph.

Definition 12.1

A *directed graph* G is a set E of *edges*, a set V of *vertices* or *nodes*, and functions

$$\delta_0: E \to V \quad \text{and} \quad \delta_1: E \to V$$

that denote source and target, respectively. G is finite if both V and E are finite sets. The following notation is used:

$$n \xrightarrow{e} n' \quad \text{or} \quad e: n \to n'$$

where e is an edge that connects node n to n'. This connection can be represented by either of these forms. In addition, two functions can be defined, δ_0 and δ_1. These functions define the process of moving from n to n' and n' to n, respectively:

$$\delta_0 e = n$$
$$\delta_1 e = n'$$

EXAMPLE 12.1

$$V = \{a, b, c, d\} \; E = \{(a, b), (a, c), (b, d), (c, d)\}$$

The corresponding graph is

EXAMPLE 12.2

$$V = \{a, b, c, d\} \; E = \{1, 2, 3, 4, 5\} \text{ where}$$

	1	2	3	4	5
δ_0	a	a	a	b	c
δ_1	b	b	c	d	d

The corresponding graph is:

Definition 12.2

Let e, e' be edges. Then e' follows e iff $\delta_0 e' = \delta_1 e$. A *path* p in G is a list $e_1, \ldots, e_n$ of edges such that e_i follows e_{i-1}. The source of $p = e_1, \ldots, e_n$ is $\delta_0 e_1 = \delta_0 p$, and the target is $\delta_1 e_n = \delta_1 p$. The path from n to n' is represented by

$$n \xrightarrow{p} n'$$

Node n' is said to be reachable from n iff there is a path $n \to n'$. A *cycle* in G is a path with $\delta_0 p = \delta_1 p$. A graph is *acyclic* iff it has no cycles.

Definition 12.3

A *root* is a node r such that all nodes are reachable from r. A *rooted graph* is a graph with a root. A *tree* is a rooted graph with a root r such that for all nodes n there is exactly one path $r \to n$. A *forest* is a graph G with a set $\{r_1, \ldots, r_k\} \subseteq G$ such that for each node $n \; \varepsilon \; G$ there is exactly one r_i and one path $p_i: r_i \to n$ in G. The r_i's are *semiroots*. Any forest is a disjoint union of trees.

EXAMPLE 12.3

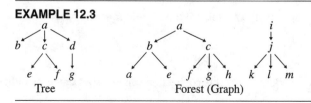

Tree   Forest (Graph)

Definition 12.4

The *unfoldment Ur(G)* is defined by

i. Its nodes are paths, $p{:}r \to n$ in G

ii. Its edges are pairs (p, p_e) such that p, p_e are nodes in $U_r(g)$; that is, p, p_e are paths from r in G, e is an edge in G. $\delta_0(p, p_e) = p$, $\delta_1(p, p_e) = p_e$.

EXAMPLE 12.4

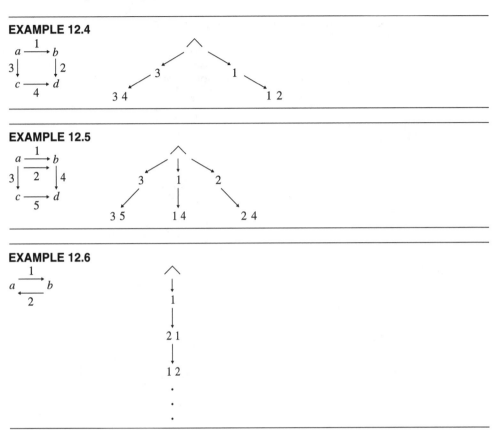

EXAMPLE 12.5

EXAMPLE 12.6

Note that this is an infinite graph!

12.2.2 Binary Trees

One of the most important searching structures is the binary tree.

Definition 12.5

A *binary tree B* is a set V of vertices or nodes, an element r called the root, and two functions σ_0 and σ_1, called the left and right successors, respectively, such that

i. $\sigma_i(\wedge) = \wedge$ for $i = 0,1, \ldots$, where $\wedge$ indicates a null node

ii. For each node $v \,\varepsilon\, V$, there is a unique list $\rho \,\varepsilon\, \{\sigma_0, \sigma_1\}$ of successors such that $p(r) = v$ where for $p = \sigma_i\sigma_j \ldots \sigma_k$ $i,j, \ldots, k\varepsilon \{0, 1\}$ we define $p(r) = \sigma_i(\sigma_j(\ldots \sigma_k(r)))$.

EXAMPLE 12.7

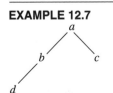

$$V = \{a, b, c, d\}$$
$$\sigma_0(a) = b \qquad\qquad \sigma_1(a) = c$$
$$\sigma_0(b) = d \qquad\qquad \sigma_1(b) = {}^\wedge$$

If the word "unique" is omitted from the definition, the result is a binary graph rather than a binary tree.

It is important to note that any finite ordered directed forest can be represented by a binary tree B by using the following:

$$\sigma_0(v) = \text{first offspring of } v, \text{ else } {}^\wedge.$$
$$\sigma_1(v) = \text{next sibling of } v, \text{ else } {}^\wedge$$

This is a one-to-one, onto mapping.

EXAMPLE 12.8

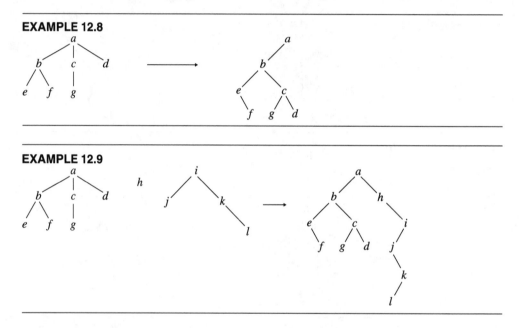

EXAMPLE 12.9

12.2.3 State-Space Representations

For many problems, it is useful to make definitions in terms of *states* and *operators* that transform one state to another. Almost any type of data structure can be used to represent states. A state space can be considered a directed graph in which the operators transform one state to another. The set of attainable states is called the state space, which may be very large or even infinite. Consider as an example the 8-puzzle in which the goal is to move tiles around to achieve the configuration (Nilsson, 1971):

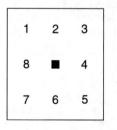

Possible operators for this problem are, UP, DOWN, LEFT, RIGHT, which refer to the direction in which the blank moves. Not all of these operators will be applicable to every state. For the initial state

only LEFT and DOWN are applicable. We will see a graph representation of this puzzle later in this chapter.

12.2.4 Problem Reduction Representations

The purpose of a problem reduction representation is to take a general problem and break it into subproblems. A problem representation is defined by the following:

1. An initial problem description
2. A set of operators that transform the initial problem into subproblems
3. A set of primitive problem descriptions

Reasoning proceeds backwards until the initial goal is reached.

A general method for problem representation is the AND/OR graph (Nilsson, 1971). The start node corresponds to the original problem. Each node represents either a single problem or a set of problems to be solved. A node that represents a primitive problem is a terminal node. An arc indicates an AND node. All others are OR nodes. As an example, consider the following integration problem that is broken into subproblems using integration by parts.

EXAMPLE 12.10: AND/OR Graph for $\int \{x \cos x + x^5)dx$

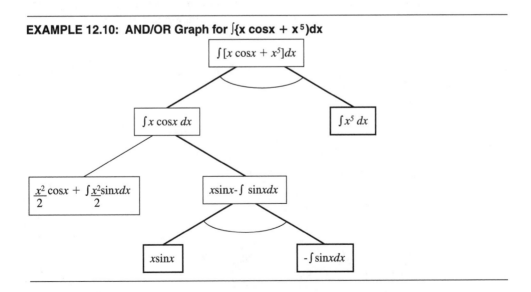

The boxes with the heavy border are terminal nodes. The dark arrows indicate the solution path. Methods for searching AND/OR graphs are discussed in Section 12.7.3.

12.2.5 Game Trees

Game trees are similar to state-space representations, with the important exception that moves (or operators) are performed by two opposing players. Terminal states represent win, lose, or draw. An AND/OR tree can be used to represent the game from one player's perspective in which his or her moves are represented by OR nodes and the opponent's moves by AND nodes.

12.3 BLIND SEARCHING

The first categories of searching algorithms that we examine are blind or exhaustive search techniques. The basic idea is to examine nodes in a graph or tree until a goal node is found. The process represents a search for specific information that is specified by the problem. The methods differ in the order in which the nodes are visited. For the following techniques, we will utilize the tree in Figure 12.1 for illustrative purposes.

12.3.1 Depth-First Search

The basic idea of the depth-first search is to find a path to a goal node by starting at the top node and proceeding down levels to the bottom. In depth-first algorithms, a depth bound is generally used, as some trees may have very large or infinite depth. This bound limits the possibility of pursuing a fruitless path for an extended period. Care must be taken, however, in establishing this bound, for premature truncation of search may result in loss of solutions. The algorithm is

1. *Put start node on OPEN list.*
2. *If OPEN is empty, exit with failure; otherwise continue.*
3. *Remove the first node* n *from OPEN and put it on a list called CLOSED.*
4. *If the depth of* n *equals the depth bound, go to 2; otherwise continue.*
5. *Expand node* n, *generating all successors of* n. *Put the successors (in arbitrary order) at the beginning of OPEN and provide pointers back to* n.

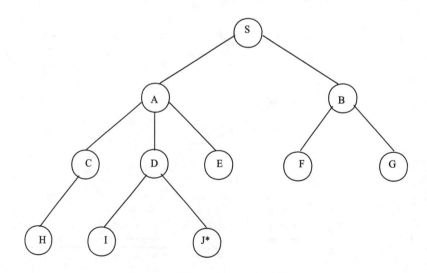

Figure 12.1 Example of a Search Tree.

6. *If any of the successors are goal nodes, exit with the solution obtained by tracing back through the pointers; otherwise go to 2.*

EXAMPLE 12.11

	OPEN	CLOSED
Iteration 1:	*S*	
Iteration 2:	*A, B*	*S*
Iteration 3:	*C, D, E, B*	*S, A*
Iteration 4:	*H, D, E, F, G, B*	*S, A, C*
Iteration 5:	*D, E, B*	*S, A, C, H*
Iteration 6:	*I, J, E, B*	*S, A, B, C, H, D*
Iteration 7:	*J, E*	*S, A, B, C, H, D, I*

J is the goal node, so the search is terminated.

12.3.2 Breadth-First Search

The breadth-first algorithm scans the width of the tree first rather than the depth:

1. *Put start node on OPEN*
2. *If OPEN is empty, exit with failure; otherwise continue.*
3. *Remove the first node* n *from open and put it on closed.*
4. *Expand node* n, *generating all its successors. If there are no successors, go to 2. Put all the successors at the end of OPEN, and provide pointers back to node* n.
5. *If any of the successors are goal nodes, exit with the solution obtained by tracing back through the pointers; otherwise go to 2.*

EXAMPLE 12.12

Using Figure 12.1, we find that the breadth-first method generates the following steps:

	OPEN	CLOSED
Iteration 1:	*S*	
Iteration 2:	*A, B*	*S*
Iteration 3:	*B, C, D, E*	*S, A*
Iteration 4:	*C, D, E, F, G*	*S, A, B*
Iteration 5:	*D, E, F, G, H*	*S, A, B, C*
Iteration 6:	*E, F, G, H, I, J*	*S, A, B, C, D*

At this point, the goal node *J* is on the list of successors, so the search terminates.

12.4 ORDERED SEARCH

The above methods relied only on the order of the nodes. The methods in this section use additional information to guide the search process.

12.4.1 Uniform Cost Method

A generalization of the breadth-first method is the uniform cost method that is guaranteed to find a minimal cost from the start node to a goal node. The breadth-first method relies on equal path length, while the uniform cost relies on equal path cost. We define $c(n_i, n_j)$ as the cost of going from node i to node j, and $g(n)$ as the minimal cost of going from S to n. The algorithm is:

1. *Put S on OPEN. Let* g(S) = 0.
2. *If OPEN is empty, exit with failure; otherwise continue.*
3. *Remove from OPEN the node* n *with the smallest* g *and put on CLOSED.*
4. *If* n *is a goal node, exit with solution; otherwise continue.*
5. *Expand* n, *generating all its successors. If no successors, go to 2. For each successor* n_i *compute*

$$g(n_i) = g(n) + c(n, n_i) \tag{12.1}$$

Put on OPEN with corresponding pointers.
6. *Go to 2.*

Note that if $c(n_k, n_j)$ is set equal to the path length, then this is the breadth-first algorithm. If all costs are positive and bounded, it can be shown that this algorithm will produce the optimal search strategy (Nilsson, 1971).

12.4.2 Using Heuristic Information

Frequently, the use of heuristic information can greatly reduce search effort at the expense of finding a minimal cost path. In heuristic search, the nodes are reordered at every step through the use of an evaluation function that indicates the promise of a node. Heuristic information is contained in a function f, where $f(n)$ is the value of this function at node n. If $g(n)$ in the uniform cost algorithm is replaced with $f(n)$, the result is the heuristic search algorithm. The difficult part is the definition of $f(n)$. An example that is often used for illustrative purposes is the 8-puzzle in which the objective is to place all tiles in order. The heuristic for this problem is

$$f(n) = g(n) + w(n) \tag{12.2}$$

where $g(n)$ is the path length and $w(n)$ is the number of misplaced tiles. The idea then is to expand the node for which $f(n)$ is a minimum. An example is shown in Figure 12.2 (Nilsson, 1971). Sample computations for each node are:

Level 0
  Node 1: $f(n) = 0 + 4 = 4$
Level 1
  Node 2: $f(n) = 1 + 5 = 6$
  Node 3: $f(n) = 1 + 3 = 4$
  Node 4: $f(n) = 1 + 4 = 5$ —————————→ Expand node 3
Level 2
  Node 5: $f(n) = 2 + 4 = 6$
  Node 6: $f(n) = 2 + 3 = 5$
  Node 7: $f(n) = 2 + 4 = 6$ —————————→ Expand node 6

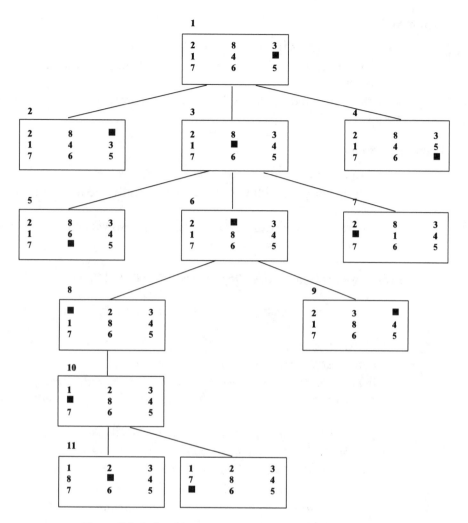

Figure 12.2 Ordered Search for Puzzle 8 (based on Nilsson, 1971).

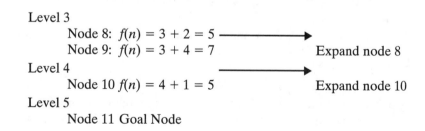

Level 3

    Node 8: $f(n) = 3 + 2 = 5$ ⟶

    Node 9: $f(n) = 3 + 4 = 7$ Expand node 8

Level 4

    Node 10 $f(n) = 4 + 1 = 5$ ⟶   Expand node 10

Level 5

    Node 11 Goal Node

12.5 AND/OR TREES

An AND/OR tree is used in general as a problem reduction tool as described earlier. A number of strategies are available for searching AND/OR trees. The objective of these methods is to find a solution by showing that the goal node (or start node) is solved. The tree will consist of solved nodes and unsolvable nodes, defined by the following:

Solved Nodes

1. The terminal nodes (primitive problems) are solved.
2. A nonterminal node with OR successors is solved if at least one of its successors is solved.
3. A nonterminal node with AND successors is solved if all of its successors are solved.

Unsolvable Nodes

1. Nonterminal nodes with no successors are unsolvable.
2. A nonterminal node with OR successors is unsolvable if all of its successors are unsolvable.
3. A nonterminal node with AND successors is unsolvable if at least one of its successors is unsolvable.

12.5.1 Breadth-First Search and Depth-First of AND/OR Tree

The following is the breadth-first searching algorithm for an AND/OR tree:

1. *Put S on OPEN*
2. *Remove first node* n *on OPEN, put it on closed.*
3. *Expand* n. *Put these successors at the end of OPEN, and provide pointers back to* n. *If there are no successors, label* n *unsolvable and continue; otherwise go to 8.*
4. *Apply the unsolvable-labeling procedure to the search tree.*
5. *If the start node is labeled unsolvable, exit with failure; otherwise continue.*
6. *Remove from OPEN any nodes having ancestors that are unsolvable.*
7. *Go to 2.*
8. *If any of the successors are terminal nodes, label them solved and continue; otherwise go to 2.*
9. *Apply the solve-labeling procedure to the search tree.*
10. *If the start node is labeled solved, exit with the solution tree; otherwise continue.*
11. *Remove from OPEN any nodes that are solved or that have ancestors that are solved.*
12. *Go to 2.*

The only differences in this algorithm for depth-first search is the modification of step three to put new nodes on the beginning of the OPEN list and checking the depth limit.

12.5.2 Costs of Solution Trees

For AND/OR trees one of two cost methods is generally used:

1. Sum of all arc costs in a tree.
2. Cost of the maximum path.

If unit costs are used, the sum method is the same as the number of nodes, and the maximum cost is the longest chain of steps. The cost of the optimal solution $g(n)$ is determined by the following where $c(n_i, n_j)$ is the cost of going from node i to node j and $g(n_i)$ is the minimum cost from the root to node n_i.

1. If n is a terminal node, $g(n) = 0$
2. If n is a nonterminal node having OR successors $n_1, \ldots, n_k$ $g(n) = \min_i [c(n, n_i) + g(n_i)]$
3. If n is a nonterminal node having AND successors, $n_1, \ldots, n_k$

$$g(n) = \sum_{i=1}^{k} [c(n, n_i) + g(n_i)] \qquad \text{(sum costs)} \quad \text{or}$$
$$\max_i [c(n, n_i) + g(n_i)] \qquad \text{(max costs)}$$

$g(n)$ is undefined for unsolvable nodes.

12.5.3 Ordered Searching of AND/OR Trees

Heuristic information, represented by $h(n)$, can be defined as we saw before for tree searching. The search process generates an AND/OR tree. At each stage, at the bottom of the tree there will be

1. Nodes that have been discovered to be terminal.
2. Nodes that have been discovered to be nonterminal but have no successors.
3. Nodes whose successors have not yet been generated.

All of these are called *tip nodes*.
If n is a tip node

1. If n is terminal, $h(n) = 0$.
2. If n is nonterminal and has no successors, $h(n)$ is undefined.
3. If n's successors have not yet been generated, then heuristic information must be used.

If n is a non-tip node, then the same procedure as outlined in steps 2 and 3 of the minimum cost algorithm applies.
The general ordered search algorithm for AND/OR trees is (Nilsson, 1971):

1. *Put S on OPEN and compute* h(s).
2. *Compute potential solution tree* τ_0 *using* h *values of nodes.*
3. *Select some tip node* n *that is on OPEN; put it on CLOSED.*
4. *If* n *is a terminal node, label it solved and continue; otherwise go to 9.*
5. *Apply solve-labeling procedure to* τ_0.
6. *If start node is solved, exit with* τ_0 *as solution tree.*
7. *Remove all nodes having ancestors that are solved.*
8. *Go to 2.*
9. *Generate all successors of* n. *If none, label* n *unsolvable and continue; otherwise go to 14.*
10. *Apply unsolvable labeling procedure to* τ_0. *If start node is unsolvable, exit with failure; otherwise continue.*

11. *Remove from OPEN any nodes having ancestors that are unsolvable.*
12. *Go to 2.*
13. *Put these successors on OPEN, and compute* h *values for successors. Recompute* h *for* n *and its ancestors.*
14. *Go to 2.*

12.6 SEARCHING GAME TREES

Game tree searching requires different searching techniques. Remember that in general game trees are represented as AND/OR trees from the point of view of one of the players. Two approaches will be discussed: minimax and alpha-beta.

12.6.1 Minimax

In the minimax procedure, an evaluation function is used. The evaluation function will be in favor of player A, so A will choose the maximum value of tip node evaluations, while player B will choose the minimum. The procedure works by computing backed-up values. As an example of an evaluation function, consider tic tac toe. An evaluation function may be (Nilsson, 1971):

$E(p)$ = (number of complete rows, columns, or diagonals that are still open for X) $-$
     (number of complete rows, columns, or diagonals that are still open for O).

If p is a win for A, then $E(p) = \infty$; if p is a win for B, then $E(p) = -\infty$. The strategy depends on the depth used for the backed-up values. In this procedure, the search tree is first generated and then evaluated.

12.6.2 Alpha-Beta

In the alpha-beta procedure, tip node evaluation and backed-up values are done simultaneously with tree generation, resulting in a much more efficient algorithm. It relies on the creation of a provisional backed-up value (PBV). The PBVs of AND nodes are called alpha values, and those of OR nodes are called beta values. The PBV of an AND node is set equal to the current largest of the final backed-up values of its successors. The PBV of an OR node is set equal to the smallest of the final backed-up values of its successors. Search is discontinued by one of the following rules:

1. Search can be discontinued below any OR node having a PBV≤ the PBV of any of its AND node ancestors. This OR node can then be assigned a final backed-up value equal to its PBV.
2. Search can be discontinued below an AND node having a PBV value ≥ the PBV of any of its OR node ancestors. This AND node can then be assigned a final backed-up value equal to its PBV.

When search is terminated by rule 1, an alpha cutoff has occurred, and, under rule 2, a beta cutoff. For more details on this procedure, see Nilsson (1971).

12.7 SEARCHING GRAPHS

The preceding algorithms were based on searching trees. There are some additional provisions if graphs are to be searched.

12.7.1 Breadth-First Graph Searching

The general algorithm applies to graphs, with the proviso that it is necessary to determine if a node is already on OPEN or CLOSED; if it is, do not put it on OPEN again.

12.7.2 Uniform Cost Algorithm

The uniform cost algorithm requires the following modifications:

1. If a newly generated successor is already on OPEN, do not add it again. However, its g value may now be smaller. Use the smallest g value. Direct pointers to the cheapest parent.
2. If a newly generated successor is already on CLOSED, the smallest g value has already been found.

12.7.3 AND/OR Graphs

For searching of AND/OR graphs, the following complications arise:

1. Breadth first
   Expand nodes with the least depth first
      Depth of start node is 0.
      Depth of any other node is 1 plus the depth of the shallowest parent.
2. Pointers can point to more than one parent.
3. It is necessary to check to see if successors are on CLOSED and previously labeled solved or unsolvable.

12.8 RULE BASE SEARCHING

In the first part of this chapter, we have discussed knowledge representation at a low level. What about higher-level knowledge such as production rules? As it turns out, the same methods apply. There are two basic strategies for rule searching, backward-chaining and forward-chaining, along with numerous variations on the two.

12.8.1 Backward-Chaining

If the purpose of a production system is to check out hypotheses, then backward-chaining is generally used. Backward-chaining can be used to establish only one particular hypothesis rapidly, or it can be used, as in MYCIN (Shortliffe, 1976), to check all hypotheses but in a manner that seems structured in that it tries to establish one hypothesis at a time. Searching the rule base generates the equivalent of an AND/OR tree. Because the information in MYCIN is uncertain, the AND/OR tree is also used to compute certainty factors. Figure 12.3 shows an AND/OR tree with certainty factor computations. The user supplies the F values as an indication of the degree of certainty of the facts. These are essentially equivalent to degrees of presence in the EMERGE system (Hudson and Cohen, 1988). The Cs are computed certainty factors, and the As are attenuation factors based on the reliability of the production rule itself. All of these generate values between 0 and 1. The computations are done according to the following:

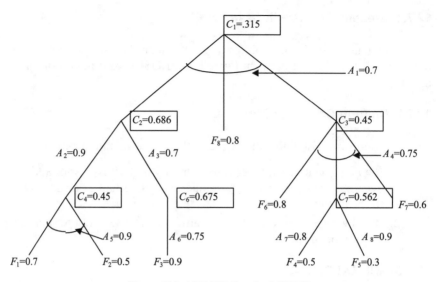

Figure 12.3 AND/OR Tree for MYCIN.

AND Nodes
>   The smallest certainty factor on the premise branches is multiplied by the attenuation factor of the production. The product is passed upward.

OR Nodes
>   The certainty factors of the branches reinforce each other according to the following:

$$C = C_1 + C_2 - C_1{}^*C_2$$

where each certainty factor is also multiplied by the attenuation factor. If the plausibility sinks below a prespecified level, the hypothesis is suppressed.

12.8.2 Forward-Chaining

Forward-chaining collects information that appears in antecedents of rules. When enough information is accumulated, one or more rules may be substantiated. As opposed to backward-chaining, which concentrates on confirming one hypothesis at a time, forward-chaining systems may appear to the user to be in random order, for the information collected may not be confined to one rule. Forward-chaining also uses the basic AND/OR tree structure.

12.9 HIGHER-LEVEL REASONING METHODOLOGIES

12.9.1 Inference Engines

Rule-based expert systems use inference engines to determine when a rule has been substantiated. The rule base searching techniques described earlier are used to accumulate information that the inference engine employs to make the determination of substantiation. There are a number of types of inference engines.

12.9.1.1 Binary Logic Engines.   The early expert systems such as DENDRAL (Buchanan and Feigenbaum, 1978) and MYCIN (Shortliffe, 1976) used binary logic engines in which rules were of the form:

```
IF      Antecedent 1
AND
        Antecedent 2
AND
        .
        .
        .
        Antecedent n
THEN Conclusion
```

A number of variations on this structure are possible while still maintaining a binary inference engine, including the use of disjunctions (ORs) and counts (a specified number in a list) as in the original implementation of the EMERGE system (Hudson and Estrin, 1984).

12.9.1.2 Approximate Reasoning Engines. Early expert systems used binary search engines in conjunction with a certainty factor to account for uncertain information, uncertain implications, and missing information. Later systems used more complex reasoning that incorporated these concepts into the inference engine itself. For example, consider the approximate reasoning implementation of the EMERGE system:

	Weighting Factor	Degree of Presence
Antecedent 1	w_1	d_1
Antecedent 2	w_2	d_2
.		
.		
.		
Antecedent n	w_n	d_n

Rule is substantiated if $D_s > T$

where w_i = Relative weight of antecedent i
d_i = Degree of presence of ith symptom
D_s = Degree of substantiation
T = Rule threshold

Thus a process of evidence aggregation must be used to determine D_s. This inference engine is discussed in detail in the case study presented in Chapter 18.

12.9.1.3 Fuzzy Logic Engines. A number of approaches to the development of inference engines have grown out of the application of fuzzy logic that replaces traditional binary logic. Some methods for implementing fuzzy logic engines along with applications are discussed in Chapter 16.

12.9.1.4 Probability-Based Engines. Traditional probability approaches such as Bayes' Rules can be used as the reasoning methodology in an inference engine. A number of extensions, such as Patrick's complex classes and the Dempster–Shafer theory of evidence can also be used. (Refer to Chapter 15 for details regarding these methods.)

12.9.2 Cognitive Models

Cognitive models use techniques from human reasoning to construct programs that can solve problems (Cohen and Feigenbaum, 1982). Early work in this area was done by Newell and Simon (1956). Their initial work on the logic theorist program (LT) resulted in a method for problem solving that did not appear to mimic the human process. LT worked backward from theorems to axioms. As a result, they rewrote the system. The result was the general problem solver (GPS) (Newell and Simon, 1963) which used means-ends analysis as a reasoning methodology. Other approaches included the use of beliefs to guide the reasoning of the system. One of the best known systems that used this approach was PARRY (Colby, 1975), a system that modeled a set of paranoid beliefs. These systems are outside the scope of this book; for those readers who are interested, some good references are Barr and Feigenbaum (1982), Jackson (1974), and Winston (1977).

12.9.3 Automatic Deduction

A large part of AI research has been devoted to automatic deduction. Much of this work is based on the resolution principle, which is a method for deducing conclusions from statements that have been formulated using predicate calculus. Representation strategies for predicate calculus were discussed in Chapter 10. Although this topic is also outside the scope of this text, an example is given here for those who are interesting in pursuing this topic.

The connectives that are used are $\wedge$ (AND), $\vee$ (OR), $\Rightarrow$ (implies), and $\sim$ (NOT). The idea is to devise a well-formed formula (wff) for which a predicate (T or F) can be established. Universal quantifiers ($\forall$) and existential quantifiers ($\exists$) are also used. Consider the statement: *All diabetics have elevated blood sugar*. This statement would be written as:

$$\forall x\ [diabetics(x) \Rightarrow blood\ sugar(x, elevated)] \qquad \text{(universal)}$$

while the statement *There is an uncontrolled diabetic* would be written as:

$$\exists x[(x, diabetic) \wedge (x, uncontrolled)] \qquad \text{(existential)}$$

There is a set of rules for converting statements into wff's whose truth-values can then be determined. These techniques are used in automated theorem proving as well as in the implementation of any binary logic reasoning procedure. For more details, see Nilsson (1971).

12.9.4 Natural Language Processing

Natural language processing is another broad topic in artificial intelligence research. It is useful in decision-support systems in the development of user interfaces. Most decision-support systems use a subset of a natural language, thus simplifying the problem. For example, MYCIN (Shortliffe, 1976) uses a subset of natural language processing in its question-answering routine. The DOCTOR system, which was the interpretive part of ELIZA (Weizenbaum, 1966) uses a more complex subset in asking questions. More complex natural language processing is seen in the STUDENT (Bobrow, 1968) program that does translation and in Quillian's work on language understanding (Quillian, 1968). For recent work on natural language interfaces, refer to Krulu (1991).

12.10 EXAMPLES IN BIOMEDICAL EXPERT SYSTEMS

One of the major areas of expert systems development has been that of biomedical applications (Barr and Feigenbaum, 1982). Many of these systems have been described in Chapter 9. Some of the major systems include DENDRAL (Buchanan, Sutherland, and Feigenbaum, 1969), MYCIN (Shortliffe, 1976), CASNET (Weiss et al., 1978), INTERNIST (Miller, Pople, and Myers, 1982), ONCOCIN (Shortliffe 1981), Taking the Present Illness (Pauker et al., 1976), Digitalis Therapy Advisor (Jelliffe, Buell, and Kalabe, 1972), and EMERGE (Hudson and Estrin, 1984). A survey of early systems is given in Andriole (1985). Several of these systems have been expanded to include tools for general rule base development such as EMYCIN and EXPERT (U.S. Department of Health, 1980). A number of biomedical expert systems with fuzzy logic components are discussed in Chapter 16.

12.11 SUMMARY

Artificial intelligence research covers a broad range of topics, some of which have been mentioned here briefly. This chapter focuses on the methods that are most relevant to developing decision-support systems for the biomedical sciences. For those readers who are interested in a more general view of artificial intelligence, there are a number of texts that cover a broad range of AI topics, such as problem solving, game playing, theorem proving, semantic interpretation, and perception (Jackson, 1974; Dean, Allen, and Aloimonos, 1995).

Although the methods described here have resulted in a number of useful and impressive decision-support systems, much work remains to be done. Some of the unsolved problems that remain include better representation of high-level knowledge, more adequate understanding of the human reasoning process, and better understanding of physiological concepts that could produce more systems that utilize deep or causal reasoning strategies.

EXERCISES

1. (a) Show the unfoldment of the graph:

(b) Give an example of an application for which the unfoldment would be useful.

2. (a) Convert the following binary tree to a directed ordered forest:

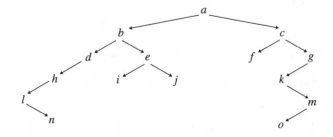

(b) Give an example of a problem that could be represented by a directed ordered forest.

3. Given the tree:

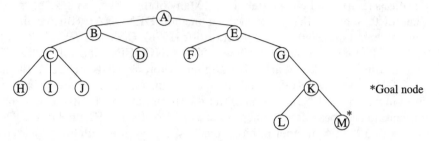

*Goal node

(a) List the order in which the nodes are evaluated in a depth-first search.
(b) Do the same for a breadth-first search.

4. For the tree

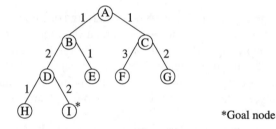

*Goal node

give the order of node evaluation for the uniform cost algorithm, with the cost indicated on each branch.

5. For the AND/OR tree, where □ indicates an AND node and ○ indicates an OR node,

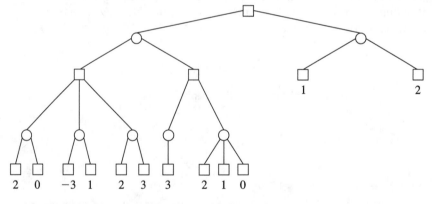

(a) Evaluate the start node using the minimax technique. Show the value of each node.
(b) Indicate which nodes would not have to be evaluated if alpha-beta was used instead.

6. Assume you have the following two rules in a knowledge base:

IF   BP < 100/60
        AND
        Skin cold and clammy
        AND
        Dizzy
THEN There is evidence that the patient has an MI.

IF ECG shows multiple PVCs
  AND
  BP < 100/60
  AND
  Abnormal mental state
THEN There is evidence the patient has an MI.

 (a) Construct an AND/OR tree corresponding to the searching of these rules.
 (b) Show the backward-chaining procedure for the AND/OR tree.
 (c) Show the forward-chaining procedure for the AND/OR tree.

7. What are the advantages of using a fuzzy or probabilistic inference engine in place of an inference engine based on Boolean (or binary) logic? What are the disadvantages?

REFERENCES

Andriole, S.J. 1985. *Applications in artificial intelligence.* Princeton, NJ: Petrocelli Books.

Barr, A., and Feigenbaum, E.A. 1981. *The handbook of artificial intelligence.* Vol. 1. Los Altos, CA: William Kaufmann.

Barr, A., and Feigenbaum, E.A. 1982. *The handbook of artificial intelligence.* Vol. 2. Los Altos, CA: William Kaufmann.

Bobrow, D.G. 1968. Natural language input for a computer-problem solving system. In M. Minsky, ed., *Semantic information processing.* Cambridge, MA: MIT Press. pp. 146–226.

Buchanan, B.G., and Feigenbaum, E.A. 1978. Dendral and Meta-Dendral: their applications dimension. *Artificial Intelligence* **11(1,2):** 5–24.

Buchanan, B., Sutherland, G., and Feigenbaum, E. 1969. Heuristic DENDRAL: A program for generating explanatory hypotheses in organic chemistry. In *Machine Intelligence* **4.** New York: American Elsevier.

Cohen, P.R., and Feigenbaum, E.A. 1982. *The handbook of artificial intelligence.* Vol. 3. Los Altos, CA: William Kaufmann.

Colby, K.M. 1975. *Artificial paranoia.* New York: Pergamon.

Davis, R. 1982. *Knowledge-based systems in artificial intelligence.* New York: McGraw-Hill.

Dean, T.L., Allen, J., and Aloimonos, Y. 1995. *Artificial intelligence, theory and practice.* Redwood City, CA: Benjamin/Cummings.

Hudson, D.L., and Cohen, M.E. 1988. An approach to management of uncertainty in a medical expert system. *International Journal of Intelligent Systems* **3(1):** 45–58.

Hudson, D.L., Deedwania, P.C., Cohen, M.E., and Watson, P.E. 1984. Prospective analysis of EMERGE, an expert system for chest pain analysis. *Computers in Cardiology.* IEEE Computer Society Press, pp. 19–24.

Hudson, D.L., and Estrin, T. 1984. EMERGE, a data-driven medical decision-making aid. *Transactions on Pattern Analysis and Machine Intelligence, IEEE,* **PAMI-6:** 87–91.

Jackson, P.C. 1974. *Introduction to artificial intelligence.* New York: Petrocelli Books.

Jelliffe, R., Buell, J., and Kalabe, R. 1972. Reduction of digitalis toxicity by computer-assisted glycoside dosage regimens. *Annals of Internal Medicine* **77:** 881–906.

Krulu, G.K. 1991. *Computer processing of natural language.* Englewood Cliffs, NJ: Prentice Hall.

Miller, R.A., Pople, H.E., and Myers, J.D. 1982. INTERNIST-I, An experimental computer-based diagnostic consultant for general internal medicine. *New England Journal of Medicine* **307:** 468–476.

Newell, A., and Simon, H.A. 1956. The logic theory machine, *IRE Transactions on Information Theory* **2:** 61–79.

Newell, A., and Simon, H.A. 1963. GPS, a program that simulates human thought. *CT:* 279–293.

Nilsson, N.J. 1971. *Problem-solving methods in artificial intelligence*. New York: McGraw-Hill.

Pauker, S.G., Gorry, G.A., Kassirer, J., and Schwartz, W. 1976. Towards the simulation of clinical cognition: Taking a present illness by computer. *American Journal of Medicine* **60:** 981–996.

Quillian, M.R. 1968. Semantic memory. In M. Minsky, ed., *Semantic information*. Cambridge, MA: MIT Press.

Shortliffe, E. 1976. *Computer-based medical consultations—MYCIN*. New York: American Elsevier.

Shortliffe, E.F., Scott, A.C., Bischoff, M.B., Campbell, A.B., Van Melle, W., and Jacobs, C.D. 1981. On COCIN: an expert system for oncology protocol management. *International Joint Conference on Artificial Intelligence* **7:** 876–881.

United States Department of Health. 1980. *Report on artificial intelligence in medicine.*

Weiss, S.M., Kulikowski, C., Amanel, S., and Safir, A. 1978. A model-based method for computer-aided medical decision making. *Artificial Intelligence* **11:** 145–172.

Weizenbaum, J. 1966. A computer program for the study of natural language communication between man and machine. *Comm. ACM* **9(1):** 36–45.

Winston, P.H. 1977. *Artificial intelligence*. Reading, MA: Addison-Wesley.

Validation and Evaluation

13.1 INTRODUCTION

In Chapter 8, we discussed validation and evaluation of decision-support systems based on neural network algorithms. Although some of the issues are the same for knowledge-based systems, there are some inherent differences. The algorithm must be validated separately, but this process is not as straightforward as is the case for neural network algorithms. The knowledge base itself, as it is usually expert-derived, poses totally different problems for validation than the neural network approach that relies on database information. Standard techniques can be employed to verify the soundness of algorithms (Yourdan, 1975). These approaches are discussed in this chapter.

13.2 ALGORITHMIC EVALUATION

As in neural network models, the inference engine and knowledge base are considered to be separate entities. In practice this is not always the case. Most systems become more efficient when they are designed for a specific application. One method for achieving this end in knowledge-based systems is to allow the inference engine to remain independent and to incorporate knowledge to optimize the process for a particular application through the use of meta rules. Often, however, some changes are made either in searching strategies or in the inference engine that makes it domain-dependent.

13.2.1 Searching Algorithm

Some strategy must be developed for searching the rules, frames, or other knowledge representation structure.

13.2.1.1 AND/OR Trees. Evaluation of AND/OR tree searching algorithms is fairly straightforward. A number of aspects must be evaluated:

1. Searching
   (a) Proper branching under all possible conditions.
   (b) Proper handling of termination conditions either through the arrival at a terminal node, termination at a specified level, or pruning.
   (c) Return of proper Boolean value under all circumstances.
2. Conversion of rules to the AND/OR structure

For rule-based systems, the rules must be represented in a knowledge structure that can be utilized by the AND/OR tree searching. As the knowledge base will change, this conversion should be automated.

13.2.1.2   Control by Meta Rules.   As we saw in Chapter 11, meta rules are used to supply information to the system regarding the organization of knowledge. The algorithm must recognize the meta rules and implement the strategies they suggest. In general, the algorithm for accomplishing this must be reevaluated for each set of meta rules because the action portions will change and will themselves affect the flow of control of the system.

13.2.1.3   Data-Driven Search.   Systems that use data-driven search provide additional problems for evaluation. In a data-driven search, the information entered by the user determines the starting point of the rule search. For example, in the data-driven version of the EMERGE system, the user may enter any pertinent information that is available, such as:

Syncope
Low blood pressure
Dizziness

An attempt is made to find these data in the antecedent portion of the rule. If a match is found, the search begins at that point. If the initial rule is not substantiated, an order of search for the remainder of the rules must then be determined. This may be done through the use of meta rules or through some other structure built into the system. As with the testing of meta rules, testing of data-driven approaches must be done in general in conjunction with the specific application.

13.2.1.4   Hierarchical Search.   Hierarchical search algorithms are among the easiest to test. However, most knowledge-based systems use some additional form of searching in addition to hierarchical searching, although hierarchical searching may be done at a meta level to organize subsets of information.

13.2.2 Inference Engine

As we have seen in earlier chapters, there are a number of types of inference engines, including those based on binary logic, fuzzy logic, probabilistic reasoning, and other techniques of approximate reasoning. Some of these methods pose serious problems in the evaluation phase.

13.2.2.1   Binary Engines.   Binary engines usually correspond to AND/OR searching. The objective of the binary engine is to attempt to substantiate a rule. For these engines, the implementation is straightforward: the function of each binary operator must be verified. These generally include conjunction, disjunction, and verification of a fixed number in a list.

13.2.2.2 Complex Engines. As we will see in the following chapters, there are a number of complex variations of inference engines based on probability theory, fuzzy logic, approximate reasoning, or some combination. Checking the accuracy of these engines can be more complex, but as they are all algorithmic their accuracy is verifiable. The major difficulty in verifying complex engines arises in conjunction with knowledge content, a subject to be addressed in the next section.

13.2.3 Aggregation of Evidence

In many knowledge-based systems, evidence is aggregated through substantiation of a series of rules. Many methods can be used to accomplish the aggregation of evidence, including the Dempster–Shafer Theory of Evidence (discussed in Chapter 15) and fuzzy logic techniques for evidence aggregation (discussed in Chapter 16). Testing the algorithm for evidence aggregation is straightforward for well-defined theoretical approaches. Whether or not the outcome of this process makes clinical sense must be verified in conjunction with the knowledge base.

13.2.4 Use of Meta Knowledge

The use of meta knowledge that is usually represented in the form of rules is inherently nonalgorithmic. The appropriateness of the use of meta knowledge must be evaluated in the combined system.

13.3 KNOWLEDGE BASE EVALUATION

Evaluation of the knowledge base itself has nothing to do with the type of algorithm used. The purpose of this phase of evaluation is to certify that the knowledge base represents sound clinical judgment. In Section 13.4, we will discuss the interface between the knowledge base and the algorithm.

13.3.1 Expert-Derived Information

Once the knowledge base has been constructed, its final form should be verified with the original expert or experts from whom the information was obtained. If possible, it should also be verified with another recognized expert in the field to ascertain its appropriateness. None of these actions, however, will assure completeness and consistency of the knowledge base. Another possible approach is to try to verify the rules through use of a learning algorithm that operates on a database of relevant information. This approach is fraught with practical difficulties. First, it is very difficult to find one database, or even a collection of databases, that will correspond to the information contained in the knowledge base. Second, use of a learning algorithm in conjunction with an adequate database will probably not produce knowledge in the same format contained in the knowledge base. This approach may, however, have some utility in verifying the breadth of the knowledge base and may in some cases expose some contradictory aspects.

13.3.1.1   Individual Units of Knowledge.   Individual units of knowledge, usually rules, must be verified for accuracy. This part is fairly straightforward. The difficulty of confirming units of knowledge depends to some extent on the knowledge representation. If the knowledge is represented by binary rules, it is only necessary to verify that the antecedents are correctly stated and that the combination of the antecedents through use of the specified binary operator leads to the stated action or conclusion. If the implication carries a certainty factor, then some means of evaluating the appropriateness of the value of the certainty factor must be established. If, however, approximate reasoning techniques are used, this process may become much more complex. For example, each antecedent may carry with it a relative degree of importance. The suitability of this relative degree must be verified. Very often different experts will disagree on the numerical values for the relative degree of importance. In addition, the rule itself is substantiated if it exceeds a specified threshold. This suitability of the value for the threshold must be established in the same manner as the relative degree of importance of each antecedent.

13.3.1.2   Combination of Knowledge.   We mentioned briefly in Section 13.1.3 the verification of knowledge aggregation. In order to succeed in knowledge aggregation and in general consistency of the system, the knowledge base must adhere to the following:

1. No contradictory rules
2. No rules that result in the same information contributing to a different degree
3. Sufficient rules to cover the domain

Points 1 and 2 are relatively easy to verify; point 3 at best can only be approximated.

13.3.2 Learned Information

As we saw in Chapter 11, some knowledge-based systems derive their knowledge from learned information. If some form of learning is used, then the database or examples from which this information came must be verified. In general, the points outlined in Chapter 8 for validation and evaluation of systems dependent on learning algorithms apply here.

13.3.3 Meta Knowledge

If meta knowledge is used to control flow of information, the usefulness of this information must be addressed. Usually meta knowledge is still domain-specific as this information is intended to optimize flow for the domain under consideration. This knowledge is usually subjective and is often evaluated in a trial-and-error format.

13.4 SYSTEM EVALUATION

The true test of an expert system is to evaluate the algorithmic base in conjunction with the domain knowledge. Obviously, this portion of the evaluation must be performed with each knowledge base and, ideally, repeated if the knowledge base is modified. A number of articles have addressed knowledge base verification, usually in conjunction with a specific clinical support system (Einbinder, Remz, and Cochran, 1996; Karlsson et al., 1997; Nathwani et al., 1997; Vadher, Patterson, and Leaning, 1997).

13.4.1 Evaluation with Original Knowledge Base

An extensive evaluation should be done that is geared to utilizing all rules in the knowledge base. Appropriate case studies must be designed to accomplish this task. Several questions must be answered in this phase:

Does the system produce the expected output?
Does the system produce consistent output?
Do the results make sense for the domain?

As an example of the third question, if it is a clinical decision-support system, do the results make clinical sense? To answer this question properly, the domain expert must review the results.

13.4.2 Evaluation with Updated Knowledge Base

In many knowledge-based systems, the substantiation of one rule may do one or more of the following:

Alter the order of invocation of additional rules.
Influence the substantiation of other rules.
Contribute to aggregation of evidence.

If one or more of these actions occur, then changing one rule can change the functioning of the entire system. Because of this sensitivity, care must be taken to restrict the alteration of the rule base to true experts. If substantial changes are made, the entire combined system should be reevaluated.

13.4.3 Evaluation of User Interaction Parameters

One of the strong points of knowledge-based systems compared to decision-support systems based on numerical computation is their enhanced ability to communicate with users in a more "human-like" fashion, both in terms of collecting information and providing not only decisions but also explanations of these decisions.

13.4.3.1 Interpretation of Input. Many knowledge-based systems allow input in natural language and provide such features as partial matching of input and interpretation of synonyms. Care must be taken, especially with partial matching, to ensure that inappropriate matches do not occur. For example, consider the partial matching capabilities of the EMERGE system. Both words and phrases are matched to a threshold level that can be adjusted. Thus, if the word match threshold is 0.75, the following scenario could occur.

User input: Normal mental status
Antecedent: Abnormal mental status

Word 1 matches six out of eight letters for a 75 percent match, while words 2 and 3 match exactly. This antecedent would then be substantiated. This situation is avoided in the EMERGE system by only attempting matches on words that differ in length by no more than 1, and not allowing the threshold to go below 80 percent. However, in practice, unanticipated problems such as these often arise.

13.4.3.2 Explanation Capabilities. Explanation capabilities usually rely on regurgitating the substantiated rules. The usefulness of the explanation depends on the clarity of expression in the rules and in the order in which they were substantiated. For example, if fifteen rules were substantiated, perhaps only eight of them would be related to the final decision results. Depending on the order, rules that had no bearing on the final outcome might be interspersed with relevant rules. The order of the rules will depend on the searching strategy—that is, backward- versus forward-chaining searches, as well as on the meta knowledge.

13.4.4 Validation with Clinical Data

Consider that we are developing a clinical decision-support system for a specific problem domain. The ultimate test is to evaluate it with clinical data, either retrospectively or prospectively. In this section, we examine some practical problems that may arise in this evaluation process.

13.4.4.1 Sources of Clinical Data. The first step in this process is to identify sources of clinical data that can be used for the evaluation. The first question to resolve is whether the data set will be retrospective or prospective. There are advantages and disadvantages for both approaches. These factors must be considered in terms of the problem itself.

13.4.4.1.1 RETROSPECTIVE STUDIES

Advantages
1. The data set is available and can be used immediately.
2. There is a possibility of obtaining followup data.

Disadvantages
1. The study is limited by the data that were collected.
2. The problem of missing information is certain to arise.

13.4.4.1.2 PROSPECTIVE STUDIES

Advantages
1. A comprehensive set of data items can be collected.
2. Missing values can be reduced.

Disadvantages
1. The time frame for collection may be lengthy.
2. Cooperation from clinical staff must be assured.

13.4.4.2 Selection of Cases. The selection of cases is crucial. The number and type must be selected to fully evaluate the system. Cases must be selected to cover the following:

1. All possible diagnoses or outcomes.

2. The use of all rules at least once.

3. The use of combinations of rules.

13.4.4.3 Actual Outcome.   One important parameter is the actual outcome for the case. The medical record will contain the diagnosis, treatment, or outcome as interpreted by the physician or other medical professional. This may not be the actual diagnosis or the correct treatment. Thus the comparison is between the recommendation of the system and what was actually done, not what should have been done. Some of these problems can be alleviated by using followup information to see if the actual diagnosis or treatment was borne out by subsequent information.

13.4.4.4 Results from Clinical Decision-Support System.   In general, the form of the clinical decision-support results is dependent on the objective. This decision must be matched with the actual outcome as described earlier. It is often useful to divide the analysis into categories to emphasize the performance of the system under different circumstances.

EXAMPLE: EMERGE Evaluation

The objective of the EMERGE system is to determine if patients presenting to the emergency room with chest pain should be admitted as inpatients. The EMERGE system was evaluated using both retrospective and prospective data. Data were used from three hospitals: a public county hospital, a private hospital, and a Veterans Affairs hospital. The data were mixed so that the patients were not identified with a particular hospital. In the retrospective study, charts were obtained from the files of each emergency room for a specified three-year time period. These cases were identified as having presented with chest pain. Admission decisions made by EMERGE were compared with admission decisions as indicated on the charts. Followup records were used to ascertain the appropriateness of the actual hospital decision.

Table 13.1 indicates three categories of patients: (a) those who were subsequently found to have a problem warranting admission, (b) those with no discernible problem warranting ad-

TABLE 13.1   EMERGE Evaluation

	Admit	Discharge
(a) Patients with Serious Illness		
EMERGE Recommendation	112	4*
Actual Hospital Decision	114	2

	Admit	Discharge
(b) Patients with No Serious Illness		
EMERGE Recommendation	0	93
Actual Hospital Decision	11	82

	Admit	Discharge
(c) Borderline Cases		
EMERGE Recommendation	20	15
Actual Hospital Decision	29	6

*Admitted for reasons other than chest pain

mission, and (c) borderline cases (Hudson and Cohen, 1984). These results illustrate a number of points that should be considered in evaluating systems. Referring to part (a), although four patients were admitted to the hospital for whom EMERGE did not recommend admission, it was found that these patients were admitted for psychiatric reasons, not for cardiac reasons. Hence it is important to consider the scope of the expert system in both the evaluation and use of the expert system. In part (a), it was also found that the hospital did not admit two patients for whom EMERGE recommended admittance. Subsequent records showed that these patients returned within a 24-hour period with confirmed diagnoses of myocardial infarction. In part (b), the hospitals actually admitted eleven patients unnecessarily for whom EMERGE did not recommend admittance. Thus important resources were used that could have been better directed to the seriously ill. Part (c) demonstrates a different point. These patients were borderline cases for whom the actual correct decision could not be ascertained. None of these patients was subsequently found to have any serious illness. EMERGE admitted many fewer of these patients than the hospitals, thus demonstrating that use of the system could result in considerable cost benefits to the hospital, an outcome that was not the intent of the original system. Because of the sizable number of borderline cases, EMERGE was subsequently revised to use approximate reasoning techniques that have been shown to have the most impact in borderline cases (Hudson and Cohen, 1988).

Grouping patients into these three categories for evaluation was important for a number of reasons as illustrated by the following example. Assume all patients were instead put into a chart indicating whether the correct decision was made. The result is the following table:

	Admit	Discharge
EMERGE Recommendation	132	112
Actual Hospital Decision	154	90

In this format it is not possible to draw implications regarding the risk that is incurred by the decision. For example, the risk of life is great if a seriously ill patient is discharged, but there is little risk if a well person is admitted. On the other hand, admittance of a well person is a costly decision in economic terms, whereas the discharge of an ill person is not.

13.5 SUMMARY

Validation of a knowledge-based system should guarantee the following to the highest degree possible:

1. The algorithm is accurate.
2. The knowledge base is:
   Accurate.
   Consistent.
   Complete within its scope.
   Up-to-date.
3. The combined system produces credible results.

Evaluation of a knowledge-based system should provide information regarding:

1. The scope of the system.
2. The accuracy of the system.
3. The analysis of risk and/or cost incurred by the use of the system.

EXERCISES

1. (a) Write an algorithm to compute a truth table for two binary variables A and B and the logical constructs AND, OR, Exclusive OR, and NOT.

(b) Make up a data set that will completely test your algorithm.

2. Name three methods that could be used to evaluate an expert-supplied knowledge base. Which do you think would be the best approach of the three? Why?

3. Give two examples of meta rules that might be used in a decision-support system for diagnosis of pneumonia. How do these rules differ from domain knowledge rules? How could you evaluate the effectiveness of these meta rules?

4. Because of the rapid increase in medical knowledge, how often do you feel that a knowledge base for a clinical support system should be updated? Can you think of ways in which the medical literature can be effectively used to help in the updating process?

REFERENCES

Einbinder, L.H., Remz, J.B., and Cochran, D. 1996. Mapping clinical scenarios to functional requirements: A tool for evaluating clinical information systems. *AMIA Fall Symposium:* 747–751.

Hudson, D.L., and Cohen, M.E. 1988. An approach to management of uncertainty in an expert system. *International Journal of Intelligent Systems* **3(1):** 45–58.

Hudson, D.L., Deedwania, P.C., Cohen, M.E., and Watson, P.E. 1984. Prospective analysis of EMERGE, an expert system for chest pain analysis. *Computers in Cardiology:* 19–24.

Karlsson, D., Ekdahl, C., Wigertz, O., and Forsum, U. 1997. A qualitative study of clinicians ways of using a decision support system. *AMIA Fall Symposium:* 268–272.

Nathwani, B.N., Clarke, K., Lincoln, T., Berard, C., Taylor, C., Ng, K.C., Patil, R., Pike, M.C., and Azen, S.P. 1997. Evaluation of an expert system on lymph node pathology. *Human Pathology* **28:** 1097–1110.

Vadher, B., Patterson, D.L., and Leaning, M. 1997. Evaluation of a decision support system for initiation and control of oral anticoagulation in a randomised trial. *British Medical Journal* **314(7089):** 1252–1256.

Yourdan, E. 1975. *Techniques of Program Structure and Design.* Englewood Cliffs, NJ: Prentice-Hall.

PART III
ALTERNATIVE APPROACHES

14

Genetic Algorithms

14.1 FOUNDATIONS

As the name implies, *genetic algorithms (GAs)* are based on the biological concept of genetic combination to produce *offspring*. The general idea is that through survival-of-the-fittest, the natural selection process will retain those individuals whose genetic characteristics best suit them to the environment in which they must exist. The terminology used is derived from genetics. An *individual* (also called a *genotype* or *structure*) is one member of the group to be considered. Individuals may also be referred to as *strings* or *chromosomes*. Of course, in biological systems, every organism is made up of a number of chromosomes. For the purposes of this discussion all individuals are assumed to have only one chromosome. *Diploidy* dominance, which deals with pairs of chromosomes, is sometimes used to generate characteristics for future generations of individuals. Chromosomes are made up of units called *genes,* which are equivalent to features that were discussed earlier in pattern recognition applications. Genes for specific characteristics are located at specific *loci* or *string positions*. Each gene may be in one of several states, called *alleles,* which are equivalent to feature values.

Each genotype in a genetic algorithm sense represents a potential solution to a problem. An evolutionary process is analogous to searching a space for possible solutions. Genetic algorithms attempt to strike a balance between optimal and exhaustive search.

A genetic algorithm must have five components (Michalewicz, 1992):

A genetic representation of potential solutions.

An initial population of potential solutions.

An evaluation function that determines fitness for the environment.

Genetic operators that alter the composition of offspring.

Values for parameters used by the GA.

14.2 REPRESENTATION SCHEMES

In many genetic algorithms, only binary genes are used. Thus a binary vector of length n represents a chromosome with n genes. Consider the binary vector of length 8:

$$(1\ 0\ 1\ 0\ 0\ 1\ 0\ 1) \tag{14.1}$$

If this vector is meant to represent a decimal number, it is easily converted by

$$\sum_{k=0}^{n-1} a_k\, 2^k \tag{14.2}$$

where a_n is the nth value from the right, $n = 0, 1, \ldots, n - 1$. The value of this vector is thus 165. However, the binary vector could also represent values of eight features, for example, the presence or absence of each of eight symptoms. Although the original approach to genetic algorithms used only binary representations, the method can be easily extended to include vectors made up of real numbers.

14.3 EVALUATION FUNCTIONS

Once a problem is described in terms of vector notation, each vector is evaluated in terms of its suitability as a solution to the problem. The idea is based on the principle of natural selection in nature that postulates that those individuals who are most suited to the environment will survive and produce offspring—a principle often referred to as *Darwinian fitness*. Evaluation functions take a number of forms. Some examples include conversion of the binary representation into a decimal quantity that is compared to the other individuals in the population, with either the highest value or lowest value selected as most suitable. Other evaluation functions may be based on distance measures such as the Hamming distance.

14.4 GENETIC OPERATORS

Individuals are combined using basic genetic principles such as *mutation* and *crossover*.

14.4.1 Mutation

A mutation occurs within a chromosome, usually in just one location. For example, the individual

$$(1\ 0\ 1\ 0\ 1\ 1\ 0\ 1) \tag{14.3}$$

is a one-bit mutation in location 5 of the individual in (14.1).

14.4.2 Crossover

Crossover takes place between two individuals to produce offspring. For example, for the two individuals:

$$(1\ 1\ 1\ 0\ 0\ 0\ 0\ 0) \tag{14.4}$$

$$(0\ 1\ 0\ 1\ 1\ 1\ 1\ 1) \tag{14.5}$$

a crossover of locations 3–6 results in the offspring:

$$(0\,1\,0\,0\,0\,0\,1\,1). \tag{14.6}$$

Crossover is a *recombination technique*.

14.5 EVOLUTION STRATEGIES

In the following strategies, the common goal is to search a set of binary strings **b** of length n. The objective is to maximize an evaluation function f. For purposes of demonstration, we will define the evaluation function

$$f(\mathbf{b}_i) = d(\mathbf{b}_i, \mathbf{b}_g) = \sum_{j=1}^{n} \delta(j) \tag{14.7}$$

where $\delta(j) = \begin{bmatrix} 1 & \text{if } \mathbf{b}_{ij} = \mathbf{b}_{gj} \\ 0 & \text{if } \mathbf{b}_{ij} \neq \mathbf{b}_{gj} \end{bmatrix}$

where d is the Hamming distance between a string $\mathbf{b}_i$ in the set and the goal vector $\mathbf{b}_g$. The function has a global maximum n when $\mathbf{b}_i = \mathbf{b}_g$ and a global minimum 0 when $\mathbf{b}_i = [\mathbf{b}_g]^C$.

14.5.1 Genetic Algorithms

The general concept of a genetic algorithm can be described by the following (Adeli and Hung, 1995):

Genetic Algorithm
Encode the decision variables as a chromosome.
Initialize an initial set of chromosomes as the first generation.
Repeat until the stopping criterion is met:
   Evaluate the objective function values for the current population.
   Select some chromosomes with higher fitness values to reproduce children for the next generation.
   Apply crossover and mutation to the parent chromosomes selected in the previous step.
   Replace the entire population with the next generation.

14.5.2 Optimization Strategies

Optimization techniques, as we saw in earlier chapters, are geared to maximizing or minimizing criteria functions. Two optimization approaches are briefly outlined here.

14.5.2.1 Hill Climbing. There are a number of approaches to hill climbing. Here we consider steepest ascent hill climbing. An algorithm for an iterative procedure for hill climbing follows (see Michalewicz, 1992):

Hill-Climbing Algorithm
Initialize
   i = 0

Repeat until i > *number of iterations.*
Randomly select a string $\mathbf{b}_j$.
Evaluate $\mathbf{b}_j$.
Repeat if $f(\mathbf{b}_j) < f(\mathbf{b}_k)$.
Create n *new strings by mutation of subsequent bits in* $\mathbf{b}_j$.
Select $\mathbf{b}_k$ *with the largest evaluation function.*
If $f(\mathbf{b}_j) < f(\mathbf{b}_k)$, *then replace* $\mathbf{b}_j$ *with* $\mathbf{b}_k$.
i = i + 1

14.5.2.2 Simulated Annealing.

Another approach is simulated annealing, which is a stochastic process derived from statistical mechanics whose goal is to find near globally minimum cost solutions to large optimization problems (Davis, 1987). It was first applied to very large scale integration (VLSI) design. Statistical mechanics studies the behavior of large numbers of interacting components such as atoms in thermal equilibrium. The probability that the system is in a certain state is given by the Boltzmann distribution:

$$\pi_T(s) = \exp[(-E(s)/kT)]/\left[\sum_{w\varepsilon S} \exp[(-E(w)/kT)\right] \qquad (14.8)$$

where k is the Boltzmann constant and S is the set of all possible configurations. In annealing processes, the nature of low-energy states is investigated. To achieve a low-energy state, an annealing process must be used in which the temperature of the system is first elevated and then gradually lowered in stages to achieve thermal equilibrium at each stage. To apply this process to optimization, the energy function is changed to the objective function, the particle configuration becomes the configuration of parameter values, and the temperature becomes the control parameter for the process. The simulated annealing algorithm for optimization follows.

Simulated Annealing Algorithm
Initialize
i = 0
Select $\mathbf{b}_j$ *at random.*
T = 0
Evaluate $\mathbf{b}_j$.
Repeat until stop criterion.
Repeat until termination condition.
Select a new string $\mathbf{b}_k$ *by mutating a single bit of* $\mathbf{b}_j$.
If $f(\mathbf{b}_j) < f(\mathbf{b}_k)$, *then replace* $\mathbf{b}_j$ *with* $\mathbf{b}_k$.
Else if random[0, 1] < exp {(f($\mathbf{b}_j$) − f($\mathbf{b}_k$))/T}, *then replace* $\mathbf{b}_j$ *with* $\mathbf{b}_k$.
T = g(T, i)
i = i + 1

14.5.3 Genetic Search

Most genetic algorithms rely upon searching the space of individuals; hence many of the techniques mentioned in Chapter 12 apply. In all searching problems, there is a tradeoff between exhaustive search that produces the best solution and optimal search that produces an acceptable solution at a lower cost. Some special considerations are involved when dealing with the genetic approach. Using the basic survival-of-the-fittest approach, we find that the proportions of better schema increase and the proportions of less desirable schema decrease that should lead to convergence of the system. However, premature convergence can occur before the optimal solution is found.

A problem studied in population genetics is *genetic drift* in which useful schemata disappear from the population. This occurs because a parent string can only produce an integral number of offspring and the number of instances in a schema cannot reflect the desired proportion with arbitrary position in a finite population. This results in a source of sampling error with stochastic selection processes and is believed to be a primary source of premature convergence in genetic algorithms (Davis, 1987; DeJong, 1975). One solution to counter the loss of diversity of the population has been proposed (Mauldin, 1984). A uniqueness value is computed which is the minimum Hamming distance allowed between any offspring and all existing strings in the population. If a new individual is too close, the allele values are randomly changed until the required distance is achieved. See Davis (1987) for details on improving efficiency for genetic searching. Zurada, Marks, and Robinson (1994) presents a number of extensions of genetic algorithms.

14.6 BIOMEDICAL EXAMPLES

14.6.1 Literature References

The medical literature for the last five years has over 200 applications of genetic algorithms to problems in biomedicine. Many of these are, naturally enough, in the area of DNA (Evans et al., 1997) and RNA (Notredame, O'Brien, and Higgins, 1997) analysis and other genetic studies (Bansal, Cannings, and Sheehan, 1997). However, the applications are diverse. One application is generation of sleep profiles using EEG data (Baumgart-Schmidt et al., 1997). In this work, genetic algorithms are used to reduce the number of features and to optimize the topologies of the networks. Another application in which a genetic algorithm is used for feature selection involves analysis of radiological images to classify mass and normal breast tissue (Sahiner et al., 1996). Genetic algorithms have also been used in analyzing spectroscopy data (Bangalore et al., 1996). A kth-nearest-neighbor genetic algorithm has been applied to ligand interactions in proteins (Raymer et al., 1997). In most of these applications, genetic algorithms are used in conjunction with other techniques, resulting in hybrid genetic approaches.

EXAMPLE: Selection of Wavelengths in Near-Infrared Spectroscopy

As an example, consider the application of a genetic algorithm applied to near-infrared spectroscopy (Bangalore et al., 1996). The approach is used for automated wavelength selection while optimizing the number of latent variables. We will look at each component of a genetic algorithm in terms of this example.

Data Representation

Inclusion of a particular spectral point is represented by a one and noninclusion by a zero. For the sets employed in the study, there are a total of 519 spectral points. Each chromosome consists of 520 genes, the first 519 of which represent these spectral points and the last of which is a decimal integer representing the model size, which is the number of latent variables to be used in building the calibration model.

Initial Population

A starting point is taken in a spectral range in which the analyte is known to observe. For this model, the three absorption bands of glucose are used, which is represented by setting genes 101–400 to 1s. The initial model size (gene 520) is set to 20. The initial population is then formed by randomly perturbing this initial chromosome, genes 1–519. The perturbation of gene 520, the model size, is performed according to:

$$h_{\text{new}} = (rsh_{\text{initial}}) + h_{\text{initial}}$$

where h_{new} is the new model size, h_{initial} is the old model size, r is a Gaussian-distributed random deviate $[N(0, 1)]$, and s is a user-controlled step size.

Genetic Operators

The recombination technique involves a one-point crossover method in which all genes up to a randomly chosen crossover point are swapped between parents to create two children.

Evaluation Function

The chromosomes are evaluated according to a fitness function. The samples are randomly split, with 80 percent comprising the calibration set and 20 percent comprising the prediction set. The replicate sample associated with a particular sample are kept together. The prediction set spectra are set aside for final testing of the optimized calibration models. The calibration set is split randomly into calibration and monitoring subsets. The fitness function is defined by the following:

$$1/\left\{\left[\sum_{i=1}^{n_c}(c_i - c_i')^2\right]/(n_c - h - 1) + \left[\sum_{i=1}^{n_m}(m_i - m_i')^2\right]/(n_m - h_w)\right\} \tag{14.8}$$

where n_c and n_m are the numbers of spectra in the calibration and monitoring subsets, respectively; c_i and m_i are the actual analyte concentration in the calibration and monitoring subsets, respectively; c_i' and m_i' are the predicted analyte concentration in the calibration and monitoring subsets, respectively; h is the number of partial least squares (PLS) factors in the model; and w is a weighting factor to control the influence of h on the fitness function.

Configuration

The configuration of the genetic algorithm (GA) is made up of control parameters. Important configuration variables include the population size, the mutation probability (P_m), the initialization probability, the recombination probability (P_r), and the method of recombination.

14.7 SUMMARY

Although genetic algorithms offer an interesting approach for optimization and classification problems, most of the examples given to illustrate genetic algorithms are so-called toy or game problems, such as the traveling salesman problem. Use of genetic algorithms in large-scale practical applications can present difficulties. In these applications, the original idea of binary input is generally altered to use more sophisticated data structures.

Many of the implementations of genetic algorithms employ ad hoc techniques either to improve the efficiency or to enhance the outcome of the system. Many of these approaches lack any theoretical basis. Performance enhancements are discussed in Davis (1991). In spite of these limitations, the use of genetic algorithms has produced some interesting applications, especially when combined with other techniques such as neural networks or decision theory.

EXERCISES

1. Given the following initial population of 5-gene individuals:

(1 0 1 0 1)
(1 1 1 0 0)
(0 1 0 1 0)
(1 0 1 0 1)

   (a) Show the result of crossover between individuals 1 and 2 in bit positions 3 and 4.
   (b) Perform the same crossover for individuals 3 and 4 and show the new population.
   (c) Perform one iteration of the hill-climbing algorithm and one iteration of the simulated annealing algorithm using the original population.

2. (a) Define a practical problem that can be represented as a binary string of features.
   (b) Define an evaluation function for this problem.
   (c) Define one pass through a genetic algorithm for your problem using crossover and mutation.
   (d) Is this the best way to define the problem? If not, give an alternative formulation that you feel is more effective.
   (e) Can you still use the genetic algorithm on your reformulation? Explain.

REFERENCES

Adeli, H., and Hung, S.L. 1995. *Machine learning: neural networks, genetic algorithms, and fuzzy systems*. New York: John Wiley & Sons.

Bangalore, A.S., Shaffer, R.E., Small, G.W., and Arnold, M.A. 1996. Genetic algorithm-based method for selecting wavelengths and model size for use with partial least-squares regression: application to near-infrared spectroscopy. *Analytical Chemistry* **68(23):** 4200–4212.

Bansal, A., Cannings, C., and Sheehan, N. 1997. An evaluation of the application of the genetic algorithm to the problem of ordering genetic loci on human chromosomes using radiation hybrid data. *IMA Journal of Mathematics Applied to Medicine and Biology* **14(3):** 161–187.

Baumgart-Schmitt, R., Herrmann, W.M., Eilers, R., and Bes, F. 1997. On the use of neural network techniques to analyse sleep EEG data. First communication: application of evolutionary and genetic algorithms to reduce the feature space and to develop classification rules. *Neuropsychobiology* **36(4):** 194–210.

Davis, L. 1987. *Genetic algorithms and simulated annealing*. Los Altos, CA: Morgan Kaufmann.

Davis, L. 1991. *Handbook of genetic algorithms*. New York: Van Nostrand Reinhold.

DeJong, K.A. 1975. Analysis of behavior of a class of genetic algorithm adaptive systems. Ph.D. Dissertation, Computer and Communication Sciences, University of Michigan, Ann Arbor.

Evans, S., Lemon, S.J., Deters, C., Fusaro, R.M., Durhan, C., Snyder, C., and Lynch, H.T. 1997. Using data mining to characterize DNA mutations by patient clinical features, *Proceedings, AMIA Fall Symposium:* 253–257.

Mauldin, M.L. 1984. Maintaining diversity in genetic search. *Proceedings of the National Conference on Artificial Intelligence:* 247–250.

Michalewicz, Z. 1992. *Genetic algorithms + data structures + evolution programs*. Berlin: Springer-Verlag.

Notredame, C., O'Brien, E.A., and Higgins, D.G. 1997. RAGA: RNA sequence alignment by genetic algorithm. *Nucleic Acids Research* **25(22):** 4570–4580.

Raymer, M.L., Sanschagrin, P.C., Punch, W.F., Venkataraman, S., Goodman, E.D., and Kuhn, L.A. 1997. Prediction conserved water-mediated and polar ligand interactions in proteins using K-nearest-neighbors genetic algorithms. *Journal of Molecular Biology* **265(4):** 445–464.

Sahiner, B., Chan, H.P., Wei, D., Petrick, N., Helvie, M.A., Adler, D.D., and Goodsitt, M.M. 1996. Image feature selection by a genetic algorithm: application to classification of mass and normal breast tissue. *Medical Physics* **23(1):** 1671–1684.

Yu, Y., Schell, M.C., and Zhang, J.B. 1997. Decision theoretic steering and genetic algorithm optimization: application to stereotactic radiosurgery treatment planning. *Medical Physics* **23(11):** 1742–1750.

Zurada, J.M, Marks, R.J., and Robinson, C J. 1994. *Computational intelligence imitating life.* New York: IEEE Press.

15

Probabilistic Systems

15.1 INTRODUCTION

Statistical analysis remains one of the mainstays for analysis of medical data (Glantz, 1992). Statistical techniques can be used not only for direct analysis and determination of significance but also for classification. Duda and Hart (1973) provide an in-depth analysis of statistical techniques for pattern classification.

15.2 BAYESIAN APPROACHES

One of the earliest learning algorithms was based on the Bayes theorem and is referred to as Bayesian Learning.

15.2.1 Bayes' Rule

Bayesian Learning is based on Bayes' Rule, which in its simplest form separates two categories based on one variable, according to the following:

$$P(\omega_j|x) = p(x|\omega_j) \, P(\omega_j)/p(x) \tag{15.1}$$

where $p(x) = \sum_{j=1}^{2} p(x|\omega_j) \, P(\omega_j)$ (15.2)

x: value of feature
ω_1:   class 1
ω_2:   class 2
$p(x|\omega_j)$:   state conditional probability density given that the state is class j (a priori)
$P(\omega_j)$:   Probability of class j
$P(\omega_j|x)$:   Probability of class j given x (a posteriori)

Consider the following example:

x:	Cholesterol level
ω_1:	Presence of coronary artery disease (CAD)
ω_2:	Absence of CAD
$P(x\|\omega_1)$:	Probability of x given presence of CAD
$P(x\|\omega_2)$:	Probability of x given absence of CAD
$P(\omega_1)$:	Probability of CAD
$P(\omega_2)$:	Probability of no CAD
$P(\omega_1\|x)$:	Probability of CAD given x
$P(\omega_2\|x)$:	Probability of no CAD given x

$P(\omega_1)$ is the presence of CAD in the general population, and $P(\omega_2)$ is $1 - P(\omega_1)$. In general, decision making is not this simple, and more than the one feature will be required to make a decision. Thus we require the n-dimensional version of Bayes' Rule:

$$P(\omega_j|\mathbf{x}) = P(\mathbf{x}|\omega_j)\, P(\omega_j)/P(\mathbf{x}) \tag{15.3}$$

$$P(\mathbf{x}) = \sum_{j=1}^{c} P(\mathbf{x}|\omega_j)\, P(\omega_j) \tag{15.4}$$

This version also assumes c classes instead of 2.

15.2.2 Bayes' Decision Theory

Bayes' Decision Theory is based on the following construct for the probability of error:

$$P(\text{error}|\mathbf{x}) = \begin{cases} P(\omega_1|\mathbf{x}) \text{ if we decide } w_2 \\ P(\omega_2|\mathbf{x}) \text{ if we decide } w_1 \end{cases} \tag{15.5}$$

Therefore, decide

$$\omega_1 \text{ if } P(w_1|\mathbf{x}) > P(\omega_2|\mathbf{x})$$
$$\omega_2 \text{ if } P(\omega_2|\mathbf{x}) > P(\omega_1|\mathbf{x})$$

Applying Bayes' Rule, we find that this translates into

Decide ω_1 if $p(\mathbf{x}|\omega_1)\, P(\omega_1) > P(\mathbf{x}|\omega_2)\, P(\omega_2)$.
Otherwise, decide ω_2.

Figure 15.1 graphically illustrates the objective of a decision strategy with two overlapping probability distributions. The objective is to shift the dividing point so that the fewest errors are made. This decision may not be straightforward, however, for some decisions may carry more risk than other decisions. This is especially true in medical problems.

15.2.3 Risk Analysis

The conditional risk can be defined by the following (Duda and Hart, 1973):

1. Observe **x**.
2. Take some action a_i.

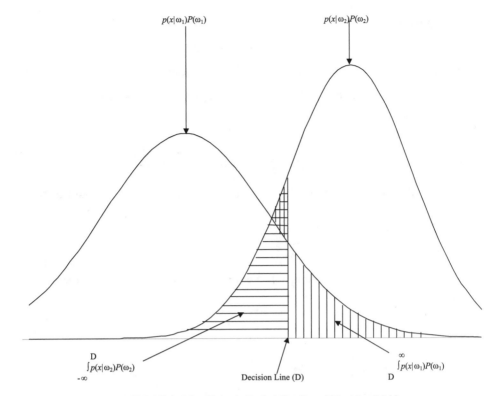

$p(x|\omega_1)P(\omega_1)$ $p(x|\omega_2)P(\omega_2)$

D
$\int p(x|\omega_2)P(\omega_2)$
$-\infty$

Decision Line (D)

∞
$\int p(x|\omega_1)P(\omega_1)$
D

Figure 15.1 Minimizing Error in Probability-Based Decision Making.

3. If the true state of nature is ω_j, then the loss is $\lambda(a_i|\omega_j)$.
4. The probability that the true state of nature is ω_j is $P(\omega_j|\mathbf{x})$.
5. The expected loss associated with taking this action is thus

$$R(a_i|\mathbf{x}) = \sum_{j=1}^{c} \lambda(a_i|\omega_j)\, P(\omega_j|\mathbf{x}) \tag{15.6}$$

where $R(a_i|\mathbf{x})$ is the conditional risk.

The objective is to minimize the overall risk, which is given by

$$R = \int R(\mathbf{a}|\mathbf{x})\, p(\mathbf{x})\, d\mathbf{x} \tag{15.7}$$

If $R(\mathbf{a}|\mathbf{x})$ is as small as possible for all $\mathbf{x}$, the overall risk will be minimized.

Bayes' Decision Rule is the following:

1. Compute the conditional risk $R(a_i|\mathbf{x})$ for $i = 1, \dots, k$.
2. Select the action a_i for which $R(a_i|\mathbf{x})$ is minimum.
3. The resulting minimum risk is called the Bayes' Risk.

The following example shows two-category classification using Bayes' Risk. Assume that a_i represents the decision that the true state of nature is ω_i. Then $\lambda_{ij} = \lambda(a_i|\omega_j)$ is the loss incurred for deciding ω_i when the true state is ω_j. Define the conditional risks

$$R(a_1|\mathbf{x}) = \lambda_{11}\, P(\omega_1|\mathbf{x}) + \lambda_{12}\, P(\omega_2|\mathbf{x}) \tag{15.8}$$

$$R(a_2|\mathbf{x}) = \lambda_{21}\, P(\omega_1|\mathbf{x}) + \lambda_{22}\, P(\omega_2|\mathbf{x}) \tag{15.9}$$

The general decision rule is

$$\text{Decide } \omega_1 \text{ if } R(a_1|\mathbf{x}) < R(a_2|\mathbf{x})$$

In terms of a posteriori probabilities, this is the same as

$$\text{Decide } \omega_1 \text{ if } (\lambda_{21} - \lambda_{11}) P(\omega_1|\mathbf{x}) > (\lambda_{12} - \lambda_{22}) P(\omega_2|\mathbf{x})$$

The likelihood ratio is

$$\left[\frac{P(\mathbf{x}|\omega_1)}{P(\mathbf{x}|\omega_2)}\right] > \left[\frac{(\lambda_{12} - \lambda_{22})P(\omega_2)}{(\lambda_{21} - \lambda_{11})P(\omega_1)}\right] \tag{15.10}$$

A special case of this procedure is the minimum error rate classification with the zero–one loss function:

$$\lambda(a_i|\omega_j) = \begin{bmatrix} 0 & i = j \\ 1 & i \neq j \end{bmatrix} \quad i, j = 1, \ldots, c \tag{15.11}$$

In this case, all errors are considered equally likely. The conditional risk is then

$$R(a_i|\mathbf{x}) = \sum_{i=1}^{c} \lambda(a_i|\omega_j) P(w_j|\mathbf{x}) \tag{15.12}$$

$$= \sum_{i \neq j} P(\omega_j|\mathbf{x}) \tag{15.13}$$

$$= 1 - P(\omega_i|\mathbf{x}) \tag{15.14}$$

The classification rule is then

Decide ω_i if $P(\omega_i|\mathbf{x}) > P(\omega_j|\mathbf{x})$ for all $i \neq j$; in other words, maximize $P(\omega_i|\mathbf{x})$.

15.2.4 Supervised Bayesian Learning

The general objective of Bayes' Decision Theory is to compute the a posteriori probabilities $P(\omega_i|\mathbf{x})$. What happens if the a priori probabilities $P(\omega_i)$ and class-conditional probabilities $p(\mathbf{x}|\omega_i)$ are unknown? One solution is to try to use all information that is available. Assume that we have a set of samples X. Then

$$P(\omega_i|\mathbf{x}, X) = \frac{p(\mathbf{x}|\omega_i, X) P(\omega_i|X)}{\sum_{j=1}^{c} p(\mathbf{x}|\omega_j, X) P(\omega_j|X)} \tag{15.15}$$

We then assume that the true a priori probabilities are known:

$$P(\omega_i|X) = P(\omega_i). \tag{15.16}$$

We then have a supervised learning problem defined by the following:

There are c sets of samples $X_1, \ldots, X_c$ where samples in X_i belong to ω_i. Thus $P(\mathbf{x}|\omega_i, X)$ can be determined separately for each class:

$$P(\omega_i|\mathbf{x}, X) = \frac{p(\mathbf{x}|\omega_i, X) P(\omega_i)}{\sum_{j=1}^{c} p(\mathbf{x}|\omega_j, X) P(\omega_j)} \tag{15.17}$$

Since there are c separate problems, we can drop the class notation and treat each problem separately. The objective is to determine $p(\mathbf{x}|X)$. The following assumptions are made (Duda and Hart, 1973):

The desired probability density $p(\mathbf{x})$ is unknown.

$P(\mathbf{x})$ has known parametric form.

The only unknown parameters are contained in a vector θ; thus $p(\mathbf{x}|\theta)$ is completely known.

Prior information about θ is contained in $p(\theta)$.

The general procedure is:

Observe samples.

Convert $p(\theta)$ into $p(\theta|X)$.

$p(\theta|x)$ should peak around the true value of θ.

The goal is to compute $p(\mathbf{x}|X)$ as an approximation to $p(\mathbf{x})$.
The following equations are necessary:

$$p(\mathbf{x}|X) = \int p(\mathbf{x}, \theta|X) \, d\theta \tag{15.18}$$

$$p(\mathbf{x}, \theta|\mathbf{x}) = p(\mathbf{x}|\theta, X) \, p(\theta|X) \tag{15.19}$$

Since the selection of each x is done independently

$$p(\mathbf{x}|\theta, X) = p(\mathbf{x}|\theta) \tag{15.20}$$

Therefore

$$p(\mathbf{x}|X) = \int p(\mathbf{x}|\theta) \, p(\theta|X) \, d\theta \tag{15.21}$$

The algorithm for general Bayesian Learning, for any distribution, is:

The form of the density $p(X|\theta)$ *is assumed to be known, but* θ *is not known exactly. The initial knowledge about* θ *is assumed to be contained in a known a priori density* $p(\theta)$.

The remainder of our knowledge about θ *is contained in a set* X *of n samples,* $x_1, \ldots, x_n$ *drawn independently according to the unknown probability law* $p(\mathbf{x})$.

$$p(\mathbf{x}|X) = \int p(\mathbf{x}|\theta) \, P(\theta|X) \, d\theta \tag{15.22}$$

$$p(\theta|X) = \frac{p(X|\theta) \, p(\theta)}{\int p(X|\theta) \, p(\theta) \, d\theta} \text{ (Bayes' Rule)} \tag{15.23}$$

$$p(X|\theta) = \prod_{k=1}^{n} p(\mathbf{x}_k|\theta) \tag{15.24}$$

This is an example of parameter estimation. In the next section we will discuss this subject in more detail.

15.2.5 Decision Trees

Decision trees were discussed briefly in Chapter 10. Referring to Figure 10.2, each branch has an associated probability with it. These probabilities are often determined using Bayes' Decision Theory. Decision trees can be used in a number of ways and can include risk factors, utility factors, and/or cost factors. Consider the following example:

A single vaccination costs $100.

The average cost per case of hepatitis B is $453.

The vaccine is 95 percent effective.

The prevalence of hepatitis B is 6 percent.

Figure 15.2 shows a decision tree with the original probabilities, the cumulative probabilities in parentheses, the utility values in brackets, and the costs in braces. Absence of these measures on a node indicates that their values are zero. The expected utility U_E and the expected cost C_E are computed by:

$$U_E = \sum P_i U_i \qquad (15.25)$$

$$C_E = \sum P_i C_i \qquad (15.26)$$

where P_i = Cumulative Probability
U_i = Utility value of each node
C_i = Cost value of each node

Thus

$$U_E(\text{vaccination}) = 0.997$$
$$U_E(\text{no vaccination}) = 0.94$$
$$C_E(\text{vaccination}) = \$101.36$$
$$C_E(\text{no vaccination}) = \$27.18$$

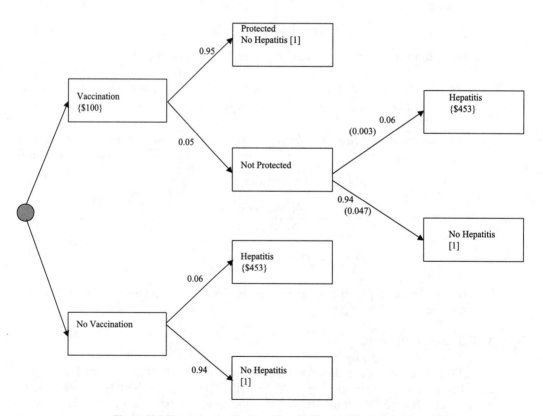

Figure 15.2 Example of a Decision Tree for Vaccination against Hepatitis B.

The cost effectiveness C is then computed by:

$$C = U_E/U_C \tag{15.27}$$
$$C(\text{vaccination}) = 101.664$$
$$C(\text{no vaccination}) = 28.9$$

15.3 PARAMETER ESTIMATION

In parameter distribution problems, we assume a known probability distribution. Most commonly, the normal distribution is assumed. The objective is to determine the parameters that define the distribution. For the normal distribution, these parameters are the mean μ and the standard deviation σ. We will examine two methods: maximum likelihood estimation and Bayesian estimation.

15.3.1 Maximum Likelihood Estimation

Let $X_1, \ldots, X_c$ be sets of samples, one set per class, drawn according to $p(\mathbf{x}|\omega_j)$. Assume $p(\mathbf{x}|\omega_j)$ is uniquely determined by the parameter vector θ_j. (For the normal distribution $\theta_j = (\mu, \sigma)$.) Assume that the classes are independent and that for each class X we have n samples $x_1, \ldots, x_n$. Then

$$p(X|\theta) = \prod_{k=1}^{n} p(\mathbf{x}_k|\theta) \tag{15.28}$$

The maximum likelihood θ is the value that maximizes

$$p(X|\theta) = (\theta_1, \ldots, \theta_p)^T. \tag{15.29}$$

Define the gradient

$$\nabla\theta = [\delta/\delta\theta_1, \ldots, \delta/\delta\theta_p]^T \tag{15.30}$$

The log likelihood is

$$l(\theta) = \log p(X|\theta) \tag{15.31}$$

$$= \sum_{k=1}^{n} \log p(\mathbf{x}_k|\theta) \tag{15.32}$$

Then

$$\nabla\theta l = \sum_{k=1}^{n} \nabla\theta l \log p(\mathbf{x}_k|\theta) \tag{15.33}$$

Setting

$$\nabla\theta l = 0 \tag{15.34}$$

gives a set of c equations.

EXAMPLE: Multivariate Normal Distribution with Unknown Mean

$$\log p(\mathbf{x}_k|\mu) = -(1/2) \log \{(2\pi)^{\mathrm{d}}|\sigma|\} - (1/2) (\mathbf{x}_k - \mu)^{\mathrm{T}} \sigma^{-1} (\mathbf{x}_k - \mu) \tag{15.35}$$

$$\nabla_\mu \log p(\mathbf{x}_k|\mu) = \sigma^{-1} (\mathbf{x}_k - \mu) \tag{15.36}$$

$$\sum_{k=1}^{n} \sigma^{-1} (\mathbf{x}_k - \mu) = 0 \tag{15.37}$$

$$\sum_{k=1}^{n} \mathbf{x}_k = \sum_{k=1}^{n} \mu \tag{15.38}$$

$$n\mu = \sum_{k=1}^{n} \mathbf{x}_k \tag{15.39}$$

$$\mu = (1/n) \sum_{k=1}^{n} \mathbf{x}_k \ \text{(Sample Mean)} \tag{15.40}$$

EXAMPLE: Univariate Normal Distribution with Unknown Mean and Variance

$$\text{Let } \theta_1 = \mu, \theta_2 = \sigma^2 \tag{15.41}$$

$$p(x) = (1/(2^{.5}\pi\sigma)) \exp\left(-1/2\right)((x - \mu)/\sigma)^2) \tag{15.42}$$

$$\log p(x_k|\theta) = -1/2\log 2\pi\theta_2 - (1/2\theta_2) (x_k - \theta_1)^2 \tag{15.43}$$

$$\nabla\theta \log p(x_k|\theta) = \begin{bmatrix} (1 - \theta_2) (x_k - \theta_1) \\ -(1/2 \ \theta_2) + (x_k - \theta_1)/2\theta_2{}^2 \end{bmatrix} \tag{15.44}$$

$$\sum_{k=1}^{n} (1/\theta_2) (x_k - \theta_1) = 0 \tag{15.45}$$

$$\mu = (1/n) \sum_{k=1}^{n} x_k \tag{15.46}$$

$$\sigma^2 = (1/n) \sum_{k=1}^{n} (x_k - \mu)^2 \tag{15.47}$$

15.3.2 Bayesian Estimation

The Bayesian estimator follows the following procedure (Duda and Hart, 1973):

Assume the probability density $p(x)$ is unknown but has a known parametric form.

Assume that the only unknown is the parameter vector θ.

Assume that the function $p(x|\theta)$ is completely known.

Prior information about θ is contained in a known a priori density $p(\theta)$.

Through sample observation, the a posteriori density $p(\theta|X)$ is computed.

The final goal is to compute $p(x|X)$ through Bayesian Learning, discussed in the previous section.

EXAMPLE: Learning the Mean of a Univariate Normal Density

$$p(\mu|X) = \frac{p(X|\mu) \, p(\mu)}{\int p(X|\mu) \, p(\mu) \, d\mu} \tag{15.48}$$

Initialize

$$\mu_0: \text{Initial guess for } \mu$$

σ_0: Uncertainty about the guess for μ_0

$p(\mu) \sim N(\mu_0, \sigma_0{}^2)$

$X = \{x_1, \ldots, x_n\}$

Then

$$p(\mu|X) = \alpha \prod_{k=1}^{n} p(\mathbf{x}_k|\mu)\, p(\mu) \tag{15.49}$$

$$p(x_k|\mu) \sim N(\mu, \sigma^2), p(\mu) \sim N(\mu_0, \sigma_0{}^2) \tag{15.50}$$

$$p(\mu|X) = \alpha \prod_{k=1}^{n} (1/(2^{.5}\pi\sigma))\, \exp\left[(-1/2)((x - \mu)/\sigma)^2\right](1/(2^{.5}\pi\sigma_0)) \\ \exp\left[(-1/2)((\mu - \mu_0)/\sigma_0)^2\right] \tag{15.51}$$

$$= \alpha' \exp[(-1/2)\left[\sum_{k=1}^{n}((\mu - x_k)/\sigma))^2 + (\mu - \mu_0)/\sigma_0)^2\right] \tag{15.52}$$

$$= \alpha'' \exp[(-1/2)[((n/\sigma^2) + (1/\sigma_0{}^2)^2) - 2(1/\sigma^2))\sum_{k=1}^{n} x_k + (\mu_0/\mu_0{}^2)\mu]] \tag{15.53}$$

Equate coefficients with $(1/(2^{.5}\pi\sigma n))\, \exp\left[(-1/2)((\mu - \mu_n)/\sigma_n)^2\right]$:

$$1/\sigma_n{}^2 = n/\sigma^2 + 1/\sigma_0{}^2 \tag{15.54}$$

$$\mu_n/\sigma_n{}^2 = (n/\sigma^2)m_n + \mu_0/\sigma_0{}^2 \quad \text{where} \tag{15.55}$$

$$m_n = (1/n)\sum_{k=1}^{n} x_k \quad \text{(Sample Mean)} \tag{15.56}$$

Solving for μ_n and $\sigma_n{}^2$:

$$\mu_n = [n\sigma_0{}^2/(n\sigma_0{}^2 + \sigma^2)]\, m_n + [\sigma_0{}^2/(n\sigma_0{}^2 + \sigma^2)]\, \mu_0 \tag{15.57}$$

$$\sigma_n{}^2 = (\sigma_0{}^2\sigma^2)/(n\sigma_0{}^2 + \sigma^2) \tag{15.58}$$

μ_n lies between m_n and μ_0.

If $\sigma_0 \neq 0$, μ_n approaches the sample mean as n approaches ∞.

If $\sigma_0 = 0$, $\mu = \mu_0$.

This learning procedure is illustrated in Figure 15.3.

15.4 DISCRIMINANT ANALYSIS

In Chapter 4, we discussed the Fisher Linear Discriminant, which is the basis for discriminant analysis. Many standard statistical packages include discriminant analysis algorithms for classifying data into one of two categories (Dixon et al., 1990). In general, a linear discriminant is used. The procedure identifies the parameter that accounts for the most variance between the two classes. It then selects the parameter that accounts for the highest remaining variance, and so forth. The procedure uses all but one sample to obtain a dividing surface and then tests its accuracy on the remaining sample. This procedure is repeated leaving out all samples once. The classification results are termed the jackknife classification.

It is also possible to include nonlinear parameters in this process by defining new variables. For example, assume you have the following three parameters for determining the presence or absence of CAD:

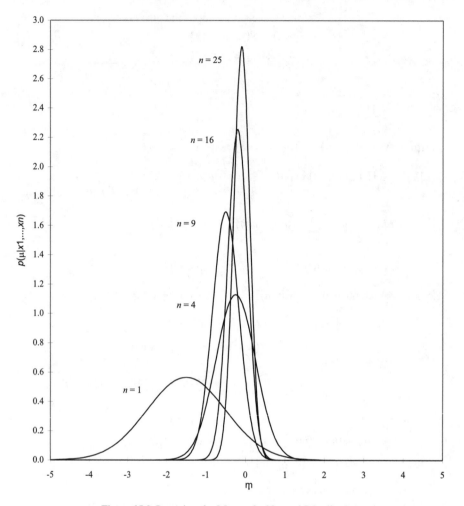

Figure 15.3 Learning the Mean of a Normal Distribution.

$$x_1: \qquad \text{heart rate}$$
$$x_2: \qquad \text{blood pressure}$$
$$x_3: \qquad \text{ST depression}$$

If you believe that the combination of heart rate and blood pressure is important, the so-called double product, which is often used as an indicator, can be defined:

$$x_4: \qquad x_1{}^*x_2$$

This new variable is treated the same as any other parameter in the discriminant analysis procedure.

15.5 STATISTICAL PATTERN CLASSIFICATION

Many of the methods we have used earlier in the book fall under the category of statistical pattern recognition. For example, the backpropagation model is essentially a statistically based method. Obviously, Fisher's Linear Discriminant and discriminant analysis in general are methods of statistical pattern classification, as are all the other supervised and unsupervised learning approaches discussed in this chapter. Patrick and Fattu (1986) present an interesting extension to techniques for statistical pattern classification with the introduction of complex classes. In this approach, a feature vector can belong to more than one category. The general idea is the following. Assume that there is a set C of primitive classes that contains m classes:

$$C: \omega_1, \ldots, \omega_m$$

Categories ω_i^* are then developed using these primitive classes:

$$\omega_i^* = \omega_1\, \omega_2\, \omega_3 \ldots \omega_m \text{ (only class 1)} \qquad (15.59)$$

$$\cdot$$
$$\cdot$$
$$\cdot$$

$$\omega_i^* = \omega_1\, \omega_2\, \omega_3 \ldots \omega_m \text{ (only class m)}$$

$$\Omega^*_{abc} = \omega_a \omega_b \omega_c \ldots \cap \qquad (15.60)$$

where $\cap$ indicates all class complements not to the left of $\cap$.
Ω^*_{abc} denotes a complex class. In general, a complex class Ω^*_ε is defined as:

$$\Omega^*_\varepsilon: \text{Set containing classes } \omega_{\varepsilon 1}, \omega_{\varepsilon 2}, \ldots$$

A posteriori class probability can then be extended by Patrick's theorem (Patrick and Fattu, 1986):

$$p(\omega_i|\mathbf{x}) = [p(\mathbf{x}|\omega_i^*) + \Sigma\, p(\mathbf{x}|\Omega^*_\varepsilon)\, p(\Omega^*_\varepsilon)]/p(\mathbf{x}), i = 1,2, \ldots, m \qquad (15.61)$$

Patrick et al. have developed the CONSULT system which has been applied to numerous applications in medical decision making using pattern classification (Patrick, 1994).

15.6 UNSUPERVISED LEARNING

Some statistical approaches to unsupervised learning were introduced in Chapter 5; additional methods are presented here.

15.6.1 Parzen Windows

The Parzen window approach is similar in some ways to the potential function approach discussed in Chapter 4. The objective is to compute the probability of a sample falling within a specified area, or window:

$$p_n(\mathbf{x}) = (k_n/n)/V_n \qquad (15.62)$$

where k_n is the number of samples in the d-dimensional hypercube r_n whose volume is

$$v_n = h_n^d \qquad (15.63)$$

where h_n is the length of a side.
The window function $\phi(\mathbf{u})$ is defined by:

$$\phi(\mathbf{u}) = \begin{bmatrix} 1 \text{ if } |u_j| \leq 0.5, j = 1, \ldots, d \\ 0 \text{ otherwise} \end{bmatrix} \qquad (15.64)$$

Thus

$$\phi(\mathbf{x} - \mathbf{x}_i)/h_n = \begin{bmatrix} 1 \text{ if } \mathbf{x}_i \text{ falls within the hypercube} \\ 0 \text{ otherwise} \end{bmatrix} \qquad (15.65)$$

The number of samples k_n in the hypercube is

$$k_n = \sum_{i=1}^{n} \phi(\mathbf{x} - \mathbf{x}_i)/h_n \qquad (15.66)$$

Then

$$p_n(\mathbf{x}) = (1/n) \sum_{i=1}^{n} (1/v_n)\, \phi(\mathbf{x} - \mathbf{x}_i)/h_n \qquad (15.67)$$

The window function can be any density function such that

$$\phi(\mathbf{u}) \geq 0 \quad \text{and} \qquad (15.68)$$

$$\int \phi(\mathbf{u})\, d\mathbf{u} = 1 \qquad (15.69)$$

The drawback of the Parzen window approach is that the data are very sensitive to the choice of cell size. A better approach is to let the cell volume be a function of the data, which is done in the kth nearest neighbor approach.

15.6.2 Nearest Neighbor Algorithms

In the kth nearest neighbor algorithm, the volume v_n is allowed to expand until it captures k_n samples that are the k_n nearest neighbors of $\mathbf{x}$. The density of the samples determines v_n. As an example, let $k_n = n$. Then

$$v_n \approx (1/n^{.5})\, p(\mathbf{x}) \qquad (15.70)$$

Thus v_n has the form $v_1/n^{.5}$.
The initial volume v is determined by the nature of the data rather than in an arbitrary manner. For $n = 1$ and $k_n = n^{.5} = 1$

$$p_1(\mathbf{x}) = 1/2\, |\mathbf{x} - \mathbf{x}_1| \qquad (15.71)$$

The estimation of a posteriori probabilities $p(\omega_i|\mathbf{x})$ can be done using either Parzen windows or the kth nearest neighbor procedure. For the Parzen window, v_n is specified as a function of n such as $1/n^{.5}$. For the kth nearest neighbor, V_n is expanded until a specified number of samples are captured, such as $k = n^{.5}$.

15.6.3 Mixture Densities and Maximum Likelihood Estimates

The mixture density approach uses the following assumptions (Duda and Hart, 1973):

1. The samples come from a known number of classes, c.
2. The a priori probabilities $P(\omega_j)$ are known, $j = 1, \ldots, c$.
3. The forms of the class-conditional probabilities $p(\mathbf{x}|\omega_j, \theta_j)$ are known.
4. The c parameter vectors $\theta_1, \ldots, \theta_c$ are unknown.

The method is based on

$$p(\mathbf{x}|\theta) = \sum_{j=1}^{c} p(\mathbf{x}|\omega_j, \theta_j)\, p(\omega_j) \text{ where} \tag{15.72}$$

$p(\mathbf{x}|\theta)$ is the mixture density

$p(\mathbf{x}|\omega_j, \theta_j)$ are the component densities

$P(\omega_j)$ are the mixing parameters

The objective is to estimate θ.

One method of finding θ is through the use of maximum likelihood estimation. Assume $X = \{x_1, \ldots, x_n\}$ is a set of unlabeled samples drawn from the mixture density. Then

$$p(X|\theta) = \prod_{k=1}^{n} p(x_k|\theta) \tag{15.73}$$

The objective is to find θ', the value that maximizes $p(X|\theta)$. This results in c equations, one for each parameter vector. An approximate procedure for accomplishing this is the Basic Isodata Algorithm described earlier.

15.6.4 Unsupervised Bayesian Learning

In unsupervised Bayesian learning, the following assumptions are made (Duda and Hart, 1973):

1. The number of classes is known.
2. The a priori probabilities $P(\omega_j)$ are known for each class.
3. The forms of the class-conditional probabilities $p(\mathbf{x}|\omega_j, \theta_j)$ are known, but the parameter vector θ is not known.
4. Part of the knowledge about θ is contained in $p(\theta)$.
5. The remainder of the knowledge about θ is contained in a set X of n samples drawn independently from the mixture density.

$$p(\mathbf{x}|\theta) = \sum_{j=1}^{c} p(\mathbf{x}|\omega_j, \theta_j)\, P(\omega_j) \tag{15.74}$$

The parameter vector is learned according to the following:

$$p(\theta|X) = p(X|\theta)\, p(\theta)/[\int p(X|\theta)\, p(\theta)\, d\theta] \tag{15.75}$$

Due to independence considerations:

$$p(X|\theta) = \prod_{k=1}^{n} p(\mathbf{x}_k|\theta) \tag{15.76}$$

If X_n represents the set of n samples:

$$p(\theta|X^n) = [p(\mathbf{x}_k|\theta)\, p(\theta|X^{n-1})][\int p(\mathbf{x}_k|\theta)\, p(\theta|X^{n-1})\, d\theta] \tag{15.77}$$

The samples in Eq. (15.77) are unlabeled. If the mixture density $p(\mathbf{x}|\theta)$ is identifiable, $p(\theta|X^n)$ can be shown to converge to a Dirac delta function centered at the true value of θ. Although this procedure appears to be almost exactly the same as supervised Bayesian Learning, there are some significant differences. When θ cannot be determined uniquely, the mixture cannot be decomposed into its true components. In addition, computational complexity increases with unsupervised learning. The sample must be assumed to be drawn from a mixture density. See Duda and Hart (1973) for a complete discussion of these problems.

15.7 REGRESSION ANALYSIS

Regression is a standard statistical technique that can be used to relate independent variables to a dependent variable (Afifi and Clark, 1990). The results can be used to produce a regression line that best fits the data. The method can be extended to nonlinear regression to produce higher order curves. The same approach can also be used for classification.

A number of commercial packages, such as CART (California Statistical Software, 1985), are available which will produce decision trees when given a data set. Figure 15.4 shows a regression tree, and Figure 15.5 a classification tree. Note that the only difference is in the terminal nodes. For regression, values for the dependent variable are generated, while for classification the class is determined. Consider the following example.

The problem is to determine the presence or absence of pneumonia. The sample consisted of thirty-eight cases, six of which were negative. The following variables are used:

WBC: White blood count

CRP: C-reactive protein

These measurements were repeated for each patient at five different time intervals; thus there were ten independent variables in all. Using the CART classification tree method, node 1 was split on CRP3 = 19.7. This was the only variable used. If CRP3 > 19.7, pneumonia was assumed to be present. Terminal node information is produced by this method. CART output is shown in Table 15.1.

The same problem approached by using discriminant analysis results in the following:

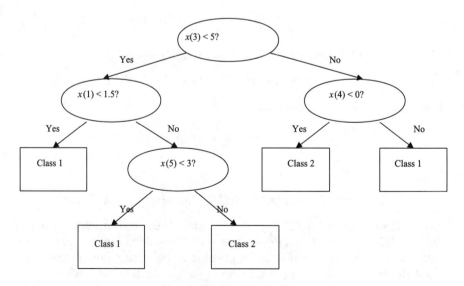

Figure 15.4 Classification Tree.

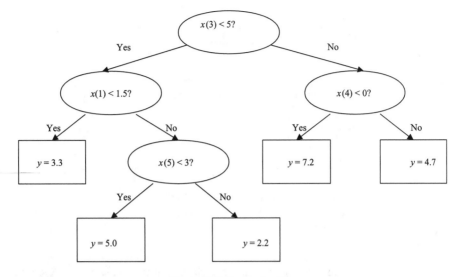

Figure 15.5 Regression Tree.

$$c(\text{no}) = -8.18 + 0.82 \text{ WBC3} + 0.25 \text{ CRP4}$$

$$c(\text{yes}) = -20.11 + 1.23*\text{WBC3} + 0.47 \text{ CRP4}$$

The probability of pneumonia is then given by:

$$p(\text{pneumonia}) = 1/[1 + \exp(c(\text{no})-c(\text{yes}))]$$

Table 15.2 shows the classification results for the discriminant analysis.

Several interesting points are illustrated by this example. First, note that the samples are not evenly balanced between the two classes. The pneumonia class contains

TABLE 15.1 CART Analysis

Terminal Node Information				
Node	Cases	Probability	Class	Cost
1	4	0.1053	1	0.0000
	34	0.8947	2	0.0588

Classification Results		
	True Classification	
Predicted Classification	No Pneumonia	Pneumonia
No Pneumonia	4	0
Pneumonia	2	32

Accuracy Measures	
Sensitivity	100%
Specificity	67%
Accuracy	95%

TABLE 15.2   Discriminant Analysis Classification Results

Classification Results		
	True Classification	
Predicted Classification	No Pneumonia	Pneumonia
No Pneumonia	5	1
Pneumonia	4	28
Accuracy Measures		
Sensitivity	88%	
Specificity	83%	
Accuracy	87%	

thirty-two samples, and the no-pneumonia class contains six samples. A skewed sample will affect the training results in almost all classification algorithms. Note also that a shift in one or two samples in the no-pneumonia class greatly affects the specificity. It also points out one of the basic reasons for using sensitivity and specificity measures as well as overall accuracy. In this example, all samples in the no-pneumonia class could be misclassified; that is, all samples could be put into the pneumonia category, with an overall accuracy of 85 percent! Here is a result with fairly high accuracy that is totally useless! Note that in this case the discriminant analysis approach yielded a better balance between sensitivity and specificity, which is in general a desirable outcome. The CART approach often results in an unstable system in which a small change in the data can produce a totally different decision tree.

15.8 BIOMEDICAL APPLICATIONS

Uses of statistical approaches abound in all fields. Commonly used methods include discriminant analysis and regression. A recent article (Raymond et al., 1997) compares methods of analysis for heart rate variability for the detection of mild hypertension. Up to six features are used; they are derived from both the spectral domain and the time domain. The best performance of 90 percent accuracy was obtained using a nearest neighbor classifier with the Euclidean distance. The corresponding Bayes' classifier had 84 percent accuracy. It should be noted that the sample size was small and each method was evaluated by the "leave one sample out" method. For a sample size of n, the training is done with $n - 1$ samples, and the remaining sample is then classified and checked for accuracy. The method is repeated until all samples have been used as the test. In general, this method will produce higher accuracy than dividing the data into a training set and a test set.

15.9 SUMMARY

Probabilistic approaches can be used for both supervised and unsupervised learning problems. These methods have strong theoretical bases. However, in the theoretical development certain assumptions are made, such as independence of variables. When considering probabilistic approaches, care must be taken to determine if these assumptions hold for your data set. Because many commercial packages are available for many of the techniques described in this chapter, they offer a good means for comparison with newer, less well-tested approaches such as neural networks.

EXERCISES

1. For a two-class problem, the following is known. The a priori probabilities are $P(\omega_1) = 0.4$, $P(\omega_2) = 0.6$. The risk values to be used are:

   $$\lambda(\alpha_1|\omega_1) = 0.0$$
   $$\lambda(\alpha_2|\omega_1) = 0.0$$
   $$\lambda(\alpha_1|\omega_2) = 0.9$$
   $$\lambda(\alpha_2|\omega_1) = 1.1$$

   (a) Set up the Bayes' Risk $R(\alpha_i|\mathbf{x})$, $i = 1, 2$ in terms of the class-conditional probabilities $p(\mathbf{x}|\omega_i)$.
   (b) If it is known that $p(\mathbf{x}|\omega_1) = 0.4$, and $p(\mathbf{x}|\omega_2) = 0.6$, what classification should be made for sample $\mathbf{x}$?

2. For the Poisson distribution

   $$p(x|\theta) = \theta^x \exp(-\theta)$$

   find θ by the maximum likelihood procedure.

3. The recursive approach to Bayes' Learning is represented by

   $$p(\theta|X^n) = [p(\mathbf{x}_k|\theta)\, p(\theta|X^{n-1})][\int p(\mathbf{x}_k|\theta)\, p(\theta|X^{n-1})\, d\theta]$$

   Explain the meaning of each variable in this equation.

4. Given the feature vectors

   $$X_1 = \{(2, 1), (1, 4)\} \qquad \text{(class 1)}$$
   $$X_2 = \{(-1, -1), (-3, -1)\} \qquad \text{(class 2)}$$
   $$X_3 = \{(1, -5), (2, -3)\} \qquad \text{(class 3)}$$

   (a) Compute the mean for each class.
   (b) Using the mean as the prototype, classify the sample $(1, -1)$ by the nearest neighbor algorithm using the following three metrics:
      i. Euclidean
      ii. City-block
      iii. Maximum coordinate

5. (a) What is the objective of the Parzen window technique?
   (b) What are the restrictions on the function that can be used for $\phi(u)$?
   (c) If $\phi(u) = (1/(2\pi)^{1/2}\exp(-1/2\, u^2)$, what is the interpretation of $\phi[(x - x_i)/h_n]$?
   (d) In the formula $p(x) = [k/n]/V$, how should k compare to n?

6. For the decision tree in Figure 15.2, show how the cumulative probabilities are calculated. Using the information in this tree, what decision would you make regarding vaccination for hepatitis? Do you think other factors should be considered? If so, how would these be incorporated into the decision tree structure?

REFERENCES

Afifi, A.A., and Clark, V. 1990. *Computer-aided multivariate analysis*. 2nd ed. New York: Van Nostrand Reinhold.

California Statistical Software, Inc. 1985. *An introduction to CART methodology*. Lafayette, CA.

Dixon, W.J., Brown, M.B., Engleman, L., and Jennrich, R.I. 1990. *BMDP statistical software*. Berkeley: University of California Press.

Duda, R.O., and Hart, P.E. 1973. *Pattern classification and scene analysis*. New York: Wiley-Interscience.

Glantz, S.A. 1992. *Primer of biostatistics*. 3rd ed. New York: McGraw-Hill.

Patrick, E.A. 1994. Statistical pattern recognition. *Proceedings, IPMU:* 142–147.

Patrick, E.A., and Fattu, J.M. 1986. *Artificial intelligence with statistical pattern recognition*. Englewood Cliffs, NJ: Prentice-Hall.

Raymond, B., Taverner, D., Nandagopal, D., and Mazumdar, J. 1997. Classification of heart rate variability in patients with mild hypertension. *Australasian Physical and Engineering Sciences in Medicine* **20(4):** 207–212.

16

Fuzzy Systems

16.1 INTRODUCTION

This chapter presents an overview of fuzzy techniques as they are used in neural networks and expert systems, with the goal of acquainting the reader with the broad range of tools that are available. The field of fuzzy logic is very well developed theoretically and has many practical applications. References are provided as a guide for those who wish to investigate any of these areas in depth.

16.2 FUZZY INFORMATION

We begin this chapter with a short overview of fuzzy information with examples of its role in biomedical applications.

16.2.1 Input Data

As a starting point, most data items used for decision making are considered to be crisp, that is, not fuzzy. Some data items that appear to be crisp are listed here, along with their data types (Hudson and Cohen, 1993):

x_1:   Duration of chest pain (duration data)
x_2:   Change in diastolic blood pressure (Δ data)
x_3:   Number of PVCs per minute (normalized Δ data)
x_4:   Pain occurring before sweating occurring before nausea (sequence data)
x_5:   Abnormal ECG (binary data)
x_6:   Type of arrhythmia (categorical data)
x_7:   Blood gas values (continuous data)

Some of these variables can in fact be fuzzy variables. For x_1, the duration of chest pain may be approximate; instead of reporting two hours duration, a more likely response is "about two hours." This value can be represented as a fuzzy number, as illustrated above. For x_2, the change in blood pressure can be interpreted as fuzzy owing to the approximate nature of the blood pressure reading. In this case, both readings would be approximate, and the difference would be computed using fuzzy subtraction. For details on fuzzy arithmetic, see Dubois and Prade (1980). As x_3 is an actual count, it is inherently crisp. For x_4 an algorithm for partial presence of a sequence would be invoked. This method will be discussed later in this section. Although x_5 appears to be a straightforward binary variable, in fact more information is imparted by indicating the degree of abnormality. Instead of entering a 0 or 1, a number between 0 and 10 can be entered, which indicates the level of abnormality. As x_6 is strictly categorical, it could be fuzzified only if each category were considered separately and a degree of membership were established for each category. In the case of x_7, the blood gas levels can be considered fuzzy numbers because of the test's limited accuracy.

The decision of whether these variables should be included as crisp or fuzzy depends on the impact that the fuzzified version will have on the decision. This can be determined experimentally by establishing different models and comparing classification results. The introduction of fuzzy input causes substantial problems in most neural network learning algorithms.

16.2.2 Fuzzy Logic and Fuzzy Set Theory

Fuzzy set theory was introduced by Zadeh in the mid-1960's (Zadeh, 1965). The basic concept is that propositions are not necessarily true or false but rather have a degree to which they are true, represented by a number between 0 and 1, inclusive. Traditional propositional binary logic is replaced by new mathematical concepts that permit conjunctions, disjunctions, and implications in terms of these partial truth-values. A component of fuzzy logic, fuzzy set theory allows partial set membership, a concept that is useful in classification problems.

Since the introduction of fuzzy logic, the field has expanded enormously in terms of both theoretical developments and practical applications. For an overview of the theory behind fuzzy systems, see Kaufmann (1985) and the journal *Fuzzy Sets and Systems,* which contains both theory and applications. Fuzzy techniques have found their way into a number of commercial products, including elevators, trains, cameras, and rice cookers. Earlier we mentioned fuzzy biomedical applications in neural networks and artificial intelligence; we will present some more examples in this chapter.

16.2.3 Representation of Fuzzy Variables

When we discussed variable types, we briefly mentioned fuzzy variables. In general, a fuzzy variable is represented either as a triangular or trapezoidal function, as illustrated in Figure 16.1. As an illustration, consider a test result such as systolic blood pressure. For a patient with a reading of 117, there is a margin of error due to the measure's degree of accuracy. If it is known that the margin of error is ±3, then the true reading is somewhere between 114 and 120. If this information is represented as a triangular fuzzy number, then 117 is the most likely value and has a corresponding membership of 1, while the membership drops to zero the further you are from this value. If a trapezoidal representation is used instead, then all values between 114 and 120 have a membership of 1, with the membership dropping to zero beyond these limits.

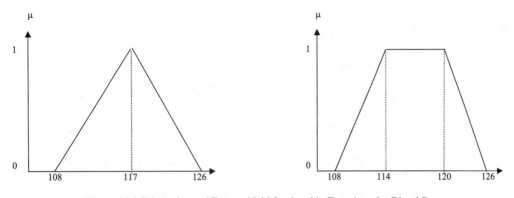

Figure 16.1 Triangular and Trapezoidal Membership Functions for Blood Pressure Readings.

16.2.4 Membership Functions

Biomedical variables can be defined as fuzzy sets, along with membership functions that indicate the degree to which an item belongs to a fuzzy set. For example, normal systolic blood pressure is a fuzzy subset of possible ranges of blood pressure. A particular value assumes a membership function in this fuzzy subset. A specific blood pressure value for a patient can be interpreted as a fuzzy number that accounts for the imprecision in the measurement. These concepts were illustrated in Figure O.1 in the Overview.

16.3 FUZZY NEURAL NETWORKS

Medical data often defy precise interpretation because diseases come in different states or in combination with other diseases. It is difficult to represent multiclass membership. Patients also suffer from a particular disease to different degrees (e.g., mild, moderate, severe). The degree of illness can be expressed as the patient's degree of membership in the class representing the disease. Furthermore, one disease may cause, complicate, or alleviate another. The dependence between classes corresponds to the dependence between diseases.

The overlapping nature of classes contributes to uncertainty. Fuzzy feature vectors can simultaneously have degrees of membership in these overlapping classes, exploiting the notion of similarity to conflicting classes. Crisp partitioning fails to exploit this similarity. A fuzzy partition algorithm indicates high partial memberships in multiple classes. Fuzzy sets are useful during feature analysis to represent input data with linguistic variables rather than exact numerical definitions. Fuzzy sets are also used for classification to maintain partial class memberships and to estimate missing information in terms of membership values (Ruspini, 1969).

A traditional neuron performs a summation of weighted input values and fires if the summation exceeds a prespecified threshold. The fuzzy neuron is similar except that it can process vague information via the membership function. The inputs to the fuzzy neuron, fuzzy sets $X_1, X_2, \ldots, X_N$, are weighted differently from those in the nonfuzzy case. The weighted inputs are then aggregated not by summation but by the fuzzy aggregation operation. The fuzzy output may remain with or without further operations. A number of researchers have developed approaches to fuzzy neural networks (Kuncicky and Kandel, 1989; Lee and Lee, 1975).

The difference between clustering and classification is that clustering algorithms label given data sets $X \varepsilon R^p$ as a group, whereas a classifier can label every data point in the entire space as R^p. Usually, classifiers are designed with labeled data (supervised learning). The partitioning decision functions may be computationally explicit discriminant functions, nearest prototype rules, or implicit multilayered perceptions, or k-nearest neighbor rules. Like fuzzy clustering, fuzzy classification preserves multiclass membership in similar classes and typically results in a hard design. This idea can be attributed to embedding: finding a better solution to a crisp problem by initially looking in a larger space with different constraints, thereby allowing the algorithm more freedom to avoid errors by making hard decisions in intermediate stages. As an example, consider the crisp k-nearest neighbor algorithm as opposed to the fuzzy k-nearest neighbor algorithm (K-NN). Both the fuzzy and crisp algorithms search the labeled sample set for the K-nearest neighbors. Other than obtaining these K samples, the procedures differ considerably. The fuzzy K-NN algorithm assigns class membership to a sample vector rather than assigning the vector to a particular class. Thus the algorithm makes no arbitrary assignments, assigning membership as a function of the vector's distance from its k-nearest neighbors and those neighbors' memberships in the possible classes.

The following sections outline a number of approaches to this problem. These approaches fall into two main categories: introduction of a pre-processor in order to handle the fuzzy input and direct modification of the learning algorithm to handle interval data. As a third alternative, a more radical reinterpretation of neural networks using an analogue model has been proposed. This model uses additional properties of biological nervous systems.

16.4 FUZZY APPROACHES FOR SUPERVISED LEARNING NETWORKS

Neural networks lend themselves well to dealing with uncertainty in that weights are adjusted according to input data. A number of issues arise in neural network research in handling uncertain or fuzzy information. These can be divided into several areas:

Input data.

Propagation of results through the network.

Interpretation of final results.

In terms of the fuzzy implementation of neural networks, none of these aspects has currently been totally resolved.

16.4.1 Pre-Processing of Fuzzy Input

In work by Sanchez (1989), a first layer to the neural network is established which represents linguistic information. Primary weights are in linguistic form and are interpreted as labels for fuzzy sets, such as decreased, normal, or increased. In addition, secondary weights in the interval [0, 1] indicate the connection's degree of weakness. The linguistic weights are then used to produce values at the intermediate, or hidden level. At this level, numeric values are then used in a learning algorithm to produce the values for the third, and final, layer.

Yager (1984) concentrates on the aggregation at each neuron and its relationship to fundamental ideas from fuzzy logic. Specifically, a degree of membership is associated with the level of firing of a neuron. The process that determines the firing level of a neuron can be associated with the evaluation of the truth of a fuzzy proposition. This can be extended to define a model for competitive firing of neurons.

In work by Gupta and Gorzalczay (1991), a fuzzy neuro-computational model is established in three steps: (1) quantization of the fuzzy variable spaces, definition of fuzzy sets, and choice of model structure; (2) derivation of rules describing the system behavior and application of appropriate learning technique; and (3) assessment of the model quality. Nonfuzzy (crisp) and fuzzy data are transferred to the perception level, determined by the primary fuzzy sets that are then processed by the neural network structure.

16.4.2 PROPAGATION OF RESULTS

16.4.2.1 Max–Min Networks. Saito and Mukaidono (1991) propose a max-min algorithm to replace the traditional sum-product algorithms that are used traditionally in neural network learning algorithms. A number of self-consistent fuzzy systems can be designed using *t*-norms and *t*-co-norms (Dubois and Prade, 1980). These are defined in Section 16.6.4.1. Thus the traditional sum-product paradigm for weight combination is replaced by one of these constructs. The minimum and maximum of membership functions are often used in place of AND and OR operations, respectively. A max-min network generally consists of a number of nodes that use either the min or the max operation to combine weights. The max-product networks are similar to the max-min networks except that the product is used in place of the min.

16.4.2.2 Learning Algorithms for Interval Data. Fujioka et al. (1991) describe a learning algorithm that handles interval data. The learning algorithm maps interval-valued data into an interval that becomes the final result. Sums are computed for the lower and upper values of the input intervals. A cost function is defined. The objective of the learning algorithm is to minimize the cost function. The algorithm can handle non-interval-input in a degenerated interval with equal limits.

In the simplest case, a fuzzy number can be represented by a membership function considered symmetric and triangle, and can thus be interpreted by the endpoints of the interval. Even in this case, however, the learning algorithm must be able to handle interval data, which requires a major revision in most established learning algorithms.

In order to handle interval data as input, the following is proposed. For a data set with n variables, define a vector (Cohen and Hudson, 1992)

$$\mathbf{x} = [(x_1, y_1), (x_2, y_2), \ . \ . \ . \ ,(x_n, y_n)] \tag{16.1}$$

where (x_i, y_i) represents the interval range for the ith variable. The values for (x_i, y_i) will be determined by the input data in the training set for the learning algorithm. The objective is to obtain a decision surface that will separate data at any point in the interval. This can be accomplished if the extreme values are accommodated. In order to do this, all possible combinations of interval endpoints must be considered. For a data set with n variables, 2^n combinations will be produced. A new set of $2n$ vectors is then defined:

$$\mathbf{z}_k = [z_1, z_2, \ . \ . \ . \ ,z_n] \qquad k = 1, \ . \ . \ . \ ,2^n \tag{16.2}$$

where $z_i \, \varepsilon \, (x_i, y_j) \ni$ all possible combinations of x_i, y_j are generated for $i,j = 1, \ldots, n$. The learning algorithm is run for each of the 2^n cases. The weights attached to the decision surface that produces the poorest classification are chosen in order to form a robust model (Hudson and Cohen, 1992).

16.4.2.3 Analogue Models.   Another approach suggested by Rocha, Theoto, and Rocha (1991) for the design of future neural network models is the introduction of an analogue, rather than a digital component, which would more closely represent the analogue nature of the neurotransmitters in actual biological nervous systems. Such an analogue system could directly interpret fuzzy information without progressing through the digitization stage that requires some type of approximation.

16.5 FUZZY GENERALIZATIONS OF UNSUPERVISED LEARNING METHODS

A number of the methods we saw in Chapter 5 can be generalized to use fuzzy concepts.

16.5.1 Fuzzy Associative Memories

The purpose of associative memories is to map data to data. Fuzzy association refers to the storage and recall of uncertain associations. Either the associations or the patterns, or both, can be uncertain. Traditional associative memories rely on *modus ponens* of traditional logic where the stored pair (A, B) represents $A \rightarrow B$. For fuzzy associative memories the approximate data item $A' \approx A$ results in the recall of $B' \approx B$. For those who are interested in more details, Kosko (1991) analyzes a number of associative memory structures in terms of fuzzy techniques, including BAMs, Hopfield nets, and the Cohen–Grossberg auto-associations, along with such topics as fuzzy cognitive maps.

Carpenter and Grossberg (1996), along with other workers, have developed fuzzy ARTMAP algorithms that use, among other techniques, linguistic variables, in which the min operator defines features that are critically present, while the max operator defines features that are critically absent. The min operator is translated into cells in the neural network which are turned on, while the max operator is represented by cells that are turned off.

16.5.2 Fuzzy Clustering

The purpose of clustering is to partition data into a number of subsets (Akay, Cohen, and Hudson, 1997). Within a set, the elements are as similar as possible to each other; elements from different sets are as different as possible. Given any finite data set, the purpose of clustering is to assign object labels that identify subsets within the given data set. Because the data are unlabeled, this problem is often called unsupervised learning, that is, learning the correct labels for subsets. Fuzzy methods can be used for clustering in several ways (Bezdek, 1987):

> **Relation Criterion Functions:** Clustering controlled by an optimization of a criterion function of the grouped data.
> **Object Criterion Functions:** Clustering controlled by an optimization of an objective function based directly on the data on an n-dimensional feature space.

This subdivision is the most popular with fuzzy c-means (number of classes known a priori).

Fuzzy Isodata: Iterative, self-organizing data analysis techniques, number of classes unknown.

Convex Decomposition: Decomposing a set of fuzzy clusters into a combination of convex sets.

Numerical Transitive: Extracting crisp equivalence relations from fuzzy similarity relations.

Generalized Nearest Neighbor Rules (Keller, Gray, and Givens, 1985): Degree of cluster membership based on metrics.

An example is the following algorithm for hard/fuzzy c-means clustering (HCM/FCM) (see Bezdek, 1981):

HCM/FCM Clustering Algorithm

Given an unlabeled data set $X = \{x_1, \ldots ,x_n\}$, *fix* c *(number of clusters),* T, $\| \|_A$ *and* $\varepsilon > 0$.

Initialize

$U_0 \varepsilon M_{fcn}$. *Choose* $m \geq 1$. *Compute weight vectors*

$$\mathbf{v}_i = \left[\sum_{k=1}^{n} u_{ik}\,\mathbf{x}_k\right] / \left[\sum_{k=1}^{n} u_{ik}^{\,m}\right] \qquad for\ i = 1,2, \ldots ,c \qquad (16.3)$$

where: $m\ \varepsilon\ [1, \infty)$:   *constrained fuzzy partitioning of* X

$\mathbf{v}\ = (v_1, \ldots , v_c)$: c *vector prototypes in* R^p

A: *any positive definite* (s x s) *matrix*

For $t = 1,2, \ldots ,T$

Compute all cn *fuzzy memberships* $\{u_{ik,\,t}\}$ *by one of the following*

If HCM

$$u_{ik} = \begin{cases} 1 & \|\mathbf{x}_k - \mathbf{v}_t\|_A < \|\mathbf{x}_k - \mathbf{v}_j\|_A, j = 1, \ldots ,c, j \neq i \\ 0 & otherwise \end{cases} \quad (16.4)$$

If FCM

$$u_{ik} = [\textstyle\sum_{l}(\|\mathbf{x}_k - \mathbf{v}_t\|/\|\mathbf{x}_k - \mathbf{v}_j\|_A)^{2/m-1}]^{-1} 1 \leq i \leq c, 1 \leq k \leq n \quad (16.5)$$

Update all c *weight vectors using (16.3).*

Compute $E_t = \|v_{t+1} - v_t\| = \sum^{c} \|v_{i,t+1} - v_{i,t}\|$ $\qquad\qquad\qquad (16.6)$

If $E_t \leq \varepsilon$, *stop; else next* t.

16.6 REASONING WITH UNCERTAIN INFORMATION

As we saw in Chapter 9, the need to deal with uncertain information was recognized in the earliest medical expert systems and was generally dealt with through the use of certainty factors. Since that time, more sophisticated techniques taken from a number of theoretical concepts have been employed. There are numerous examples of expert systems that utilize fuzzy techniques (Adlassnig, 1982; Esogbue, 1983; Gupta and Gorzalczay, 1985; Kandel and Langholz, 1991; Cohen and Hudson, 1995). In the following sections, we look at different aspects of uncertainty in knowledge-based systems.

16.6.1 Uncertainty in Input Data

16.6.1.1 Degree of Presence Input.   Although the above procedure utilizes fuzzy matching for words and phrases, the effect on the invocation of rules is still binary: either an antecedent is substantiated or it is not. A simple modification to this procedure is to allow a degree of presence to be entered instead of a yes/no/? response. Thus the questioning mode will change to

Questioning Mode

Blood pressure low? 8
Syncope? 3
Abnormal mental status? 9

and the data-driven mode will change to:

Data-Driven Mode
Enter any clinical findings followed by a value between 0 and 10 indicating degree of presence.

Low blood pressure 8
Abnormal mental state 9

The values are normalized by dividing by 10. Note that the entry of these numbers does not change the word and phrase matching described earlier but does affect the operation of the inference engine to be discussed later in this chapter.

16.6.1.2 Linguistic Input.   Another possibility for user input is to present the questions in the following format:

Question Mode
Indicate the range of symptoms according to the following (low, medium, high), or (normal, abnormal)

Blood pressure: low
Mental status: abnormal

The first entry requires numeric interpretation that is most easily done by predefined membership functions as shown in Figure O.2 of the Overview. The inference engine interprets the value obtained in the same manner as the values entered in the previous section. The second entry is treated simply as binary input.

16.6.2 Uncertainty in Knowledge Base

The knowledge base itself traditionally contains production rules in the format illustrated above:

IF   ALL OF
        Antecedent 1
        .

.
.
.
       Antecedent n
THEN   Conclusion

This structure can be altered by the introduction of linguistic quantifiers that were first presented by Zadeh (1978). There are two types of linguistic quantifiers: Kind 1 and Kind 2. Kind 1 quantifiers, or absolute quantifiers, represent a specified amount, such as about three, at least four, or all. Kind 2 quantifiers, or relative quantifiers, represent an approximate amount, such as most or some. An absolute quantifier can be expressed as a fuzzy subset of nonnegative real numbers, whereas a relative quantifier can be expressed as a fuzzy subset of the unit interval.

Using Kind 1 quantifiers, we can change the rule structure to:

IF   At least m of
            Antecedent 1
.
.
.
            Antecedent n
THEN   Conclusion

where $1 \leq m \leq n$.
Use of this type of quantifier results in minor modifications to the inference engine. If Kind 2 quantifiers are used:

IF   Most of
            Antecedent 1
.
.
.
            Antecedent n
THEN   Conclusion

then more major modifications are required.

Further modifications to the rule base include the possibility that the antecedents do not contribute equally (i.e., quantifiers are associated with each antecedent) and that each antecedent may be partially substantiated. Incorporation of this type of knowledge base is discussed below under other approximate reasoning techniques.

16.6.3 Inference Engines for Uncertain Information

The heart of the decision process in knowledge-based system is the inference engine. Although rule searching may be done by a number of strategies, a particular rule is confirmed by matching the premises with case information.

16.6.3.1 Binary Logic Engines. Traditional rule-based systems used binary logic inference engines with rules that were only conjunctions. Thus each antecedent had to be substantiated for the rule to fire. The original EMERGE system modified this structure to permit the inclusion of a subset of Kind 1 quantifiers represented by "at least m of" where $0 \leq m \leq n$, where n was the number of antecedents. Thus the input was still binary, but different degrees of substantiation were permitted.

16.6.3.2 Fuzzy Logic Engines. The normal production rule format has un-qualified antecedents. For a one-antecedent rule,

$$\text{IF } (X \text{ is } A) \text{ THEN } (Y \text{ is } B)$$

These statements are considered all or nothing. However, membership functions $f_A(x)$ and $f_B(x)$ can be defined which describe to what degree X is A and Y is B, respectively, at every point x and y of the universes, U_x and U_y—in other words to what degree these propositions are satisfied at each point.

16.6.4 Evidential Reasoning

Evidential reasoning implies that evidence to support a premise is aggregated by some method. In systems that use binary logic, a proposition is either confirmed or it is not, but if uncertainty is present, evidence is aggregated to support a conclusion. It is seldom possible to aggregate sufficient evidence to be 100 percent certain of the out-come. Some approaches to evidence aggregation include possibility theory which uti-lizes fuzzy techniques, probability-based techniques, and the Dempster–Shafer Belief Theory, which is an extension of probability theory.

16.6.4.1 Possibility Theory. A possibility distribution can be defined by as-signing to every element x in U_X a degree of possibility (Zadeh, 1983):

$$\pi_X(x) = f_A(x) \tag{16.7}$$

Let $r(x, y)$ represent the strength of the implication. There are a number of possibili-ties for the definition of $r(x, y)$, which are described in Bouchon-Meunier (1992). An example is the Mamdani Implication:

$$r(x, y) = \min(f_A(x), f_B(y)) \tag{16.8}$$

As an example, consider the rule

IF (blood pressure is low) THEN (shock is present)

$f_A(x)$ and $f_B(y)$ must be defined. The respective universes of discourse are the range of all possible values, $U_x = [0, 300]$, $U_y = [0, 1]$, where 0 indicates absent and 1 indicates present.

In order to implement a reasoning process, these rules must be combined with data to produce conclusions. In ordinary binary logic, *modus ponens* is used for this purpose. Again, several possibilities have been proposed for a fuzzy *modus ponens* (Bouchon-Meunier, 1992). Assume the actual data for the above rule is

$$X \text{ is } A'.$$

Define an operation T such that

$$g_{B'}(y) = \max (T(g_{A'}(x), r(x, y))). \tag{16.9}$$

where $g_{A'}(x)$ and $g_{B'}(x)$ are membership functions. Usually, T is a *t*-norm (Kosko, 1986), which is a function satisfying the following properties:

$$T(x, 1) = x \qquad\qquad \text{(Boundary)} \tag{16.10}$$

$$T(x, y) = T(y, x) \qquad\qquad \text{(Symmetry)} \tag{16.11}$$

$$T(x, z) \le T(y, z) \text{ if } x \le y \quad \text{(Monotonicity)} \tag{16.12}$$

$$T(x, T(y, z)) = T(T(x, y), z) \quad \text{(Associativity)} \tag{16.13}$$

The most common choice for a t-norm is the minimum. T must be chosen in conjunction with $r(x, y)$ to preserve the conclusion when the observation is identical with the premise.

Usually, production rules have multiple antecedents and take the form

IF $(V_1$ is $A_1)$ and $(V_2$ is $A_2)$ . . . and $(V_n$ is $A_n)$, THEN U is B (Yager, 1984).

The possibility distribution discussed earlier can be generalized to

$$\pi_{v_1, v_2, \ldots, v_n, u} \text{ on } X_1 \, X \, X_2 \ldots, X_n \, X \, Y$$

such that

$$\pi_{v_1, v_2, \ldots, v_n, u} = 1 \, \hat{} \, (1 - A_1(x_1) \, \hat{} \, A_2(x_2) \ldots \hat{} \, A_n(x_n) + B(y)) \tag{16.14}$$

where $\pi_i(x) = A_i(x)$ are the individual possibility measures and $\hat{}$ is the min operator. For example,

IF $(BP < 100/60)$, THEN (shock is present)

must be separated into the components

IF   (Systolic BP $<$ 100) AND (Diastolic BP $<$ 60)
THEN (shock is present)

or alternately

IF   (Systolic BP is low) AND (Diastolic BP is low)
THEN (shock is present)

16.6.4.2 Probabilistic Approaches. Many probabilistic approaches, such as Bayes' Theory, lend themselves to evidence aggregation. These approaches have been discussed in Chapter 15. We include them here to emphasize their possible uses in dealing with uncertain information.

16.6.4.3 Dempster–Shafer Belief Theory. The Dempster–Shafer Theory of Evidence is based on set theory. A very brief description is given here. For those interested in theoretical details, refer to Shafer (1976). For applications to expert systems, see Buchanan and Shortliffe (1984).

Assume that there are n possible hypotheses that are mutually exclusive and exhaustive. Each piece of evidence is assigned a probability called a bpa (basic probability assumption). $M(A)$ is the measure of the probability or belief assigned to the element A. $m(\theta)$ is the measure of the portion of total belief that remains unassigned. A belief function (Bel) assigns to every subset S the sum of beliefs specified by a specific bpa, that is, for two hypotheses h_i and h_j (Fu, 1994):

$$\text{Bel}(h_i, h_j) = m((h_i, h_j)) + m(h_i) + m(h_j) \tag{16.15}$$

The belief interval for A is $[\text{Bel}(A), 1 - \text{Bel}(A^C)]$ where A^C is the complement of A. Evidence is combined for two bpa's by

$$m_1 \oplus m_2 \, (S_0) = \sum m_1(S) \, m_2(S) \tag{16.16}$$

where ⊕ is the combining operator $S_i \cap S_j = S$.

Römer and Kandel (1995) draw interesting comparisons between the Dempster–Shafer theory and the use of fuzzy evidences in Bayesian systems. They apply these principles in medical reasoning using the concept of partial beliefs conditioned on fuzzy events.

16.6.5 Compatibility Indices

Fuzzy matching can be used as a direct means of classification (Sanchez, 1989). Applying this method to the heart disease example, consider the three-category problem of differentiating among normal heart function, myocardial infarction, and angina pectoris. Assuming four possible variables apply, we get fuzzy set descriptions summarized in Table 16.1 using the variables blood pressure (BP), pulse rate (PR), white blood count (WBC), and postventricular contractions (PVCs). The last of these (PVCs) is a type of arrhythmia. The corresponding membership functions are illustrated in Figure 16.2 (Hudson and Cohen, 1994).

TABLE 16.1   Ranges for Angina and MI

	BP	PR	WBC	PVC's
Angina Pectoris	Increased	Increased	Normal	None
Myocardial Infarction	Decreased	Increased	Elevated	>3

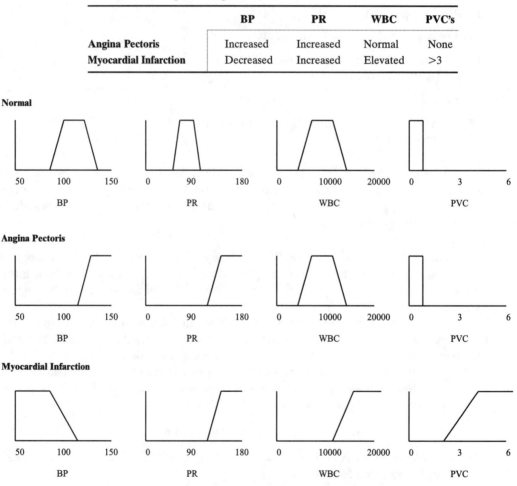

Figure 16.2 Membership Functions Corresponding to Table 16.1.

Classification of a patient case using this information can be done through use of compatibility indices, which are illustrated in Figure 16.3. This figure shows the matching of patient data represented as a triangular fuzzy number F (heavy triangle) with a possible membership function M (heavy trapezoid). The complement of F is shown as a thin line consisting of an inverted triangle with lines on each end with a membership value of 1.

The first measure is the possibility measure. It is defined as

$$\pi(M, F) = \text{Sup } (M \cap F) \tag{16.17}$$

The second is the necessity measure:

$$v(M, F) = 1 - \pi(M', F) = 1 - \text{Sup}(M' \cap F) = \text{Inf}(M \cup F') \tag{16.18}$$

The third is the truth-possibility index

$$\rho(M, F) = \pi(\tau_0, \tau_1) \tag{16.19}$$

With the fuzzy sets described here, the truth-possibility index is "around f" with the following holding

$$v \leq \rho \leq \pi$$

The index to be used is chosen according to optimistic or pessimistic considerations. These three indices yield slightly different results. It is up to the user to decide on the choice depending on how conservative he or she wishes to be in the matching process. The characterizations given here can also be weighted according to relative importance, as with the rules described above, in which case relative heights are adjusted.

16.6.6 Approximate Reasoning

In order to accommodate Kind 2 quantifiers, we need to change the rule structure. To use quantifiers, each proposition P in a rule is replaced with

P: QVs are A

or more commonly

Q(RVs) are A

where the second type of statement can be interpreted as, for example,

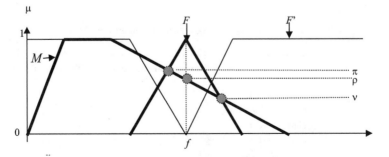

Figure 16.3 Compatibility Indices (F: Fuzzy number for input data, M: Membership function).

(At least n) (important) objectives are satisfied by x

where Q is "at least n" and R is "important."

   Again, a number of possibilities exist. In order to determine the truth-value of P, we consider some subset C of V such that (1) the number of elements in C satisfies Q, or (2) each element in C satisfies the property A. The degree to which P is satisfied by C will be denoted as $V_P(C)$. The overall validity is then (Hudson and Cohen, 1988):

$$V(P) = \max_{C \, \varepsilon \, 2^A} \{V_p(x)\} \qquad\qquad (16.20)$$

where 2^A is the power set of A. If Q is a Kind 1 quantifier, then

$$V(P) = \max[Q \, (\sum_{i=1}^{n} c_i \wedge q_i) \wedge \min_{i=1,\ldots,n} a_i^{c_i \wedge q_i}] \qquad\qquad (16.21)$$

$c \, \varepsilon \, [0, 1]$ indicates the membership status, r_i the weighting factor for the ith antecedent that indicates its relative importance, and a_i the degree of presence of the ith finding, entered by the user. The values for r_i are determined through expert consultation or through use of a neural network model. For an example of an antecedent with weighting factors, refer to Table 16.2. In the general case, Q may also be a Kind 2 quantifier, in which case the summation in Eq. (16.20) is normalized by dividing by the summation over i of the r_i values.

16.7 PRE-PROCESSING AND POST-PROCESSING USING FUZZY TECHNIQUES

At the final level, a decision must be made as to whether results should be de-fuzzified. Depending on the algorithm employed, the de-fuzzification may have occurred at an earlier stage. In the case of the systems that use pre-processing of fuzzy information, the result will in general be de-fuzzified. In systems that use learning algorithms for interval data, the final result will in general be an interval that must be properly interpreted according to the application. Some neural network learning algorithms provide a classification as well as a degree of membership in that classification.

   Another approach (Yager, 1991) concentrates on the aggregation at each neuron and its relationship to fundamental ideas from fuzzy logic. Specifically, a degree of

TABLE 16.2   Sample Antecedent with Weights and Degree of Presence

Symptom	Degree of Presence	Weighting Factor
Low blood pressure	0.8	0.5
Abnormal mental status	0.9	0.1
Cold, clammy skin	1.0	0.1
Gray, cyanotic skin	0.3	0.1
Weak peripheral pulses	0.7	0.1
Low urinary output	0.6	0.1

membership is associated with the level of firing of a neuron. The process that determines the firing level of a neuron can be associated with evaluation of the truth of a fuzzy proposition. This can be extended to define a model for competitive firing of neurons.

In a more complex structure (Gupta and Gorzalczay, 1991), a fuzzy neuro-computational model is established in three steps: (1) quantization of the fuzzy variable spaces, definition of fuzzy sets, choice of model structure; (2) derivation of rules describing the system behavior, application of appropriate learning technique; and (3) assessment of the model quality. Nonfuzzy and fuzzy data are transferred to the perception level determined by the primary fuzzy sets that are then processed by the neural network structure.

16.8 APPLICATIONS IN BIOMEDICAL ENGINEERING

One of the common applications of fuzzy logic is in control. Many commercial products now use fuzzy control. The list includes elevators, cameras, washing machines, and even rice cookers! Fuzzy control can be used effectively in some medical devices. Potential applications of fuzzy control are outlined in Rau et al. (1995). Rau et al. are developing two prototype devices using fuzzy rules. The first is for fuzzy control of a total artificial heart (TAH). Fuzzy rules are used to control the filling phase and the ejection phase of the heart. The fuzzy rule base consists of twenty-five rules. A sample rule is

IF   Filling is fast
        AND
        Pump rate is good
THEN   Pump rate a little faster

These rules are represented in the form of membership functions for each premise, in this case filling rate and pump rate. A membership function is also used for change of pump rate. Inferences are made using the methods described above. Figure 16.4 shows these membership functions.

The second application is the establishment of intelligent alarms for use in cardioanesthesia. The goal of this system is to monitor vital parameters such as blood pressure, temperature, and blood gases. The alarm sounds if the parameters are outside of an acceptable state, but it is up to the anesthesiologist to make the decision regarding changes in treatment (Becker et al., 1997). The system is knowledge-based and uses a fuzzy logic process model. The knowledge base was designed in consultation with a cardiac anesthesiologist. The patient's vital parameters are gathered from conventional monitoring devices and information systems and are then evaluated using fuzzy logic. A sample rule in the system is:

If "AP_{sys}" is good and "LAP" is too high, then "preload" is too high (0.8).

Where AP_{sys} is arterial systolic pressure, LAP is left arterial pressure, and preload is a state variable. Linguistic variables are used to describe input parameters. Membership functions are then defined for each linguistic variable. The prototype system has been evaluated and shows sensitivity, specificity, and predictability to be very good compared to conventional systems.

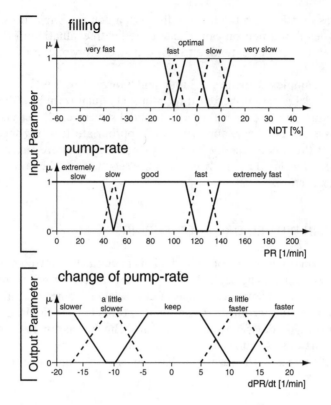

Figure 16.4 Membership Funtions for the Fuzzy TAH Controller (Rau et al., 1995).

16.9 SUMMARY

Use of techniques from fuzzy logic, approximate reasoning, and evidence aggregation can enhance the performance of decision-support systems, especially when dealing with borderline cases in which nuances are important. The advantages of these methods must be balanced against the increased complexity of the reasoning process along with the accompanying higher computational demands. In addition, it may be more difficult to interpret the reasoning processes of these approaches. Use of fuzzy approaches in combination with other methods is discussed in Chapter 17.

EXERCISES

1. What are the advantages of defining input variables in terms of fuzzy numbers? What are the disadvantages?
2. Give examples of test results that would best be represented by:
   Triangular fuzzy numbers
   Trapezoidal fuzzy numbers
3. In fuzzy supervised learning algorithms, is the training time likely to be slower or faster than that in crisp learning algorithms? Explain.
4. Define a problem that would best be solved using fuzzy clustering. How will the output differ in fuzzy clustering and crisp clustering?

5. Show that the minimum satisfies the four conditions of a *t*-norm. Can you think of another function that would satisfy these conditions?

6. Set up an example for which you can use the concept of compatibility indices and construct a figure similar to Figure 16.3. Calculate the possibility measure and the necessity measure for your example.

7. For the example in Table 16.2, compute $V(P)$ from Eq. (16.20).

REFERENCES

Adlassnig, K.P. 1982. A survey on medical diagnosis and fuzzy subsets. In M.M. Gupta and E. Sanchez, eds., *Approximate reasoning in decision analysis,* pp. 203–217, Amsterdam: North-Holland.

Akay, M., Cohen, M.E., and Hudson, D.L. 1997. Fuzzy sets in life sciences. *Fuzzy Sets and Systems* **90(2):** 221–224.

Becker, K., Thull, B., Kasmacher-Leidinger, H., Stemmer, J., Rau, G., Kalff, G., and Zimmermann, H.J., 1997. Design and validation of an intelligent monitoring and alarm system based on a fuzzy logic process model. *Artificial Intelligence in Medicine* **11:** 33–53.

Bezdek, J.C. 1987. Some non-standard clustering algorithms. *NATO ASI Series G14.* Berlin: Springer-Verlag.

Bezdek, J.C. 1981. *Pattern recognition with fuzzy objective function algorithms.* New York: Plenum.

Bouchon-Meunier, B. 1992. Inferences with imprecisions and uncertainties in expert systems. In A. Kandel, ed., *Fuzzy expert systems.* pp. 43–54. Boca Raton, FL: CRC Press.

Buchanan, B.G., and Shortliffe, E.H. 1984. *Rule-based expert systems: the MYCIN experiments of the Stanford Heuristic Programming Project.* Reading, MA: Addison-Wesley.

Carpenter, G.A., and Grossberg, S. 1996. Learning categorization, rule formation, and prediction by fuzzy neural networks. In C.H. Chen, ed., *Fuzzy logic and neural network handbook*, pp. 2.1–2.33. New York: McGraw-Hill.

Cohen, M.E., and Hudson, D.L. 1995. *Comparative approaches to medical reasoning.* World Scientific, New Jersey.

Cohen, M.E., and Hudson, D.L. 1992. Approaches to handling of fuzzy input data in neural networks. *Proceedings, IEEE Conference on Fuzzy Systems:* 93–100.

Dubois, D., and Prade, H. 1980. *Fuzzy sets and systems: theory and applications.* Vol. 144. Orlando, FLA: Academic Press.

Esogbue, A.O. 1983. Measurement and valuation of a fuzzy mathematical model for medical diagnosis. *Fuzzy Sets and Systems* **10:** 223–242.

Fu, L.M. 1994. *Neural networks in computer intelligence.* New York: McGraw-Hill.

Fujioka, R., Ishibuchi, H., Tanaka, H., and Omae, M. 1991. Learning algorithm of neural networks for interval-valued data. In R. Lowen and M. Roubens, eds., *Proceedings, International Fuzzy Sets Association (IFSA):* 37–40.

Gupta, M.M., and Gorzalczay, M.B. Fuzzy neuro-computational techniques and its application to modeling and control. In Lowen and Roubens, eds., *Proceedings, IFSA:* 46–49.

Gupta, M.M., Kandel, A., Bandler, W., and Kiszka, B., eds. 1985. *Approximate reasoning in expert systems.* Amsterdam: North Holland.

Hudson, D.L., and Cohen, M.E. 1994. Fuzzy logic in medical expert systems. *IEEE EMBS Magazine* **13(5):** 693–698.

Hudson, D.L., and Cohen, M.E. 1993. The impact of fuzzy logic implementations on knowledge-based systems. *International Society for Computers and Applications:* 151–154.

Hudson, D.L., and Cohen, M.E. 1992. Approaches to handling of fuzzy input data in neural networks. *IEEE Conference on Fuzzy Systems:* 93–100.

Hudson, D.L., and Cohen, M.E. 1988. Approaches to management of uncertainty in an expert system. *International Journal of Intelligent Systems* **3:** 45–58.

Kandel, A. 1991. *Fuzzy expert systems,* Boca Raton, FL: CRC Press.

Kandel, A., and Langholz, G., eds. 1992. *Hybrid architectures for intelligent systems.* Boca Raton, FL: CRC Press.

Kaufmann, A., and Gupta, M.M. 1985. *Introduction to fuzzy arithmetic, theory, and applications.* New York: Van Nostrand Reinhold Co.

Kaufmann, R., Becker, K., Nix, C., Rau, G., and Reul, H. 1995. Fuzzy control concept for a total artificial heart. *Artificial Organs* **19(4):** 355–361.

Keller, J.M., Gray, M.R., and Givens, J.A., Jr., 1985. Fuzzy K-nearest neighbor algorithm. *IEEE Trans. Sys., Man, Cyber.,* **SMC 15(4):** 580–585.

Kosko, B. 1986. Fuzzy knowledge combination. *International Journal of Intelligent Systems.* **1:** 293–320.

Kosko, B. 1991. Fuzzy associative memory systems. In A. Kandel, ed., *Fuzzy expert systems.* pp. 135–162. Boca Raton, FL: CRC Press.

Kuncicky, D.C., and Kandel, A. 1989. A fuzzy interpretation of neural networks. *Proceedings, International Fuzzy Set Association* **3:** 113–116.

Lee, S.C., and Lee, E.T. 1975. Fuzzy neural networks. *Mathematical Biosciences* **23:** 151–177.

Rau, G., Becker, K., Kaufmann, R., and Zimmermann, H.J. 1995. Fuzzy logic and control: principal approach and potential applications in medicine. *Artificial Organs* **19(1):** 105–112.

Rocha, A.F., Theoto, M., and Rocha, M. 1991. Investigation medical linguistic variables. R. Lowen and M. Roubens, eds. *Proceedings, IFSA:* 180–183.

Rocha, A.F. 1990. Proposed methodology for knowledge acquisition: a study on congenital heart disease diagnosis. *Methods of Information in Medicine* **29:** 30–40.

Römer, C., and Kandel, A. 1995. The application of Bayesian inference with fuzzy evidences in medical reasoning. In M. Cohen and D. Hudson, eds., *Comparative approaches to medical reasoning,* pp. 199–201. Singapore: World Scientific.

Ruspini, E. 1969. A new approach to fuzzy clustering. *Information and Control* **15:** 22–32.

Saito, T., and Mukaidono, M. 1991. A learning algorithm for max-min network and its application to solve fuzzy relation equations. R. Lowen and M. Roubens, eds. *Proceedings, IFSA:* 184–187.

Sanchez, E., and Bartolin, R. 1989. Fuzzy inference and medical diagnosis, a case study. *Proceedings, First Annual Meeting, Biomedical Fuzzy Systems Association:* 1–18.

Shafer, G. 1976. *The theory of evidence.* Princeton, NJ: Princeton University Press.

Yager, R.R. 1991. Modeling and formulating fuzzy knowledge bases using neural networks. *Iona College Machine Intelligence Institute Report #MII-1111,* 1–29.

Yager, R.R. 1984. General multiple-objective functions and linguistically quantified statements. *International Journal of Man-Machine Studies* **21:** 389–400.

Zadeh, L.A. 1983. The role of fuzzy logic in the management of uncertainty in expert systems. *Fuzzy Sets and Systems* **11:** 199–227.

Zadeh, L.A. 1978. Fuzzy sets as a basis for a theory of possibility. *Fuzzy Sets and Systems* **1:** 3–28.

Zadeh, L.A. 1965. Fuzzy sets. *Information and Control* **8:** 338–353.

17

Hybrid Systems

17.1 HYBRID SYSTEMS APPROACHES

The term *hybrid system* has been used to describe any decision support approach that includes more than one methodology. A recent edited volume by Kandel and Langholz (1992) contains twelve papers combining different approaches for the design of medical decision aids and an additional six chapters describing applications of hybrid systems. The approaches used include knowledge-based systems, neural networks, fuzzy logic, learning systems, distributed systems, connectionist models, optimization, and hierarchical structures. Applications include data analysis, robotic skill acquisition, medical diagnosis, wastewater treatment, and scheduling of manufacturing systems.

The objective of the hybrid system approach is to bring as many tools to bear as possible on the problem at hand. Traditionally, many researchers have become advocates of their methodology and have sought to promote it as the preferred method. The hybrid system approach requires a step back from this advocacy to a more pragmatic approach to problem solving. A typical argument for using hybrid systems is the ability to include both expert-derived and data-derived knowledge in the same system, thus allowing all information to be incorporated.

Problems that arise in hybrid systems include the combination of diverse methods in a seamless manner to provide a system that is easy to use, the development of interfaces so that information derived from one technique can be used by another, and the validation of the overall model. Since the number of possibilities for combination of methods is quite large, it is not possible to discuss all problems that may arise. This chapter summarizes some of the techniques that have been discussed earlier in this book, emphasizing features important for the development of hybrid systems.

17.2 COMPONENTS OF HYBRID SYSTEMS

The major difficulty in combining different reasoning strategies arises in the combination of knowledge-based approaches and data-based approaches, as the sources of information are completely separate. It is this combination, however, that has the most to offer for the inclusion of all available information.

Basic strategies for combining two approaches include:

1. Using output of one method directly as input to another method.
2. Restructuring the output of one method to produce input to another method.
3. Running two methods independently and combining output information.
4. Using one methodology to significantly alter the structure of another.

The remainder of the chapter illustrates these combinations of methods.

17.2.1 Knowledge-Based Approaches

As we have seen in Part II of this book, a number of knowledge-based approaches have been developed. Salient attractive features of knowledge-based systems for the development of hybrid systems include:

Use of expert-supplied information.

Human-like reasoning processes.

Ability to provide explanations of conclusions.

Figure 17.1 shows a general system diagram for a knowledge-based system. The knowledge base is developed through consultation with experts in the application domain. It consists of rules or other appropriate knowledge structures, along with supplementary information such as certainty factors. The box with the heavy border represents the actual functioning of the expert system in which the inference engine uses the case data to try to substantiate rules. The list of substantiated rules is created, along with computation of certainty factors. The output from the system consists of the recommendations based on the substantiated rules, an explanation of the reasoning process, and specific information that can be recorded in the patient record.

Major difficulties are presented in combining the knowledge-based approach with data-driven approaches. Next we examine four components of the system: knowledge base, input, decision-making algorithm, and output.

17.2.1.1 Knowledge Base.   The knowledge structure is symbolic, with the only numerical component consisting of the certainty factors. The knowledge is derived from consultation with experts. Is there any way in which other approaches can augment this structure?

A number of researchers have tried to generate rules automatically from accumulated data rather than through consultation with experts (Cimino and Barnett, 1993; Dzeroski and Lavrac, 1996; Yager, 1991). Techniques that can be used for automatic rule generation include neural networks and genetic algorithms. (Specific techniques were discussed in Chapter 11.) The advantage of automatic rule generation is the reduction in time required for knowledge base development as well as the ability to develop knowledge bases without expert input. A number of disadvantages are also apparent. Rules that are derived automatically will require verification, and there is no guarantee that they are consistent, exclusive, and/or exhaustive. A more reasonable approach appears to be the combination of expert-supplied rules with generated rules.

A major area that can impact the structure of the knowledge base is fuzzy logic and fuzzy set theory. Techniques from multivalued logic permit the inclusion of more subtle reasoning strategies and more complex structures. They also permit the cer-

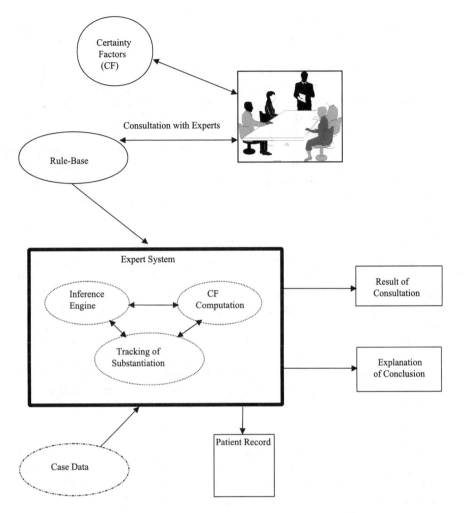

Figure 17.1 General Structure of a Knowledge-Based System.

tainty factor to be replaced with membership functions and degrees of substantiation that have stronger theoretical bases. Note that the use of fuzzy techniques does not remove the necessity for expert consultation and may actually increase the development time of knowledge bases because of the need to determine membership functions and rule thresholds (Hudson et al., 1992). (These techniques have been discussed in Chapter 16.) These numerical items can also be obtained through use of data-based approaches such as neural networks. Automatic generation of weights, membership functions, and thresholds will be discussed later in this chapter.

17.2.1.2 Input Data. In a knowledge-based system, what form does the input data take? Since the goal is generally to substantiate rules, the system attempts to collect information that is relevant to the premises. This can be done in a number of ways, depending on the user interface. The user may be asked to answer questions regarding the presence or absence of symptoms or previous history of disease and enter test results or other relevant data, including interpretations of medical images and ECG data. In traditional systems, these items are indicated as present or absent. Fuzzy techniques can be applied to allow the user to respond with degrees of presence rather than with simple presence or absence. Test results that are entered as numeric values can be interpreted as fuzzy numbers, as described in Chapter 16.

In some hybrid system approaches, output from data-driven models can be used as input for knowledge-based models. As an example, a neural network model can be used to determine the presence or absence of a certain condition that is then used as one premise in a more complex rule. In addition, other automatic processing models can be used to generate input for knowledge-based systems. One very common numerical method that is often overlooked as part of numerical processing because it has become so common is the output from automatic ECG processing algorithms. A related example is the processing of time series data using techniques such as chaotic analysis. In the next chapter, we will see an example of chaotic processing of Holter tapes (Cohen et al., 1994).

17.2.1.3 Decision-Making Algorithm.   As we saw in Chapter 12, traditional inference engines in knowledge-based systems use standard binary logic to confirm rules. They most often use some form of certainty factor to deal with uncertain information in the reasoning process. In Chapter 16, we looked at ways in which fuzzy techniques and other techniques in approximate reasoning can significantly expand the binary model to provide systems that indeed appear to reason in more humanistic terms. The combination of fuzzy logic with knowledge-based systems has been one of the major extensions of the basic inference engine concept. An example of an expert system that uses approximate reasoning is given in Chapter 18. Many researchers have developed fuzzy medical expert systems that employ different methodologies (Cohen and Hudson, 1995; Hudson, 1991; Rocha, 1989; Sanchez, 1989).

17.2.1.4 Output Data.   What kind of output do we expect from knowledge-based systems? For diagnostic systems, the primary goal is, of course, the diagnosis or perhaps a differential diagnosis. This is usually in the form of a statement of the probable disease, with an indication of the degree of certainty with which the system believes this is the actual situation, or in the case of differential diagnoses, a list of possibilities with allied certainty factors. Along with the outcome, an explanation of the reasoning that led to the conclusion is usually provided. Is it possible to use this information in other approaches? A simple extension would to be to include the outcome as a node (or for differential diagnosis multiple nodes) in a neural network or genetic algorithm that would then be used to generate a higher-level model. This approach is seldom utilized, for the diagnosis is usually the final decision. One exception would be to use this information in a model that established treatment possibilities. For differential diagnoses, this approach is potentially useful if the outcome from the knowledge-based system can be used in a data-based model in an attempt to narrow the possibilities or increase the likelihood of some of the possibilities.

17.2.2 Data-Based Approaches

Figure 17.2 shows a typical structure of a data-driven approach using a supervised learning algorithm. Note that our input is now entirely numeric, as is the output. In what ways can this information be used in knowledge-based systems? We will summarize a few possibilities for several data-based approaches.

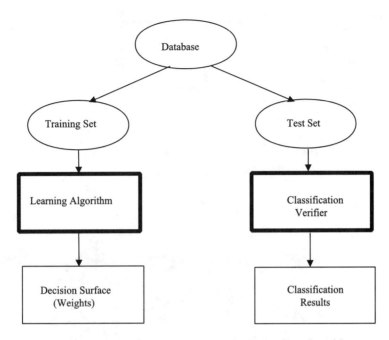

Figure 17.2 General Structure of a Supervised Learning Data-Based System.

17.2.2.1 Neural Networks. As mentioned earlier, one problem inherent in the knowledge-based approach is the determination of certainty factors. This problem is exacerbated if approximate reasoning techniques are employed, as in addition one requires membership functions, antecedent weights, and rule thresholds, discussed earlier in Chapters 10 and 16. The introduction of fuzzy techniques automatically combines the numeric with the symbolic. Neural networks can be used to derive these values if sufficient data are available. (One method of accomplishing this is given in Chapter 18.) As mentioned above and described in Chapter 11, neural networks can also be used for automatic derivation of rules.

Additional approaches include using the output from neural networks to feed into a symbolic reasoning system. For example, assume that you have a neural network for differential diagnosis with the structure illustrated in Figure 17.3. We will use a simple linear neural network for illustration, although the same approach can be used for three-layer nonlinear networks. At each of the five output nodes at level 2 in the neural network, a decision surface has been generated. Each decision surface may use different input nodes with different weights to arrive at its conclusion. For each of the five nodes, we thus have the following information:

$X_{i1}, \ldots, X_{in}$:	Contributing input nodes to output node i
$W_{i1}, \ldots, W_{in}$:	Weights associated with each input node
$O_1, \ldots, O_s$:	Output nodes
$D_i(\mathbf{x})$:	Degree to which diagnosis i has been confirmed

This information can then be fed into a symbolic reasoning layer that uses this information along with other information solicited from the user. The symbolic layer may have rules of the type:

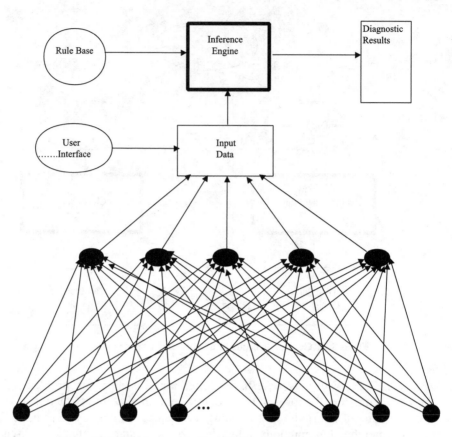

Figure 17.3 Combination of a Neural Network with Symbolic Reasoning.

IF   disease i is suspected
AND   symptom x_j is >100
AND   the patient has a family hx of diabetes
THEN obtain a liver enzyme panel.

All information except the family history was taken from the neural network model. Additional rules may be used to try to confirm or rule out the conditions from the neural network model. Another type of neural network combined with a symbolic layer will be shown in Chapter 18.

     17.2.2.2 Genetic Algorithms.   Although the paradigm is different, input and output from genetic algorithms can be treated the same as input and output from neural networks. Genetic algorithms can also be used to generate rules automatically (Oliver, 1994), although little research has been done in this area.

17.2.3 General Methodologies

     17.2.3.1 Fuzzy Logic.   As we saw in Chapter 16, fuzzy logic and other techniques from approximate reasoning can be used to alter the actual reasoning structure of decision-support systems. In knowledge-based systems, the use of approximate reasoning techniques alters the rule structure by permitting antecedents to contribute to varying degrees and to allow more complex combinations than binary logic allows. Derivation of the knowledge base requires additional information regarding the relative importance of antecedents and the degree to which they must be substantiated. In addition, input information is altered. Rather than yes/no responses, either degrees of presence are entered or a linguistic quantifier is used, such as low, medium, and high, which is then interpreted by predefined membership functions. Thus ANDs and ORs are replaced by evidence aggregation and partial substantiation of rules. Because of the altered rule structure and input data structure, the inference engine must be totally replaced. Hybrid systems that use fuzzy logic thus fall into category 4 described at the beginning of this chapter.

Fuzzy neural networks also fall into category 4. In general, the sum-product paradigm used as the basis for most neural networks is replaced by a MIN/MAX network that implements the idea of ANDs and ORs in the fuzzy logic concept. In addition, some fuzzy neural networks allow fuzzy numbers as input variables.

17.2.3.2 Statistical Approaches. Less work has been done in the combination of decision analysis with other types of decision-support systems. Three approaches to evidential reasoning—Bayesian probability theory (Lee, 1989), fuzzy set theory (possibility theory) (Zadeh, 1978), and Dempster–Shafer theory (Shafer, 1976)—exist and are discussed in detail in Chapter 16. One attempt to combine Bayesian inference with fuzzy evidence using the basic Dempster–Shafer logic is illustrated by Römer and Kandel (1995) in an application to diastolic dysfunction in congestive heart failure. Symptoms are entered in linguistic terms. This approach alters the input to the system as well as the reasoning structure of the system.

17.3 USE OF COMPLEX DATA STRUCTURES

As discussed earlier, one of the outstanding problems in biomedical decision-support systems is the incorporation of complex data such as ECGs, EEGs, and medical images into the reasoning structures. Hybrid systems offer some possibilities for solving this problem.

17.3.1 Time Series Data

17.3.1.1 Automatic ECG Analyzers. For a number of years, automatic ECG analyzers have been available commercially. In-depth study of the techniques used is beyond the scope of this book, but these methods generally rely on Fourier analysis and pattern matching techniques. These systems have been used successfully to identify arrhythmias and to classify ECGs as normal or abnormal. The diagnostic information obtained from these automated systems is used as input to knowledge-based systems. As an example, consider the following rule from the EMERGE system:

Rule 10a

IF   ALL OF
        Unifocal PVCs
        Frequency > 10/min
        Not proved old
        BP < 100/60
        ANY OF
            Abnormal mental status

          Cold, clammy skin
          Gray, cyanotic skin
          Weak peripheral pulses
          Urinary output < 30cc/hr
THEN   Patient should be admitted to CCU

The user is asked to answer questions regarding the ECG. These answers may be obtained by manual evaluation but often are obtained from the automatic ECG analysis. This information is exceedingly important in cardiology decision-support systems. In fact, in the EMERGE system, the ECG analysis consists of 40 percent of all rules (Hudson, 1981). As an alternative to asking the user to enter the results, the automatic analyzer can be used as direct input to the expert system.

17.3.1.2 Summary Methods.   Various methods of summarizing time series can also be used. These include chaotic analysis of times series, which has been discussed in detail in Chapter 3. The next chapter illustrates the use of chaos theory as part of a hybrid system. In another application, Xiao et al. (1997) describe the use of chaotic parameters in the analysis of EEG data. It uses a combination of frequency-domain threshold extraction and neural network pattern recognition to detect 40-Hz EEG bursts. The neural network is a backpropagation algorithm. The system was used to analyze left and right brain activity during different states that included quiet, subtraction trial (for logical thought), and spatial trial (for image processing). The fractal dimension is used as a summary measure.

17.3.2 Image Data

Image data remains a difficult element to include in automated decision processes. It is usually reduced to linguistic evaluations, such as radiograph interpretations: normal, abnormal, suggestive of pneumonia, and so on. Numerical information can be obtained under some circumstances. For example, for digitized images, relative computation of tumor size can be performed. Based on digital subtraction, other changes from previous images can be determined. Many technical problems remain, for both of these procedures require normalization of images in size and orientation, as well as in gray levels. Automatic edge detection and other image enhancement features can be employed. New advances in imaging technology make three-dimensional imaging possible, a technique that is extremely important for treatment of tumors and surgical interventions. However, these techniques currently do not provide information that is readily usable in decision-support systems.

17.4 DESIGN METHODOLOGIES

17.4.1 System Structure

Figure 17.4 shows an overall diagram of a decision-support system, with the impact of different paradigms indicated at the point where they might affect the system. The structure of the system may be quite complex using one or a combination of the reasoning paradigms indicated in the center box. These paradigms may be supplemented by additional methods as indicated in the boxes attached with dotted lines.

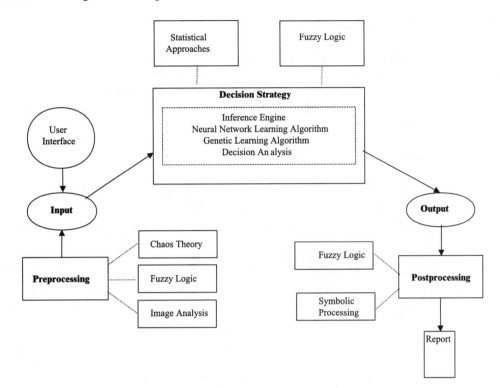

Figure 17.4 General Structure of Hybrid Systems.

17.4.2 User Interfaces

The user interface may be used to combine various decision strategies so that the method of reasoning is transparent to the user. Information is solicited and then directed to the appropriate algorithm. An example is shown in the next chapter in the combination of three reasoning strategies in the same system.

17.4.3 Pre-Processing

Pre-processing is often necessary with medical data, in particular nontextual data such as images and time series. In addition, fuzzy or linguistic variables may require pre-processing to become acceptable to the system.

17.4.4 Post-Processing

Post-processing is often used to interpret results. For example, numerical output from a neural network may be rephrased in linguistic terms or detailed explanations may be provided with knowledge-based systems. Post-processing may also involve the application of another paradigm, such as a neural network feeding into a symbolic analyzer. Fuzzy results may need to be de-fuzzified, or numeric results may be interpreted in fuzzy or linguistic terms.

17.4.5 Presentation of Results

Presentation of results to the user is usually a synopsis of the decision, a list of parameters that contributed to the decision, and possibly an explanation. Results may also be automatically added to a patient file or a database for future use.

These components are illustrated in a specific example of a hybrid system in the next chapter.

17.5 SUMMARY

The hybrid system approach has a number of advantages. Combination of knowledge-based and data-based methods allows all sources of information to be brought to bear on the problem at hand. In addition, use of other techniques, such as approximate reasoning and probabilistic models, can help establish more robust models for reasoning with uncertain information. The goal of computer-assisted decision support in biomedicine is to build realistic, useful models. The hybrid approach overcomes dependency on one methodology and thus has a great deal to offer in the quest for an accurate, realistic model.

EXERCISES

1. What major components present in Figure 17.1 are absent in Figure 17.2? Is it easier to establish a database than it is to establish a knowledge base? Explain.

2. Re-draw Figure 17.2 for an unsupervised learning system. Does the output from this system differ? Can it be combined with other approaches in the same manner as the supervised learning system?

3. What are the main advantages of incorporating fuzzy logic techniques in decision-support systems? Does the incorporation of these techniques make the system easier or harder to implement? Why?

4. Draw a membership function for the low, normal, and high ranges of heart rate. Give an example of how these ranges could be incorporated into a rule-based expert system. How would the use of membership functions improve the system? Could you represent this same information using probability theory? Explain.

5. Explain the conceptual difference between probability theory and fuzzy logic. Are these tools interchangeable? Give an example in which probability theory would be better suited in representing a problem than fuzzy set theory.

6. What kind of information in a CT scan is relevant to the decision process? Is this the same information that would be relevant in an MRI scan?

REFERENCES

Adlassnig, K.P. 1982. A survey on medical diagnosis and fuzzy subsets. In M.M. Gupta and E. Sanchez, eds., *Approximate reasoning in decision analysis,* pp. 203–217. Amsterdam: North-Holland.

Cimino, J.J., and Barnett, G.O. 1993. Automatic knowledge acquisition from MEDLINE. *Methods of Information in Medicine* **2:**120–130.

Cohen, M.E., and Hudson, D.L. 1995. *Comparative approaches to medical reasoning.* New Jersey: World Scientific.

Cohen, M.E., Hudson, D.L., Anderson, M.F., and Deedwania, P.C. 1994. A conjecture to the solution of the continuous logistic equation. *International Journal of Uncertainty, Fuzziness and Knowledge-Based Systems* **2(4):** 445–461.

Dzeroski, S., and Lavrac, N. 1996. Rule induction and instance-based learning applied in medical diagnosis. *Technology and Health Care* **4(2):** 203–221.

Esogbue, A.O. 1983. Measurement and valuation of a fuzzy mathematical model for medical diagnosis. *Fuzzy Sets and Systems* **10:** 223–242.

Hudson, D.L. 1981. *Rule-based computerization of emergency room procedures derived from criteria mapping,* Ph.D. Dissertation, UCLA.

Hudson, D.L., Cohen, M.E., and Anderson, M.F. 1991. Use of neural network techniques in a medical expert system. *International Journal of Intelligent Systems* **(6,2):** 213–223.

Hudson, D.L., Cohen, M.E., Banda, P.W., and Blois, M.S. 1992. Medical diagnosis and treatment plans derived from a hybrid expert system. In A. Kandel and G. Langholz, eds., *Hybrid architectures for intelligent systems,* pp. 329–344. Boca Raton, FL: CRC Press.

Kandel, A., and Langholz, G., eds. 1992. *Hybrid architectures for intelligent systems.* Boca Raton, FL: CRC Press.

Lee, P.M. 1989. *Bayesian statistics, an introduction.* New York: Oxford University Press.

Oliver, J. 1994. Finding decision rules with genetic algorithms. *AI Expert* **9(3):** 32–38.

Rocha, A.F. 1990. Proposed methodology for knowledge acquisition: a study on congenital heart disease diagnosis. *Methods of Information in Medicine* **29:** 30–40.

Rocha, A.F., Deoto, M., Rizzo, I., and Laginha, M.P.R. 1989. Handling uncertainty in medical reasoning. *Proceedings, IFSA* **3:** 480–483.

Römer, C., and Kandel, A. 1995. The application of Bayesian inference with fuzzy evidences in medical reasoning. In M.E. Cohen and D.L. Hudson, eds., *Comparative approaches to medical reasoning,* pp. 190–201. New Jersey: World Scientific.

Sanchez, E., and Bartolin, R. 1989. Fuzzy inference and medical diagnosis, a case study. *Proceedings, First Annual Meeting, Biomedical Fuzzy Systems Association:* 1–18.

Shafer, G. 1976. *A mathematical theory of evidence.* Princeton, NJ: Princeton University Press.

Xiao, D., Yang, H., and Zhou, S. 1997. Extraction of 40 Hz EEG bursts for chaos analysis of brain function. *IEEE Engineering in Medicine and Biology Magazine* **16(4):** 27–32.

Yager, R.R. 1991. Modeling and formulating fuzzy knowledge bases using neural networks. *Iona College Machine Intelligence Institute,* Report #MII-1111, 1–29.

Zadeh, L.A. 1978. Fuzzy sets as a basis for a theory of possibilities. *Fuzzy Sets and System* **1:** 3–28.

18

HyperMerge, A Hybrid Expert System

18.1 INTRODUCTION

The hybrid system HyperMerge is a combination of the knowledge-based system EMERGE and the neural network model HyperNet (Cohen and Hudson, 1992a). HyperMerge is illustrated here as a decision-support aid for cardiology. It deals with several facets of heart disease, including myocardial infarction, coronary artery disease, and congestive heart failure. Components of the system have been discussed earlier. EMERGE knowledge structures were presented in Chapter 10 and approximate reasoning techniques in Chapter 16. HyperNet, whose algorithm uses a type of supervised learning, was discussed in Chapter 4. Pertinent aspects of each system are summarized here along with methods for building the combined hybrid system. The application of this hybrid system to heart disease is illustrated (Cohen and Hudson, 1995; Hudson, Cohen, and Deedwania, 1995). A pertinent feature of the system is the inclusion of summary time series information through the use of continuous chaotic modeling (Cohen, Hudson, and Deedwania, 1996).

18.2 KNOWLEDGE-BASED COMPONENT

In its current configuration, different components of the expert system can be activated depending on the aspects of uncertainty that are present. They fall into three categories (Hudson, Banda, and Blois, 1992):

- Crisp implementation.
- Partial substantiation of antecedents.
- Weighted antecedents and partial substantiation of rules.

18.2.1 Crisp Implementation

The crisp implementation allows rule antecedents in three forms: conjunctions (AND), disjunctions (OR), and a specified number in a list (COUNT) (Hudson and Estrin, 1984). These constructs are summarized in Figure 18.1. Remember that

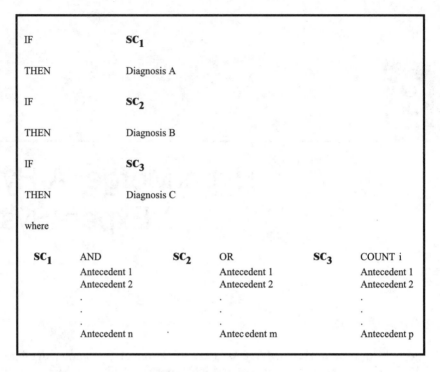

Figure 18.1 Rule Structure.

COUNT is followed by an integer that indicates how many in the list must be substantiated. The inclusion of these three logical constructs permits the types of reasoning most often identified in the human thought process. The AND and OR are special cases of the COUNT, with AND equivalent to COUNT m, where m is the number of antecedents, and OR equivalent to COUNT 1 (as discussed in Chapter 10).

When using the crisp form of the expert system, the presence of all symptoms and the results of all tests are considered to be all or nothing, with no degrees of severity indicated. Thus all operations are implemented in straightforward binary logic. The only uncertainty included is the presence of certainty factors associated with each rule that indicate the certainty that the substantiation of the rule points to the presence of the relevant condition.

In reality, seldom is it acceptable to ignore degrees of presence of symptoms, for important nuances in the data may be lost. These nuances are more important in borderline cases, the exact cases for which it is important that the expert system function properly.

18.2.2 Partial Substantiation of Antecedents

Partial substantiation of antecedents can be accomplished in a number of ways. The most straightforward implementation changes the user interaction with the system so that, instead of yes/no responses, the user responds with a degree of presence (a number between 0 and 10), which indicates a degree of severity. In this case, it is necessary to provide some guidelines to guard against individual differences in interpretation of severity. For example, the following may be used.

0	No evidence of presence
1–3	Moderate
4–6	Substantial
7–9	Extremely high
10	Maximum possible

This is still a controversial area, and no completely satisfactory solution has been found. However, for subjective evaluations of symptoms such as pain, no better solution has presented itself.

Once partial presence of symptoms is allowed, the binary logic inference engine will no longer suffice. Each of the three conditions in Figure 18.1 must be reimplemented.

For the conjunctive case

$$V_1 \text{ is } A_1 \text{ AND } V_2 \text{ is } A_2 \text{ AND} \ldots V_n \text{ is } A_n \tag{18.1}$$

A function P is defined on the set $V = \{V_1, \ldots, V_n\}$:

$$P_v(\mathbf{x}) = \min_{i = 1, \ldots n} [A_i(x_i)] \tag{18.2}$$

where $x = (x_1, \ldots, x_n)$ are the input values for the current case and A_i is the value of the membership function for x_i (degree of substantiation). Similarly, for disjunctions

$$P_v(\mathbf{x}) = \max_{i = 1, \ldots n} [A_i(x_i)] \tag{18.3}$$

For the case where neither a conjunction nor a disjunction is appropriate (e.g., COUNT), linguistic quantifiers are used (Yager, 1984; Hudson and Cohen, 1988a). Let:

$D_i(\mathbf{x})$ be the ith largest element in the set $\{A_1(x_1), \ldots, A_n(x_n)\}$.

Then for any quantifier Q

$$H(\mathbf{x}) = \max [Q(i)^\wedge D_i(\mathbf{x})] \tag{18.4}$$

This definition suffices for the special cases AND and OR also. For AND,

$$Q(i) = 0, i = 1, \ldots, n - 1 \tag{18.5}$$
$$Q(n) = 1$$

18.2.3 Weighted Antecedents and Partial Substantiation of Rules

The following rule structure illustrates the combination of weighted antecedents along with the partial substantiation of each antecedent. The w_i's must be determined by some means, which is discussed later. The a_i's are determined by information entered from the user, perhaps in conjunction with predefined membership functions (equivalent to $A_i(x_i)$ described above).

	Antecedent	Weighting Factor	Degree of Substantiation
IF	Antecedent 1	w_1	a_1
	Antecedent 2	w_2	a_2

.
.
.

Antecedent n w_n a_n
THEN Conclusion (If S > Threshold)

In order to determine S, the degree of substantiation, let Q be a Kind 1 linguistic quantifier (such as all, most, and some), replacing the statement "QVs are A" with

$$Q_1(Q_2V\text{'s}) \text{ are } A \tag{18.6}$$

The quantifier Q in this case replaces traditional binary logic operations, such as AND, OR, or more generally, m out of n conditions required for substantiation. The truth of the proposition is then determined by assuming there exists some subset C of V such that (1) the number of elements in C satisfies Q; or (2) each element in C satisfies the property A. The degree S to which P is satisfied by C is given by

$$S = \max_{C \, \varepsilon \, A} \{V_P(c)\} \tag{18.7}$$

where

$$V_P(c) = \max \left[(Q \sum_{i=1}^{n} c_i \wedge w_i) \wedge \min_{i=1,\dots,n} (a_i{}^{c_i \wedge w_i}) \right] \tag{18.8}$$

where $\wedge$ indicates minimum, a_i and d_i are the weighting factor and degree of substantiation, respectively, of the ith antecedent, and n is the number of antecedents.

18.2.4 Handling of Temporal Data

Temporal data are difficult to handle in knowledge-based systems. In general, temporal information is treated in special rules. For example, an antecedent of one rule in the chest pain rule base is "Duration of pain." The consequent of the rule is dependent on this temporal information. Usually, temporal reasoning is incorporated by adding specific rules to the knowledge base that may be purely temporal or may combine temporal and other data items.

18.3 NEURAL NETWORK COMPONENT

18.3.1 Learning Algorithm

The neural network component, HyperNet, has been discussed in Chapter 4 as a supervised learning system (Cohen and Hudson, 1992a; Hudson, Cohen, and Anderson, 1991). As we saw earlier, the basis of the technique is generalized vector spaces that permit the development of multidimensional nonlinear decision surfaces. As we saw in Chapter 4, the general form of the decision function is

$$D_i(\mathbf{x}) = \sum_{i=1}^{n} w_i x_i + \sum_{i=1}^{n} \sum_{j=1}^{n} w_{ij} x_i x_j \tag{18.9}$$

where n is the number of input nodes. This is the simplest nonlinear case; higher order equations can also be generated.

18.3.2 Special Data Types

18.3.2.1 Temporal Data. These data types can be handled in a straightforward manner, according to the following schemes (Hudson and Cohen, 1993a). Let $n(t_i)$ be the value of the nth variable at time t_i, and let

$$\Delta n = n(t_i) - n(t_{i-1}) \tag{18.10}$$

$$\Delta t = (t_i - t_{i-1}) \tag{18.11}$$

Assign a new node in the network for Δ data such that

$$p_n = \Delta n \tag{18.12}$$

The original network is then expanded by the number of nodes required to accommodate the items for which the change is important. For normalized Δ data, follow the same procedure as before, except let

$$q_n = \Delta n/\Delta t \tag{18.13}$$

Duration data can also be handled simply, by establishing

$$r_n = \Delta t \tag{18.14}$$

The most difficult type of temporal data to handle is sequence data because a new variable cannot be created to deal with this entity. A major modification must be made to the neural network structure for accommodating this type of reasoning. These data are handled by embedding a procedure at each sequence node. To analyze for the presence of a sequence, let $s_i, i = 1, \ldots, k$ be the ith symptom out of k and let t_i be the ith time interval. Define the matrix

$$S = [a_{ij}] \text{ where}$$

$$a_{ij} = \begin{bmatrix} 1 \text{ if event } s_i \text{ occurred at time } t_j \\ 0 \text{ otherwise} \end{bmatrix} \tag{18.15}$$

Then $tr\,[S] = k$ if the proper time sequence occurred, where $tr\,[S]$ is the trace of the matrix S. There are two options for determining the value of node u:

$$u = \begin{bmatrix} 1 \text{ if } tr\,[S] = k \\ 0 \text{ otherwise} \end{bmatrix} \tag{18.16}$$

$$\text{or} \qquad u = \{tr\,[S]\}/k \tag{18.17}$$

These choices will be discussed later with respect to fuzzy data.

18.3.2.2 Crisp versus Fuzzy Temporal Data. For the first three temporal data types, there are two parameters that may assume fuzzy rather than crisp values: the time-dependent finding $n(t_i)$ and the time interval itself t_i. The $n(t_i)$'s can be of four types: binary, categorical, integer, or continuous. For these types of temporal data, the values themselves are not important; only the differences in the values are significant. (If the value itself is important, it is included as a separate node in the network.) Thus the generalization of the difference operation is required. The most straightforward generalization appears to be extended subtraction for fuzzy sets defined in Dubois and Prade (1980). According to the algorithm established by Dubois and Prade, this operation can be applied to continuous variables, with a simpler, direct computation possible for the discrete case. If the data itself is binary or categorical, these variables can first be fuzzified, if appropriate. In the case of normalized data, the extended division, also discussed in Dubois and Prade (1980), can be applied. It can be shown that if M and N are fuzzy numbers, then

$$M \ominus N = M \oplus (-N) \text{ (subtraction)} \tag{18.18}$$

is also a fuzzy number, where $M \oplus N$ is extended addition, as well as

$$M \oslash N = M \otimes (N^{-1}) \text{ (division)} \tag{18.19}$$

where $M \otimes N$ is extended multiplication.

For the sequence data, the occurrence of a sequence in the correct order is a crisp result. However, the degree to which the sequence occurred in the correct order can be considered. Instead of setting node u_n as in Eq. (18.16), Eq. (18.17) is used. This definition provides a degree to which the sequence occurred in the required order. For example, consider the $k \times k$ matrix S:

$$\begin{bmatrix} 1 & 0 & 0 & 0 & \ldots 0 \\ 0 & 0 & 1 & 0 & \ldots 0 \\ 0 & 1 & 0 & 0 & \ldots 0 \\ 0 & 0 & 0 & 1 & \ldots 0 \\ \cdot & & & & \\ \cdot & & \cdot & & \\ \cdot & & & & \\ 0 & 0 & 0 & 0 & \ldots 1 \end{bmatrix} \tag{18.20}$$

Then $u_n = (k - 2)/k$, the degree to which the required sequence was met. Each row in this matrix represents a point in time, and each column represents a symptom. $S_{ij} = 1$ if at time i symptom j is present.

18.3.2.3 Time Series Data.   Time series can be incorporated into the neural network if a summary measure can be found that allows it to be represented in numerical terms. A number of methods exist for quantifying the degree of chaos in the system, including the fractal dimension and the Lyapunov exponent. The method used here is the central tendency measure of the second-order difference plots derived from a continuous approach to chaotic modeling of nonlinear systems.

18.4 ANALYSIS OF TIME SERIES DATA

18.4.1 Chaos Theory

The basic common thread in chaos theory is the recursive evaluation of seemingly simple functions that produce unexpectedly complex results. An iterative function does not suddenly become chaotic, but rather goes from the stage of convergence to a single value to a bifurcation, or convergence to two values. Additional bifurcations occur, and finally chaos results.

The logistic equation is one of the best known chaotic functions:

$$a_n = A \, a_{n-1}(1 - a_{n-1}) \quad 2 \leq A \leq 4 \tag{18.21}$$

where A is a constant whose value changes the behavior of the function. The recursion is dependent on the selection of a_0, which must be chosen between 0 and 1. For increasing values of A, the equation progresses from single-value convergence to chaos. Within the chaotic area, regions of stability unexpectedly appear. It has been shown (Cohen et al., 1994) that these regions of stability are only a matter of perception when discrete values of n are considered. They do not exist if continuous values are taken. For integer values of n, this function exhibits chaotic properties for $A > 3.57$. These properties include apparent lack of periodicity and sensitivity to initial conditions.

Many processes in medicine appear to exhibit chaotic properties. These analyses have become increasingly useful, especially in cardiology (Goldberger and West, 1987; Goldberger, 1989). Chaotic analysis is still in its infancy, with new techniques needed to determine the degree to which a data set appears to be chaotic.

18.4.2 Continuous versus Discrete Chaotic Modeling

In the traditional approach to chaotic modeling, a recurrence relation is established which is evaluated at integer values, generally with each integer corresponding to a fixed time interval. These values are then plotted and connected with straight lines. However, the actual noninteger values of these recurrence relations are unknown. We have developed an approach (Cohen, Hudson, and Deedwania, 1996) which permits an approximate solution of the logistic equation not only for integer values but also for all real values of n and for any value of A in the important range $2 \leq A \leq 4$.

These results show that the chaotic behavior of the logistic function is not apparent when viewed as a continuous, and not as a discrete, model, except in the narrow mathematical definition. This work emphasizes the danger of approximating any continuous process by a discrete model when the underlying principles are not understood (Cohen, Hudson, and Anderson, 1992b).

In Eq. (18.21), only integer values are considered. The exact solution of Eq. (18.21) presents a different picture. In order to get a perspective on the behavior of chaotic systems, we first examine the exact solution of the logistic equation at $A = 4$. The solution is

$$a_n = 1/2\,[1 - T_{2^n}(1 - 2a_0)] \tag{18.22}$$

where $T_n(x)$ is the Chebyshev function (Szego, 1939).

This solution has a number of interesting properties which emphasize that it is indeed a well-behaved function (Cohen et al., 1994). We have found that it is indeed orthogonal, satisfying the relation:

$$\int_0^1 f_n(a_0)\,f_m(a_0)\,[a_0\,(1 - a_0)]^{-1/2}\,da_0 = \begin{cases} 0 & n \neq m \\ B & n = m \end{cases} \tag{18.23}$$

where

$$f_n(a_0) = \frac{(a_{n+1})^l}{1 - 2a_{n+1}} \qquad \begin{aligned} &\text{for } l = 1, 2, 3, \ldots \\ &n = 1, 2, 3, \ldots \\ &m = 1, 2, 3 \ldots \end{aligned}$$

$$B = \frac{(l\pi)4^{l+1}\,(1/2)_2^l\,(1/2)_2^{l-1}}{(4l)!}$$

where

$$(c)_k = \begin{bmatrix} c\,(c + 1)\ldots\,(c + k - 1), k \geq 1 \\ 1 \qquad\qquad\qquad k = 0 \end{bmatrix}$$

Note that B reduces to π for $l = 1$, an interesting special case.

The solution given in Eq. (18.23) is valid only for $A = 4$, a point in the region of chaos. As no exact solution is available for other values within the region of chaos, we constructed a method for approximating solutions for any value of A, $2 \leq A \leq 4$.

Assume a solution of the type

$$a_n = \sum_{k=0}^{l} \alpha_k T_k(2^n x) \tag{18.24}$$

where $T_k(x)$ is the Chebyshev function of the first kind and n is a real number. We assume l to be the number of points in the interval $0 \leq n \leq 1$. Thus

$$a_n^2 = \sum_{k=0}^{l} a_k^2 T_k^2(2^n x) + 2 \sum_{\substack{j>i \\ i=0,1,\ldots,l-1 \\ j=1,2,\ldots,l}} \alpha_i \alpha_j T_i(2^n x) T_j(2^n x) \tag{18.25}$$

In the conjecture, progression from one point to another implies adding a Chebyshev polynomial. Hence

$$a_{n+1} = \sum_{k=0}^{2l} \beta_k T_k(2^n x) \tag{18.26}$$

where n is assumed to be a real number.

Feeding (18.24), (18.25), and (18.26) in the logistic equation (18.21) and simplifying and comparing coefficients give nonlinear equations involving the unknowns α_i's and β_j's and the arguments x of the Chebyshev polynomials. We have solved 300 equations involving 300 variables and have chosen the appropriate α_i's and β_j's and the argument of the Chebyshev to satisfy a_n to be strictly monotonic increasing in the interval $0 \leq n \leq 1$. It should be pointed out that the nonlinear equations give a multitude of solutions. By imposing appropriate boundary conditions, one obtains a unique solution to these nonlinear equations involving 300 variables. Values for $n > 1$ are obtained by applying the logistic equation to the points obtained for $0 \leq n \leq 1$.

This theoretical result is used to generate a new type of difference graph that can be used in analysis of time series data.

18.4.3 Difference Equations and Graphs

Chaotic equations are sometimes used to generate graphs that are known as Poincaré plots. Using the logistic equation (18.22), we obtain a Poincaré plot by plotting a_{n+1} versus a_n. The resulting plot is a measure of the degree of chaos in the system. We produced similar graphs using the continuous solution (Cohen, Hudson, and Anderson, 1993a). Figure 18.2 shows two discrete Poincaré plots, at $A = 3.5$ and $A = 4.0$. Figure 18.3 shows the continuous Poincaré plot for the same two values. Note that the character of these plots is totally different.

Another useful graph for practical applications is the second-order difference: $(a_{n+2} - a_{n+1})$ vs. $(a_{n+1} - a_n)$. This method produces plots that are centered around the origin and is useful in modeling dynamic biological parameters, such as hemodynamic flow and heart rate variations. The difference approach appears to give a more robust picture of the problem and fits well within our theoretical results of the continuous logistic equation (Cohen, Hudson, and Anderson, 1993b). Examples for $A = 3.75$ and $A = 4.0$ are shown in Figure 18.4.

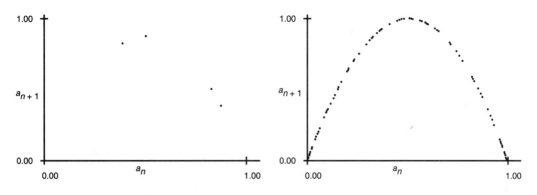

Figure 18.2 Discrete Poincaré Plots, $A = 3.5$ and $A = 4.0$.

18.4.4 Central Tendency Measure

Although the second-order difference plots provide a useful graphical display of the distribution of the time series, in order to use this information for inclusion in a neural network model, it must be quantified. One method of numerically describing the data distribution is through the use of the central tendency measure (CTM), computed by selecting a circular region around the origin of radius r, counting the number of points that fall within the radius, and dividing by the total number of points. Let $t =$ total number of points, and $r =$ radius of central area. Then

$$n = \left[\sum_{i=1}^{t-2} \delta\,(d_i) \right] / (t - 2) \tag{18.27}$$

where

$$\delta(d_i) = \begin{bmatrix} 1 \text{ if } [(a_{i+2} - a_{i+1})^2 + (a_{i+1} - a_i)^2]^{.5} < r \\ 0 \text{ otherwise} \end{bmatrix}$$

The node value n will thus be a number between 0 and 1, inclusive, and can be added to the network like any other node.

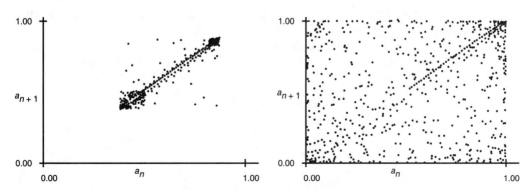

Figure 18.3 Continuous Poincaré Plots, $A = 3.5$ and $A = 4.0$.

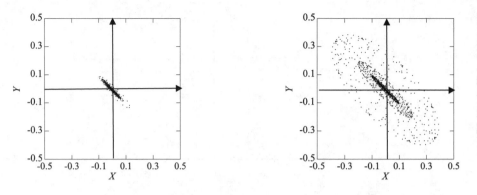

Figure 18.4 Second-Order Difference Plot, $A = 3.75$ and $A = 4.0$,
$x = a_{n+1} - a_n, y = a_{n+2} - a_{n+1}$.

18.5 COMBINED SYSTEM

The techniques described earlier are combined in a number of ways that address some of the shortcomings of each system in isolation.

18.5.1 Weighting of Antecedents

First, the neural network structure can be run independently for each rule to determine the appropriate weighting of antecedents. In the simplest approximation, a hyperplane is obtained from Eq. (18.9), generating an equation of the form

$$D_i(\mathbf{x}) = \sum_{i=1}^{n} w_i x_i \tag{18.28}$$

The weight a_i for the ith antecedent is then determined by

$$a_i = \frac{w_i}{\sum_{i=1}^{n} w_i} \tag{18.29}$$

Note that these weights are normalized to sum to 1.

18.5.2 Determination of Thresholds

In addition, the neural network can be used to determine appropriate threshold levels for each rule (Hudson and Cohen, 1993b). The maximum and minimum values for the decision surface $D(\mathbf{x})$ must be determined. Let $A_i = \{m_1, \ldots, m_k\}$ denote the set of all values which x_i can assume, where $m_i > 0$ for all i. Then to obtain the maximum value $D_{\max}(\mathbf{x})$:

$$\text{If } w_i > 0, \text{let } x_i' = \max [A_i] \tag{18.30}$$
$$\text{If } w_i < 0, \text{let } x_i' = 0 \text{ for all } i = 1, \ldots, n$$

Then

$$D_{\max}(\mathbf{x}) = \sum_{i=1}^{m} w_i x_i' + \sum_{i=1}^{m} \sum_{\substack{j=1 \\ i \neq j}}^{m} w_{i,j} x_i' x_j' \tag{18.31}$$

Similarly, $D_{\min}(\mathbf{x})$ is obtained by the following:

$$\text{If } w_i > 0, \text{let } x_i' = 0 \tag{18.32}$$
$$\text{If } w_i < 0, \text{let } x_i' = \min[A_i]$$

and by application of Eq. (18.31) for $D_{\min}(\mathbf{x})$.

All decisions are then normalized by

$$D_n(\mathbf{x}) = \begin{array}{lll} D(\mathbf{x})/D_{\max}(\mathbf{x}) & \text{if } D(\mathbf{x}) > 0 & \text{(class 1)} \\ D(\mathbf{x})/|D_{\min}(x)| & \text{if } D(\mathbf{x}) < 0 & \text{(class 2)} \\ 0 & \text{if } D(\mathbf{x}) = 0 & \text{(indeterminate)} \end{array} \tag{18.33}$$

The result is a value between -1 and 1, inclusive, which gives a degree of membership in that category. The values are then shifted to give an answer between 0 and 1, inclusive by

$$V(\mathbf{x}) = [1 + D_n(\mathbf{x})]/2 \tag{18.34}$$

18.5.3 Neural Network with Symbolic Layer

The nonlinear decision function produces a normalized numerical value between 0 and 1, inclusive (Hudson and Cohen, 1993c). A separate decision function $D_i(\mathbf{x})$ is attached to each output node. A threshold value $T_i(\mathbf{x})$ (or values) is also attached to each level three node. If the value of the decision function exceeds the corresponding threshold value, a certain symbol is produced; if it does not, a different symbol is produced. This process can be extended by expanding the number of threshold values to produce as many symbols as desired. An additional layer is added to the network that combines the symbols generated by adjacent nodes according to a well-structured grammar. A grammar provides the rules by which a symbol can be combined. The following notation is used. A grammar G is defined by (V_n, V_t, P, S), where V_n are the variables, V_t are the terminals, P are productions, and S is the start symbol. A simple grammar would be

$$V_n = \{S\}$$
$$V_t = \{0, 1\} \tag{18.35}$$
$$P = \{S \rightarrow 0S1, S \rightarrow 01\}$$

The result of this grammar is to produce the sequence $0^n 1^n$.

EXAMPLE: Combined System

Consider a medical application in which it is necessary to choose among three conditions. It is possible that none, one, or a combination of two or more conditions is present. A neural network is set up to learn using data of known classification, determining which variables are pertinent to making the decision and the appropriate weighting factors for each of these variables (Hudson and Cohen, 1993c). The decision algorithm is represented by a three-layered network: input, intermediate, and output. The output level is the decision level. In traditional neural networks, this would be the final level. In the combined system described here, the output from this level is used to produce an additional level, denoted the action level. In the case of medical decision making, level $n - 1$ would determine which condition or conditions are present, and level n would determine what treatment or followup testing should be done based on these results. This network structure is shown in Figure 18.5. Table 18.1 shows a sample grammar. A possible interpretation is the following. Each node has a potential excitatory action (represented by a) or inhibitory action (represented by b). This is determined by threshold values: If $D_i(\mathbf{x}) > T_i$,

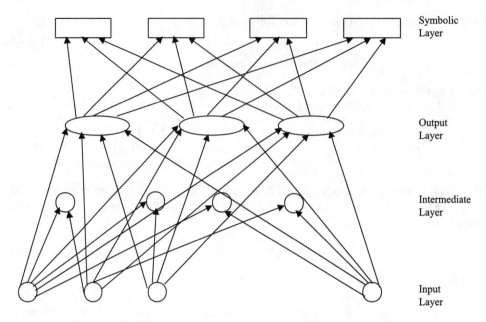

Figure 18.5 Neural Network with Symbolic Layer.

then *"a"* else *"b."* In the grammar, each node is numbered N_i. A response of *"a"* at node i indicates that condition C_i is present. To simplify the grammar, a sequential evaluation of nodes is assumed. If random evaluation is done, additional entries in the grammar are required. For the example, four possible actions are assumed:

$$r_1: \text{No action}$$
$$r_2: \text{Re-do test}$$
$$r_3: \text{Do additional tests}$$
$$r_4: \text{Begin treatment}$$

18.6 APPLICATION: DIAGNOSIS OF HEART DISEASE

18.6.1 Categories of Heart Disease

These methods are illustrated in a decision-support system for analysis of chest pain in the emergency room. When a patient comes to the emergency room with chest pain, it is vital to make a rapid decision regarding whether the patient should be hos-

TABLE 18.1 Sample Grammar

$V_n = \{S,A,B,C,D,T\}$		$V_t = \{a,b,r_1,r_2,r_3,r_4\}$
P: $\qquad S \to N_1$	$N_1 \to aN_2$	$aaaT \to r_1$
	$N_1 \to bN_2$	$bbbT \to r_4$
	$N_2 \to aN_3$	$bbaT \to r_3$
	$N_2 \to bN_3$	$baaT \to r_3$
	$N_3 \to aT$	$abbT \to r_2$
	$N_3 \to bT$	$aabT \to r_2$
		$abaT \to r_2$
		$babT \to r_2$

pitalized, and if so, if he or she should be assigned to a coronary care unit. Relevant information for this decision comes from a number of sources, including description of symptoms, observable symptoms, patient history, ECG results, X-ray results, and blood analysis. The objective is to combine these data into one model, which is capable of producing a rapid and accurate decision. The variables illustrated here have been selected to illustrate the different data types described previously.

18.6.2 Knowledge-Based Information

Typical rules and standard conditions (SCs) are illustrated in Figure 18.6. Note that a number of types of information are represented in these rules. Data types include integer, categorical, continuous, and binary. Variable types may be fuzzy or crisp, and temporal data are also included. The information in these rules was derived through expert input over a ten-year period. Expert-derived rules are always subject to change as medical knowledge improves; thus it is necessary to continually update the rule base.

18.6.3 Data-Based Information

Some information may not be available through expert consultation. This is particularly true for new areas in which data are in the collection process or for areas in which experts disagree about the relative importance of contributing factors. This data-based information is included in the system through the use of HyperNet. In the example shown here, all analysis of exercise treadmill testing is done using HyperNet.

18.6.4 Chaotic Data

Chaotic analysis is useful in many aspects of heart disease. For example, data obtained from twenty-four hour Holter monitoring of patients produces a record of electrocardiogram activity during normal day-to-day activities. Analysis of R-R intervals for the Holter data, which is the time between heartbeats, yields interesting patterns.

Rule 010	IF		Blood Pressure < 100/60
		AND	SC_1
	THEN		Patient should be admitted to CCU
Rule 020	IF		SC_{10}
	THEN		Patient should be admitted
Rule 030	IF		SC_{15}
		AND	Associated with onset
	THEN		Patient should be observed
	SC_1	(OR)	Abnormal mental s tatus
			Cold, clammy skin
			Grey, cyanotic skin
			Weak peripheral pulses
			Urinary output < 30 cc/hr
	SC_{10}	(AND)	Pain excruciating
			Pain unremitting
	SC_{15}	(COUNT 2)	Sweating
			Nausea
			Dizziness

Figure 18.6 Rules and SC's for Chest Pain Analysis.

Typically, around 100,000 points are included in the twenty-four hour period. Figure 18.7 shows a second-order difference graph for the R-R intervals for a normal patient. By comparison, Figure 18.8 shows a patient with congestive heart failure (Cohen, Hudson, and Deedwania, 1996). The visual difference is quite dramatic. The total number of points for each plot is the number of R-R intervals in a twenty-four hour period. For the two cases, shown, these are:

$$t_{\text{normal}} = 104443 \qquad t_{\text{chf}} = 109374$$

Using Eq. (18.27), the central tendencies for these two plots are computed:

$$n_{\text{normal}} = 0.986 \qquad n_{\text{chf}} = 0.232$$

These numerical representations of central tendency can thus be included in the neural network model. Note that a rule could also be established in which a subjective measure of the degree of chaos is used. As it turns out, the CTM measure is quite successful alone in distinguishing between CHF patients and normal individuals. We analyzed fifty-four Holter tapes: twenty-six for patients with congestive heart failure (CHF) and twenty-eight for normal subjects. Central tendencies were evaluated using $r = 0.1$ in Eq. (18.27). The mean CTMs for CHF (0.69) and normals (0.90) were significantly different ($p < 0.01$). Only three normal individuals had a CTM less than 0.8, while fifteen CHF subjects fell into this category. No normal subjects were found with a CTM less than 0.62. Figure 18.9 shows the distribution of CTM values for these two groups (Cohen, Hudson, and Deedwania, 1996). Use of this value in conjunction with clinical parameters in a neural network model provides a useful clinical decision aid for diagnosis of CHF.

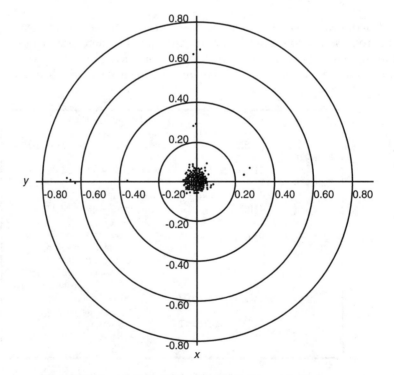

Figure 18.7 Second-Order Difference Graph, Normal Patient,
$x = hr_{t+1} - hr_t, y = hr_{t+2} - hr_{t+1}.$

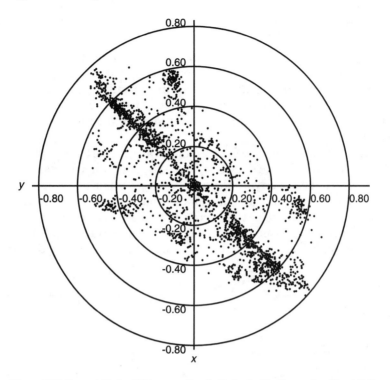

Figure 18.8 Second-Order Difference Graph, Patient with Congestive Heart Failure. $x = hr_{t+1} - hr_t, y = hr_{t+2} - hr_{t+1}.$

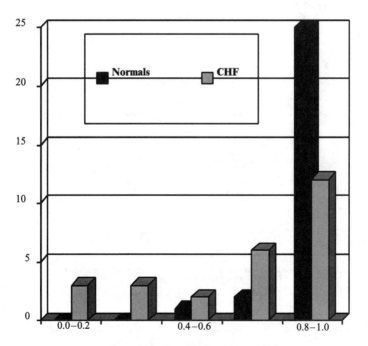

Figure 18.9 Classification Using CTM.

18.6.5 Sample System

Figure 18.10 shows a consultation as it appears to the user, invoking both the rule-based system and the neural network model where appropriate. The neural network model is embedded in the rule-based model and is triggered by the invocation of certain rules. In addition to this direct connection, the neural network model is used to obtain weighting factors and thresholds for many of the rules in the knowledge-based program.

The italicized entries in the consultation are not part of the system but are added to indicate the origin of the data. Note that the consultation contains a mixture of data types. However, the underlying complexity of the system is not apparent to the user.

As shown, the user can obtain an explanation. In the explanation phase, for the rule-based portion, the rules that were substantiated are given. Note that these rules use the approximate reasoning format described in Section 18.2. When the neural network model is invoked, the variables used and their relative ranking are provided in-

```
Patient name: SRM
Age: 67
Chief complaint: Recurrent chest pain
Hx of coronary problems y/n?  y
Hx CAD y/n?  y
Recent ETT data available y/n ?:  y
From ETT                                              (Neural Network)
        Max ST depression in mm:  2.8
        HR at beginning of ETT:  89
        HR at end of ETT:  100
        BP at beginning of ETT:  135
        BP at end of ETT:  133
Hx of CHF y/n?  y
Computer file of holter data available y/n?  y
Enter file name:  SRMholter                          (Chaotic Analysis)
List current symptoms, followed by a degree of severity between 0 (n) and 10 (y):
        Chest pain 9                                 (Knowledge-Based System)
        Sweating 7
        Syncope 7
        Cold, Clammy Skin 8
             *
BP < 100/60?  y
Dizziness?  8
Nausea?  6
Associated with onset?  y

Patient should be admitted to hospital as inpatient.
ETT data indicate 2 vessel CAD
Holter data indicates significant chaos in R-R intervals related to CHF

Do you want an explanations of these conclusions?  y

The following rules from the knowledge-based chest pain analysis were substantiated (in reverse order):

        IF      Sweating              .25
                Dizziness             .25
                Nausea                .25
                Associated with onset .25
        THEN    Patient should be admitted    (Threshold 0.5)


        IF      BP < 100/60           .5
                Abnormal Mental Status .1
                Cold, Clammy, Skin    .1
                Dry, Cyanotic Skin    .1
                Weak Peripheral Pulses .1
                Urinary Output < 30cc/hr  .1
        THEN    Patient should be admitted to CCU    (Threshold 0.6)

        IF      Chest pain
        THEN    Proceed to other symptom analysis

The neural network model for ETT concluded 2-vessel disease based on change in HR during test, change in BP during test, double produce of HR and BP, and maximum ST depression.

Chaotic analysis of R-R intervals from the 24-hr Holter tape indicates a central tendency of 43%, indicating a high level of variability.
```

Figure 18.10 Consultation.

stead of a rule. For the chaotic analysis, the CTM value for $r = 0.1$ is given for the Holter tape analysis.

18.7 SUMMARY

Although many clinically useful systems have been developed, they have been put to little practical use for a number of reasons. In order to become useful decision aids, these systems must provide relevant advice, be easy to use, and incorporate all available medical knowledge. The combination of expert input and information derived from accumulated data through automated learning algorithms ensures that all available information can be used in the same system. In the hybrid system presented here, the knowledge structure developed by the authors expands the usual production rule format to permit more complicated reasoning structures and to allow complete departure from binary logic leading to reasoning with uncertainty.

These two approaches not only are adaptable to new medical knowledge, but also allow the same system to be utilized for different medical applications by replacement of the knowledge and databases. Although in theory this is true, some systems will incorporate specific design features that may change with the application.

EXERCISES

1. For the sample consultation shown in Figure 18.10, assume that the crisp implementation was used and that all values > 0.5 are assumed to correspond to yes, and all values < 0.5 correspond to no. Using the rules and SCs in Figure 18.6, which rules would be substantiated?

2. Using the weighting factors given in the explanation portion of Figure 18.10 along with the values entered for each finding, compute the level of substantiation using Eq. (18.8). Do these results correspond to the results from exercise 1? Explain.

3. Instead of using the neural network model for analysis of ETT data, write a rule or series of rules. What information do you need in order to write these rules?

4. For the two rules given in the explanation portion of Figure 18.10, how many input nodes would be needed if you wanted to set up a neural network model to analyze this information?

5. For the plots in Figures 18.7 and 18.8 that show degrees of chaos, which plot has a higher degree of chaos? What would you expect a plot to look like for a time series with no chaos present? with a maximum amount of chaos?

6. It has been found that including more information to describe the distribution of points in the second-order difference plot results in better classification results. The following were used:
   CTM with $r = 0.05$
   CTM with $r = 0.10$
   Value of r for which CTM includes 99 percent of points
   Total number of R-R intervals.
   (a) Illustrate a neural network design that could be used to develop a classifier using this information.
   (b) Devise a set of rules that would accomplish the same purpose.

REFERENCES

Cohen, M.E., Hudson, D.L., and Deedwania, P.C. 1996. Application of continuous chaotic modeling to signal analysis. *EMBS Magazine* **15**(5): 97–102.

Cohen, M.E., and Hudson, D.L. 1995. *Comparative approaches to medical reasoning*. New Jersey: World Scientific.

Cohen, M.E., Hudson, D.L., Anderson, M.F., and Deedwania, P.C. 1994. A conjecture to the solution of the continuous logistic equation. *International Journal of Uncertainty, Fuzziness and Knowledge-Based Systems* **2(4):** 445–461.

Cohen, M.E., Hudson, D.L., and Anderson, M.F. 1993b. Blood flow data exhibit chaotic properties. *International Journal of Microcomputer Applications,* **12(3):** 37–40.

Cohen, M.E., Hudson, D.L., and Anderson, M.F. 1993a. A conjectured continuous approach to chaotic modeling. In D. Gakkai, ed., *Nonlinear theory and its applications,* pp. 783–786. Honolulu, HI: Research Society of Nonlinear Theory and Its Applications.

Cohen, M.E., Hudson, D.L., and Anderson, M.F. 1992b. Importance of sampling rate for analysis of hepatic blood flow data demonstrated by non-chaotic solution of Poincaré equation. In J.P. Morucci et al., eds., *Engineering in Medicine and Biology,* pp. 982–983. Piscataway, NJ: IEEE.

Cohen, M.E., and Hudson, D.L. 1992a. Integration of neural network techniques with approximate reasoning techniques in knowledge-based systems. In A. Kandel and G. Langholz, eds., *Hybrid Architectures for Intelligent Systems,* pp. 72–85. Boca Raton, FL: CRC Press.

deDombal, F.T., Leaper, D., Horrocks, J., Staniland, J., and McCann, A. 1974. Human and computer-aided diagnosis of abdominal pain. *British Medical Journal* **1:** 376–380.

Dubois, D., and Prade, H. 1980. *Fuzzy sets and systems: theory and applications.* Vol. 144, Orlando, FL: Academic Press.

Goldberger, A.L. 1989. Cardiac chaos. *Science* **243 (2987):** 1419.

Goldberger, A.L., and West, B.J. 1987. Fractals in physiology and medicine. *Yale Journal of Biology and Medicine* **60:** 421–435.

Gorry, G.A. 1973. Computer-assisted clinical decision making. *Methodology for Information in Medicine,* **12:** 45–51.

Hudson, D.L., and Estrin, T. 1984. EMERGE, a data-driven medical decision-making aid. *IEEE Transactions on Pattern Analysis and Machine Intelligence* **PAMI-6:** 87–91.

Hudson, D.L., and Cohen, M.E. 1988a. An approach to management of uncertainty in a medical expert system. *International Journal of Intelligent Systems* **3(1):** 45–58.

Hudson, D.L., and Cohen, M.E. 1988b. Fuzzy logic in a medical expert system. In M. Gupta and T. Yamakawa, eds., *Fuzzy computing: theory, hardware realization and applications,* pp. 273–284. Amsterdam: North Holland.

Hudson, D.L., Cohen, M.E., and Anderson, M.F. 1991. Use of neural network techniques in a medical expert system. *International Journal of Intelligent Systems* **6(2):** 213–223.

Hudson, D.L., Cohen, M.E., Banda, P.W., and Blois, M.S. 1992. Medical diagnosis and treatment plans derived from a hybrid expert system. In A. Kandel and G. Langholz, eds., *Hybrid architectures for intelligent systems,* pp. 329–344. Boca Raton, FL: CRC Press.

Hudson, D.L., and Cohen, M.E. 1993a. Combination of spatial and temporal variables in a neural network model, *Proceedings, International Society for Computers and Their Applications:* 69–73.

Hudson, D.L., and Cohen, M.E. 1993b. Use of fractional powers to moderate neuronal contributions. *IEEE Conference on Neural Networks:* **I,** 517–522.

Hudson, D.L., and Cohen, M.E. 1993c. A nonlinear neural network combined with symbolic processing. In D. Gakkai, ed., *Nonlinear theory and its applications,* pp. 937–940. Honolulu, HI: Research Society of Nonlinear Theory and Its Applications.

Hudson, D.L., Cohen, M.E., and Deedwania, P.C. 1995. Hybrid system for diagnosis and treatment of heart disease. In M.E. Cohen and D.L. Hudson, eds., *Comparative approaches to medical reasoning,* pp 289–310. Singapore: World Scientific.

Szego, G. 1939. *Orthogonal polynomials,* American Mathematics Society Colloquium Publications, XXIII, 59.

Yager, R. R. 1984. Approximate reasoning as a basis for rule-based expert systems. *IEEE Transactions on Systems, Man, and Cybernetics* SMC-14 (4): 636–643.

19

Future Perspectives

19.1 INTRODUCTION

Predicting the future is always dangerous. One is reminded of some famous predictions of the last fifty years relating to computer technology. In the early 1950s an IBM executive was asked how many of the new computers would be needed for the United States. His prediction was that five would suffice! On the software side, a famous conference was held in 1956 of leaders in the then fledging field of artificial intelligence. They predicted that most of the important problems of AI would be solved within twenty years. At a twenty-five year reunion of the group at the 1981 Vancouver, Canada, meeting of the American Association for Artificial Intelligence (AAAI, 1981), they admitted that the problems had been slightly underestimated. Nonetheless, with these examples in mind, we will attempt to project some future prospects of computerized decision-support aids.

19.2 EFFECTS OF HARDWARE ADVANCES

As anyone with a passing acquaintance with computers can confirm, the changes in computer hardware in terms of both memory capacity and speed have been phenomenal in the last few years. With the recent introduction of new chip technologies, it appears that the rate of increase in speed is likely to continue to escalate. Although these changes prompt users to buy new computers, do they have any effect on basic software technology?

19.2.1 Faster Computing Speeds

Faster computational speeds not only allow us to retrieve information and do calculations more rapidly, but they open up new possibilities for software. As an example, consider the Windows 95 package running on a 486-based computer versus a Pentium-based processor. On the former, the speed is slow enough to discourage use of the package. Thus faster speeds do lead to the development of more complex software packages.

How does this affect the methods we have discussed here? In the 1960s and 1970s, many pattern recognition algorithms were considered infeasible because of the lengthy training time, which could run into days. With current computers, training algorithms can be run on large data sets that were completely out of the question with slower computers. The faster speeds are also important in applications that require real-time answers, such as intensive care unit (ICU) monitoring systems: the faster the computer, the more complex the computation that can be done in real time. Many other applications that require rapid decision-making algorithms include emergency situations, either in the ER or by paramedics in the field. Some of the early systems, such as MYCIN, could take as long as twenty minutes to arrive at a decision. Fast computers can allow complex decision algorithms to produce results that are rapid enough to use in these situations.

19.2.2 Increased Memory

Increased memory provides important advantages for many pattern classification and AI systems. Many early algorithms were abandoned because they required that all data be stored in the computer simultaneously. This is no longer an important consideration except for image databases. Increased memory in the future will permit more automated decision making with nontextual data such as images and time series, which may still consume several megabytes per item. Memory size is no longer a problem for storage of algorithms, as it was in the 1960s and early 1970s when problems had to be paged in and out of memory.

19.2.3 Parallel Machines

Although parallel machines exist today, they are rare, and even for those that do exist, the software rarely takes full advantage of the parallel processing capabilities. One motivating factor for neural network approaches is that they were based on the parallel structure of the biological nervous system. Even so, because of the widespread use of the sequential computer, virtually all of these algorithms were implemented in a sequential fashion. Once parallel processors are widely available, the software will have to be rewritten to take advantage of parallel computation. The drive to do this has been diminished by the faster speed of sequential computers. Again, an area that can benefit greatly from parallel computation is image processing. For knowledge-based systems, much more complex rule structures could conceivably be searched in a simultaneous fashion, although in many cases this would completely alter the rule searching strategy.

19.2.4 Miniaturization

In the process of becoming faster, computer chips have also become smaller. This is very important in the field of implantable medical devices and in orthoscopic surgical instruments. The smaller chips that can hold more instructions open up new possibilities in the design of intelligent biomedical products.

19.2.5 Organic Semiconductors

One intriguing new area of research is the study of organic semiconductors. If a successful commercial organic semiconductor were developed, what effect would this have? There are probably many unforeseen possibilities, but one immediate advantage may be their increased biocompatibility that will aid in the development of implantable medical devices, as will the miniaturization process.

19.3 EFFECTS OF INCREASE IN KNOWLEDGE

The hardware is the tool that we use to implement decision-support strategies. The underlying software is limited only by the imagination of the developer.

19.3.1 Information Explosion

We are currently in the midst of an information revolution, in terms not only of volume but also of delivery of information. Worldwide communications have been facilitated through the use of electronic mail, and an increasing proportion of the population gets information directly from the Internet. The current drawback of the Internet, which appears to be inherent in its nature, is the lack of organization. There is, however, unlimited potential for the development of decision-support systems that can seek out and use relevant information. In the decade to come, Internet information will pose a number of challenges, including:

1. How can relevant information be located?
2. How can the reliability and accuracy of the information be ascertained?
3. How can the information be updated?
4. How can Internet information be incorporated directly into decision-support aids?

Of all these questions, the second is the most crucial.

19.3.2 Human Genome Project

The human genome project has been ongoing for some years now and has shown some remarkable progress. The rate at which genes are being located for specific disorders has increased dramatically. Is any of this information relevant to biomedical decision-support systems? There are some obvious connections:

1. Genetic diagnosis.
2. Genetic algorithms.
3. New information techniques for gene identification.

This project has also brought into focus research on new information technology dealing with gene sequencing. Although this research is currently focused on the human genome project, it has future potential for applications in many areas since it addresses problems of searching, matching, and storing large volumes of information. The impact of the human genome project will probably not be fully realized for a number of years.

19.3.3 Proliferation of Databases

In addition to the human genome database, numerous biomedical databases exist. These include site-specific databases at hospitals, clinics, and research facilities that are generally not shared with other researchers; collaborative databases established through cooperative efforts; federal and state government databases such as the National Institutes of Health collection of databases and state-based tumor registry data;

as well as a growing number of Internet databases, including chemical abstracts, conference papers, dissertation abstracts, federal research in progress, pharmaceutical abstracts, science citation index, and social science citation index (Galvin et al., 1995). The National Library of Medicine maintains a number of bibliographic databases, including AVLINE, BIOETHICSLINE, CANCERLIT, CATLINE, HEALTH, HISTLINE, HSTAR, POPLINE, and TOXLINE as well as factual databases, including CHEMID, DENTALPROJ, PDQ, and TOXNET. Another active area of database creation is radiology. These databases in general contain archived images representing the healthy and diseased conditions of various body systems. For example, a system called CHORUS (Collaborative Hypertext of Radiology) was developed to facilitate collaboration among physicians (Kahn, 1995). It consists of a computer-based radiology handbook that was developed and published electronically via the World Wide Web on the Internet. This system allows physicians without computer expertise to read documents, contribute knowledge, and critically review the handbook's content by using a simple, graphical user interface from virtually any type of computer system. These databases offer potential for large-scale epidemiological studies if the issues discussed in Chapters 8 and 13 can be adequately addressed.

A topic of growing interest is evidence-based medicine (Gray, 1997). The basic premise is that medical decisions should be based on well-founded research. There are major obstacles to using the medical literature in this manner. An overview of the subject is given by Sackett et al. (1997) and emphasizes formulating clinical questions that can be answered, searching for, critically appraising, and evaluating evidence. This approach to medical decision making attempts to utilize the growing body of information in a rational framework. It can also offer a framework for developing computer-assisted medical decision-making systems. The coming of age of the digital library should facilitate evidenced-based approaches (Lucier, 1995).

19.3.4 Communication of Information

In addition to online databases and digital libraries, advanced communications will allow the immediate transfer of information that can be put to good use in biomedical applications. Clinical applications are already in place for such fields as teleradiology and telepathology. Direct telemedicine applications, in which a physician located elsewhere conducts physical examinations, will no doubt increase in number and sophistication (Hudson et al., 1998). These technologies can be particularly useful for patients in rural areas. Remote monitoring of online systems may also become feasible with high-speed reliable networks.

19.4 THE FUTURE OF SOFTWARE

19.4.1 Hybrid Systems

As discussed in Chapters 17 and 18, hybrid systems that encompass a combination of techniques appear to hold promise in addressing complex problems encountered in the biomedical field. If these systems are designed in a modular fashion, they will also be able to add new approaches as they become available.

19.4.2 Parallel Systems

The development of software that is written specifically to take advantage of parallel processing will allow problems with large numbers of variables to be solved in real time. This is particularly important in patient care situations such as the emergency room and the ICU.

19.4.3 Nontextual Data

Problems associated with image information remain largely unsolved. The use of parallel processing greatly enhances image manipulation capabilities, but new software techniques are still needed for pattern recognition and automated image analysis. Methods for analysis of biomedical time series data are also needed which permit the extraction of patterns from large data sets and nonstationary patterns such as EEGs.

19.4.4 Neural Network Models

Most neural network models are based loosely on the structure of biological nervous systems. There is a growing body of information about nervous systems and brain function that is not incorporated into the computer models. New paradigms may be developed which more closely resemble the human information processing system.

19.4.5 Artificial Intelligence Approaches

As many of the advances coming from artificial intelligence approaches become commonplace, their origins are lost. For example, the time-sharing computer originated from research in artificial intelligence. Neural networks also had their foundations in artificial intelligence but are now generally considered as a separate topic. Certainly, the field of artificial intelligence provides unlimited opportunities for growth because it is broad enough to encompass any computer approach that appears to demonstrate intelligence. The future of artificial intelligence in the field of medical decision making is difficult to predict but will probably rely on more sophisticated reasoning paradigms than current systems use and may benefit from the evidenced-based approach to medical decision making.

REFERENCES

American Association of Artificial Intelligence. 1991. *Proceedings.* Cambridge, MA: AAAI Press.

Galvin, J.R., D'Alessandro, M.P., Erkonen, W.E., Smith, W.L., el-Khoury, G.Y., and Weinstein, J.N. 1995. The virtual hospital. Providing multimedia decision support tools via the Internet. *Spine* **20(15):** 1735–1738.

Gray, J.A.M. 1997. *Evidenced-based healthcare.* New York: Churchill Livingstone.

Hudson, D.L., Cohen, M.E., Anderson, M.F., and Moazamipour, H. 1998. Design of a telemedicine network to facilitate rural health care. *International Society for Computers and Their Applications. CAINE:* 278–287.

Kahn, C.E., Jr. 1995. CHORUS: a computer-based radiology handbook for international collaboration via the World Wide Web. *Radiographics* **15(4):** 963–970.

Lucier, R.E. 1995. Building a digital library for the health sciences: information space complementing information place. *Bulletin of the Medical Library Association* **83(3):** 346–350.

Sackett, D.L., Richardson, W.S., Rosenberg, W., and Haynes, R.B. 1997. *Evidenced-based medicine.* New York: Churchill Livingstone.

Index

About the Authors

Donna L. Hudson received the B.S. and M.S. degrees in Mathematics from California State University, Fresno, in 1968 and 1972, respectively, and the Ph.D. in Computer Science from the University of California, Los Angeles, in 1981. Dr. Hudson is a professor of Family and Community Medicine, University of California, San Francisco (UCSF), and director of Medical Information Resources at UCSF Fresno Medical Education Program. She is also a founding member of the Executive Committee for the Medical Information Sciences Program at UCSF and a member of the Bioengineering Graduate Group at UC Berkeley and UCSF. In 1987 she received the Faculty Research Award for her work on reasoning with uncertainty in medical expert systems.

Dr. Hudson's research interests include approximate reasoning techniques in medical decision making, expert systems, neural networks, image processing, and chaotic modeling of medical data; she has published over 150 papers in these areas. Also, she is coauthor of two books and associate editor for Intelligent Systems for the ISCA *International Journal of Computers and Their Applications*.

Dr. Hudson is a senior member of the Institute of Electric and Electronics Engineers (IEEE), a member of the Administrative Committee of the IEEE Engineering in Medicine and Biology Society, a Fellow of the American Institute of Medical and Biological Engineering, and president of the International Society for Computers and Their Applications.

Maurice E. Cohen received his Ph.D. in Applied Mathematics and Theoretical Physics from the University of Wales in the United Kingdom. He was subsequently a research fellow at the French Atomic Energy Commission before coming to the United States in 1968. Presently, he is a professor of Radiology at the University of California, San Francisco, professor of Mathematics at California State University, Fresno, and a founding member of the Graduate Group in Medical Information Science at UCSF and Bioengineering Graduate Group at UCSF and UC Berkeley.

In 1977 he solved a problem involving Jacobi functions, which had been considered impossible. In 1985 he was coauthor of a paper on detection of coronary artery disease from exercise test data which won the American Medical Informatics Association Best Paper Award; in 1991 he was named Outstanding Professor at California State University, Fresno; in 1996 he won the Faculty Research Award at UCSF for the use of chaos theory in early detection of heart disease; in 1997 he was named Phi Kappa Phi Centenary University Scholar. Also in 1997, Dr. Cohen was inducted as a Fellow of the American Institute for Medical and Biological Engineering for "pioneering work in decision making in cardiology." Dr. Cohen has written over 170 publications in applied mathematics, artificial intelligence, neural networks, chaos theory, automated medical decision making, and medical imaging and is coauthor of *Comparative Approaches to Medical Reasoning* (World Scientific, 1995). Dr. Cohen is an artist who uses chaos theory in the creation of oil paintings and has shown his work at a number of exhibitions, including a one-man show in Paris, France. The cover art for this book, an oil painting entitled "Yosemite Vignettes," was created by Dr. Cohen.